Nicholas Rhea is the pen-name of Peter N. Walker, formerly an inspector with the North Yorkshire Police and the creator of the *Constable* series of books from which the Yorkshire TV series *Heartbeat* is derived. In the three *Constable* books in this volume, *Constable in Disguise*, *Constable Among the Heather* and *Constable by the Stream*, Nicholas Rhea tells of some of the colourful incidents and eccentric Yorkshire characters encountered by a country constable, stories which have provided the basis for the adventures of PC Nick Rowan, played by Nick Berry in the TV series. Peter N. Walker is also the author of *Portrait of the North York Moors* and, married with four children, lives in Ampleforth in North Yorkshire.

Heartbeat:
Constable Among the Heather and Other Tales of a Yorkshire Village Bobby

Nicholas Rhea

HEADLINE

First published in paperback in 1992 under the title HEARTBEAT
by HEADLINE BOOK PUBLISHING

Re-issued in this edition in 1993
by HEADLINE BOOK PUBLISHING

10 9 8 7 6 5

ISBN 0 7472 4012 4

Printed and bound in Great Britain by
Cox & Wyman Ltd, Reading, Berkshire

HEADLINE BOOK PUBLISHING
A division of Hodder Headline PLC
338 Euston Road
London NW1 3BH

CONTENTS

Constable
in
Disguise

1

Detection is, or ought to be,
an exact science, and should be
treated in the same cold and un-
emotional manner.

Sir Arthur Conan Doyle (1859-1930)

In the large and uncertain world outside the police service, the letters CID are widely assumed to mean 'Criminal Investigation Department'. In the minds of countless citizens, particularly those approaching the autumn of their years, these initials conjure up near-romantic images of trilby-hatted men in overlarge raincoats who go about mysterious work which is far too important and intellectual to be trusted to uniformed police officers.

Most of us possess a mental picture of a typical detective but there is no modern requirement for them to wear trilbies or belted raincoats. Indeed, the ideal detective should look nothing like a police officer. Too many bygone sleuths looked too much like off-duty police officers, with their short haircuts, big polished shoes, trilby hats and belted raincoats — they wore what was in effect a civilian uniform, which often defeated the purpose of wearing plain clothes. Happily, many of today's detectives do not look like police officers in their designer jeans, trainer shoes and expensive casual wear.

And this is where the real meaning of CID ought to be mentioned — it means 'Constable in Disguise'.

Constables in Disguise, or detectives as they are better known, are usually depicted entering or leaving the mighty

portals of the original Scotland Yard which stood on the banks
of the River Thames in London, England, in the manner of
some legendary and impenetrable castle. Associated with this
image are black Wolsley police cars, Black Marias, turned-up
raincoat collars, loosened belts, short haircuts, magnifying-
glasses and the habit of addressing all other male persons as
'sir', particularly those under investigation. The number of
'sirs' emitted during an interview varies proportionately with
the importance of the interview or the social class of the
interviewee.

An adjunct to this perpetual image of Scotland Yard's
famous detectives was the notion that all really serious crime
in the United Kingdom was solved by them and that the
bumpkins in the shire forces were fit only for riding bikes in
pursuit of poachers or telling the time.

It is surprising how many Americans and other foreigners,
and indeed what a high level of British folk, still think that
Scotland Yard investigates every British murder or indeed
every British crime. This is a myth, of course, but it has been
fostered by many past crime writers who have dramatized
Scotland Yard departments like the Flying Squad, the Murder
Squad and the Fraud Squad. Their heroic members swooped
around Britain keeping the streets free from villainy.

Those detectives never walked anywhere, nor did they
proceed, travel, gallop or simply move. They always swooped,
or so it seemed from contemporary novels and newspaper
reports. The outcome of this PR exercise was that many
authors, and thus many of their readers, constantly failed to
appreciate that the provincial police forces had, and still have,
some very good detectives. The truth is that all provincial
criminal investigation departments are very capable of solving
their own crimes. Indeed, there seems no reason why the Yard
should not call them in to solve a few of London's trickier
cases.

Another oft-repeated myth perpetuated by some crime
writers is that all murders are committed either on express
trains or in the libraries of country houses during dinner.
Followers of this mythology may also believe that dead bodies
do not mess the carpets or smell after an hour or so of lying
around the house. In fact, dead bodies are not very nice

things. The truth is they are terribly cumbersome and something of a problem to deal with, a fact known to most police officers. Furthermore, dead bodies that have been subjected to the inhuman treatment dished out by some murderers and rapists are very nasty, messy and smelly indeed. Furthermore, criminals of all types are not very nice people, in spite of what some sociologists would have us believe. They are so often the dregs of society who are able to masquerade as decent folk until the police are able to prove otherwise.

It follows that it takes a rather special person to become a successful detective. That person must have intelligence, which is not necessarily the same as intellectual ability; he or she must also have a deep working knowledge of criminal law and the legal procedures involved in the prosecution of criminals, as well as an immense understanding of people and their behavioural traits, plus, of course, a keen eye for detail, good powers of observation, a very alert and enquiring mind and infinite patience. The latter quality is needed to cope with those long moments of drudgery and the wealth of interminable, plodding and fruitless enquiries.

It might be prudent to mention here that police officers are not necessarily promoted when they join the CID. They are often transferred to plain clothes duties without promotion to a higher rank; an officer may be a police constable (PC) one day and a detective police constable (D/PC) — abbreviated to Detective Constable (D/C) — the next. Such a move is not a promotion, because the detective remains in the rank of constable — it is a sideways transfer. But a detective constable *can* be promoted either to a uniform sergeant (Sgt), or to a detective sergeant (D/S). Within the ranks of the CID, there is detective sergeant, detective inspector (D/I), detective chief inspector (D/C/I), detective superintendent (D/Supt) and detective chief superintendent (D/Chief Supt).

All police officers begin their careers in uniform, but there can be promotion right through the ranks of the CID or, alternatively, elevation to the senior heights of the service is sometimes gained by switching from uniform to CID and back again as the opportunities arise. Young constables often join the police service having read books about the great detectives or even about Sherlock Holmes, Hercule Poirot *et al*; their desire is sometimes to become a famous sleuth, albeit within the ranks of the police service and not as a private investigator. So they opt for at least two years plodding the beat in uniform before being eligible to further their careers as members of the elite CID.

But becoming a detective is not easy.

It requires the initial ability to make known one's skills to those who select recruits for the CID, and in my young constabulary days selection was followed (or occasionally preceded) by a thirteen-week intensive Detective Training Course. This included criminal law, legal procedures and methods of detection, in the form of lectures, and practical work on fingerprints, forensic science, scientific aids, the administration of a murder investigation or serious crime inquiry, identification methods and that host of worldly necessities that makes a good CID officer.

There was the TIC procedure to understand too.

This can be somewhat complicated, but in simple terms it is where an arrested person confesses to the police that he or she has committed other crimes which have not, up to that stage, been prosecuted or even detected. When an arrested person is charged with a crime, therefore, he or she is questioned about other undetected crimes of a similar nature for which he or she may be responsible. If the arrested person admits any further crimes, they are added to the charge sheet and presented to the court as admissions of guilt. When determining the cases, the court will 'take into consideration' those other confessed crimes, although a case of careless driving would not be dealt with at the same time as fifteen burglary charges. The crimes which are TIC'd must be similar in nature to each other. The chances are that the villain will receive a sentence lighter than if his list of crimes had been detected and presented to a court individually. Thus the TIC system is beneficial to convicted criminals because it allows them to wipe clean their proverbial slate and, when they are released, to start committing a whole range of new crimes.

This system is also useful to the police. It means that strings of crimes can often be written off as 'detected,' a pleasing state of affairs when submitting returns for publication in the Home Office's annual *Criminal Statistics for England and*

Wales. A good example would occur where a burglar is arrested, his house is searched and a veritable Aladdin's Cave of stolen goods is discovered. Those objects are the loot from several earlier crimes. He then admits breaking into other premises from which he stole those items. If the arrested person agrees, those other crimes would, in police jargon, be TIC'd 'taken into consideration' by the court when passing sentence.

Another important thing to learn was when, or when not, to 'crime' a complaint. If a complaint is 'crimed', it means that the investigating officer is satisfied that indeed a crime has been committed. For example, lots of women rush into police stations on Saturday afternoons to complain that their hand-bags have been stolen or that their purses have been stolen from the top of their shopping-bags. In truth, how many of these are really lost or mislaid? The answer is: quite a lot! So if a detective is informed by a woman that her handbag has been stolen, he will first make sure that she has not mislaid it. This is not an easy assessment to make but it is one that must be done.

It is a fact that people do feel they are the victims of crime when a loss is either their own fault or a misunderstanding of some kind. I knew a dear lady pensioner who was convinced someone was stealing her coal, whereas she was simply using it faster than she thought. I knew a man who complained that his garden spade had been stolen, whereas he had lent it to a friend and had forgotten about the loan until he wanted to dig his garden six months later. I knew a woman who left her handbag on a park bench. She realized she'd left it behind and returned within minutes, but it was missing upon her return, so she reported it stolen. In those few moments, it had in fact been found and handed in to the park authorities by an honest finder.

There are thousands of such losses every day. If every lost item was 'crimed', the crime rate would soar and the detection rate would slump. So crimes are recorded as such only when the police are sure they are genuine crimes; hence they are *crimed*.

Bearing in mind the hard work that is needed to become a fully fledged detective, I felt I would like to know more about this branch of police work. I had read my Sherlock Holmes books, I had puzzled over the loopholes in Agatha Christie's efforts, I had seen films about the work of the master detectives and I warmed to the notion of dramatic battles in court when I could prove, by clever reasoning, that my arrested person was guilty of the crime I had alleged. But was it wise for a rural constable to join those whose work deals almost entirely with crime and criminals? Could this jaundice my view of the great British public whom I had sworn to serve? Would I still regard every human being as someone basically decent and honest?

And besides, how does a uniformed village constable break into those hallowed ranks?

In my time, the mid-1960s, the answer lay in a system known as 'Aide to CID' which was an officer's short-term attachment to the Criminal Investigation Department. It involved a six-month period of work with the CID, during which time one's efforts were assessed to see if one was capable of becoming a full-time CID officer. An aptitude for the work would be rewarded by that thirteen-week course at a convenient Detective Training School.

The snag with a North Yorkshire moorland village like Aidensfield was that very little crime was committed and so it was not easy to show one's potential for this specialized work. Another factor was that the crime figures that I had to submit quarterly to my superiors were open to wide interpretation. If I recorded a meagre annual total of twelve crimes upon my beat, the official attitude was that there was no need for a constable to live and work in Aidensfield, as the crime rate was far too low to justify his presence.

Besides, the crimes themselves were at the lower end of the scale of seriousness. For example, some of those crimes might involve little more than the theft of a gallon of petrol from a car (or a crime wave of twelve thefts from twelve cars), or the theft of poultry or sheep, shoplifting from the village stores or the work of a sneak thief in the local council estate who prowls about stealing radios or cash from houses whose doors have been left open while the ladies gossip or drink tea. It was hardly serious crime or Holmesian stuff, and it was not likely to worry the senior officers of the force. However, it was highly upsetting to the victims and to the general morale and well-being of a small community.

But *my* interpretation of such figures was that I was out and about on my beat, keeping down the volume of crime. I claimed that a low rate of crime indicated some very positive policing. In my view, it showed I was doing a good job and that my presence as a resident constable was necessary to keep it that way. I said, and I maintain, that the village constable was and still is an asset to the community. After all, crime prevention is a very sophisticated art, and much of it is achieved by the presence of a patrolling constable in uniform who has the time and the will to stop and chat to his public. Those chats could reveal villains and they could produce crime-prevention advice for those who are less aware of such risks. In addition, the sight of a local constable going about his daily routine does provide a feeling of security within the community.

In several discussions with senior officers about the merits of a resident village constable, I suggested that a high crime rate on Aidensfield beat would be proof that I was *not* doing my job, irrespective of any detection percentage. It is worth mentioning here that most crimes on a rural beat were investigated by the resident officer, and not by the CID.

I followed my arguments with the logic that my beat's annual low crime rate was clear evidence of the value of my presence and also proof of my localized crime-beating efforts. The bosses countered this by saying that, if the village constable was taken away from Aidensfield and not replaced, the volume of crime would not show a significant increase. I agreed with this, but *not* for the same reason as the bosses. I knew that, if there was no constable at Aidensfield, many local crimes would never be reported; the villagers would not bother to contact an anonymous and distant police officer, especially by telephone, to report their losses unless it was a very serious matter. As a consequence, the outcome would be a continuing low number of *reported* crime, but another important aspect was that, in the absence of someone handy to whom to report the smaller crimes, the incidence of true crime could be a lot higher. The absence of a convenient constable would mean that more actual crime would be committed but much less would be reported.

I could not make my superiors understand that, for the type of crimes suffered in the villages, the local people would not contact a distant police station. They'd wait until they met the constable to report matters like,

'Oh, Mr Rhea, I thowt I'd better mention this — somebody got into my implement shed and nicked a coil o' rope last week.'

Or I would receive reports like, 'There's somebody about, Mr Rhea; five or six of us have had money taken, milk money we left on our doorsteps on a morning for t'milkman . . . only a few pounds . . . '

Another example is that someone would tell me, 'Mr Rhea, awd Mrs Barthram's had somebody in her greenhouse, pinching her garden tools. Two trowels and a spade have gone; she doesn't like bothering you, so I thought I'd mention it . . . '

Crimes of this kind would never be reported other than to the local constable as he passed by, and although officers might patrol the villages in cars and vans, who would halt a passing police van to complain of the theft of a coil of rope a week earlier, or that someone had stolen a cactus from dad's greenhouse? Removal of village constables is a fine way of reducing the volume of reported crime, but their absence can never permit the real level of rural crime to be calculated — and the same argument pertains to acts of vandalism, damage and general anti-social behaviour.

It was while entertaining such thoughts and concern about the future of the village constable that I was on patrol in Ashfordly one autumn morning in 1966. I was standing beside a telephone kiosk, making a point there in case the office wished to contact me (even though I had a radio in the van!), when I noticed the rangy figure of Detective Sergeant Gerry Connolly, who was heading towards me with strong, purposeful strides.

He was the man in charge of the CID at Eltering. Ashfordly and Aidensfield were within his area of responsibility. He was a pleasant man in his early forties who sported a mop of thick fair hair over a face that was as pink and fresh as a child's. Clad in brown brogue shoes, a Harris tweed jacket and cavalry twill trousers, he looked every inch a countryman, which indeed he was. He bred golden retrievers and seemed to be friendly with everyone.

Of course, he wore a brown trilby hat. It was similar to those worn by men who resort to racecourses; I have often wondered why so many male racegoers wear brown trilby hats. There is a sea of them at any racecourse, where they are a group-identifying feature, in the form of mass adornment or professional lids. Gerry had one too, and I do know he liked attending the races, whether on duty or off.

Gerry Connolly addressed everyone by their Christian names, even those of higher rank than himself, the only exceptions being the chief constable and the deputy chief constable. I knew that his small staff enjoyed working with him; it comprised Detective Constable Paul Wharton, who played bowls and kept tropical fish, and Detective Constable Ian Shackleton, who liked beer, haddock-and-chips and trout fishing. The trio made a good, effective and popular team.

'Morning, Nick,' he beamed as he came to a halt at my side. 'It's a pleasant day to be patrolling this pretty place.'

'And what brings the might of the sub-divisional CID to Ashfordly?' I asked with interest. 'Have we a crime in town?'

'Not unless you know something I don't,' he returned. 'No, we've been having a few raids on the local Co-Ops. A team is breaking in through the back windows of the storerooms and nicking thousands of fags each time. Six or seven Co-Ops have been raided in the county since the summer. I've just been for words with your local manager; I've tried to persuade him to have bars fitted to all his back windows and better locks fitted on the doors.'

'We've been telling him that for months,' I said. 'We read about the raids in our circulars, but he seemed to think it could never happen to his shop.'

'I'm going round all those that haven't been hit,' he said. 'I reckon he's got the message now; he says it's a decision which has to be made by higher authority, and they're a bit tight with their budgets for improvements and alterations to premises. They're not too concerned about the thefts because the insurance will cover the losses.'

'The poor old insurance companies, they do fork out for a

lot of carelessness, don't they?'

'Some are tightening up their conditions now, Nick; they insist on proper safeguards.'

We chattered awhile about professional matters and personal affairs, and then, quite unexpectedly, he said, 'Look, Nick, you're about due for a spell as an Aide, aren't you?'

'I'd enjoy that,' I said, for it was true.

'Right, leave it with me,' he beamed. 'I'll submit your name. It'll take a few weeks to be processed and considered, but I reckon, if I ask for you, they'll approve.'

I returned home feeling very pleased at this promise and explained to my wife that CID duties would entail long hours albeit with no night shifts. One difference would be that I should be expected to spend my evenings at work, visiting the pubs and clubs in the area to quaff pints with the best and the worst elements of society. I would receive a small detective allowance to help defray such expenses, but it would not cover the actual cost. Mary was happy for me and we both knew that I would enjoy this kind of work.

And so it was that in the early summer of the following year I received a formal note from the superintendent to say that I was to be seconded to the CID at Eltering as an Aide for a period of six months.

On the appointed date, therefore, I dressed in a sports jacket, flannels and comfortable shoes, kissed Mary and our four infants farewell and set out for Eltering. I was due to start work at 9 a.m. that Monday but had no idea when that first day's duties would finish. I would be working some very long days during the next six months.

Mary would have to suffer some extended periods alone with our little family, and for me it would be an expensive time.

I did ponder the moral issues of whether I should be spending necessary cash in the pursuit of villains when, all the time, the growing family needed it. But I came to regard my forthcoming period of high expenditure as an investment, believing that, if I did well in my new task, I might get promoted.

But as I drove to Eltering that morning, I decided I would not spend my money on one certain item — I would not buy a trilby hat.

2

The two divinest things this world has got,
A lovely woman in a rural spot!
James Henry Leigh Hunt (1784-1859)

My first morning in the bustling CID office at Eltering Police
Station was spent among a pile of old books, because my three
new colleagues were each telephoning all over the place,
writing reports, interviewing callers and liaising with the
uniform duty inspector on current criminal matters within the
sub-division. There seemed to be an inordinate amount of
frantic activity, but that is often the impression gained when
entering the sanctum of another; people always appear to be so
busy, and they generally have little time for the newcomer. I
simply sat at the end of a desk and observed it all.

I heard them discussing a spate of local motor-car thefts
and, of much more interest, a series of confidence tricks on the
landlords of local inns.

That latter series was based on the simple premise that we
all like to get summat for nowt – in this case, the temptation
was oceans of whisky at cut price. It was being offered by the
con men for cash in advance, with a free bottle as a symbol of
good faith. Those landlords with tied houses were not allowed
to sell their own selections of beer or spirits, and so this system
offered them a few bottles which they could sell without the
brewery's knowledge. This in turn would produce cash sales,
so offering the dream of tax-free and accounts-free money for
themselves from unauthorized and surreptitious sales. A nice

way of earning a bit of pocket-money.

As a result, when the trickster called with his offer of
whisky at a bargain price, the very favourable terms involving
cash in advance, many landlords saw it as a means of earning a
quick tax-free profit. They gave cash to the con man, enough
to buy several crates, but got one bottle of whisky. They never
saw their money again nor any of the other promised bottles.
Some had ordered dozens and laid out hundreds of pounds.

Members of the uniform branch were instructed to visit all
the local pubs to warn landlords of this ploy, but in some
instances their warning was too late. The lure of easy cash had
cost them dear.

The three detectives had no time to explain things that
morning, and I entertained myself by browsing through old
records. Boring as they were, the battered books were of some
value. There was a photograph album of local criminals, some
of whom must have been dead for at least half a century; it was
an ancient volume whose original entries were in splendid
copperplate writing and whose contents were a list of MOs of
local criminals – an MO being, in criminal jargon, a 'method
of operation', from the Latin *'modus operandi'*.

MOs were an important means of identifying the work of a
criminal – one local housebreaker, for example, always broke
in through rear kitchen windows of the houses he attacked. He
always smashed the glass by sticking treacle and brown paper
over it, then hit it with a brick. This muffled the noise of the
breaking glass and held most of the pieces together so he could
quickly and easily dispose of them. We always recognized his
method of operation.

A more modern book contained details of those awful
tricksters who wheedled cash out of pensioners and simple
folk by their smooth-tongued lies. In North Yorkshire, the
dialect term for such evil operators is 'slape-tongued varmints'
– 'slippery-tongued vermin'. 'Slape' is a dialect word for
'slippery', and there are 'slape-faced 'uns' too (people with
untrustworthy faces).

So far as the slape-tongued varmints were concerned, it was
the laying or repairing of drives to houses and farms and the
repairing of roofs which were a popular form of deception at
that time. It worked like this – a team of rogues would arrive

unannounced and offer to tarmac a drive to a house or farm and then charge an abortive sum for their shoddy work. Another device was to inform pensioners that, while driving past their home, they had noticed that the chimney-stack was on the point of collapse or that a hole had developed in the roof. Having thus alarmed the old folks, the villains offered to repair it immediately out of the kindness of their hearts (!). They would then ask for cash in advance, 'to buy the materials', or they would fix the defect (which often did not exist) for a fee which was well above normal.

They would either disappear with the advanced cash or do the job and then terrify the pensioners into paying a ridiculously high fee. Every one of us wanted to catch these scoundrels, and so those accounts of their trickery were very closely studied. A lot of these villains came from Leeds, and so the crimes became known as the work of 'the Leeds Repairers'.

Sadly, in most cases, it was difficult getting a clear story or a description of the varmints from the pensioners. Even if we did get a coherent story and identified the slape-tongued varmints, it was difficult proving they had committed a crime rather than an act which was merely an unsatisfactory business transaction. There were many times when their activities did not come within the province of the police or the scope of the criminal law. It often depended upon the precise wording they used at the time of committing their evil deeds. Hoping to arrest some of them or their ilk, I swotted up lists of outstanding crimes, some going back ten or twelve years without being solved.

I was then shown the finer points of compiling a crime report and how to complete the necessary statistical forms that accompanied such a report. It was all very baffling, and there seemed to be so much paperwork to complete, but I knew it would all become clearer when I had to record my first real crime as an Aide. And that baptism occurred that very same afternoon.

It was three o'clock and I was in the office with D/PC Ian Shackleton. He was explaining the problems of investigating the crime of shopbreaking. He was highlighting the fact that some shopowners or their managers claimed that items had been stolen because they needed to cover up deficiencies in the stock which were of their own making, through either carelessness or dishonesty. There were some who set fire to their premises in order to claim from their insurance companies, and I was rapidly realizing that genuinely honest people seemed to be somewhat rare members of the community, especially in towns. I quickly realized why the CID trusted no one.

Shackleton explained that, when investigating a crime, we had to have a very, very open mind indeed and, difficult though it was to accept, we had to be suspicious of everyone, even the supposed victims. That sounds terrible on paper, but it is a fact of police life – some people do claim to be the victims of crime to cover their own crimes and deficiencies, and sometimes they do so in an attempt to gain revenge upon others. Police officers are taught to be very much aware of this tendency, especially when dealing with reports of rape or indecent assault by some women. We were mindful of Francis Bacon's works, 'Revenge is a kind of wild justice, which the more man's nature runs to, the more ought law to weed it out.'

In the police service, one soon learns that, in the world of criminal investigation especially, nothing must be taken for granted. The possibility of deviousness by members of the general public, particularly those with deep secrets of their own, must never be ignored or overlooked.

It was during this earnest and valuable talk with Shackleton that a call came through. Eltering Police Station's duty constable, PC John Rogers, came into the CID office from the enquiry counter. He was a calm individual; having done his job for years nothing surprised him or troubled him. In his quiet way, he had received calls about matters which would panic the most calm, terrify the fearless and horrify the sensitive. But John was unflappable, and he sailed through it all with characteristic equanimity.

'Ian,' he addressed Shackleton, 'we've a funny call just come in. A body's been found at Lover's Leap. It's a male. He's dead. He's been attacked, by all accounts. I've sent Echo Three Seven to the scene to investigate.'

'Genuine corpse, is it?' asked Shackleton.

'It could be a load of rubbish, of course, a false alarm

probably with good intent. It'll be a tramp or a drunk sleeping in the sunshine; it's a tourist area.'

Rogers had received many reports of this kind, and I recalled one of my own at Aidensfield. A motorist had reported a corpse lying on the side of a country lane, having apparently been knocked down by a hit-and-run car. When I went to investigate, I found a happy tramp fast asleep with his legs sticking out of the grass into the carriageway. I found it amazing that his legs had not been broken by passing vehicles, for he said he often lay down in this manner. It seems he loved to sleep on the grassy lanes of England. Such calls about corpses were all treated with a little caution, but all had to be dealt with.

'Where's Lover's Leap?' Ian asked.

'I can take you there. It's on my beat,' I said, recalling an incident involving a naked couple in a van who managed to set fire to the moor at that point.*

'Right, you'd better come with me, Nick,' said Shackleton, lifting his jacket from behind the door. 'John, if Gerry Connolly comes in, tell him where we are and what it's all about. Who found the supposed body, by the way?'

'A hiker. He rang in from a kiosk. He's waiting to show Echo Three Seven where it is. They're rendezvousing at the car-park nearby — there's a picnic site there.'

And so we jumped into the CID car, a small red Ford Anglia, and headed for the splendour of the North York Moors. There were no blue lights to flash during this trip, no sirens to sound and no uniforms to indicate the importance of this journey. To all intents and purposes, we were just two men in a little car going about our routine business.

I showed Ian the route to Lover's Leap. It is a splendid beauty spot with stunning views across the surrounding moors and countryside. From a small plateau, the ground falls steeply away down a heather and bracken-covered hillside into a ravine. There are young pines and silver birches, and at the bottom of the ravine is a moorland stream of crystal clarity and icy coolness. The views embrace scores of scenic square miles. You can see the radomes of the Ballistic Missile Early Warning

*See *Constable on the Prowl*.

Station at Fylingdales, with the North Sea in the background, and in the valleys are tiny villages with church spires and cottages huddled beside streams or clinging to the steep-sided dales. It is a beautiful place and, as the name suggests, very popular with courting couples. They come at night, like moths flying towards a bright light, but this was a mid-afternoon in the early summer.

We arrived within forty minutes, and I could see the little police car, Echo Three Seven, waiting for us; two other cars occupied the parking-area. The driver of Echo Three Seven, PC Steve Forman was standing beside it talking to a well-dressed man and to another in hiking gear. We halted, parked and walked towards them. Apart from this little party and the two cars, the picnic area was deserted.

Shackleton took control.

Forman told a simple tale. 'This is Stuart Finch,' he introduced the hiker. 'He was walking up the side of this hill, and when he was a few yards from the edge of the car-park, he saw the man lying in the bracken. He spoke to him, got no reply, then touched him.' Finch nodded his agreement as Forman continued: 'He thought the man was dead, and so he rang us, and he had the sense to ring for a doctor.'

'Good thinking, Mr Finch,' said Shackleton. 'Well done.'

'And I'm Doctor Gregson from Malton,' the smart man said. 'I've had a look at the man. He *is* dead. I'll confirm that, but I cannot certify the cause of death.'

'How long's he been dead, Doctor? Any idea?' asked Ian.

'Not long,' said Gregson. 'A couple of hours maybe. He's still fresh, no *rigor mortis*. I can't be more specific than that.'

'Any views on the cause then?'

'I didn't examine the body for marks — I thought I'd leave that to your experts — but it has all the appearances of a heart attack. The odd thing is that his clothes are in disarray, and that's a puzzle. Had his clothes been correctly worn, I'd have said it was nothing more than a heart attack, that he collapsed and died while walking here, although you appreciate I cannot certify that without knowing the casualty's medical history.'

There being no time like the present, Ian asked me to take a brief statement from the doctor before he left; he and the hiker, guided by PC Forman, went to examine the body.

I wrote the brief account of the doctor's findings in my pocket-book, and he signed it. I allowed Doctor Gregson to leave in his Rover and went to join the others at the corpse.

They were standing near the body when I arrived. I noticed a patch of smooth grass on a small, flat plateau in this sea of tall bracken; until one arrived at the patch of grass, it was impossible to see the body, so high and thick was the surrounding bracken. Finch had struck through the bracken to gain access to the car-park and had found the dead man. It was almost pure luck that he had come by this route, for there was no formal footpath. Ian had quizzed him closely about his discovery and felt no suspicion could be attached to Finch.

I looked down upon the corpse. It was that of a heavily built man in his early fifties; he had an almost bald head with wisps of dark hair around the sides, a dark moustache and a soft, flabby face. He was lying on his back with his arms spread rather wide but his legs very slightly apart. He wore a light-coloured jacket and an open-necked shirt with most of the buttons undone, and his trousers were round his ankles, although it did seem an attempt had been made to draw them up. His white underpants were down too, and they stopped his legs from falling apart. I could understand Finch's thinking he had been attacked, but the odd thing was that a bunch of fresh sweet peas lay near his head.

Having quizzed the hiker and taken a written statement from him, Shackleton thanked him for his co-operation and allowed him to leave.

'So, what do we make of this?' asked Shackleton, puzzling as he stared at the recumbent form.

'Parked up there,' said Forman, 'there is a car that might be his, that blue Morris. A businessman, pausing for lunch maybe, was taken short and came down here because there's no toilets up there. Hence the dropped pants. Strained himself while at it, and his heart stopped?'

'That doesn't explain the sweet peas,' I said.

'They might not be his,' said Shackleton. 'Somebody else could have been here before him. Anyway, the point is: have we a natural-causes death or a suspicious one? If it's suspicious, we'd better notify the coroner and call in the cavalry — photographer, forensic pathologist, my boss, scenes of crime, the lot. We might have to set up a murder inquiry.'

'We'll need a PM to determine the cause of death,' I added for good measure.

'Right, decision time. We can't move the body until we have had it photographed *in situ*; I mean, it does look odd and I think we'd better treat it as suspicious. Right, Steve, radio Control, will you? Tell them we have a suspicious death here, and I'd like a senior detective to attend. Now, do we know who he is?'

'I haven't searched his clothing yet. I thought I'd better not touch anything. But that car might be his,' Steve reminded us of the blue Morris. 'You could do a check of the number for starters.'

'Nick, that's one for you.'

While Steve Forman made his call from Echo Three Seven, I went to examine the Morris. It was a blue saloon, two years old and in good condition; it was taxed and bore an excise licence issued at the North Riding Vehicle Taxation Office at Northallerton. This was before the days of the Police National Computer, but I knew we could discover the owner of the car very quickly through its registration number. I radioed Eltering from the CID car and gave them a situation report (a 'sit-rep'), then asked them to check the car number with the Taxation Department at Northallerton. It would take a few minutes, and in the meantime I took a closer look at the Morris, albeit without touching it. On the back seat were a brief-case and some coloured file jackets but I could see no names or identifying marks on them. Besides them was a length of floral wrapping-paper. I could see that it was printed with 'Gowers for Flowers' and a Scarborough address. And a solitary red sweet pea petal lay beside it.

Then I realized I knew this car. Or at least, I had seen it before. Because Lover's Leap was on my beat, I had made regular patrols to the locality over the past few months, and sometimes I had parked for a few minutes on the car-park, both at night and during the daytime hours. And I was sure I had seen this blue Morris several times, always parked in this very place. I stood back from it now and walked away to the road, to gain the view I would normally see.

And the more I stared at it, the more I realized it was the

same car, parked in precisely the same spot. But something was missing, some extra detail I had noticed before. And I could not recall that detail . . . As I examined the scene before me, some parts of those memories came back to me, but not all, and I wondered if I had made a note of those occasions in my pocket-book. Recording such a sighting would hardly be necessary unless there was a reason, but I could not recall any official reasons for noting the registration numbers of cars parked here. Maybe this sighting had triggered off a memory of an incident in the past?

Then I heard my call-sign on the CID car radio: 'Echo Control to Echo One-Six.'

I lifted the handset of the CID car and responded: 'Echo One-Six receiving. Go ahead. Over.'

'Echo One-Six, reference your enquiry about the blue Morris, the registered owner is George Frederick Halliwell,' and I was given an address in Scarborough.

We could not assume that the dead man *was* Halliwell — this man might have borrowed his car — and we would now have to make enquiries in Scarborough to see if it could be him. We'd have to be very discreet, because we must not upset his relatives if Halliwell was still alive. A search of the body might confirm that name, but we would need a relative to come and view the corpse to make a formal, positive identification. That would be done when the body had been tidied up and placed in a mortuary.

Within an hour, the CID had arrived in a succession of vehicles. The force photographer, a detective chief inspector, scene-of-crime experts and other officers gathered to examine the body and commence their own specialist work.

The car-park and bracken area were cordoned off as we awaited a forensic pathologist, and in the meantime official photographs were taken of the body, the location and the car, with its empty flower wrappings. The full might of a murder investigation was launched as the car-park seemed suddenly full of police officers and official vehicles.

And then, as the formal investigation got under way, I remembered the circumstances of that blue Morris. About a year or eighteen months earlier, I had parked my police motor cycle here for a few moments during a patrol, and a woman had approached me with a purse she had found.

She'd found it on this car-park a few moments before my arrival, and it had contained several pounds, a pair of silver ear-rings and other jewellery. As she was touring the area, she would not retain the purse, and so I entered it into our Found Property system. Before leaving the car-park, however, I had approached the drivers and occupants of all the parked cars to see if it belonged to any of them. It did not — and the only two cars that remained empty were this blue Morris and a small green Austin mini.

I had noted the registration numbers of each, so that I could later trace the owners and contact them about the found purse. But before that need arose, a woman had reported losing the purse and it had been returned to her. I had never tried to trace the owners of the blue Morris and the green Mini. But I had noticed the green Mini parked beside the blue Morris on several successive occasions at the very spot, and those sightings had occurred over a period of around a year. The green Mini was not here today, it was not parked close to the Morris — and that was the missing item.

I would have to examine my old notebooks to trace those numbers but said nothing to the other officers at this stage, just in case my theories were incorrect.

The pathologist had examined the body and expressed an opinion that the fellow had been having sex with a woman immediately prior to his death. The flowers, the pants around the ankles and evidence of some seminal fluid found by the scientist supported that theory. The body, its mode of dress and position had all the hallmarks of such a situation.

In the pathologist's words, 'He was going at it hammer and tongs; he was right here with his fancywoman, just reaching the exciting bit, when his heart stopped. He literally died on the job, gents, and rolled off her, or she heaved him off, dead as a door nail. What a way to go. She's fled the scene, terrified . . . It's just a theory, mind, but I've seen it all before.'

'You mean this often happens?' smiled Forman, intrigued.

'Illicit affairs like this happen everywhere,' continued the pathologist. 'Poor old sod. You'd be surprised how many old codgers die on the job when they've found a young bit of stuff to keep their peckers up. But at least he died happy. I'll have to do a PM, but I'll bet my cotton socks it's natural causes, heart failure. The excitement was too much for him. If so, there'll be no need for an inquest, no need to drag his name through a coroner's court, or hers if you can find her.'

When the scientific examinations were finished, the body was searched and a wallet containing a driving licence added strength to the belief that this was indeed the remains of Mr Halliwell, but we still needed a positive identification. And so the body was removed to a mortuary at Eltering as discreet efforts were made by Scarborough police to determine whether or not this was the late George Frederick Halliwell. A CID officer drove his car to Eltering Police Station, and the wrapping-paper was removed; Mrs Halliwell, if there was a Mrs Halliwell, would never see that scrap of evidence of her husband's unfaithfulness. The enquiries to confirm his identity had to be undertaken before his family was told of his death, and I wondered what the newspapers would make of it all.

I went home after a full day, and after my meal unearthed my old pocket-books. I searched every page for my notes on that purse and found them, having made the entry fifteen months earlier. The two car numbers were there — one agreed with that of today's blue Morris and the other was the green Mini. Tomorrow I would check that Mini number with the Taxation Department.

Next morning I learned that the man had been positively identified as George Frederick Halliwell. He was a county councillor and restaurant-owner from Scarborough. His wife had had the awful task of viewing the body to confirm his identity, but she was not told of his reason for being at Lover's Leap. She was simply informed he had had a heart attack there, for that was the result of the pathologist's post-mortem examination. In other words, it appeared that his death was from natural causes, even if the circumstances were a little unusual. For us, the state of his clothing continued to be a worry, for it could be an indication of a struggle of some kind, instead of the aftermath of sex. Could his death be the result of manslaughter? Had there in fact been a struggle, a fight to the death? About a woman, even?

The morning paper carried a brief note of the death, saying only that we were investigating the death of a man found at a local beauty spot in Ryedale. The paper did not name Halliwell because, at the time of going to print, we could not confirm his identity. I was pleased that no sordid details were published. Having read the account, I rang Taxation and learned that the owner of the green Mini was a Mrs Dorothy Pendlebury, from a village near York, also a county councillor. I told Gerry Connolly of my findings.

'That's great, Nick, a real piece of detective work. Well done! Now, let's go and see her,' he said. 'You come with me, and we'll do it during the day, when her husband's at work. She'll never tell us if he's hanging around listening to every word. If she was the last person to see Halliwell alive, we need to know what happened.'

Dorothy Pendlebury was a tall, heavily built woman who was handsome rather than beautiful; in her early forties, she had a head of fine blonde hair and a bearing which could be described as almost aristocratic. In expensive clothes, she answered our knock and promptly assumed we were brush salesmen.

'I'm not seeing anyone today.' There was a haughtiness in her voice which was perhaps a means of covering her current uncertainty and misery. 'You'll have to see my husband if it's anything to do with the house, and he will be at work till seven.'

Gerry Connolly was all charm. 'Mrs Pendlebury, we are not salesmen, we are police officers,' and he introduced us by our names and ranks. 'I believe you knew the late George Frederick Halliwell of Scarborough, the restaurateur and county councillor.'

His opening words were designed to shock. There was but a moment's hesitation before she snapped, 'Yes, of course, I know him. We're on the county council, we serve on the same committees.'

'Mrs Pendlebury,' said Gerry in his quiet voice, 'I would like to have a word with you about him, in confidence.'

'Really? Why, might I ask?'

'I would prefer to talk inside the house if you don't mind,' continued Gerry.

She hesitated; I realized later that her mind must have been in turmoil at that moment, but her face never revealed anything of her emotions.

'I have an appointment in half-an-hour,' she said. 'I cannot break it . . . ' but she stepped back into the house and we followed her into the kitchen.

She indicated two chairs at the pine table but did not offer us coffee or tea.

'Well?' She stood near the window, looking out, her face away from our scrutiny. It was a clever move on her part.

I wondered how Gerry Connolly would tackle this interview, for I could guess she would deny any allegation he made. She was the sort of woman for whom appearances and social acceptance were of paramount importance, and any hint of a scandal, particularly a sordid sexual one, would be ruinous. There, in her mind, it would never happen – it had never happened . . .

'I have reason to believe,' he said slowly, 'that you were the last person to see George Frederick Halliwell alive.'

Her head dropped slightly forward at this, but her face remained out of our sight as she gazed from her window.

'Is he dead?' her voice was hoarse now. 'No one told me.'

Gerry, in his soft, friendly voice, explained the circumstances surrounding the discovery of Halliwell's body, and he ended by repeating his earlier remark: 'I have reason to believe you were the last person to see him alive, Mrs Pendlebury. I have reason to believe you were with him at Lover's Leap.'

'We were good friends.' Her voice was a mere whisper now. 'He was a fine man . . . '

'But yesterday were you with him at Lover's Leap?' Connolly stood up to ask the direct question.

'No!' she flung the answer at him. 'How dare you make such insinuations! I am a respectable married woman, the mother of two adult children, and a councillor; how dare you suggest that I was with him, on a secret liaison . . . '

'I did not suggest any such thing, Mrs Pendlebury. I merely suggested you were the last person to be with him, to see him alive. You might have met there for business reasons, to discuss county council matters . . . '

'I have nothing more to add, Inspector,' she snapped, and

added, 'Now I must go. I have an urgent appointment to keep.'

Gerry stood his ground. 'Mrs Pendlebury, I need to know your movements yesterday around lunchtime. Mr Halliwell is dead, and his death is being investigated as suspicious. We know that he was not alone when he died.'

He allowed those words to register in her mind before he continued: 'And furthermore, we have every reason to believe that he was engaged in the act of sexual intercourse with a woman at the moment of his death. If that is true, his death will be regarded as being due to natural causes — there will be no inquest and no publicity. If, however, we have to make more detailed enquiries, probably along the lines of a murder investigation, of course there will be publicity.'

He paused again to allow his words to take effect, then said, 'Now, so far as you are concerned, we could demand the clothes you were wearing yesterday, for fibres were found clinging to Mr Halliwell's clothes; we could ask you to submit to a medical examination to determine whether or not you engaged in sexual intercourse yesterday, and a forensic test might even confirm it was with Mr Halliwell . . . our forensic experts are very clever at matching stains and fibres — and we could make very searching enquiries about your movements over the past year or so.'

She did not say a word but remained on her feet, staring out of her kitchen window; she was totally composed and in command of her own emotions.

'If he did die in the manner you describe,' she said quietly, 'and if his death was due to a heart attack, there will be no inquest, no publicity? That is what you said?'

'That's true. But we do need to know the truth, and we will respect anything confidential.'

'I'll make some coffee,' she said suddenly, moving across to the cupboard for some mugs. Connolly winked at me but said nothing more as she busied herself in the kitchen. Finally, with three steaming mugs in her hands, she settled at the table, tearless and utterly composed, and faced Detective Sergeant Connolly.

'What do you want me to say, Inspector?' she asked.

'Just the truth,' he said.

'I panicked,' she licked her lips now. 'I ran away and I am ashamed of that; I am not ashamed of my liaison with him. I needed him and he needed me; there was no love, no risk of marriage breakdowns on either side, just sex. We fulfilled each other, Inspector, we made each other happy. Yes, I was with him yesterday, and yes, we were making love when he collapsed. I did my best to revive him but failed. Then I heard someone climbing towards us through the bracken, so I ran away, leaving him to find George. I recognize a heart attack when I see one. So what happens next?'

'I need a written statement from you, to complete my investigation — I need no more than what you have just told me.'

'But will it reach a court of any kind?'

'No,' he promised her. 'I must submit a report to the coroner, but as you have explained how he came about his heart attack, how you were present at his death, and as the pathologist's findings agree with your story, there will be no inquest. His death will be recorded as natural, not suspicious.'

'His wife will have to be told that he died during an act of adultery, will she?'

'No,' said Connolly. 'She has been told he died at Lover's Leap, but we have spared her the details.'

'And my husband?'

'He need never know of your involvement unless you tell him.'

'I will not tell him,' she said. She paused a long time as she sipped her coffee, then continued: 'You must both think I am evil, leaving him like that, running away, but I knew he was dead. I was a nurse, you know. I ran off to protect him from scandal. There was nothing I could do, nothing could be done to save him, and he did give me pleasure and happiness, and I gave it to him. There is nothing wrong in that, is there, Inspector? Not when you have an impotent husband . . . '

'We are not concerned with the moral aspects of your relationship, Mrs Pendlebury, just the facts. Now, can we get this statement written down officially?'

'Yes, of course,' and I thought I detected a note of relief in her voice.

But there were no tears, no signs of sorrow and no hint of

any regret. She was an amazing woman and I did wonder whether the hinted aristocratic breeding in her bearing was genuine. Whether she would cry when we left, I could not say, but she did not mention her appointment any more. Instead, she allowed Gerry to write down her statement, and it catered for those final minutes of George Frederick Halliwell. As he had rolled off her, dead but happy, she had tried to re-establish his clothing for decency's sake, but the weight of his body had defeated her.

She bade us farewell, still addressing Gerry as 'Inspector', and we were all relieved.

'I wonder why she left the sweet peas behind,' said Gerry as we drove away.

'They were probably her wreath,' I said. 'She won't attend the funeral, will she?'

'She will,' he said firmly, 'but as a county councillor and a colleague, not as his mistress. She will regard that as her duty,' he smiled.

'You know, Sarge, I think you are right,' I added.

And he was. She turned up at the funeral looking splendid and self-assured, but sorrowful. And she donated another wreath, this time without any sweet peas.

3

The law's made to take care o'
raskills.

George Eliot (1819-80)

During one of those quiet moments in the CID office, it
dawned on me why I might have been selected as an Aide to
the constabulary's detectives. It was surely the outcome of two
cases in which I had been involved during my very youthful
days. At the time I was patrolling a town beat as a raw and
unconfident constable at Strensford, but my actions had been
recorded in my personal file and, indeed, I received a chief
constable's commendation following one of the investigations.
I guessed that, on the strength of these, I was thought to
possess Sherlockian qualities, and so these cases are worthy of
record here, even though they did not occur during my
attachment to Eltering CID.

The first story began one New Year's Eve. In the North
Riding of Yorkshire, this is a time of celebration. There are
lots of parties, dancing, feasting, drinking and general *bonho-
mie*. As the desire to have a good time manifests itself in constables as well as ordinary mortals, most of us tried to avoid
working night shift as the old year became the new one. Often
lots were drawn to avoid argument and hints of favouritism
but even then there were grumbles. To be off duty on New
Year's Eve was indeed a bonus; to be on duty was a real chore.

On this particular New Year's Eve, a colleague of mine,
who was doing his best to woo the lady of his dreams, had an

invitation to a dinner dance with her family. He desperately
wanted to go. The sergeant said he could have the night off
provided someone worked his night shift for him. He asked
me. At first I was horrified at the thought but, with an
understanding wife who was a close friend of his lady-love and
who wished to see a successful conclusion to this ardent
wooing, I capitulated. We swapped shifts and I found myself
patrolling the deserted streets to the sound of happy people
making merry behind closed doors. There is something akin
to real distress within one's soul while patrolling a town alone,
listening to the sounds of happy voices in warm interiors along
every street. It produces a massive feeling of being unwanted,
and it echoes the loneliness of the diligently patrolling police
officer.

In spite of being on duty as the old year became the new, we
did have a good time. In the chill of that happy night, girls
kissed us to wish us a Happy New Year, we honoured the
time-old tradition of First Footing* and we joined in many
parties, albeit with the decorum of the constabulary uppermost in our minds. We regarded it as a good public relations
exercise, a social mingling of the police and the people whom
they serve and for whom they care.

By two o'clock that morning, with the first hours of the new
year now history, it was snowing. The fall was gentle but it
was dry, and it rapidly covered the ground with a blanket of
beautiful white. Soon the entire landscape was glistening in
the flickering lights of partying households and traffic-free
streets, but we knew that on the lofty moorland roads there
would be drifting in the bitter north-east wind.

My refreshment break that cold morning was timed to begin
at 2.15 a.m. and to finish at 3 a.m. I welcomed the warmth of
the police station with its blazing coal fire, a blaze that was
never allowed to go out between 1 October and 31 May. It
burned for twenty-four hours a day, and it was a wonderful
tonic during a chill night duty. I settled down with my
bait-bag, which contained my snack of sandwiches and an
apple, plus a flask of coffee. My only companion was the office
duty constable, Joe Westonby. We chatted about the cheerful

*See *Constable Around the Village*

events of the night; even Joe had had visitors from the nearby
houses, people who came in to wish him a Happy New Year in
his lonely job.

And then, at 2.30 a.m., the telephone rang. It was the
ambulance station, who announced they had received a telephone call from a moorland farmer to say that a car had
overturned in his gateway and two people had been injured.
They were now in the farmhouse but not too seriously hurt.
He added that the moorland roads were treacherous and filling
in rapidly with heavy drifting and a steady fall of snow, but the
ambulance had to make an attempt to cover those five hilly
moorland miles and bring the casualties to hospital.

'Take one of our lads with you,' Joe suggested to the
ambulance station's duty officer. 'If it's not urgent, he can be
with you in five minutes.'

This step agreed, partly to assist us in our duty of dealing
with the accident and partly because in those days we did not
have the regular use of official cars, Joe rang PC Timms at a
kiosk in town and told him to accompany the ambulance. He
suggested he take a shovel too, and some wellies, as it could
develop into a hazardous trip.

With that drama now being dealt with, I resumed my town
patrol and returned to the office at 4.30 a.m. for a warm-up
before the lovely fire. The sergeant said we could all come in
for a break as we were covered in snow and our extremities
were freezing. The steady pace of patrolling a beat does not
warm the circulation, and it is not dignified to break into a
trot, even on the coldest of Yorkshire nights. My toes and
fingers were frozen, and I was ready for bed, but there was
another hour and a half before I could book off duty at 6 a.m.

As I entered the station, I saw the ambulance struggling up
the slippery slope to the hospital; it had to pass the police
station to get there, so I grabbed a shovel and scattered gravel
along its path. But it halted outside. 'There's snow up yonder
that'll block us in before sun-up,' said the driver. 'We nearly
got snowed up in t'farmhouse. Anyroad, we made it; one of
'em'll need hospital treatment, t'other's in t'back with your
mate. T'car's a right-off.'

I opened the rear doors of the ambulance and out climbed
PC Graham Timms and another man. In the darkness, the

ambulance struggled to finish its journey to the hospital with spinning wheels and a few sideways slithers as I accompanied Timms and his companion into the station. He had brought the man in so that he could obtain the details for his accident report.

Even in the gloom, I recognized the motorist and he recognized me; we had been brought up in neighbouring moorland villages, and in those small communities we all knew each other.

'Now then, Ben,' I said. 'You're not hurt then?'

'Hello, Nick. No, I was lucky. Harry's got a broken arm, I think. It could have been worse.'

'Who was driving?' I asked, merely out of interest.

'Me,' said Ben Baldwin as I followed him down the dark passage into the enquiry office.

As he walked into the light of the office, I saw that he was wearing a smart pale blue raincoat that was a shade too long for his short figure and more than a shade too wide at the shoulders. As he and PC Timms settled into the office, with Timms arranging a cup of tea for Baldwin, I was sure I recognized that coat. It was exactly like one that had been stolen from a village dance hall about two years earlier. Baldwin took it off and hung it on a hook on the office wall, so I poured myself a cup of tea and studied it carefully. Baldwin was taken into another office by Timms, and I was alone with PC Westonby.

'Joe,' I said, 'that coat hanging there, I'm sure it's one that was stolen two years ago from a dance hall at Fieldholme.'

'Don't be daft, Nick,' he grinned. 'A coat's a coat. You can't tell one from another, especially not after two years!'

'I can,' I confirmed. 'Because it's mine.'

'Yours?' he puzzled. 'You mean somebody nicked your coat and this is it?'

'Yes,' I said.

He stared at me, unbelieving, then said, 'Try it on while Baldwin's out.'

I did, and it fitted perfectly; I knew it was mine. I returned it to the coat hook.

'Tell me more,' invited Joe.

I explained that, before I joined the police service, I did my

two years National Service with the RAF and upon leaving
bought myself a smart new raincoat. It was expensive, and it
was RAF blue in colour. With my new coat on, I took my
fiancée to a dance at Fieldholme Village Hall one Saturday
night. It was during the three weeks holiday I had allowed
myself between leaving the RAF and joining the police force.
When the dance was over, I went to the cloakroom for my
coat. It had gone. In its place there was a filthy brown raincoat
that was covered in grease and oil stains and which was far too
small for me. I reported the theft to the village constable.

'And you maintain this is yours?'

'Yes,' I said, without a shadow of doubt in my mind.

'But how can you tell?' he asked me.

'I dunno,' I had to admit. 'I just know it's mine – the
colour's unusual for one thing, and it's too big for Baldwin
anyway. That is my coat, Joe, and he's pinched it.'

'That's no good for our purposes, Nick,' he said. 'You
know very well that we need to *prove* it's yours. Believing is no
good; if we try to prosecute him on your say-so, no court
would convict him.'

'So he gets away with theft of my coat?'

'Look, Nick, you know the ropes as well as I do. I know this
seems different because you claim it's yours, but look at it on a
broader plane – after all, anyone could claim property in this
way, by merely saying it's theirs. People do make mistakes,
you know. They think they recognize something they've
lost . . . '

I was aware of the problems and the need for positive
identification, and in this case it highlighted the value of
having some means of personalizing one's goods, especially
when there are hundreds or thousands of identical copies.

'I've still got the brown one at home,' I said. 'I've been
keeping it in case this sort of thing happened – I guessed the
thief was local.'

'I'll have a go at Baldwin when Graham's finished with
him,' promised Joe. 'You'd better not be the one to interview
him – you're biased! In the meantime, I'll dig out your crime
complaint – when was it, exactly?'

I told him the date of the dance two years earlier.

When Baldwin had given his account of the accident,

Timms brought him back into the enquiry office to collect his raincoat. I stood to one side as Joe said, 'Put that coat on, Mr Baldwin.'

He did; it looked huge.

'Nice coat,' said Joe. 'Where did you get it?'

'Middlesbrough,' said Baldwin.

'New, was it?'

'Yes, brand new, but I can't remember the shop.'

'What did it cost?'

'Twenty five quid,' he said; it had cost me £30, in fact.

Joe looked at me. How could we disprove this story? It lacked any detail that could be challenged — like the familiar thief's tale that 'I got it off a chap in a pub' or 'It fell off the back of a lorry.' I said nothing, knowing that I could jeopardize the enquiry if I wasn't careful.

Joe must have believed my claims because he tried shock tactics. 'Well, Mr Baldwin, I don't believe you. And I'll tell you what, you've just dropped the biggest bollock of your life. That coat isn't yours, it's this lad's. It belongs to PC Nicholas Rhea, and you nicked it from a dance hall at Fieldholme two years ago.'

Baldwin's eyes showed his guilt and his horror, but he recovered quickly and said, 'Bollocks! It's mine and I bought it new.'

Then I remembered a detail which no one else knew. It came to me as Baldwin was affirming his ownership, and I said, 'Joe, there is a way of proving it's mine.'

'You need something good, Nick,' was all he said.

'It is.' I was confident now. 'When I was in the RAF, we had tags bearing our service numbers; we sewed them into our clothes. My number was 2736883, and it was on a white tag; I had some of those tags spare when I left the RAF, and I sewed one under the flap on the wrist of the right sleeve of that coat.'

I saw by the expression in Baldwin's eyes that he knew I was the true owner of that coat, but I also reckoned he would never admit stealing it. I had known him long enough to know his character, but had he found that tag?

Joe beamed. 'Come here, Mr Baldwin,' he said, and as Baldwin stood before him, Joe loosened the button on the flap on the cuff of the right sleeve and turned it back. But there was no service number tag inside — although there were some tiny remnants of white cotton where it had been removed.

'Evidence of guilt, Nick,' said Joe, pointing to the shreds of cotton. 'He's removed the number — that's good enough for a court.'

We looked at Ben Baldwin, guilt all over his face as he said, 'Sorry, Nick, I had no idea it was yours . . . '

And he confessed to the theft two years earlier.

Due to my personal interest in the case, it was unwise for me to undertake the formalities that ensued. I was merely a witness, a victim of that crime, so Joe arrested Ben and he was formally charged. But it did not end there.

The first problem was that there was no record of my original report of the theft. The crime records did not show that I had reported it, and this threatened to cause administrative problems until the CID realized the entry might be in the lost-property book! And so it was. My coat was recorded as 'lost', not stolen, but at least there was a note of it in official records. But how on earth anyone could assume it was 'lost', when another of completely different size, colour, appearance and quality had replaced it, was baffling.

I reckoned it was one way of keeping down the crime figures!

But there were more developments. When the local crime records were searched, it was learned that several other coats had been stolen from dance halls in the locality. They had disappeared over four or five years, and with the arrest of Ben Baldwin, we now had a prime suspect. He was a part-time barman and general dealer, who lived alone in a small cottage at a village called Kindledale. As common law permitted, the CID decided that his home should be searched for material evidence of those other crimes. Ben was told of these plans and did not object, so the search went ahead while he was in custody at Strensford.

If he had objected, a seach warrant would have been obtained, although it was not necessary in these circumstances. The Royal Commission on Police Powers and Procedures expressed an opinion that the authority for such searches of the premises occupied by arrested persons was now enshrined in common law.

And in this case no further coats were found. But Ben's home did reveal a huge cache of other stolen goods. It was filled to overflowing with tins of food, bottles of whisky, brandy and gin, bottles of beer and stout, packets of sugar, flour and cereals and a host of other odds and ends. When confronted with this, Ben admitted stealing the lot from the various inns and hotels where he had worked.

In many instances, the owners had not missed the goods, although, with the volume involved, it was felt that any stocktaking would reveal these deficiencies. And so Ben was charged with several more thefts; as we say, these were 'TIC'd' when he appeared in the magistrates' court to answer the charge of stealing my coat. A hefty fine was imposed upon him.

The newspapers were full of the story due to the odd circumstances which had led to his arrest, and I had my coat returned to me, a little more battered and worn than it had been when I 'lost' it but still wearable after a thorough cleansing. And for my powers of observation in recognizing the stolen coat, I received a commendation from the chief constable.

But the story continues. A week after the court case, my wife's cousin rang me from Fieldholme. A large cardboard box had mysteriously appeared in his garden overnight, and when he opened it, it contained several overcoats. One belonged to him but he had no idea to whom the others belonged. Our records showed they had all been stolen in that vicinity.

And we never did find out who had stolen those other coats, nor who had dumped the box in that garden.

Some twenty years later, there was a further sequel to this yarn. I appeared before a Promotion Board at Police Headquarters where my career was discussed; that commendation was mentioned and I had to give an account of it. It was only as I discussed it with the chief constable and his senior officers that it dawned on me that nowhere in the Headquarters files was it mentioned that it was my own coat.

Maybe, if that early report had included that point, I would never have been commended?

However, it is clear that, if I had not swapped shifts that New Year's Eve, a lot of crimes would have remained unsolved.

The second investigation which came my way as a youthful constable at Strensford was one which involved 'discreet enquiries'. In this case, our neighbouring police force at Middlesbrough had received an application from a gentleman who wished to be granted a liquor licence. His request was for the grant of a restaurant licence which was issued by the justices.

He had bought some small parts of an old factory premises and wanted to turn them into a licensed restaurant. At that time, restaurant licences were a new idea, having recently been given statutory approval, for it meant that intoxicants could be sold with table meals away from the established hotels and inns, provided the premises were suitable and, of course, that the applicant was also suitable.

It was known that the applicant's expansive plans included future development of the site until it became a noted club, restaurant and even gaming centre. But all that was in the future – his immediate concern was to be granted that first liquor licence so that his restaurant could become a reality and so that he could establish himself on his chosen site.

He had submitted his plans and his application through the proper channels, and the role of the police, in forwarding these to the magistrates, was to establish whether or not he was a 'fit and proper' person to hold such a licence. He had no criminal record, and so it seemed his fitness to be granted such a licence was not in doubt. But, because he had given an address in Strensford, which was in a police area different from the one through which he was applying, we had to make discreet enquiries in the town. These were merely to strengthen his fitness claim; it was a routine enquiry for us, one of many we had to make.

At the start of my late shift one morning, Sergeant Andy Moorhouse called me into his office.

'Nick,' he said, holding a sheaf of papers, 'I've a grand job here for you. It involves some discreet enquiries and you can take a day or two over it; there's no rush, so long as you do a thorough job.'

He explained about the application for the restaurant

licence and said, 'The applicant is a Mr Ralph Charles Swinden; he's forty-one years old and a native of Wakefield. But it seems he lived in Strensford for a year or two, and has given an address in town — No. 7 Belford Place. He doesn't live there now, by the way, but it seems he came to live there just over two years ago. We've been asked to make discreet enquiries in the area to see if there's any reason why he should not be granted his licence.'

I said I understood, but he continued:

'Now, have you done one of these enquiries?'

'No,' I admitted.

'There's no problem with them at all. They're an interesting way of occupying your time. Swinden has no criminal record, so it's just a case of asking local tradesmen whether he's honest and trustworthy. Get around the shops and businesses near where he lived and see if they know anything against him. Be discreet, Nick, and then submit your report through me. OK?'

'We've nothing in our files, have we?' I asked.

'No,' he said. 'I've never come across the chap, and I've been here six years. I've had a word with CID and he's never crossed their paths. He's obviously led a decent and quiet life, but we need to convince Middlesbrough Police and their magistrates of that.'

I looked forward to my task and was allocated a beat which included Belford Place. I started immediately I had read the papers and decided my enquiries would begin with people in the area whom I knew and trusted. The papers did not say whether Swinden had worked in Strensford or whether he had merely lived there and worked elsewhere, but if he had been a part of the town's social or business scene, I would soon find out.

I tried to determine where a man in his late thirties, as he would then have been, would spend his money or his time and decided to start with those pubs he might have used.

I entered the Golden Lion when it was quiet and after some small talk with the landlord asked him, 'Jim, do you know Ralph Swinden? He used to live in Belford Place; he came to live in the town just over a couple of years ago.'

'What's he look like, Mr Rhea? What did he do?'

'No idea,' I confessed. 'I've just got a name.'

'Sorry,' he said. 'Ralph; I can't recall having a Ralph in here as a regular.'

There were seven pubs, two hotels and one registered club very close to Belford Place but no one associated with them knew Swinden.

He was not a member of the registered club either, but the steward did know most of the locals on the town's social round, those who frequented the golf club, the British Legion and the Strensford Working Men's Club, as well as those who had joined the Rotary Club, the Round Table, the Lions and other similar organizations. The name of Ralph Charles Swinden did not feature in his memory, but I visited the secretaries of those clubs and organizations he had suggested, just to be certain. They did not know him either.

My first tour of duty was concluded without anyone's knowing my subject, and I found that odd.

'How's it going, Nick?' asked Sergeant Moorhouse as I booked off duty.

'No one knows him, Sarge,' I said.

'Good, then no one knows anything against him,' he beamed.

'I've more people to see.' I wanted him to know I had not finished.

'No problem. Keep at it, but don't overdo it!'

The next day I continued my enquiries, for I was becoming intrigued by this nonentity. Surely a man cannot live in a small town like Strensford for two years or so and be totally unknown? I reckoned that he, or perhaps his wife, would certainly shop in town. Close to Belford Place there was a grocer's shop, the Co-Op, clothes shops, a sub-post office, vegetable and fruit shops, jewellers, an electrical supplier, stationer, newsagent and bookshop, butcher and many more. I decided to ask at them all, including those who might have called at the house, such as the postman and milkman, as well as insurance agents and travelling salesmen.

And in every case I received a negative reply. No one knew the man.

Sergeant Moorhouse said it all confirmed the notion that there was nothing known against him, nothing that would make him an unsuitable candidate for a restaurant licence. But I was not happy. Someone in town must know him.

All the following day I continued asking at shops and business premises. I knew a solicitor and asked him; I knew a bank manager and asked him; the postman shook his head, and the milkman said he had never come across Swinden. I asked the local Catholic priest, the vicar, the Methodist minister and the Salvation Army captain, none of whom knew him, and I even asked my colleagues. I found that in my off-duty time I was asking people if they had come across Ralph Charles Swinden, but no one had. After three days of doing nothing else, I had not found a single person who knew him. Sergeant Moorhouse felt this was a perfect situation, for in his opinion it indicated that Swinden was not a man who got himself into debt or into trouble or into conflict with others. He seemed such a quiet chap, law-abiding, honest and with integrity.

When the sergeant said I should submit my report accordingly, I asked for at least another day on the enquiry, for I had to find someone who knew the man.

'Tomorrow then, Nick. I can't let this go on any longer, son; you're not letting it become an obsession, are you?'

'No, Sarge!' I cried. 'I just want to find somebody who knows him. Don't you think it's odd that no one has come across him?'

'Not really,' he said. 'Some folks live very quietly and go about their lives in total anonymity.'

I hardly felt that such a style of life suited a man whose ambition was to run a thriving restaurant and club; in my view, such a life-style was more suited to a hermit than a businessman. Businessmen were rarely so elusive and unknown. I knew I must ask at the houses which adjoined his address.

Belford Place was a curious little assemblage of cottages at the end of an alley; in Strensford, those alleys are called either ghauts, ginnels or yards. They form a narrow tunnel through the houses or shops. Often with a roof at first-floor level, they reach from the streets and occasionally open into a small square around which the occupants dwell. The alleys leading from the streets are little wider than a pram, and indeed some have doors on the street so that the casual passer-by has no idea that a small community exists behind. In those instances where the alley does not open into a square, the cottage doors and windows line each side, so that people living opposite one another are almost within arm's length. But Belford Place did open into a small, irregular square; it was a pretty area with a handful of tiny stone cottages. They boasted bow windows and were built of local stone as they nestled in this quiet area just behind a busy thoroughfare. Apart from the alleyway between the houses, this place was virtually shut off from the world.

I counted eight cottages, all neatly painted, with polished numerals on the doors and colourful boxes of flowers adorning their window-ledges. The area between the cottages comprised paving-stones, and here and there were dotted half-barrels of more flowers. It was a very pretty little area, a picture-book kind of haven.

Being a methodical sort of chap, I started my enquiries at No. 1. Upon my knock, the door was opened by an elderly, stooping man whose eyes showed the initial horror that most people feel upon being unexpectedly confronted at their front door by a uniformed policeman.

I adopted an oblique approach to my search for information, for I did not want undue alarm or gossip to be created by my visit.

'I'm looking for a Mr Swinden,' I said. 'Ralph Swinden. I'm told he lives here.'

'Swinden?' shouted the old man. 'Never 'eard of 'im. Where's 'e live then?'

'In one of these houses,' I responded.

'You've got it wrong, lad,' he grunted and went back inside.

And so I tried No. 2, where a middle-aged lady, holding a ginger cat in her arms, told me she had noticed a man at No. 7 who disappeared for long periods but she didn't know his name. At No. 3 I got a similar response from a young woman with a baby who'd recently moved in, while at No. 4 a huge woman eating a bread bun produced a negative result. The man at No. 5, who looked like a holidaymaker with his colourful shirt and open-toed sandals, said he was just visiting the yard and had never heard of Swinden. The lady at No. 6

refused to open the door, but shouted her answers through the
letter-box. I think I'd got her out of the bath. I omitted No. 7,
which was Swinden's supposed address, but got the now
expected answer from No. 8; the couple living there, tiny folk
with a tiny dog that yapped at my knock, shook their heads
and said they had never known a Mr Swinden, but could it be
that man at No. 7?

I was now left with No. 7. Should I ask there? I knew that
these enquiries were supposed to be discreet, but I was now in
a position where I had to know something, anything, about
the mysterious subject of my investigation.

I decided to enquire at No. 7.

I rapped on the door and waited. My knock was answered
by a woman about thirty-five years old. She wore a cheap
frock with a flowery design and carpet slippers, and her fair,
untidy hair was wet, probably having just been washed.

'Oh, the law!' she gasped when she saw me. 'What have I
done?'

I smiled. Her approach was friendly enough, and so I went
into my new routine. 'I'm looking for a man called Swinden,
Ralph Charles Swinden . . . '

Before I could go any further, she exploded. 'That bastard!'
she cried. 'Where is he? What's he done now?'

'You know him?'

'You bet I know him! What's all this about, Constable?'

'Can I come in?' I asked, for I did not want this development to be overheard by the entire yard. She led me into a tiny
kitchen, where she had obviously been washing her hair over
the sink, for shampoos and towels lay on the draining-board.
'Sorry about the mess, I've just been tarting myself up.
Coffee?'

'I'd love one.' I was ready for a sit-down after my perambulations, and this promised to be a revealing discussion. She
made us each a mug of instant coffee, sighed heavily and then
settled opposite me at the formica-covered kitchen table.

'So,' she said, shovelling three spoonfuls of sugar into her
mug, 'what's he been up to?'

'Before I tell you, how do you know him?' I wanted to
establish the truth of this little affair right at the start.

'He was my lodger,' she said, and I guessed the term was

merely a euphemism.

'So you are not Mrs Swinden?' I asked.

'Not likely!' she said. 'I wouldn't have him for keeps.'

'So who are you?' I had to ask.

'Smithson, Jenny Smithson,' she smiled. 'And this is my house, not his. My dad left it to me; it's all mine.'

'Do you work?' I asked.

'Part-time. I'm a barmaid at the Mermaid Hotel most evenings, and then some days in the week I serve behind the counter at Turner's — that's the fruit and veg shop near the harbour.'

As I paused to write down these details in my pocket-book, she asked, 'So what's all this about?'

I was a little uncertain how much I should explain, but if this woman's description of 'lodger' was true, I could ask my 'discreet enquiries' of her. If lodger meant live-in lover or common law husband, it might be different. I decided to be honest with her; after all, she was the only person in the town who admitted knowledge of Swinden.

'He's applied for a liquor licence in Middlesbrough,' I began. 'He wants to open a restaurant, and he has given this as his former address. My job is to enquire around here to see if he is a fit and proper person to hold such a licence.'

'He most definitely is not!' she burst out. 'Oh, my word, no! Look, Constable, let me show you something.'

She went into her living-room and I heard her open a cabinet of some kind, then she returned with a small book.

'Right,' she said. 'This is my building society passbook. See that last entry?'

She handed it to me and I saw there had been a withdrawal of the entire funds, totalling £203.17s.6d.

'So?' I asked.

'He did that, Constable. He forged my signature on the withdrawal form and got away with all my savings. And he pinched money from upstairs — I keep my spare cash in a vase in my bedroom, and that's all gone. Fifty quid or so.'

'How did this happen?' I put to her, sipping the coffee.

She explained how Swinden had met her during her work in the Mermaid, and they had struck up a liaison. He had been seeking accommodation in Strensford and so, eventually, she had taken him into her home, at first as a lodger, but it wasn't long before he was in her bed too. This had happened about two years ago, and they had been moderately happy. He said he was a salesman, and so he was away quite a lot. Then she had to go to Reading to look after the two children of her sister who was ill; she had spent some six weeks there earlier this year, leaving Swinden in the cottage to care for himself. And when she had returned, only last week, he had gone; there was no note to explain his absence, but all his things had been removed and he had left no forwarding address.

'I came back unexpectedly,' she said. 'I thought I'd be away for six months or even more, and so did he. Maybe that's why he gave this address, thinking no one would be here? Anyway, here I am, back at home.'

'So what did you discover?' I asked.

'Only yesterday,' she continued, 'I went to find that passbook; I was going to buy myself a new dress and I found my money had all gone. When I asked at the building society, they said they had a withdrawal form, signed by me, and they refused to think someone else had done it. Well, somebody else has, Constable, because I was in Reading at the time of the withdrawal. Is that something you can investigate? I was wondering if I should call in the police about it.'

'Yes,' I said. 'We can investigate, and it *is* something you should make an official complaint about.'

Sergeant Moorhouse was surprised, to say the least, the CID were delighted to have a forgery to investigate and the superintendent was somewhat aghast that my discreet en-quiries had uncovered this crime.

Ralph Charles Swinden was not granted his restaurant licence, the reason being that his conviction for forgery and larceny, with its heavy fine and the order for restitution of the missing cash, meant he was not a fit and proper person.

4

You thought you were here to be
the most senseless and fit man for
the constable of the watch.
            Don Pedro: *Much Ado About Nothing*
            William Shakespeare (1564-1616)

'On obbo' or 'keeping obs', is the police jargon for 'keeping observations'; this means watching a suspect person or premises, and it usually entails long, cold and boring hours alone and in silence while accommodated in the most cramped of conditions. We could be hunched in the back of a bare and cold van or car, we could be in a filthy, draughty loft watching the street below or we might be hidden in a wood or field with only the owls, foxes, weasels and voles for companionship.

Many of these long stints ended with no positive result, but sometimes the rewards can be great, such as those occasions when one catches a suspect bank-raider or burglar. For that reason, there is always the excitement of the unknown, and this helps to sustain the observer during those worst soul-destroying times. During a long obs session, there is something of the gambler's tension, for one literally never knows whether the anticipated result will occur. Some you win, some you lose. If you win, you are exhilarated; if you lose, you know there'll be another obs job along in a moment or two, one that could produce better results and the exhilaration of catching a villain in the act of committing his crime.

'We've an obs job for you,' said Gerry Connolly to me one

morning. 'Tomorrow night, mebbe all night. Come on duty at ten o'clock, dress in something dark and warm, and fetch a flask of coffee and some sandwiches. Oh, and a torch. I'll fill you in tomorrow. There'll be a briefing at ten o'clock.'

Apart from demolishing my assurance to Mary that I would not be expected to undertake night duty when working as a CID Aide, this also caused some *angst* in her because she had no idea what I was about to do. Neither had I, so I could not explain, but policemen's wives do learn to be trusting and understanding. They have to be when neither knows what is about to happen or what involvement there will be. In some cases there can be danger, and well they know it.

'I've no idea what I'll be doing or how late I'll be,' I said as I dressed in some old black uniform trousers, several dark sweaters and a pair of black leather gloves. 'They didn't say what the job was; nobody knows. We're to be briefed when we report for duty.'

'Just be careful then.' She kissed me goodbye. 'It does sound dangerous, all those dark clothes . . . '

'They're the warmest I've got,' I said, trying to be nonchalant. 'Bye.'

I arrived at Eltering Police Station to find five other detectives, all dressed in thick, warm clothes. I knew two of them, for they had been drafted in from Strensford, but the others were strangers to me.

As we assembled in the main office, wondering what our mission was to be, Detective Sergeant Connolly came in.

'Right,' he said. 'Into the court house, all of you; we'll have our briefing there.'

The court room adjoined the police station, and there was a linking passage; no one would be using it at this time of night, and so it offered some security from flapping ears. Ears can flap in police stations, ears that can unwittingly – or sometimes deliberately – reveal the secrets of an undercover operation. This was clearly an operation of paramount secrecy, so secret that even other police officers were not to be informed. We were therefore the elite of the moment, those in the know, those selected for a mission of sensitivity and drama, an occasion to display our professional skill and competence. We all wondered what on earth was going on.

When we were seated, Gerry Connolly gave each of us a thin file containing a diagram of a street, a plan of some houses in that street, and a list of other details such as the names, car numbers and distinctive marks or habits of those whom we were soon to learn were suspects.

'Has everyone got a file?' he asked, and when there were no dissenters, he continued: 'Right. This is our task for tonight. It will be known as Operation Phrynia.'

'Frinia?' puzzled one of the men.

'Phrynia,' affirmed Gerry Connolly without explanation. He paused as he took the street plan from his own file. 'Examine the street plan first . . .'

As he spoke, we learned that the street was Pottery Terrace, Eltering. It lay in the older part of the town where, as the name suggested, there had once been a thriving pottery. The house in which we were interested was No. 15. It was a terrace house built of local stone with a front door leading directly onto the street, and a back door opening onto a closed yard. The exit from the yard led into a back lane.

'No. 15 Pottery Terrace is the home of Margot Stainton, Mrs Margot Stainton, who is thirty-two years old. Her husband is a squaddie serving in Germany, a tank regiment, I'm told, and when he's away, she gets lonely and so she goes on the game. We don't think he knows what she gets up to. She is helped in her enterprise by some of her lady friends, who, we are assured, are very enthusiastic volunteers who earn a bob or two for their efforts. That house, gentlemen, is a knocking shop, and it is attracting customers from a wide area, some of whom will make headlines if we catch them at it. It is a brothel, gentlemen, not a high-class one by any means, but a busy one if our information is correct.'

He paused to let us digest these words and went on:

'The house is jointly owned by Mr and Mrs Stainton, which means she can be prosecuted for keeping or managing the brothel; there is no question of a landlord or agent being involved. So it is our job tonight to prove that she is running a brothel.'

Most of us were now striving to remember the law on brothels, but Gerry was continuing.

'Our purpose tonight is to gain the evidence which will, in

the long term, justify a prosecution and secure a conviction. We also need to acquire sufficient evidence to enable us to obtain a warrant to search the premises and to arrest any suspects. That will be the second phase of this operation; tonight we are to be engaged on the first phase, the observations which will give us the evidence we need to justify the second phase. We are prepared to keep obs for two, three or more nights if necessary. We have had complaints from neighbours, by the way, and so we want to clean up this terrace.'

He then reminded us about the law on brothels: we had to prove that at least two women were using the house, or just a room in the house, for the purposes of illicit sexual intercourse or acts of lewdness. If just one woman was using the house for those purposes, however much she charged or whatever number of men she coped with, that was not a brothel. Two women were required in law if we were to prove the house was a brothel, but it did not matter whether or not they were paid for their work.

We had to make a note of the number of men arriving at the premises, with times and modes of transport (and car registration numbers where possible), the number of women in the house at any one time and, if possible, evidence of what they got up to when they went into the house.

A raid of the house was not planned tonight, he told us; that might come later, once the evidence had been obtained to justify it. He paused again for all this to sink into our skulls, for it was now time to allocate individual tasks. We were all given particular places to hide in, so that all entrances and exits were covered, and there was to be no radio contact with Eltering Police Station or the force control room. Our duty was simply to note everything and everyone we saw entering and leaving that house, with names if possible, conversations and other factors that would establish its role as a brothel. We were to remain at our allocated points from 11 p.m. until 2 a.m; at 2 a.m. we were to stand down, without orders being given, and we had all to rendezvous in the playground of the infants' school just around the corner. If for any reason the operation was aborted earlier, we were to rendezvous in that playground. There would be a brief résumé of our success or

otherwise, and we would then return to Eltering Police Station
to write up our notes.

As the positions were allocated, I awaited mine with
interest. Finally, he said, 'D/PC Rhea. We've a special one for
you. Now look at the plan of the house. Got it?'

'Yes, Sarge,' I said.

'You see the building that extends from No. 15 to abut the
lane at the back? It makes the house L-shaped.'

'Got it,' I said.

'That is a one-storey-high set of outhouses. There's a
washhouse, an outside loo and a coalhouse. All the houses in
that terrace have them.' I knew the kind of building to which
he referred; they were a feature of the terrace houses in this
region. 'That building forms the boundary to the east; each of
its doors opens into the yard of No. 15. The other side of that
same building has another loo, coalhouse and washhouse, and
they open into the yard of No. 13.'

'I get the picture,' I said.

'It would be nice if we could hide in one of those sheds to
watch visitors, but we daren't; for one thing it would amount
to a trespass by us, and for another they might use any of them
tonight and discover us. So, Nick, I want you on the roof of
that building. That way you will not be seen. There are no
street lights in that back lane, and from that roof, if you lie on
it, you will be able to look down into the yard of No. 15. All
those houses have flat cement roofs, by the way, so there is no
danger of falling through it or falling off it. From there, you'll
be able to see all movements through that back entrance, and
you should be able to overhear any conversations at the back
door as visitors arrive and depart. Note everything in your
pocket-book: times, names etc.

'Now, above you, if you stand with your back to the wall of
No. 15, is the window of a back bedroom. We know that room
is used by the incoming fellers and at least one of the women.'
He paused and continued: 'It would be of enormous help to
this operation if you could overhear any snatches of action or
conversation in that room.'

'Won't I be seen up there?'

'Not if you're careful. I note you've dark clothing on, and
you can climb onto the roof by shinning up the rear wall of

No. 15's yard, from the back lane. It's a high roof, and if you keep still, you'll not be spotted. If you are seen, just run for it — jump into that back lane and gallop like hell. They'll think you're a pimper or a burglar. That applies to you all — this is an undercover operation, lads, so you're on your own. Think on your feet and keep out of trouble. Right? Now, any questions?'

There were one or two points of clarification and then we were despatched to our posts, one at a time to avoid what might appear to be a bunch of hooligans marching into town. I was the last to leave.

'Sarge,' I said to Connolly, 'one point of curiosity. Why call this job Operation Phrynia?'

'A joke of sorts, Nick; we shan't be using radios, so the lads needn't remember it. But Phrynia, or Phryne as she is sometimes called, was a famous Greek prostitute some 400 years before Christ. She was gifted with extraordinary beauty and, in fact, was the model for the statue of Venus rising from the sea. She was eventually tried for being a prostitute.

'She was defended by Hyperides; the evidence was all against her, and just before a guilty verdict was about to be given, he tore her robe to expose her magnificent chest. And at that, the judges' minds went berserk and they acquitted her. So beware the wiles of women and their lawyers, and beware of Mrs Stainton. Don't forget, she might claim you and the other lads are her customers . . . '

I made a resolution to remain very carefully concealed during my forthcoming duty and left the station. It was a cool, dark night with no moon and, in those areas away from the street lights, the town was pitch dark. I arrived at the rear of No. 15 on foot, knowing that I was being observed by hidden CID men. I looked for them but could not see them, so I reckoned no casual visitor would know of our observations.

At the rear door of No. 15, the one which led into the yard, I had the task of climbing onto the wall, which was about eight feet high, and then making my way onto the roof of the outbuildings. I dare not use my torch, which was stuffed into my pocket, but I found I could mount the wall by using the handle of the yard door in conjunction with some footholds in the stonework. It was a scramble, but in a short time I was lying stomach down on the wall — facing the wrong way. I then had to stand up on the narrow top of the wall in order to turn around and walk towards the roof upon which I was to spend the next three hours. It was like walking a tightrope but I reached the edge of the roof without falling off.

The wall upon which I had walked formed the end outer wall of the outbuildings. The edge of the roof was level with the top of the wall, and it would be a simple matter to transfer from one to another. But then I was horrified to find it was *not* a flat roof. These outbuildings had a sloping, tiled roof — all the other houses had flat-roofed outbuildings. Someone had not done their research very thoroughly! So I now had an additional problem.

I could see the slates ahead of me, shining in the meagre light from the houses, and that at this end, the back street end, the roof ended with stone copings which rose steeply from the wall. I was sure Connolly had said it would be a flat roof . . . but orders were orders. In the gloom, I could see the ridge of the roof and saw that it extended to the back wall of the house. If I could creep along that ridge, I could sit there, straddling it with my legs as I kept observations. I had to prove I could do this job. Ahead of me, and joining the wall upon which I stood, was a steep slope of coping-stones which led up to the ridge. I must not step directly onto the tiles, and I knew I must climb up that slope.

Cat-like, I now began to climb towards the summit of the roof without standing on any of the blue slates. My gloved hands gripped the coping-stones at their edges as I inched my way upwards. And then I was at the top. If I crept onto the ridge now, I would be facing the wrong way, and so I decided to turn around.

I wanted to sit on the ridge of the roof with a leg dangling down each side, and my back could then rest against the wall of the house, beneath that bedroom window that was of such interest. With infinite care, and happy that no one was walking along that back lane to witness my efforts, I twisted and inched myself onto the roof. In my heavy clothes, I was perspiring by the end of my manœuvring, but eventually I was sitting astride the ridge tiles which ran along the rounded peak of this well-built outhouse roof.

It was now time to inch my way backwards towards the house. I glanced at the bedroom window which was one of my objectives but it was not illuminated and it seemed the curtains were closed. I was not too late for that task — not yet, anyway.

By executing a kind of low-level rearward leapfrogging movement, I did journey backwards two or three inches at a time towards the security of the wall of the house. I was half way through my trip when someone approached; a man suddenly materialized in the rear alley. He opened the yard door, flitted into the yard and then walked purposefully towards the back door of the house. He knocked and waited as I sat on the roof watching him. I wondered how I could reach my pocket-book in the darkness to record this moment, but the door opened and a woman's voice said, 'Come in, Ken.' He vanished inside without seeing my right foot dangling upon the sloping tiles only a few feet above his head. I would make my notes when I was settled, but what I had observed was hardly criminal material.

Then another man came the same way; he was admitted by a woman who said, 'Come in, Alec. Nice to see you,' but I could not see her. I had no idea whether it was the same woman. I wondered if the front door was now busy receiving guests. (I was later to learn that some eight or nine men and a similar number of young women were in the house by this time, having used the front door.) When a third man arrived by this route, I began to wonder if I would ever reach the security of the wall behind me, for I was still marooned midway along. I remembered he was called Gordon.

I noted their times of arrival on my watch . . . 11.15 p.m., 11.19 p.m. and 11.22 p.m. Not knowing how many women were inside, nor how many men had entered through the front door, it seemed that an orgy was planned. But not for me. I was still inching backwards, trying to be silent, trying not to send tiles spinning into the yards at each side of me, and trying to be invisible.

Then my back touched the wall. I had arrived at my place of safety. I felt very relieved at this achievement and was pleased that I could now sit here and observe. I leaned back against the welcoming wall, panting with my efforts and now feeling much more secure. For a few minutes nothing happened. I sat on my odd perch and gazed around the street scene below, my eyes now accustomed to the darkness and my ears attuned to the noises of the town.

I could hear faint music from somewhere too, a regular beat. And sometimes the sound of happy voices reached me, to provoke in me a sense of loneliness and isolation. What on earth was I doing, sitting on a roof as midnight approached, I asked myself. The ridge tiles, although rounded and made of clay, were most uncomfortable; after a few moments of sitting, I had to stretch my legs and relieve the discomfort, and I wondered if I could stand up, just for a few moments, to get my circulation moving and to ease my cramped muscles.

I decided to test the strength of the tiles. Gingerly, I placed each foot squarely upon a couple of tiles and allowed them to take my weight; they seemed to be firm enough. But to stand up, with my back against the wall, I needed some kind of assistance and recalled the window above me and to my right. There was a similar window to my left as well; it belonged to the house next door. If I could reach the window-ledges, I could use them to lever myself to my feet, and they would offer some support. I extended my right arm high to my right, and in the gloom my finger reached the ledge. But this was not enough to give me the purchase I required; I therefore extended my left hand and found the other window-ledge. Now, with both hands, I tried again, but my right hand slipped an inch or two – there was moss on that window ledge. It was enough to throw me off balance for a fraction of a second, and in so doing my left hand slid along the neighbouring window-ledge.

And then drama.

That sliding hand hit a plant pot which stood on the ledge. I turned to look; in horror, I saw it topple off. But there was worse to come. That pot had been tied to another, and another . . . there were six plant pots, all full of plants, and as the first one toppled off the ledge, its weight moved the others. And I was too far away to save them. One by one, they leapt off that ledge and crashed into the back yard of No. 13, strung together like rock-climbers, each falling away.

The first crashed into a coal bunker but the second, having escaped from its securing string, hit the window-sill at ground-floor level; the third, I think, hit the metal dustbin with a resounding clang, and the others all crashed into various objects in the yard. The noise was terrible. I heard angry shouts from No. 13, and the back door opened. A large number of men poured out . . .

One of them saw me.

How I achieved my next act, I do not know, but I galloped along the ridge of that roof as if I were a fleeing cat and leapt off it into the back lane seconds before the men burst from their own back yard. But to my surprise, they did not chase me – instead, they hurtled into the yard of No. 15. I heard shouts and curses, women screaming and the sound of men fighting . . .

Within seconds, I saw the familiar sign of a blue light racing through the darkness and decided I should remain invisible.

I decided to head for the rendezvous point in the school playground, even though it was only just midnight. Within minutes of my arrival, the others turned up. The exercise had been aborted.

'What happened?' asked Connolly in the darkness. He did not address his question to me in particular but to anyone who might answer.

'Dunno,' said one of our men. 'There was a hell of a crash, and the next thing I knew, those five brothers from No. 13, and their dad, all burst into No. 15 and began knocking hell out of the men in there.'

'And what was happening at No. 15?' asked Connolly.

'A party, I think,' said one of the detectives. 'A birthday party, nothing more than that. No orgy, nowt. Just a party with lots of blokes and girls there, some good music and a fair bit of drink and noise. No brothel tonight, Sarge.'

Later, back at the station when the beat car returned after attending the rumpus, we were to learn that there had been bad feeling between No. 13 and No. 15 for years, and each had performed nasty tricks upon the other over a long period. The crashing plant pots had been thought just another in this war of aggravation because the people at No. 13, a family called Parry, had complained about the noise of the music only minutes before. They'd rung Margot Stainton and had issued a string of abuse down her telephone, so the police took no action.

In our terms, all the participants were warned as to their future conduct. The beat man had no idea that we had been keeping watch on the premises, but no further observations were kept upon that house and there were no more complaints about it.

But I never told anyone about my part in provoking that incident.

It is a feature of observations of this kind that one branch of the service operates without the knowledge of the others, and there are many practical reasons for this, secrecy being, at times, of paramount importance. This practice was to cause problems at another obs job.

Detective Sergeant Connolly had received a tip from one of his many informants that a switch of high-value stolen goods was to occur at a place called Springbeck Farm. This was on the moors above Eltering, on the edge of a moorland village called Liskenby. According to his informant, there was to be a raid on a country house in south Durham on Friday evening when the occupants were out at a hunt ball. The raiders were intent on getting their hands on the family silver; they had an outlet for it, through some less-than-honest members of the antique trade in the Midlands and south, and so a system of transporting it to their crooked dealers had been arranged. The switch would be late on that same Friday night or in the early hours of Saturday morning.

Our information was that the unoccupied Springbeck Farm had been selected due to its remoteness. I often wondered how the CID managed to acquire such detailed information from informants, and I also pondered upon the motives of such informants. Without them, the work of the CID would be difficult, and yet the detectives who relied upon them despised them as much as the criminal fraternity hated them.

However, this information was regarded as 'good', which meant it had to be acted upon. And that meant a period of observation on the farm and its ranging buildings, with the utmost secrecy being observed. There could be some danger in this exercise, for men in possession of high-value goods are loath to relinquish them without a fight, but there was no question of being issued with firearms. We would have to make do with own strength and skill, aided by our detective staves, short truncheons which would fit into a jacket pocket.

Connolly decided that a visit to the farm for a recce was out of the question; the villains themselves might be keeping a watch on the premises, although a drive past the entrance in a plain car was agreed. Four of us undertook that mission. We discovered that a rough, unmade track led down to the farm from the moor road between Eltering and Strensford. Although the gate, bearing the name Springbeck Farm, was on the main road, the farmhouse and its buildings were out of sight in a shallow valley.

There was no road direct to the farm from the village of Liskenby, in whose parish the farm stood, but there was a second route into the buildings. That led from Liskenby Manor, the big house which was the focal point of Liskenby Estate. A private road led from the village through the estate and up to the big house, and a lane ran from that road to Springbeck Farm, which belonged to the estate.

'Whoever selected this spot knows that estate,' said Connolly. 'Not many farms have two entrances; in this case, they drive in off the main road, do the switch and drive out through that estate. And because the estate is private property, no member of the public is going to see vehicles moving around at night, and the big house is too far away from anyone there to notice them. So, let's make our plans. We'll all have to be involved in this one.'

There were several imponderables. We had no idea how many men would be involved; we did not know how many vehicles would be used, nor indeed what kind they would be. They might be stolen or hired for the job. They could be cars, vans, cattle trucks or pantechnicons, and we did not know precisely what time they would arrive. Our information did not tell us they would be armed, and so we had to assume they would not; in those days, not many villains did carry firearms. This meant a long period in hiding around the farm, but in this instance there would be radio contact, albeit using codes because some villains listened in to police broadcasts.

There needed to be a lot of careful planning. The dog section would be placed on alert too, without telling them why, and so would the traffic department. And they would be told to keep away from Liskenby and district unless ordered directly to take action there.

Our task was to catch the thieves or handlers in possession of the stolen goods; that was always first-rate proof of their villainy, for seasoned criminals were cunning enough to get rid of 'hot' goods as soon as possible or to deny they had ever been in possession of them. In this case, we felt that the transfer of goods would take place in a barn; the barns on these moorland farms were large enough to accommodate two furniture vans or certainly a couple of smaller vehicles. Even Dutch barns, especially when replete with hay or straw, offered some security. But no one knew the layout of these premises. We daren't ask either the estate or the local council's planning office for plans, due to the secrecy involved, and so we had to rely on our ability to think fast at the time.

After a lot of deliberation, which involved studying all the possible methods of tackling this problem, it was decided that the four of us, Connolly, Wharton, Shackleton and myself, would enter the farm buildings via the village; there was a footpath across the fields. Under cover of darkness, we could achieve that without being seen, and we would take portable radios. We would leave the car on the pub car-park; it was unmarked and would not attract attention there.

At the farm, we found a large and beautiful dwelling-house in a splendid setting, remote and, in the day time, with staggering views across the valley. All the doors were locked and the windows were secure; it was in very good condition in spite of its lack of use. In the adjoining yard, which had a concrete base, was a row of looseboxes and sundry small buildings. This had clearly been a stable block, and all the stable doors were closed and in good condition. There was a large barn but the doors were closed and secured with a huge padlock, while the Dutch barn did contain some bales of straw. In the darkness, we silently inspected the layout and ascertained, beyond all doubt, that the farm was totally deserted.

'Right,' said Gerry Connolly, 'I reckon they'll do the switch in that stable yard; the ground before the Dutch barn is too soft for a large vehicle to linger on it for long, and I doubt if they'll break into the barn. There are no other open buildings. And that stable yard has two ways in, or one way in and another way out. The surface is good, the buildings around it will offer some security and there's always the looseboxes to dive into if necessary.'

We listened to him and agreed with his comments.

'I think we ought to be in the Dutch barn,' he said. 'It'll provide us with cover, and we can see into the yard area of the stable block; we can also see the lights of any vehicles approaching. And we can move about fairly quietly.'

Once more, we all agreed. We adjourned to the Dutch barn and settled on the bales of straw, whereupon Connolly produced a flask of coffee and some chocolate biscuits. It was only ten o'clock in the evening, a chill autumn night, and there was a long time to wait.

Hardly had we sipped our taste of coffee when things started to happen. Lights appeared across the fields; a vehicle of some kind was coming down the lane from the main road.

'To your posts,' hissed Connolly. 'Radios on, but very low volume. And if there's only one vehicle, we take no action — we need two, and we need to catch them exchanging the stuff. Wait for the word from me . . . ' and we all slipped into the darkness to adopt our pre-arranged observation positions.

Due to the roughness of the track, it took the oncoming vehicle a few minutes to reach the farm buildings, but its lights swept the scene as it swung into the stable yard. There it dowsed its headlights as three men climbed out. One of them opened the door of a garage next to the stable block, and the car quickly reversed inside. All the lights went out and the door was closed by the driver, then all four disappeared into one of the looseboxes. That door was closed behind them, although the top half of the door remained open. They were now waiting as we watched them. They were awaiting vehicle No. 2.

My position was in an old implement shed among a lot of disused junk, spare parts of ploughs and harvesters, old bins and tools and so forth, but I had a fine long view of the yard. Now I could see nothing. Was that hidden car full of loot, or was it waiting to collect the loot from the other?

My heart was thumping as I waited; I found this session of

observation far more exciting than Operation Phrynia, for there was going to be a dramatic and positive finale. And then came trouble.

As a second set of lights burst across the far horizon to hurtle down that road to the farm, a third set appeared from the direction of the estate entrance. Two sets of lights were therefore heading towards the farm. But there was a problem − each was flourishing a flashing blue light.

They were police cars − we were later to learn that the estate gamekeeper had seen the arrival of the first car with the men who were then in the loosebox. Suspecting them to be poachers, he had alerted the local police. And no one had told them about this operation − a selection of other operational teams had been informed, but not the local police. And so these two cars, operating very strategically, were rushing into the farm to block both exits and contain the supposed poachers and their vehicle. I knew Connolly would be tearing out his blond hair, for there was no way of halting them now. Our radio sets were not on their frequency, and our car was a long way off, in the village . . .

I groaned. Unless that car in the garage contained the stolen silver, the whole exercise would be wasted.

Both police cars drove into the yard, each parking so that their headlights flooded the area, and I realized that other cars would be blocking the exits at their distant points. It was a superb operation − but it was so pointless and ruinous.

Then my old colleague from Ashfordly, Sergeant Blaketon, splendid in his uniform, emerged from one of the cars. Its blue light was still flashing as other uniformed constables climbed from the second car. And then a gamekeeper appeared.

'In there,' I heard him say, as he pointed to the garage and looseboxes.

At this stage, Detective Sergeant Connolly revealed himself to Blaketon, and so I thought I would do likewise; my two CID colleagues also appeared.

'Rhea!' cried Blaketon. 'What are you doing here . . . oh, and Gerry . . . '

'Oscar, you great oaf!' snapped Connolly. 'You've probably ruined my operation. This is a set-up. We're waiting for a cache of stolen silver to be transferred . . . '

Oscar Blaketon drew himself up to his full height and majesty and said, 'And I am here to catch poachers. Now Vincent,' he addressed the gamekeeper, 'where are they?'

'In that loosebox, Mr Blaketon, and their car's in yon garage . . . '

At this, the door of the loosebox burst open and out came three men, whose leader strode across to Blaketon.

'You rustic buffoons, you crass idiots, you utter bloody fools . . . you have just ruined our operation!' he snarled. 'There'll be hell to play over this. We nearly had 'em, the best tip in years, the top operators nearly trapped and you country bloody bumpkins go and blow the lot . . . '

'And who are you, pray?' growled Blaketon, eyeing the three scruffy individuals in their jeans and heavy sweaters.

'Regional Crime Squad, Detective Inspector Jarvis based at Durham,' and he showed his warrant card to Blaketon. 'And look what you have just done. You've just blown a major operation, you've just alerted some of the region's top villains to our plan . . . '

Jarvis did his nut, as the expression goes, while Blaketon, true to form, insisted he was seeking poachers and promptly took his men on a tour of the estate to find them. Gerry Connolly remained.

'If you bastards would tell us what's going on, this wouldn't have happened . . . '

'And if you woolly-backs let real detectives do their jobs, we'd have nailed this lot . . . '

They argued and fought for half an hour as Blaketon and his team crunched and crashed through the woodland around the farm.

'Come on, lads,' said a depressed Connolly. 'Back to Eltering. Back to local housebreakings and petty theft. Back to minnows instead of salmon . . . '

Leaving the Crime Squad to lick their wounds, we travelled back to Eltering in silence, each with his own thoughts. I felt sorry for Gerry Connolly, for, whoever his informant was, he had given superb information. As we pulled into the car-park, we had to avoid a white 30-cwt van parked there. I saw it had a broken rear-light cluster.

'That's all we're good for, lads,' said Gerry, stepping out of his car, 'nicking speeders and people with duff lights on their motors!'

But inside, PC John Rogers was waiting for us with a huge smile.

'Sarge!' he said as Connolly entered. 'Thank God you've come! Traffic have stopped that van that's outside, a duff light . . . it's full of silver, nicked from a job in Durham . . . they've got two blokes. I was just going to give Headquarters a ring, to get them to alert the Crime Squad.'

'No need,' Gerry beamed. 'This is one for us, I think, eh lads?'

'Yes, Sarge,' we chorused as we followed him into the CID office.

5

For when the One Great Scorer comes
To write against your name,
He marks, not that you won or lost
But how you played the game.

Grantland Rice (1880-1949)

Until 1968, many of the crimes which involved breaking into houses and other buildings were classified by the type of premises entered in this felonious way. For example, there were schoolhouse-breaking, warehouse-breaking, Government, municipal or public building-breaking, office-breaking, counting-house-breaking, garage-breaking, factory-breaking, store-breaking and others. To break into a church or other place of divine worship to steal or to commit any other serious crime was called sacrilege, and because those places were considered the House of God, the crime was regarded as extremely serious and, until 1968, carried a maximum penalty of life imprisonment.

To break into someone's private dwelling-house was called housebreaking if it was done during the daylight hours and burglary if it was done during the night hours, i.e. between 9 p.m. and 6 a.m. Burglary was a very serious offence, and it was classified as a felony (and so was sacrilege); other felonies included crimes like murder and rape. Housebreaking, on the other hand, was considered a lesser crime because it was common law misdemeanour, although it was made into a statutory felony by the 1916 Larceny Act. Nonetheless, criminal folklore continued to ascribe it with a lesser status, and it was infinitely more desirable to have a series of housebreakings than a series of burglaries.

The difference between the two was often a matter of timing by the burglar/housebreaker. For example, if a man woke up at 7 a.m. to find his house had been broken into during the night, how could anyone prove it had been burgled? No one knew if the villains had entered before 6 a.m. – they could have got in at 6.05 a.m., and so that crime would be logged as housebreaking, not burglary. After all, no one wanted a burglary logged in their records! As a consequence of this thinking, the volume of burglaries was kept at a minimum, while housebreakings chugged along at a fairly high rate.

With the passing of the Criminal Law Act of 1967, the distinction between felonies and misdemeanours was abolished, and so these terms became obsolete – instead we had a category of crimes known as 'arrestable offences' or, more simply, just 'crimes'. And then, in 1968, the Theft Act scrapped all those old 'breaking offences', as we called them, and placed every type of breaking offence under one heading – burglary. From being a crime which had carried the death penalty for over 700 years (from around 1124 until 1838), it was now no more serious than breaking into a henhouse to steal an egg.

Older policemen were horrified, because it meant their burglary figures would soar. They could not see that the change had reduced the status of burglary instead of elevating the status of housebreaking. They couldn't see that the artificial differences between felonies and misdemeanours no longer mattered. Another change was to call stealing 'theft' instead of larceny, and I do know these changes did alarm the elder police officers, albeit without reason.

But my period as an Aide to CID was in those halcyon days when burglaries were burglaries and felonies were felonies, and the statisticians were delighted to be able to juggle with the crime figures thus produced.

In common with most small towns, Eltering did have its outbreaks of crime. These were hardly crime waves, but they did come in identifiable types – there would be a spate of thefts from motor cars, for example, or a spate of shop-breakings, a run of thefts from public houses or a sequence of con men leaving hotels or boarding-houses without paying the bill. It was odd how these continuing crimes occurred because, quite often, a sequence of crimes was not perpetrated by the same person or gang. It almost seemed as if there were fashions for crime, fads that came and went just like any other passing craze.

But there would be outbreaks of crime that could be attributed to the same person or gang, a fact easily ascertained by the MOs of the criminals.

Such a spate involved a series of housebreakings on small estates at Eltering, but also at other small towns in the district. They had been occurring for some months and followed a similar pattern. Bungalows on small estates would be entered through ground-floor windows that had been left partially open. Country folk liked to have fresh air circulating their homes, and so they left the windows open; sensible though this might be from a health viewpoint, it is an invitation to a passing and opportunist thief or burglar. As the term 'breaking' included opening windows as well as smashing them, this series was termed 'housebreaking' because the crimes occurred during the daylight hours. The ordinary citizens, of course, did not know of these subtle categorizations, and they would report they had been burgled.

The housebreakers, to give them their official name, seemed to know when their victims were away from the premises, and a feature of their work was that they seldom caused any damage inside the houses. They rifled the premises for cash and also took valuables that were not easily identifiable, such as radio sets, binoculars, cameras, ornaments of silver and pewter and other disposable things. Cash seemed to be their main objective, however; we felt they only took those other things if cash was not quickly found. In some cases, the means of entry, through small windows high off the ground, such as toilet windows or pantry windows, suggested someone of agility and youthfulness.

Added to this was the fact that their area of operation indicated they had transport, but in every case no one had seen the villains and no one had reported a suspicious vehicle. It seemed that our crooks were invisible.

'Nick,' said Gerry Connolly one quiet morning, 'get the files on those housebreakings and go through all the reports. See if you can find any common factor we might have missed. I feel sure there's something glaringly obvious that we've over-looked. Find a quiet corner somewhere and give them your undivided attention for today.'

I enjoyed this kind of research and took all the files into the court house, which was not in use. There I began my reading and drew a chart on some lined paper; on that chart, I listed the day, date, time and estates in question, the mode of entry and all the other basic factors of each crime. I did not come to any particular conclusions, although I did discover that the earliest crime had been discovered at 11.30 a.m. and the latest at 4.30 p.m. Most had been committed on a Monday, although others had occurred on Wednesdays, Fridays and Saturdays. The victims could not be categorized either, because they included pensioners, young people, married couples, single people, rich and poor. A lot of the attacked premises were bungalows but the attacks did include semi-detached houses, terrace houses and detached properties. The majority, however, were on fairly new estates where the residents might not know all their neighbours. There, a stranger was not unusual.

I decided I would look at similar crimes in the neighbouring market towns too; while I could not obtain as much detail about them from the circulars we received, I knew I could get facts such as the dates and times, a description of the stolen goods and an idea of the kind of premises. If I needed more facts, I could obtain them from the police stations in those towns. As I worked, Gerry Connolly came in to see how I was progressing and brought me a mug of coffee; he looked at my charts and asked if I had come up with anything new, and when I said, 'No,' he smiled.

'We've tried too. Anyway, keep looking, Nick. There's nowt happening just now, so you're as well doing that. Something might click.' And he left me to my piles of paper and charts.

As I worked, nothing of note emerged until I listed the towns where the crimes had been committed together with the days when the attacks occurred.

The odd thing about Ashfordly's handful of crimes (twenty-one in the past year) was that they had all occurred on a Friday; when I checked those at Brantsford (fifteen in the year), I found they had all been committed on a Wednesday, But that did not apply to Eltering, because different days have been utilized there, and the same applied to the reported crimes at Malton. Saturday had featured prominently in Malton's tally, but so had Wednesday and Friday. Eltering's crimes had been committed on Mondays, Wednesdays, Fridays and Saturdays. There were no such crimes on Tuesdays, Thursdays and Sundays in those towns.

That seemed odd, I felt, but why? Why was it odd?

I ended that day's studies without any firm conclusions, and then the following day, Friday, I got a call from Connolly. It was half past three in the afternoon.

'Nick, there's been a housebreaking in Heather Drive, No. 18. Name of Turnbull. Cash taken. Can you attend? You'll be on your own.'

'Yes, of course.' I was a little nervous but anxious to show that I could investigate this kind of crime.

No. 18 Heather Drive was a brick-built, semi-detached bungalow on a corner site; it was on a new estate, completed only two years earlier, which occupied a sloping site on the northern edge of the town. I walked to the address and knocked; the door was opened by a solidly built man in his early sixties, and his wife stood close behind.

'Detective Constable Rhea,' I said, showing my warrant card. 'You called the office . . . '

'Aye, lad, come in,' he said warmly. 'The buggers have taken our holiday savings. Now if Ah'd been here when they got in, Ah'd have skelped 'em for sure.'

'Skelped' is an old Yorkshire dialect word for 'hit'. I could well imagine this fellow tackling them and thrashing them for their cheek in invading his home.

'Where did they get in?' I asked. 'Will you show me?'

'Pantry window,' he said, leading me through to the back of the bungalow. Mrs Turnbull followed us, wringing her hands.

'There,' he said, pointing to the window. It was only eighteen inches wide by two feet tall, but they had pushed up the bottom half from the outside and climbed through. I went outside to have a look and found they had pushed the dustbin from its position near the gate until it was beneath the window. They'd climbed upon it and had squeezed through this tiny space.

'You left the window unlocked?' I asked.

'Open,' said Mrs Turnbull. 'I allus leaves it open an inch or two, for fresh air, you see. It is a larder, you know, young man, and food needs fresh air.'

'It's sensible to screw it in position, then,' I said. 'Put screws through the frame so no one can push it further open. So they got in here, and then where did they go?'

'Into the parlour,' said Mr Turnbull, leading the way.

The parlour is what others might call the lounge. I followed the couple in. On the mantelshelf was a white vase.

'I had £85 in there,' said Mrs Turnbull. 'It's all gone.'

'In notes, was it?' I asked.

'Ten-bob notes and pound notes,' she said, 'saved up from my pension. We were going to go to Brighton, me and Lawrie.'

'I'm sorry.' I was genuinely sorry for them in their loss, and asked if anything else had been touched, or whether any other room appeared to have been searched.

None had, but I checked each one just in case.

'Now,' I said, with my notebook open, for I was recording all the necessary details, 'what about the other places you've got money hidden? People always hide money all over the house, and the burglars know exactly where to look. There's no hiding-place in this house that they would not find – and find easily,' I stressed. Pensioners in particular hide their spare cash instead of banking it, and it is such a simple matter for a thief to find it. I saw the looks in their eyes, and Mr Turnbull said, 'You go and look, Norma, while I pour this lad a cup of tea.'

I was not to be privy to their secret hiding-places, but as I sipped tea in the kitchen, Mrs Turnbull returned smiling. 'He's nivver found any of it!' she beamed proudly. I wondered if this meant their return had disturbed the intruder, for it was odd if the intruder had not made a more thorough search of the house. I asked them to show me all around, just in case he was hiding in a wardrobe or in the loft – that was not unknown, even with a policeman in the house. But he'd gone – he'd let himself out of the front door by unlocking the Yale.

I asked if they had touched anything before ringing the police, and Mrs Turnbull said she'd 'nobbut done a bit o' dusting' to tidy the place before my arrival!

'You might have destroyed any fingerprints or other evidence,' I tried to explain. 'I'll get our fingerprints people to come and check the house – leave the pantry window.'

'He might get in again!' she snapped.

'They'll be here later today,' I said. 'And then you can secure that window – and all the others. And they'll want to examine the vase where you had the cash, and the front door – and anything else he might have touched.'

'She allus cleans up afore we have visitors,' said Mr Turnbull. 'She'll hoover again afore your fingerprint fellers get here . . . '

'She'd better not!' I shook my finger at the old lady. 'Now, remember, Mrs Turnbull, don't touch anything else, not until they've done their work. It is very important that we get every scrap of evidence they might have left behind.'

'Then you'll want this!' she opened the door of the kitchen cabinet and showed me a small block of blue chalk. It was the type used by billiards and snooker-players to chalk the tips of their cues. 'Now if I hadn't hoovered before you came, I'd not have found that,' she said in some sort of triumph.

'Where was it?' I asked.

'Under t'sofa,' she beamed. 'Now it's not mine and it's not our Lawrie's, and it wasn't there when I hoovered up yesterday, and it wasn't there when I hoovered up this morning before we went off to Ashfordly market. So he must have dropped it.'

Her logic was impeccable, so I pocketed the chalk. It could be relevant. The snag was it was one of millions of such cubes – it would prove very little even if we found the owner. But it *was* of value. Every clue left at the scene of a crime is of some value, however limited.

I took particulars of all the necessary details, said we would investigate the crime and reassured them that our fingerprint experts would arrive later in the day. And then, as I walked back to the police station, I realized that Mrs Turnbull had said something highly significant.

After completing my crime report, I went to the files I'd been using the day before. Market day! Market day in Ashfordly was a Friday – and its recent housebreakings had been committed on Fridays; market day in Brantsford was a Wednesday, and its breakings were on Wednesdays. That pattern did not fit Eltering or Malton – but Eltering's market day was Monday, and a lot of its breakings had been on Mondays, while many of Malton's had been Saturdays – its market day. And then I realized that Eltering's and Malton's other breakings had been committed during market days at Ashfordly and Brantsford.

So either the villains were stopping off at Eltering and Malton on their way home to commit further crimes or they had found a way of knowing when folks were out of their homes, attending those other markets . . .

I was excited about this and was making notes when Gerry Connolly came in.

'Well, Nick, how did it go?'

I explained what had happened at the Turnbulls' home and before I could tell him about the cue chalk, he asked a few pertinent questions, then he said, 'Well, while you were out, there was a development. A minor one, but it could be important. I've been talking to D/S Miller at Scarborough; they've got a pair of suspects for us, names of two local lads who've been selling stuff to second-hand dealers and junk shops in Scarborough. They've a van which they rig up to look like a window-cleaner's vehicle with a ladder on top, and they've been spending freely lately – but not cleaning many windows. Miller says they spend their days in the snooker hall. I thought we might give them an unannounced call.'

'Then this will interest you,' I said, picking up the chalk which I had now placed in an envelope, labelled with the crime report number.

'Bloody hell!' he beamed. 'It's amazing how things come together . . . right, tomorrow then? You and I will go to Scarborough.'

'It's a Saturday,' I said. 'They might come out to Malton to do a job.'

'Then I'll give Malton police their vehicle number and we can keep our eyes open for them. But we'll do that snooker hall anyway, in the evening.'

And so we did. There was no reported housebreaking in Malton that Saturday, and we arrived at the snooker hall at six o'clock.

Gerry booked a table and we had a game of snooker; he thrashed me soundly and I said, 'You've played this game before!'

'Once or twice,' he smiled. 'Ah, these are our men,' and two men in their early twenties came to one of the tables. Before they began to play, Connolly went across.

'Got a bit of chalk I can borrow, lads?' he asked, holding his cue.

'Sure, mate,' and one of them pulled a piece from his pocket. It bore the same blue paper covering as the one I'd recovered at the Turnbulls'.

'You are Terry Leedham and Graham Scott,' he smiled charmingly at them.

'So what if we are?' responded Leedham.

'I'm Detective Sergeant Connolly from Eltering, and this is D/PC Rhea. We're investigating a series of housebreakings in the area, and think you lads might help us with our enquiries. In fact, we've brought some of your chalk back — you left it in one of the houses you raided.'

And he produced my bit of chalk, still in its envelope marked officially with the crime reference. It was clear from the expressions on their faces that they were the guilty parties, but every police officer knows that knowledge of guilt is not proof of guilt. I could see that they wondered how much we really knew. In fact, we knew nothing that would prove a case against them — we had no fingerprints, nothing.

It was just supposition and so we needed a cough, as the CID term an admission.

'We know you're the culprits,' said Connolly, 'and we can prove it . . .'

They looked at each other in amazement at this sudden confrontation, then Scott said, 'You'll get nowt from us, mate. No coughs, no admissions, you'll have to prove your case all the way, every inch . . .'

'You are sporting lads,' he smiled again. 'You like a game of snooker?'

'Yeh, course we do. We practically live 'ere.'

'I'll take the pair of you on,' offered Connolly. 'Me against the two of you. If I win, you admit those crimes, you give us a cough to save us proving the case, If you win, you don't need to give us a cough — but we'll go off and prove you've done those jobs — and mebbe lots more.'

'Gerraway, that's stupid!' laughed Scott.

'No,' said Leedham. 'We can beat a cop any day, Graham; that'll get him off our backs.'

I could see that Leedham was anxious to take on this challenge, and then, as I glanced around the walls of the hall, I knew why. He was a club champion, a winner of several trophies. I tried to warn Connolly but was too late because he said, 'Right. It's on, is it?'

'Best of three frames?' chuckled Leedham. 'Tell you what, this is the easiest interrogation I've ever had . . . '

Scott was not so willing, but he could not let his partner down and so the game was on, with Gerry Connolly playing each in turn, their scores counting as one man's. I acted as marker. It is not necessary to go into the details of that game, except to say that Gerry Connolly trounced them. He won the first two games and insisted they play the third — which he also won.

'Right, lads, time to cough those jobs, eh?' he said.

And to my surprise, Leedham agreed. He sat down with Connolly and admitted a string of housebreakings, with Connolly showing him a list of outstanding ones in Malton, Eltering, Ashfordly and Brantsford. Scott joined in too — he had no alternative. It was a most surprising gesture by these two criminals.

'What made you make that weird offer?' I put to Connolly in the car after the pair had been bailed at Scarborough Police Station.

'I was relying on a bit of gen I got from the local lads,' he said. 'They said Leedham was a superb snooker-player, a real talent, but he couldn't afford to go professional. He wasn't in work, so he couldn't pay his way in most amateur games. He took to crime to help him continue playing — and they say he's the most honest of sportsmen, he'll never cheat in a game. A curious mixture — so I issued that challenge.'

'You could have lost,' I said.

'I could,' he smiled, 'But I didn't.'

I was to learn soon afterwards that Gerry Connolly had been the National Police Snooker Champion for five successive years and runner-up on no fewer than three other occasions. He'd also won many contests outside the police service.

(*Author's note:* Some seventeen years after this incident, I found myself breakfasting at a police training centre with the then Director of Public Prosecutions. I told him of this strange case and asked him whether, in his opinion, such a confession would be admissible in court had it been challenged by the defence. He expressed an opinion that it would be admissible because it had been freely given without any duress.)

If the actions of Terry Leedham were surprising, those of a lady, the victim of a housebreaking, were touching. She rang the police station to report the theft, for someone had sneaked into her home during the morning and had stolen several items. I was sent to investigate.

'Well, Mrs Harland,' I said as she showed me into her parlour, 'what can you tell me?'

'Ah nobbut popped out for a minute.' She was a lady in her sixties, the widow of a retired farmer. 'Round to t'corner shop for some flour and lard. Ah mean, Mr Rhea, up on t'moors, there's neea need ti lock doors or owt, is there, and folks nivver come pinching.'

'That's true,' I agreed. 'But this is a town, you know, and you should lock your doors, even if you're out only for a moment or two. Now, what's been taken?'

'My housekeeping. I keep it in yon box on t'mantelshelf. Nobbut £8 and a few coppers. A pair o' brass candlesticks from t'piano top, a silver mug that my dad left me when he died, and three black cats, ebony they are. Now, they're t'worst loss, Mr Rhea, a family heirloom, they are, very old. They were my grandmother's; she worked for Queen Victoria at Buckingham Palace, as a cook, and the Queen gave her those cats. They've come right down through t'family, daughter by daughter. Not worth a lot, mind, but, well, I'm right saddened about them being taken.'

She gave me a cup of tea and a scone as I took descriptions of all the missing objects, and I assured her that details would be circulated among the local second-hand and antique dealers. The value of the missing items was low, and I could not understand why anyone had stolen them — it seemed to be the work of an opportunist thief who had taken the cash and anything else that might make a few shillings.

The three cats seemed to be the most interesting — they were each carved from ebony and, according to Mrs Harland, they had green eyes 'that shone a bit' and 'claws made oot o' gold-coloured stuff', and each wore a leather collar studded 'wi' bits o' red glass'.

Each was in a sitting position, one being six inches or so in height, one about four inches and a kitten about 2½ inches high. They were linked together with a gold-coloured chain which was threaded through their collars. Without seeing these objects, I had to rely on her description of them, but I did wonder if, in fact, those 'green eyes that shone a bit', the 'bits o' gold-coloured stuff' on their claws and the 'red glass' on their collars were genuine gold and real jewels. Mrs Harland could not put a financial value on the cats and so, for the record, I recorded them as being worth £10 for the set. In our reports, we had to show the financial value of stolen goods.

Sergeant Connolly said I should tour the second-hand shops in town and other places that might sell the stolen goods, and so I did. But no one had been offered them. After those initial enquiries, there was little more that could be done, for new crimes were being recorded and investigated and the theft from Mrs Harland looked like being just another undetected crime.

It would be a month later when I received a second call from Mrs Harland.

'Mr Rhea!' she shouted into the telephone in the manner of one unaccustomed to using such new-fangled inventions. 'Them cats o' mine, Ah've come across 'em.'

For the briefest of moments, I could not recall the cats about which she spoke, and then, just in time, I remembered.

'Have you?' I said. 'Whereabouts?'

'In a house window-ledge, up Curnow Street, No. 3. Ah've

made a note o' t'number.'

'Can you be sure they're yours?' I would have to exercise enormous discretion if I was virtually to accuse a householder of stealing them; they could be identical, or very similar, copies.

'Aye,' she sounded hurt. ''Course Ah can; yan on 'em has a claw missing, middle cat, left back leg.'

'I'll go and ask about them,' I assured her. 'I'll come back and let you know how I go on.'

'So long as I get my cats back, that's all Ah want,' and she slammed down the telephone.

I told Sergeant Connolly, and he felt she could be mistaken, but I remembered the incident of my own stolen coat. I knew my own coat, just as Mrs Harland most surely know her own cats, cats that were part of her family history. Connolly listened to my arguments on her behalf and said, 'Fine, right. Go and sort it out, Nick. But for God's sake be careful. We don't want folks complaining that we're accusing them of housebreaking and theft.'

I knew the dangers, and it was with some trepidation, therefore, that I walked to Curnow Street to sort out this dilemma.

Curnow Street comprised semi-detached and detached houses with large-paned windows overlooking tiny gardens which abutted the street. No.3 was a pleasant, brick-built semi with pretty curtains at its window. As I approached, I saw no cats sitting there. I wondered how I would tackle the delicate accusation I was duty-bound to make. But my immediate worries were solved. As I was about to walk up the short path to the front door, someone opened it. A young woman in her early thirties, with a pretty face atop a rather heavily built body, was trying to manoeuvre from the house a wheelchair containing a large child. The child was a girl of about twelve with long, dark brown hair and sad eyes, and a rug covered her lower regions and legs. The plump young woman was battling to lower the chair down two steps and, at the same time, keep the heavy door from slamming shut. I went to help her.

'Thanks.' She clearly welcomed the extra pair of hands, and I coaxed the heavy chair down the steps and onto the path.

And then I saw the three cats; they were laid on the lap of the girl, on top of the all-embracing blanket. I had to make use of this heaven-sent opportunity, so I picked up the cats and tried to make contact with the girl. But she was a spastic, I felt, and communication was not easy.

'They're nice,' I said, half to the girl and half to the woman, whom I assumed was her mother.

'They're Eve's,' I was told. 'She loves cats and we had a big black one, but she got knocked down by a bus a couple of weeks ago. She had kittens once, a year or two ago, but they died. Eve was heart-broken.'

Eve tried to speak to me about those model cats but I could not understand her. I wished I could communicate with her, for her hands were moving around in her attempt to speak. I replaced the cats in her lap, having seen that they corresponded in every detail to those stolen from Mrs Harland.

'They're lovely cats, Eve,' I said gently.

'I found them on a bric-à-brac stall in the market last Monday,' said the mother. 'Eve was with me and I knew she wanted them, so I got them. They were only £3, a real bargain.'

'They look like ebony,' I said.

'The man on the stall thought that too,' she said. 'He thought they'd been carved in Africa or India.'

I did not tell this lady, whose name I learned was Mrs Ann Reynolds, of the real reason for my visit. I allowed her to think I just happened to be passing, and I did not tell her I was a policeman; I felt a twinge of guilt at my deception but felt, in the circumstances, it was justified.

It was Monday that day, so I went to the market and found the bric-à-brac stall. It was there every Monday.

'You had some black cats here last week,' I said, without saying who I was. 'Three of them, ebony I think, linked with a gold chain.'

'Sold,' he said. 'A little lass in a wheelchair wanted them, so I let her have 'em cheap.'

'Can I ask where you got them?' I put to him.

'You the police, then?' he put to me.

'CID,' I said. 'We've had a report of some cats like that being stolen locally.'

'A feller came to me only last Monday morning with 'em,' he said. 'Scruffy chap, two or three days' growth of whiskers, bit of a down-and-outer, I'd say. He sold 'em to me, said they were his. I mean, Officer, I don't deal in knocked-off stuff, never have. Mind, I do get offered stuff that sometimes I wonder about, and if I'm worried, I leave it alone. But them cats, well, they're the sort of thing you can pick up in any souvenir shop.'

I disagreed with his assessment of their merits but did not argue with him. I believed his story and made a note of his description of the man who had sold the cats. I did not feel that this man knew he had bought stolen goods, and he was not therefore culpable, but he would have to feature in my crime report. However, who was the rightful owner of the cats, assuming they were the ones stolen from Mrs Harland?

She must inspect them and identify them as her property before any further legal proceedings could be taken. I knew I should have taken possession of those cats until the matter was determined, but I had shrunk from that action, rightly or wrongly. Mrs Harland, the loser, did have an obvious claim to the cats, but so did Mrs Reynolds, who had purchased them in good faith. If a battle over ownership did result, it was not the duty of the police to sort it out. That rested first upon the respective claimants and, if they could not agree, recourse through the civil courts was available — they would determine true ownership. But that was a last resort. In the event of a criminal prosecution of the thief, a court could order the return of the cats to Mrs Harland, and possibly some compensation to Mrs Reynolds. But first we had to catch the thief — his description would be circulated. In the meantime, I decided to pay a visit to Mrs Harland to acquaint her with the day's odd circumstances.

She welcomed me and I knew, by the expression on her face, that she had expected me to be clutching her three cats upon arrival. She took me into the parlour, produced a cup of tea within seconds, plus a buttered scone and some strawberry jam, and said, 'Well now, Mr Rhea, so you've not found my cats.'

'On the contrary,' I said, and I launched into the story of my enquiries, and of Eve's role in all this. Mrs Harland listened intently and I concluded by saying, 'What you must do now, Mrs Harland, is accompany me to the Reynolds' home to identify those cats formally. If they are yours, we can then take charge of them until the ownership has been determined or until the thief is arrested and dealt with.'

'Now that's a rum 'un,' she said, and she fell into a long silence which I did not interrupt. I wondered what she was thinking.

Then she brightened up and said, 'Mr Rhea, Ah'd like yon little lass to keep 'em. I've no daughter to pass 'em on to, no son either, and yon invalid lass is welcome to 'em. She has no idea they were stolen, has she?'

'No,' I said. 'Her mother bought them in good faith from the market. She has no idea where they came from before that.'

I now realized I had problems of my own, for the writing-off of this reported crime would create some administrative problems. I started to explain the difficulties to Mrs Harland but she was equal to the occasion.

'The way Ah sees it,' she smiled, 'is that Ah was mistaken when Ah spotted them cats in yon window. Ah've had a closer look, and they're not mine. Similar, mebbe, but definitely not mine.'

'That would keep the books straight, Mrs Harland.' I had to admire her decision.

'And it'll keep a little lass very happy, eh?'

'It will,' I said. 'Thank you.'

And as I left, I recalled the old Yorkshire belief that, if a black cat enters a house, it is a sign of good luck. I hoped three ebony ones would bring a spot of good fortune and happiness to little Eve Reynolds and her family.

6

Death, in itself, is nothing.

John Dryden (1631-1700)

In police circles, the quotation from John Dryden given above is very true. Police officers deal with death in all its forms, and it is surprising just what a large part this most unavoidable of natural states plays in their daily work. Murders, manslaughters, infanticides, homicides in all their mystery and cruelty, suicides, sudden deaths, deaths from unknown causes, deaths in mysterious circumstances, accidents with motor vehicles, firearms or other devices, drownings, poisonings and druggings, falling off cliffs or down mine shafts, leaping off bridges or out of aircraft, and a whole host of other curious forms of leaving this earthly life are the lot of the constable on duty. A straightforward natural death, where someone simply drifts cheerfully into the hereafter, is therefore of little consequence, a matter only for doctors, clergymen and undertakers, plus, of course, the friends and family of the dear departed.

On many occasions, however, the distinction between a natural death and a suspicious one is not easy to determine. Complications arise, sometimes due to the place in which the demise occurred, sometimes due to the curious manner in which the departure from life took place. In such cases, the police do have a duty to examine the circumstances and to involve others – coroners, forensic experts, doctors and pathologists – in an attempt to determine whether or not foul play is suspected.

Being involved in an enquiry into a mysterious death is truly fascinating, and most officers, when undergoing their basic training, are advised that their manner of investigating these deaths is a fine introduction to CID work. It is also a wonderful way of performing a service to the public, because a considerate but efficient investigator, when working so closely with the bereaved relatives or friends, can rapidly enhance the stature of himself and the entire police service. I have known very determined anti-police citizens revise their opinions of the force as a direct result of being involved in such an enquiry, especially when it was conducted by a sensitive and efficient constable.

In most parts of the country, the investigation of a sudden or mysterious death is the responsibility of the officer to whom the report is made, as a consequence of which many uniformed constables find themselves engaged in this work. In other areas, particularly in urban communities, a constable is appointed to the post of Coroner's Officer and undertakes all such routine enquiries. It demands a special kind of sympathy and understanding of human nature to cope with sudden death every day of one's working life, but these officers perform their duties in a cheerful and professional manner.

There are times when the police officer is the only friend the family has in their loss, the only one to offer help without complications.

The CID are called in only when the suspicious death is confirmed as being truly worthy of their interest as a possible homicide. At Eltering, because it was a small town, the CID took an interest in most suspicious deaths (as in Chapter 2), even though there was little likelihood of their being a homicide. Nonetheless, one or two further intriguing cases of death came my way during those few weeks as an Aide to CID.

One such example occurred on a Saturday morning, and it illustrated the curious way that some people have of behaving in the face of events which are outside the normal scope of their work and daily routine. As a result of this case, and the one which follows, I realized that there are people who simply cannot cope with the dramatic, unusual or unexpected; they categorically will not accept any responsibility over and above that which their job entails. To avoid such pressures, they simply behave as if the dramatic, unusual or unexpected has never occurred. There are times when I think this would make a fascinating matter for research, to show how a human being can avoid coping with something that is presented before his or her very eyes.

This trend often manifests itself during a crisis in the streets or other public places – passers-by simply ignore what is happening and walk on, even if someone is dying or being raped or mugged. I have often wondered how such passers-by can live with their consciences, knowing that their immediate action, had they done something, could have saved a life or prevented a crime, even if that action required nothing more than making a fuss or ringing 999. But so many citizens refrain from 'getting involved', as they term it – they do absolutely nothing. Police officers cannot behave like this. However terrified and uncertain they are, however young and inexperienced, they must cope with everything from lost dogs to exploding bombs via crashed aircraft, crimes, dramas of every kind, whether large or small, and, of course, sudden or unexplained deaths.

The case which follows is a fine illustration of this tendency, and it started with a telephone call from an estate agent.

'My name is Walters,' he told the duty constable, PC John Rogers. 'I'm employed by Pendle Smith and Watson, estate agents. I have just found a dead man in a house we are selling. The house is empty by the way . . . '

The only uniform constable on duty in Eltering that morning was dealing with a traffic accident at the roundabout in the High Street, and so Gerry Connolly suggested I went along, Just to have a look and see if he's not imagining things.' I said I would be pleased to do so, and off I went.

The house was a pretty terrace cottage, No. 14 High Forest Terrace in Eltering, a loftily situated row of stone-built houses overlooking Low Forest Terrace. I arrived within five minutes to find a worried-looking individual on the doorstep. He was a small, mild-mannered man with thinning dark hair and he clutched a brief-case to his chest.

'I'm D/PC Rhea,' I introduced myself. 'Are you Mr Walters?'

'I am, yes, and this is terrible, Mr Rhea, it really is. I mean, fancy coming to check a house over and finding a corpse . . . '

'Show me,' I asked him.

The body was that of a late-middle-aged man, probably in his mid-sixties, and it was fully dressed in grey trousers, a blue shirt, grey pullover and black shoes; the unfortunate fellow was lying on the bare floorboards of the main bedroom of this empty two-bedroomed property. I touched the corpse on the cheek; it was stone cold, and rigor mortis had set in; he was dead all right.

This man had died in a sleeping position, for he was laid out as if he was still in the Land of Nod, and his corpse was as stiff as the proverbial board. I could see no sign of visible injury but would have to strip him at the mortuary to check those parts of his body that were clothed. That was one of the jobs of an investigating officer – in this case, me.

There was the smell of death in the air as, with Walters following me around, I did a quick survey of the windows and doors to see if there had been any forcible entry. This death was certainly suspicious – after all, what explanation could there be for it?

'Who is he? Any idea?' I asked.

'Sorry, no. I'm new, I didn't handle the sale of this house, you see; one of my colleagues did. He's gone off on holiday, to Tenerife; he did the sale, you see, and I was just checking that the outgoing owner had cleared his furnishings, a courtesy, you know, towards the incoming owners . . . we make a practice of checks of this kind before we let the new purchasers in. They're due very soon – today, in fact.'

'So you are saying this house has been sold?' I asked.

'Yes, completion is today. The owner is a Mr . . . er . . . ' and he examined his files. 'Er . . . Mr . . . Clough, Mr Martin Clough, yes. Well, he had to be out today and our new owners are moving in this afternoon. This is rather, er, well unexpected . . . embarrassing . . . To be honest, Officer, I do not know what to do . . . '

'They won't be too happy about having a body on the floor, will they?' I said. 'So who is this dead man? Is it Mr Clough?'

'They won't be too happy about having a body on the floor, will they?' I said. 'So who is this dead man? Is it Mr Clough?'

'Well, er, I don't know. I haven't met him, you see.'

'If it is Mr Clough, where is all his furniture?' I put to the estate agent.

'Well, that's a puzzle as well, isn't it? I mean, so far as I know, the removal men were due this morning . . . maybe they've been, maybe Mr Clough came back for something and died . . . '

'Was the house locked up when you arrived?' I asked.

'Oh, yes, but we have a spare key.'

'And where will the other key be, assuming it is not lying in this poor fellow's pockets?'

'I expect the removal men will have used it. They'll bring it to the office in due course . . . They sometimes get it from the outgoing owner and lock up after themselves . . . We ask them to take charge of the keys, you see. We don't like outgoing owners keeping them . . . for security, you know. Some have been known to let themselves back in to collect things they thought the removal men had left behind . . . very thoughtless . . . illegal anyway . . . '

'Who are the removal men?' I asked in an effort to stop his waffling.

'Lapsley and Power,' he said. 'From York.'

'And where was the furniture going?'

'To York, to a bungalow Mr Clough had bought — through us, I might add.'

'Well, Mr Walters, this chap is as dead as a dodo, and the smell's going to get worse before too long, so we'd better get him shifted, hadn't we?'

'Er, well, yes, I suppose so. Do you want me to give you a lift with him?'

'Thanks, but no. There are things to do first. I'll have to get a doctor in to certify death, and if possible to state the cause of death. And then we'll see about getting this chap moved somewhere. Where can we put him, Mr Walters? We can hardly stand him in a corner to look lively, can we? Or pretend he's the gasman who's come to check the fittings. He's about as lively as some officials I've come across. And we can't have him littering the floor when folks want to put the carpets down, can we?'

'Er, no, well, I suppose not.' By now, poor Mr Walters was very worried and kept referring to his watch.

Leaving him with the corpse, I went to the cottage next

door and spoke to a lady. Yes, she knew Mr Clough very well, and her description fitted the man upstairs. I did not ask her to come and look at him; I felt we could identify him quite easily by other means, perhaps via his doctor. The neighbour said his medical practitioner was Dr Craven of Eltering, and she added that the old man had been under treatment for some weeks. I returned to Clough's cottage and used the telephone, which had not been cut off, to call Dr Craven. Fortunately he was available and would come immediately. We waited, with me puzzling about Mr Clough's furniture, and the unhappy Mr Walters worrying if his new owners would arrive to find the corpse still in their bedroom.

I wondered what the legal situation was if the owner of a property remained on the premises after completion of the purchase, albeit in the form of a corpse. Could a corpse be a trespasser? Certainly he could not be prosecuted, but could his relatives be held responsible for his refusal to move out at the correct time? Was there any negligence here? It was an area of civil law that did not come within the scope of police work, fortunately.

During my musings, Dr Craven arrived. He examined the corpse, said it was Mr Clough and announced he was prepared to certify the death as being of natural causes, a heart failure, he affirmed. He'd been treating Mr Clough for heart problems, and he could make the formal identification that we required. The old man was a widower with no family, but he had relations in York.

This matter settled, I rang Eltering Police Office and asked for the shell to be driven around in the van — the shell was a plastic coffin which we used for moving bodies. The van arrived, driven by PC Gregory, and I helped him to lift the remains of Mr Clough into the shell. We replaced the lid and as our van, with Mr Clough on board, turned away from the premises, I saw the approach of a small green Ford Anglia containing a man and woman.

'Oh, dear, here they are . . . ' said Mr Walters. 'I do hope nothing will be said. We don't want a back word to be given at this stage, good heavens no . . . '

'Mum's the word,' I said. 'But I'd open the windows if I were you, Mr Walters, to let some fresh air in. He was starting to get a bit ripe. You could always blame someone's dirty socks, I suppose. Well, I'll be off now.'

I left the house and walked back to the police station, knowing we would have to trace Mr Clough's relations in order to arrange a funeral. They would probably be waiting at his new house with the kettle on, and I would ask a York police officer to call there with the sad news, but fortunately, as his death was due to natural causes, there would be no post-mortem and no inquest.

But where was the furniture from the house, and how did poor old Clough come to be lying on the bare floor? I rang the removal firm, Lapsley & Power, and asked if the men who had removed his furniture had returned. I was told, 'No, they're still unloading at York.'

It was estimated they would return to base around 7 p.m., and so I decided I must interview them. At 7 p.m. I drove to their office and waited. They were fairly prompt, because they pulled their pantechnicon into the yard at ten past seven. They garaged the huge lorry and went into the office to book off, and so I walked in behind them. They were a pair of men in their forties, each about five feet six inches tall and rather solidly built. They were like Tweedledum and Tweedledee, I thought, one sporting a bushy black moustache and the other having his untidy hair long, straggly and probably unwashed.

'Now then,' I said, 'I'm D/PC Rhea from Eltering. Can I have a brief word?'

'We're supposed to finish at seven,' said Tweedledum.

'We're working over now,' said Tweedledee. 'The boss doesn't like paying overtime, 'specially on Saturdays . . . '

'It won't take a minute.' I stood before them as they both stared at me. 'Now, did you shift the furniture from High Forest Terrace today? A Mr Clough's house?'

'We did. 14 High Forest Terrace to 27 Henson Green Lane, York. Full house contents. Here, this is the key to the Clough job. We leave it here,' and Tweedledum plonked it in a tray on the desk, clearly proud of his firm's system for such things.

'Did you come across anything odd at Clough's house?'

They looked at each other, frowning, and then Tweedledee said, 'No, nowt really. No winding staircase. No narrow passages. No trouble at all, no wardrobe that wouldn't come downstairs, no iron-framed pianos, no fish-tanks full of guppies. No carpets nailed down. No, no problems. It was an ordinary job, really. Cheap stuff, most of it. Nowt very good, I'd say, no mirrors or marble washstands worth smashing . . . '

I found this an odd interview, to say the least, for I was sure the body must have been there as they worked. I knew I must ask the direct question.

'And Mr Clough? Was he there?'

'There was a chap there, yes.'

'Where was he? What was he doing?' I asked.

Tweedledum responded. 'He was upstairs on t'bed. Dead, I reckon. We tried to rouse him, but he wouldn't have any of it, so we thought he must have passed away.'

'So what did you do?' I asked.

'Laid him on t'floor while we shifted his bed. Rolled him over to shift the mat we'd put him on, and left him there. He'd got the stuff ready, mind, pots and pans packed in boxes, ornaments in tea-chests and such like. He'd done a fair job of packing; that's what I said at the time, didn't I? Many younger folks would have done a lot worse . . . some can't pack for toffee . . . anyroad, it wasn't a long job, not as it would have been if we'd had to pack right from the start.'

'Didn't you tell anybody — about Mr Clough, I mean?'

They looked at one another as if this was a stupid question. 'Nay, lad, that was nowt to do with us.' Tweedledee acted as spokesman now. 'We were there to shift furniture, not to do t'undertaker's job. T'only problem was finding somewhere to put him while we demolished his bed, but he was no trouble really. We got finished on time.'

'But don't you think you should have called the doctor or someone?'

'He was dead. There was nowt a doctor could do,' said Tweedledee. 'Besides, our boss says we've not to get involved in things that don't concern us. Our job is to shift furniture and to make sure it's shifted on time, with no overtime. Very particular is our boss about suchlike.'

Tweedledum then added his wisdom: 'If we did all t'things folks ask us while we're moving stuff, we'd never be finished. One woman wanted us to help paper t'ceiling, and a feller once asked if I'd help him fix his leaking toilet basin . . . so our boss says never do other folk's jobs. See to your own, he says . . . so shifting bodies is not our job, Mr Rhea. That's for t'undertaker, so we didn't get involved. We had a timetable to keep, you see, and there's no time to go chasing folks and ordering coffins and things when you've got to get loaded up and unpacked in t'same day.'

I took a statement from them and was satisfied in my own mind that poor old Mr Clough had packed his belongings the previous night and afterwards had simply passed away on his bed. He had not locked up that night, and these characters had simply let themselves in that morning to go about their work. And so they had, without letting a dead body interrupt their tight timetable.

I left them. I was amazed that they could ignore such a thing, and I wondered if they'd claim overtime from their boss for the time they spent with me.

I also wondered what they would have done if Mr Clough had been lying there in his coffin with the lid shut. I reckon they'd have moved him to his new house in York.

If the behaviour of those removal men seems bizarre, I can support it with a similar tale from a village on the moors.

I was working one Thursday morning at Eltering Police Station when a call came from a hiker. He was ringing from a telephone kiosk at Briggsby and sounded panic-stricken. I happened to be near the phone in the police station when it rang, and as PC Rogers was dealing with a motorist at the counter, I answered.

'Eltering Police,' I said.

'Hello?' the voice sounded full of anxiety. 'Hello? Oh, is that the police?'

'Detective PC Rhea speaking,' I said slowly.

'Oh, thank God for that! Look, I'm ringing from a kiosk at Briggsby. You know it?'

'I do,' I said, for it was on my own rural beat.

'There's a body in the church,' he gasped. 'Dead . . . '

'Maybe there's going to be a funeral,' I tried to soothe him. 'Bodies are taken into church before the funeral . . . '

'In coffins, yes, but this one is lying on one of the pews. Near the front. He's got a notice on him saying, "Pray for the soul of Mr Aiden Bradley".'

'Is it a joke of some kind?' I asked. 'Is someone playing a joke on you?'

'Look, Officer, I know a dead body when I see one. I'm a tutor in first aid, and I am a responsible person. If you want to check, my name is Welham, George Welham, and I live at Moorways, Albion Road, Middlesbrough.'

'Point taken, Mr Welham. I'll come straight away. Will you wait? I'll be there in twenty minutes.'

I told John Rogers where I was going and what the call had alleged, and he chuckled. He thought it was some kind of village prank, a joke against the verger or the vicar, but logged it in our occurrence book.

I drove out to Briggsby, a pretty community high on the moors. It comprises a handful of cottages, one or two farms and a tiny parish church which perches on a small patch of rising ground. I eased to a halt outside and saw a man, in full hiking gear, waiting for me. His rucksack stood on the wall of the graveyard. I could see the relief in his face as I stepped from the car. I introduced myself.

'This is a most unlikely story,' I said. 'Sorry if I sounded full of disbelief . . . '

'I think I'd have done the same!' he smiled. 'I've been back inside once or twice, just to convince myself, but he's still there. He *is* dead, Officer; he is not pretending; he is not asleep, and I don't think the notice is a joke of any sort.'

George Welham was a tall, slim man in his thirties; he wore heavy hiking boots, thick tweed trousers and a warm red sweater.

'Show me,' I invited.

He led me into the dim interior and we walked in silence towards the altar. At the front of the pews, he halted and pointed to the first pew on the left.

And there, as he had stated, was the body of an elderly man. He was fully clothed in a dark suit and was lying on the pew with his feet towards the aisle. His hands were crossed upon his chest. The solid backrest of the pew shielded him from view, and even when one was sitting in the second pew, he was almost out of sight; I wondered how long he had been here. A congregation could assemble without realizing he was lying here, unless anyone wanted to sit beside him. He could have been here for ages . . . but I felt not. Decomposition had not yet set in, although he was exuding a bit of a pong. As Welham had mentioned on the telephone, there was a handwritten notice on his chest, held secure beneath his hands, and it read, 'Pray for the soul of Mr Aiden Bradley.'

I felt his hands and face; he was cold, and rigor mortis had set in. He was as dead as the proverbial dodo. I asked Mr Welham a few pertinent questions, such as the time he had found him, whether he had moved him or called a doctor. He had done neither, and I then allowed him to leave. The problem of Mr Aiden Bradley was now mine. I searched his pockets for something by which to confirm his likely identity but, apart from a few coins, a comb and a handkerchief, there was nothing.

There were the usual formalities to arrange, such as certification of death, but how had the man come to be here and who had placed the notice on his chest? I did not know Mr Bradley and felt he was not a local man.

I decided to visit the adjoining farm to begin my enquiries, and to use their telephone to call a doctor and to arrange for the shell to be brought from Eltering.

'Bradley?' responded Joe Crawford, the farmer who lived next door to the church. 'Nivver 'eard of 'im. He's not a local, I'll tell thoo that for nowt.'

'You've no vicar here, have you?' I asked.

'Nay, lad, he comes in fre' Crampton. Covers Crampton, Briggsby and Gelderslack parishes. 'E lives in Crampton.'

'Thanks, I'll have a word with him. Does anybody in the village have a key for the church?'

'Aye, awd Mrs Dodson at Forge Cottage. She's t'cleaner.'

I explained the problem, but it didn't seem to worry Joe Crawford; as he said, 'You choch 'as a few bodies in it ivvery year, Mr Rhea, so another 'un isn't owt to shout about.'

I called Dr McGee, who had to travel from Elsinby, and in the meantime I went to see awd Mrs Dodson. She was a lady in her eighties who had been church cleaner for more than sixty years.

'I'd like to borrow your key for the church.' I spoke loudly, noticing the hearing-aid unit strapped to her belt. 'I might have to lock it until we've investigated a matter.'

'Summat wrang, is there?' she shouted at me.

'There's a dead man in church.' I knew I would have trouble explaining the matter in detail. 'We might have to seal the church until we've investigated his death.'

'I hope he hasn't made a mess,' she bellowed. 'I swept out last week. I should 'ave been in this morning, but my brush head fell off.'

'It's a Mr Bradley, I think,' I told her.

'He rents that cottage at the end of Green Lane.' The words rang in my ears. 'He comes for weekends and holidays.'

That explained why I did not know him.

'Where from?' I asked. 'Do you know? Has he any family?'

'Bradford,' she said. 'He's a retired wool merchant. I clean for him, an' all. After I do the church, I do his cottage, but my brush head's fallen off . . . '

'I'll fix it,' I said.

She brought it to me, together with a hammer and a box of nails, and I set about securing the brush head to the shaft. As I hammered in the nail, she said, 'Ah've had yon brush for thirty-five years, and all Ah've had for it is three new heads and two new shafts.'

'Really?' I wondered if this was a kind of joke, but she sounded serious and proud of her brush.

'Brushes were made to last in them days.' she beamed.

'Did you go to the church this morning?' I asked her as I finished hammering the nail through the hole in the head.

'No,' she hollered. 'Thursdays is my day, but because that head fell off . . . '

'So who would go in this morning?'

'The vicar,' she boomed. 'He has his own key. He has a service on Thursday mornings, ten o'clock. Not many folks go, mind, not like they used to. Mr Bradley allus went if he was staying here . . . '

'I'll wait at the church for the doctor,' I told her. 'And then I'll take Mr Bradley away to the mortuary. If anybody comes asking about him, relations mebbe, tell them to get in touch with me at Eltering Police Station. Rhea is the name. Then I'll lock the church and bring you the key; don't unlock it until I tell you. I'll probably ring later today, when we know whether this is a suspicious death.'

'222,' she barked. 'My number.'

'Thanks,' and I left with the key in my hand.

'Bye, Mr Rhea,' she thundered as I made my way back to the church.

Dr Archie McGee, smelling of whisky in spite of the hour, arrived and I showed him the corpse.

'Dead,' he said. 'Very dead, Nick, old son. I'll certify that but I cannot certify the cause. He was not my patient; never seen the follow before.'

So that meant a post-mortem. However, I thanked him and off he went. The van containing the shell arrived shortly afterwards, and we loaded Mr Bradley, complete with his request to God, and sent him on his way to the mortuary. Later I would ask Bradford police to trace his relatives and hoped his cottage would reveal an address at which we could begin; that had to be searched next. I did find an address in his bedroom at the cottage and would relay that to Bradford for enquiries to be made.

My immediate job now was to find the vicar. I drove to his small, modern vicarage at Crampton and found him in the garden tending a border. He was hoeing out some weeds and smiled as I approached.

'Ah, Mr Rhea. Such a nice surprise. We seldom get a visit by the police.'

The Reverend Jason Chandler was a curious man, in my view. He had done several jobs before entering the ministry of the Church of England, including being a coastguard and a salesman of women's lingerie, and he lived a life remote from the parishioners. He seldom entered the social life of the area and, as a bachelor, found it difficult to mix with the families whom his church served. In his late forties, he was always pleasant when I met him.

'Mr Chandler,' I began, 'I've an odd event to enquire about,' and I related the story of Mr Bradley's remains being found by the hiker.

'Ah, yes,' he said without hesitation. 'He was in my congregation this morning, Mr Rhea. A congregation of one, I might add. And then he collapsed and died. He was sitting in the first pew, so I laid him out and put a sign up asking for prayers. I do hope he goes to Heaven, Mr Rhea. He was a truly generous man, a keen supporter of our little church at Briggsby.'

'Did you call the doctor?' I asked.

'Well, no. I, well, had reached the most solemn part of the service, preparing for communion, you know, when it happened, I had reached the consecration of bread and wine and could not interrupt that . . . so when I got to him, it was clear he was dead. I was a coastguard, you know, very highly trained in first aid, and, well, there was no doubt about it. He was too late to receive communion, you know. He passed away just a few minutes too soon, and I know that would not have pleased him. He did like to receive communion, Mr Rhea. Anyway, calling a doctor would have been a total waste of time, far too late to revive him. Far too late. God works in mysterious ways, Mr Rhea.'

'You can say that again!' I could not help myself uttering that remark. 'So what did you do?'

'After I'd laid him out, you mean?'

'Yes.'

'Well, nothing. I felt I ought to put the sign on him to tell visitors he was dead, rather than asleep. People do fall asleep in church, as I'm sure you know, but I felt I ought to make it quite clear that this was a dead man.'

'Which you did. Then what?'

'Well, I had another service immediately afterwards, at Crampton, and had to leave straight away, otherwise I would have kept that congregation waiting — Lord and Lady Crampton always attend on Thursdays, you see.'

'It's a few minutes' drive to Crampton, eh?'

'Yes,' he oozed. 'There is not a moment to spare on that trip, and I had to be on time . . . I knew Mrs Dodson would see to Mr Bradley. She does his cottage, you know. She's the church cleaner, as well, so I knew he was in good hands. It's her day in, you see, and I knew she would find him. She was due to do the brasses today and, well, I felt she could not help noticing him.' .

'She didn't go in this morning.' I sighed, wondering how on earth people could behave like this, and added for good measure, 'The head fell off her brush.'

'Oh, dear, I do hope she gets it fixed. That church floor

does get very dusty, from the road, you know, passing traffic . . . '

I had found the last person to see poor old Mr Bradley when he was alive, and I had an account of his final moments, such as they were. After taking a formal statement from the Reverend Mr Chandler, I left him to his gardening and wondered how he would have coped as a coastguard if a ship was about to be grounded. Maybe he would have left it for a fisherman to sort out — which might explain why he was no longer a coastguard.

The post-mortem examination showed that Mr Bradley had died from natural causes, from a heart-attack, in fact. There would be no inquest.

We did find his relatives, and they took the body home for burial. I did not tell them of the odd circumstances of the discovery of his body, merely saying he had died in church while attending a service.

That knowledge seemed to offer them some consolation, so I did not say that he had missed Holy Communion.

Sad though sudden death is, there are times when coping with corpses is akin to a black comedy.

Three large policemen, one of whom was myself, once had the tricky job of manœuvring the corpse of an eighteen-stone man down a narrow, winding staircase while the grieving family sat in a room at the foot of the stairs. The problem was that the corpse had only one leg, so there was precious little to grip as we took it away for a post-mortem. The truth was the fellow got away from us on those stairs and bumped his way down the flight until he ended in a heap on the front door mat. Fortunately the door into the room was closed, and so the relatives never saw what happened; it was also fortunate that the front door was closed, otherwise the one-legged body would have rolled into the street and directly into a bus queue standing outside. The result might have been something like a game of giant skittles.

We had a similar task when a huge woman collapsed on the top of a lighthouse; we had to slide her down the winding staircase because it was impossible to lift her and impossible to manœuvre the coffin-sized shell around the tight corners. We made use of a card table top and sat her upright on that, then used it as a kind of sledge with her on board. I'm sure the trip gave her a posthumous thrill – it frightened the life out of us, for we felt sure the contraption would escape from our hands on the descent. But it didn't.

I had to admire the improvisation skills of a colleague at Strensford, when he came across a dead man at the back of a pub one Saturday lunchtime. A regular at the pub had found the corpse and thought it was merely a drunk sleeping off his over-indulgence. Because this route led in from the car-park, however, and because it was also a busy alley leading to several shops, my colleague had to think fast. He was alone, the local police van was in use at Thirsk Races, and the shell was being utilized at another sudden death. He did not like to leave his body lying on a busy thoroughfare with women and children passing by every few seconds, so he borrowed a wheelbarrow from the landlord, sat the still-warm corpse in it and placed one or two beer bottles around it. Thus the corpse had all the appearance of a drunk, and my colleague wheeled it through the town to the mortuary. He was cheered on his way by some other cheerful drinkers, but no one knew he was carting away a corpse. They thought it was a drunk being arrested in a highly unusual but very practical manner.

Perhaps the funniest that I was involved in, from a slapstick point of view, involved a body in the upper harbour at Strensford.

The call came at seven o'clock one morning, when I was patrolling in uniform, and I was despatched to the power station whose night-duty man had noticed the body with the arrival of dawn. It lay in the mud, apparently having been left high and dry when the tide had receded, and it was that of an elderly man. I went into the control room to ask where precisely this body lay and was shown from an upper window.

'You'll need wellies,' I was told. 'It's thick mud out there.'

I borrowed a pair from the power station's staff room, went down a gangway normally used by boats and started to walk across the expanse of thick black mud. I sank almost to wellington boot tops in the slime, but beneath the layer of greasy mud there was a firm surface, so I decided to continue. The body lay at least fifty yards away, and beyond it the river flowed towards the sea in a channel it had created over the years. When the tide was in, this area of mud flats would be covered with several feet of sea water, but there were some hours before this would happen.

Then, as I lifted my foot to make the next step, the wellington remained in the mud. The depth and the suction held it down, and so I had to walk across to the corpse by literally lifting each wellington up by hand as I walked. Step by step, already filthy around the legs and hands, I made my way to that body. It seemed to take an age, but I arrived to find an old man lying face down in the mud.

The clothes on his back were dry, an indication that he had fallen face down into the waters of the upper harbour. As the tide had flowed out, he had been left marooned on this mud bank. He was dead; of that, I was never in doubt, but I tried to lift the body to examine his face and to make a cursory check for any signs of life.

As I took the weight with my hands, my feet slithered backwards in that slime, and I fell flat on my own face beside the body, sending a shower of black, oily mud towards the skies. I was spreadeagled there and could feel myself sinking, but I managed to draw my legs beneath me to stand upright. I emerged like a black and greasy excrescence and wondered if the power station staff were observing this performance. Once on my feet, now oozing all over with stinking mud, I tried again. But the body would not shift; the suction of the ghastly brew held it firmly down. I splodged around in that smelly scum, trying and trying to slide or lift the body, but in that thick, oily mess it would not move. I stank like a drain now and was smothered because of frequent slips and falls.

I decided I needed help and that bare feet might be one solution, so I trudged back to the power station, leaving my wellies standing on the corpse's rump. They would act as markers for my next sortie. From an outbuilding at the power station, where my condition could not do a lot of harm, I rang for assistance.

The power station staff, now increasing in numbers as the day's work began, laughed themselves sick when they saw me, but I did manage to persuade the sergeant that I needed help. He said he would send someone to help me, and this would be a constable who lived nearby. He was summoned to my aid. When Alan arrived, he fell about laughing at me, and then we set off together across the mud, heading for the pair of wellies which were our guides. The stench from the path I had created by disturbing the mud was appalling. It was like splodging through a huge open-air sewer.

Alan had taken off his shoes and had rolled his trousers up to his knees before accompanying me, but even the act of walking made us slither and catch one another; by the time Alan arrived with me, we were both smothered in stinking black slime. We decided that the only way to turn the body over was for me to stand at one side, grip his clothing and roll him towards me, while Alan stood at the other to lift and push simultaneously. We tried. The body refused to move. Then, as we heaved and pulled, there was, without any warning, a loud sucking sound as the body suddenly moved – I fell backwards into the knee-deep mud, the body came half-way out and Alan fell flat on his face as his feet slithered away. When I stood up, the corpse was on its side with one hand sticking into the air like a mast, and Alan was crawling out of the mire with his entire face and upper body dripping with ooze. But we had dislodged the body from its anchorage.

We managed to get the unfortunate chap out of the sludge and onto his feet and, satisfied that he was really very dead, began to carry him back to the shore. I put one of the dead arms about my shoulders, and Alan did likewise; thus the three of us slithered, fell and stank our way back to the slipway, by which time a cheering crowd had assembled at the power station railings.

Once ashore, we could cope. There had to be a post-mortem on this body, and the odd thing was that he had not died from drowning – there was no water in his lungs. He had died from natural causes. How he came to be in the water was never discovered.

Afterwards I submitted a request for my uniform to be cleaned at the expense of the police, and I was told that no funds were available for that kind of thing. Keeping my uniform pressed and clean for duty was my responsibility, I was told.

But from that day forward, there was always a welcome for

me at the power station, with a cup of coffee and the offer of a pair of clean wellies any time I need them to go paddling.

7

I hope I shall never be deterred
from detecting what I think is a
cheat.

Samuel Johnson (1709-84)

One of the crimes which puzzled, and probably still puzzles, the general public was that of taking and driving away a motor vehicle without having either the consent of the owner or other lawful authority. This bafflement has arisen because this is not the same crime as stealing a motor vehicle. The two are quite distinct, and the essential difference is that stealing entails the intention of permanently depriving the owner of his property, while the unauthorized borrower has no such intention. He takes a vehicle for a joy-ride, and youths would take cars simply to get them home after a night out, after which they would abandon them with little thought of the owners' anguish or little anxiety about the damage and expense they had caused the unfortunate owner. Almost without exception, the cars were found by the police and restored to their owners.

For some years, this unlawful taking of motor vehicles was not a crime, simply because it had not been considered when the early definitions of larceny were compiled. To prosecute the 'takers' for something, they were occasionally charged with stealing the petrol they had consumed. This smacked of desperation, but what else could be done by the police?

Later, because an increasing number of cars were being 'borrowed' illicitly, the offence was written into the law, albeit not as part of the law on stealing but as part of the 1930's road traffic law. It was another thirty years or so before the law realized that other forms of conveyance were also borrowed without lawful authority and that no statute catered for them. They included bikes, hang-gliders, aircraft, boats, trains and roller-skates – in fact, it now includes anything constructed or adapted for the carriage of persons by land, water or air, whether or not such a thing has an engine fitted. However, it does not include things which are pedestrian-controlled, such as prams and lawnmowers. This long-overdue 1968 law did, of course, continue to include cars, lorries, buses and other such means of transport.

The unlawful borrowing of that mass of other conveyances was not written into the Theft Act until 1968, and so, when I was a young constable and an Aide to CID, I was not concerned with the unauthorized taking of all conveyances but merely with those which fell into the definition of motor vehicles. But we were heavily into the popular crime of Taking Without Consent, as we called it in long-hand, or TWOC as we abbreviated it. We pronounced it TWOCK.

There was no crime of TWOCing a pedal cycle, however (there is now), and so lots of illicit bike-borrowers were never prosecuted simply because they had committed no criminal offence. Now, a bike is within the meaning of a conveyance, and so illegal borrowers can be prosecuted.

One of the more popular crimes when I was an Aide to CID was the relay TWOC. A man would take a car from, say, London and drive it as far as the tank full of petrol permitted – say, Luton. At Luton he would abandon the first car and take another one, driving that until its tank was almost empty. That might have carried him to, say, Newark, where he would seek another one with the keys in the ignition. The Newark car would perhaps be driven to York and left in a side street as he took yet another to convey him to Middlesbrough or further north. And so the journey continued. In this way, a TWOC merchant could travel the length or breadth of Britain without cost to himself, but leaving in his wake a trail of abandoned motor vehicles.

The sufferers were the owners of the cars. Sometimes the cars were damaged; sometimes they were abandoned in awk-

ward places as their tanks ran dry, and sometimes they were
never found at all. If they were found abandoned, it rested
upon the unfortunate owner to recover them, and so their
owners had to travel long distances at their own expense to
fetch home their straying vehicles. Sometimes, as a matter of
courtesy and as a means of further protecting these abandoned
cars, we would take them to the police station for security.

One such case of relay TWOC occurred while I was doing
my stint as an Aide at Eltering.

The message originated from the Metropolitan Police in
London and it said that a car taken from Putney had been
found abandoned at St Albans; one taken at St Albans had
been found abandoned at Peterborough; one taken at Peterborough had been found abandoned at Doncaster, and one
had been stolen at Doncaster only that afternoon. That had
not yet been found, and so all police forces within reach of the
A1 (the Great North Road) were being alerted. It seemed that
a relay TWOC merchant was driving north via the A1,
venturing off only to abandon one car and take another.

The car stolen from Doncaster was a black Humber Snipe,
and its registration number was HMH 200. We were requested to seek this car in our area, where it might have been
abandoned. We are also advised to alert our officers to the
likelihood of a theft or TWOC in our part of the country.

At half-past seven that same evening, one of the uniformed
constables of Eltering rang in from a telephone kiosk to say he
had found the abandoned Humber Snipe. There was no one
with the car, the keys were still in the ignition, and it was
presently on a piece of waste ground in the town. He was told
not to touch it until the CID arrived. Detective Sergeant
Connolly was told of the car and said to me, 'Go and have a
look at it, Nick. There's not a lot we can do with a job of this
kind, but see if there's any stolen property stashed away in it,
fingerprints on the fascia, that sort of thing.'

I joined PC Steve Forman at the car. He had found it during
a routine foot patrol and watched as I opened the boot, lifted
the seats and did a thorough search without finding anything
of interest. With a light fingerprint brush laced with grey
powder, I dusted the steering-wheel, internal mirror, ashtray
and other points likely to have been handled by the driver, but

none was worth preserving. They were all smudged.

I made an external examination of the car. I noted that it bore the number plates MHH 200, which had not been altered or replaced by false ones, and saw that it was in a filthy condition. Its general appearance was one of neglect but it did bear a current Road Fund Licence, as the excise licence was then known. This was before the days of MOT tests, and the tyres were bald, the interior was full of dust and corn husks, old sacks and rusting tools, and there were holes under the mudguards and in the doors.

'Is there any petrol in it?' I asked Steve.

He switched on the ignition, and the gauge showed empty, although by shaking the car with the filler cap off, we could hear a faint sloshing in the tank.

'He's run it dry,' I said. 'But I reckon there's enough to get it back to the station. I'll drive it there for safe keeping.'

And so we both jumped in and I drove it to Eltering Police Station, where I parked in the compound at the rear, locked it and brought the keys into the office.

Steve and I made out our reports and settled down to await the inevitable report of a car missing from Eltering. If the Humber had been abandoned here, another one would have been stolen — unless, of course, the TWOC merchant was travelling no further than Eltering. In that case, he could be at home now, gloating over his triumph of travelling free from London. But we felt this was not the case. We felt sure we were part of a relay series of TWOCs and that soon a worried car-owner would turn up to report his or her car missing.

Sure enough, a couple of hours later, as I was typing some statements in the general office, a man arrived on a bike and came to the enquiry desk. He was dressed in rough working clothes and smelt of pigs.

'Noo then,' he said as he came in, wafting that awful pig muck aroma around as he removed his flat cap, 'Ah think this is t'right spot to come, but somebody's pinched my car.'

'This is the right spot.' PC John Rogers tried to hold his nose away from the pervading pong, but there was no escape. 'So, let's start at the beginning.'

The man was called Ralph Cross. He was a farm labourer and he lived in Eltering. After taking those details on the form he was compiling, Rogers asked, 'Now, Mr Cross, the car. What kind is it?'

'Humber Snipe,' he said. 'A black 'un. Mucky, mind, but black underneath all t' muck. Number MHH 200. They've took it from that spare land up Penthorne Lane way. They won't get far in her because she's hardly gitten any petrol in. Anyroad, Ah thowt Ah'd tell you fellers.'

Upon hearing his description, I came to the counter. 'Mr Cross,' I asked, 'where was it taken from? You've not been in Doncaster today, have you?'

'Doncaster?' he sounded horrified. 'Nay, lad, not Doncaster. That's down south, isn't it?'

'It's a long way south of here, yes,' I agreed. 'But we got a report to say your car had been stolen from Doncaster.'

I turned up the relevant message in the Occurrence Book and read it again.

'Nay, there's summat wrang there,' he frowned. 'She's nobbut been to Scarborough once and that was six month back, and she's nivver been as far south as Doncaster, nivver.'

It now began to look as if a highly improbable thing had happened. I wondered if someone had stolen Cross's Humber Snipe from Eltering that morning and had then driven it to Doncaster, there to abandon it without this man's ever realizing it had gone missing. And had someone else then stolen it again, and driven it back to its home town, a sheer fluke of circumstance, but not impossible. But no — that was not possible, because who had reported it missing from Doncaster?

If Cross had not known it was missing, he could not have reported it . . . unless the car had been involved in some other adventure we knew nothing about . . .

We had a puzzle, and I wondered whether there was some insurance fiddle going on or whether Cross was involved in some other kind of wrong-doing of a very subtle kind. Should we tell him straightaway that his car had been found and that it had been abandoned here in town after being reported missing at Doncaster? Or should we find out exactly what had occurred before releasing it? We continued with our enquiries.

'I'll ring Doncaster police,' said John Rogers, and he said to Cross, 'We had a report of your car being in Doncaster this morning,' avoiding mention of the reported theft in that town.

'It nivver was!' he cried. 'I went up to t'farm in it this morning, drove a few sacks o' taties about, and a piglet to t'vets, and then it was in t'farmyard till I left at half five tonight. She's nivver been in Doncaster today, no, nivver.'

Rogers knew he must check this tale with Doncaster, even before circulating Mr Cross's car as stolen or TWOC'd. Cross and I watched as he put through his call.

'Ah,' he said eventually as the call was connected. 'This is PC Rogers from Eltering. I'm ringing about that Humber Snipe, the black one . . . '

We could not hear any response but were to learn that the officer said, 'Forget it, Mr Rogers. It's been found abandoned in Wakefield. The owner's gone to collect it.'

'You're joking!' he cried.

'No, it's been recovered. The black Humber Snipe that we circulated as a relay runner, HMH 200.'

'But we have it here, in Eltering . . . '

'No, you haven't. Wakefield police have it, and it's safe and sound in their compound, awaiting collection. It was found abandoned there at five o'clock this evening.'

'Well, if you are sure . . . '

'We are,' said Doncaster, and Rogers put down his telephone, puzzlement showing on his face.

'They've found it in Wakefield . . . '

'Wakefield?' cried Cross. 'Does that mean I've got to go to Wakefield to get it back?'

'Five o'clock it was found, they said,' continued Rogers. 'And the owner is already on his way to collect it.'

'Now, hang on a minute, lads, at five o'clock Ah was in my car, driving home, and Ah was here in Eltering, nowhere near Doncaster or Wakefield or any o' them spots.'

In the meantime, I had picked up the occurrence book and was looking at the entry relating to the Doncaster Humber.

And then, embarrassed until my face flushed deep crimson, I said to Mr Cross,

'Mr Cross, your car has been recovered, but it is not at Wakefield. It is here, in our compound.'

'What the hell's going on then?' He looked at us one by one.

'We thought a black Humber Snipe, stolen at Doncaster

had been abandoned here. It's HMH 200.'

'That's not mine,' he said rapidly. 'Mine's MHH 200. Different number, different car.'

And so it was.

Highly embarrassed, we returned his car to him and did our best to explain, but he drove off cheerfully, saying, 'I'm glad you fellers found mine.'

'All part of our duty, Mr Cross.' I said.

And then I asked John Rogers, 'Where did he park his car after work?'

'Outside his house,' he said. 'On waste land at Penthorne Lane.'

'That isn't where we found it,' I said. 'We looked at it on waste land just off the Sycamore estate. That's on the other side of the town.'

I looked at John Rogers and he looked at me. 'So it had been nicked after all,' he said.

'And found abandoned, and returned to the owner,' I said.

'So the file is closed?' grinned John.

'Yes,' I said, with more than a hint of relief. 'One crime reported and one crime detected, with all the property recovered intact. A nice entry for our records.'

'And a piece of fine detective work,' laughed John. 'You know, we were idiots not to have noticed those car numbers were different.'

'Round numbers are always false,' I said quoting from Samuel Johnson because I could think of nothing else worth saying.

One of the most peculiar TWOC cases concerned a bus, and we never did find the perpetrator of this cheeky crime.

A Women's Institute from County Durham had hired a coach from Palatine Pullman, a local coach-hire company, to take a party of ladies on a pleasure outing to the North York Moors. One of their halts was at Eltering, where they were to be given a guided tour of Eltering Castle, known for its links with the Plantagenets, and afterwards they would have lunch at the White Hart Inn. Their total stay in the town was scheduled to take 1¾ hours; they arrived at noon and were to leave at 1.45 p.m.

The splendid coach parked in Castle Drive to disgorge its ladies, and the driver did as most drivers do — he ate his own sandwiches and drank his flask of coffee while sitting on the luxurious back seat, and then curled up on the long, relaxing seat and went to sleep. It was something he did regularly on such trips. He left the passenger entrance door unlocked, because he knew the noise and chatter of the returning ladies would rouse him. It always did. His own little cab was also unlocked — and he left the keys in the ignition; again, he always did this because there had never been any bother.

What happened next is something of a mystery, but, in reconstructing the events, it seems that a cheeky character had seen what he thought was an empty coach and had climbed aboard, seen the keys in the ignition and then driven the bus over the moors to Strensford.

News of the disappearance of the bus came from the WI's organizer who had travelled with the party. She came to the police station at Eltering, harassed and red-faced.

'Our driver's gone without us,' she panted. 'We were not late, there has been no delay, and he has left the place where we parked.'

This kind of problem occurred a lot in popular tourist areas, and invariably the panic was due to a misunderstanding of some kind. Either the ladies had not understood where the bus would be upon departure or they'd taken the wrong turning on the way back to it, or it would be in the coach-park in town. Invariably, in such cases, we managed to reunite bus and passengers.

So, well-practised in this art and with the aid of the town's uniform branch, we searched every likely parking-place, but there was no sign of the distinctive coach.

PC John Rogers, who knew every inch of the town realized the lady was right — her coach had gone and so had the driver.

'I'll ring the owners,' he offered.

He rang them and said, 'Oh, this is Eltering Police. I'm ringing on behalf of a WI outing; they've come here on one of your coaches. Yes, today.'

He waited as the receptionist plugged him through to someone else, and then he repeated his story, adding, 'Well, there is now a problem. The bus has gone, but its passengers are still here. We have about forty-five ladies marooned in Eltering. All wanting to catch their bus to its next destination. But there is no bus. We have searched the town, and there is no sign of it. And they were not late, not lost, not rude to the driver or anything like that. The bus has not been dismissed and it has not caught fire anywhere. Now, has the driver called you at all? Is there any explanation from him? No, he's not reported it missing because he's missing as well.'

From what we could overhear, it seemed the driver had not been in touch with his head office, and they could offer no explanation. It was now 2.15 p.m. and the ladies were getting anxious, either wishing to travel onwards or, in some cases, wanting to get back home. With the co-operation of the WI organizer and the coach company, John Rogers managed to persuade them to wait for an hour. His calm, unflappable response had a soothing effect upon the WI organizer.

'Things might sort themselves out,' he said, raising his eyes to Heaven. 'I'm sure the driver has not forgotten you.'

The company agreed to this compromise, threatening to discipline their driver if and when he turned up, and they agreed that, if he did not return to the pre-arranged place by 3.15 p.m., they would dispatch a duplicate coach. But it would take an hour and a half to reach Eltering. The ladies were heading for a lot of tea-drinking, some delightful window shopping and a fair bit of queueing at loos. The organizer said she would go and explain things to her clients, then return at 3.15 p.m. to see if there was any further development.

When she'd gone, I smiled at John Rogers. 'What do you make of all that?' I asked.

'He'll have gone off to the loo himself, or for a meal somewhere. Mebbe got a puncture on the way back . . . He'll turn up. They always do.' He was philosophical about it. 'We get loads of problems like that.'

As the bus had not been reported stolen and as the driver was evidently still with it, we did not circulate it as a stolen vehicle, nor did we think it had been taken without consent. In fact, that is what had happened. A man had driven it across the moors to Strensford, and all the time the driver remained asleep on that rear seat, blissfully unaware of his predicament. The warmth and the gentle motion lulled him, and so, as the bus motored its expensive way across the heights towards the coast, the driver went into an even deeper sleep.

Having arrived safely at his destination in Strensford, the thief (or, to be precise, the Taker-Without-Consent) simply drove the bus into a quiet street, parked it and walked away. There is every reason for believing he had no idea he had taken the driver with him.

The driver, a man called Jimmy Porritt, was aroused by the cessation of the relaxing motion. A few moments after the bus had stopped and its temporary driver departed, he yawned, stretched his arms and awoke from a very pleasant dream. He left his place and walked down the aisle to his driving-seat, never at this stage thinking he was in the wrong town. He settled down and then looked at his watch. It was 3 p.m.

Puzzled that his ladies had not returned on time, he looked outside and then saw he was in an unfamiliar street . . . and there was no sign of Eltering Castle. Jimmy was baffled. He felt sure he'd parked near Eltering Castle and yet, in this place, he could hear seagulls screaming, and between the houses he could see the tall shape of a lighthouse.

He clambered out of his bus, puzzled and somewhat alarmed, thinking perhaps that he had lost his senses or had a blackout of some kind. He hailed a passing lady with a baby in a pram and said, 'Excuse me, but what street is this?'

'Albion Terrace,' she said.

'Ah.' He did not wish to appear foolish, but had to ask, 'And what town is it?'

'Strensford,' she said, puzzled by his question.

He returned to his coach utterly confused by this turn of events, and in his bewilderment decided to ask the police to enlighten him. The police at Strensford listened to his odd tale and decided to seek our help in sorting out this Jimmy's dilemma.

John Rogers took the call, and I heard him chuckling. 'Yes,' I heard him say. 'We have lost a bus; it's left a load of women in town. They're overcrowding all the loos after drinking gallons of tea till we got things sorted out.'

'I'll get him to come back to Eltering,' said the Strensford constable. 'Shall I ask him to park near the castle where he was before?'

'Yes, do that,' John agreed.

When the WI organizer returned, within a few minutes of this call, we could say that her bus had been found in Strensford, but we had no idea why it had gone there. The driver was full of apologies and he would return within the hour. We also rang his head office to say the ladies and their coach had been re-united, but we left any explanations to the driver.

We never did receive a formal complaint that this coach had been the subject of a 'take and drive away' offence, but I did wonder if there was an offence of taking a driver without consent!

One vehicle which caused some legal head-scratching was the caravan.

If people lived in it, either temporarily or permanently, was it a dwelling-house? Or, if it was used only for holidays, was it a storehouse when not in use, for it then contained only furniture and crockery? Were those caravans used as temporary offices classified as offices, or was a caravan merely a trailer, as defined in the various road traffic regulations? One caravan at Aidensfield had an onion-shaped edifice on its roof and was used for Greek Orthodox Church services, so was that particular caravan a church? If so, it would be sacrilege to break into it, or burglary when such a vehicle was used as living-accommodation.

We would pose questions such as: if someone stole a residential caravan, did they steal an entire dwelling-house? But stealing a dwelling-house was legally impossible, because it was attached to the realty, i.e. the ground. To be legally guilty of stealing a real dwelling-house, it was necessary for the house to be demolished and abandoned, and then someone who stole the stones might be found guilty. So, for theft purposes, we felt a caravan should be regarded as merely a trailer. Was it a just thing to change the nomenclature of a caravan in order to accommodate particular laws? And what about the contents? If a stolen caravan contained 250 different items of furniture, crockery and food, was the thief guilty of stealing all those as well as the caravan itself?

These little puzzles were cast into the pool during our initial training, just to alert us to the legal fiction which was then so much a part of criminal law, and to attune our minds, through argument and illustration, to the wiles of both lawyers and villains in their desire to find ways around the various rules and regulations. It was interesting to realize that lawyers could spend lots of hours poring over lots of books to solve this kind of problem while earning lots of cash, but we poor constables had to carry the information in our heads. Instead of taking days or weeks to arrive at a decision, we had to act promptly and fairly in our execution of the law, without bringing the wrath of public opinion down upon our heads.

Although some of the answers to these knotty issues could be found in statutory form, others never received a satisfactory answer. But our discussions did cause some mirth and some interest while we were learning the law.

One thing we did know, however, was that a caravan could not be the subject of a TWOC charge. As TWOC then applied only to motor vehicles, there was a legal puzzle if someone took without consent a car with a caravan attached. The car could be TWOC'd, but the trailer could not. In its case, it was either theft or nothing.

However, at Eltering we were presented with another puzzle associated with a caravan.

David Crossley was a self-employed builder in his middle thirties who undertook odd jobs in and around Eltering. He could build a fine stone house if requested but seemed to spend most of his time repairing old buildings, roofing farms and cottages, constructing walls and renovating a wide range of rural edifices, from pigsties to church steeples. He was a competent workman, and we never had complaints about either his craftsmanship or his honesty. He would never be rich – he lacked the entrepreneurial skills necessary to be a tycoon, but he did earn a reasonable living for himself, his wife and two sons.

To put this story into chronological order, David was commissioned to build a row of stables for a local farmer who fancied himself as a member of the landed gentry. The farmer, Andrew Farrell, had become wealthy by the easiest possible route – he had married a rich wife. Her links with the gentry of the county and with local aristocrats meant that Andrew had to keep up appearances.

After a year or two of bliss, which included Andrew's obligatory attendance at hunt balls in country houses, fox-hunting with the nobility and shooting with golden retrievers called Rufus and Polly, it became evident that his wife was no fool. The blessed honeymoon over, Andrew found himself actually having to work to maintain the life-style to which he wanted to become accustomed.

But if he had acquired almost the right accent, almost the right clothes sense, almost the right way of holding wine glasses, and the ability to say 'grarse' instead of 'grass' and 'bass' instead of 'bus', he did lack the ability to make enough money to win over the friends he so desperately wished to cultivate.

Keeping horses for hunting, eventing and even racing was one of his ideas; horses, he knew, did open lots of doors to a finer style of living, and although his wife, Angela, spent a lot of money on herself in the way of clothes, outings and smart cars, she made Andrew work for his place in her society. Those of us on the outside of this domestic drama knew that Andrew would never achieve his social goals, but Andrew did not cease to strive in his efforts.

And so it was that David Crossley found himself building a block of eight stables in the grounds of the Farrell house, once called Honeywell Farm but now known as Honeywell Hall, in keeping with Andrew's new image.

David was sensible enough to get Andrew to pay for the materials and part of the labour costs as the building progressed. But by the time the smart new block was complete and Andrew's fine stables received their first intake of handsome fillies and colts, David had not received his final payment. He was owed some £800 in labour charges, but repeated requests did not produce the cash from Andrew.

We all suspected that Andrew's desire for social acceptance in high places had put a strain on his bank balance, a strain that was affecting other tradesfolk and business people in addition to David Crossley. News of Andrew's impending disaster had filtered through to the CID, not because getting into debt is a criminal offence but because people were openly talking about Andrew's inability to meet his rising social expenses. If his wife did indeed have money of her own, she was not letting her husband get his hands on it.

Then Andrew himself came into the office at Eltering one fine spring morning and was referred to the CID. I took him into our tiny office.

'Well, Mr Farrell,' I said, 'how can we help?'

'Someone's stolen my caravan,' he said, and I could see the theft had deeply upset him. 'It's disappeared sometime since yesterday afternoon.'

I quizzed him about it. He had bought it only a week earlier, second-hand but in excellent condition, from a supplier near York. It was a four-berth model, fully equipped with sleeping and kitchen equipment. It was worth, he felt, about £400 — that's what he'd paid for it.

He'd seen it in position the previous afternoon, at 4.30 p.m., and had missed it at ten o'clock that morning. It stood on a concrete hardstanding adjoining his new stable block, and it was to have accommodated a new groom he had appointed to care for his increasing number of horses.

'It's vital I get it back, Mr Rhea,' he said. 'I need that man to work with my horses, otherwise I shall lose valuable customers . . . and there is nowhere else for him to sleep. He has no transport, and there's no accommodation available nearby; besides, he needs to be close at hand at all times . . . '

I obtained a detailed description of the missing caravan but realized there were no distinguishing marks upon it; this was one of the Nomad range, all being very similar to each other. Farrell's caravan did bear his car's registration number but that could easily be removed. However, I assured him details would be circulated and asked him if he could point to any suspects.

I got the impression that he was reluctant to answer that question, but when I said that recovery of the caravan depended upon his total co-operation, he said, 'Yes, well, not just one suspect. Several.'

'Several?' I was surprised and must have sounded it, because he produced a handwritten note from his wallet. It was on lined paper from a cheap writing-pad, and in ballpoint pen were the words, 'When you pay your bill, you'll get your caravan back.'

'What bill is this?' I asked.

He shrugged his shoulders and had a look of defeat about him. 'I don't know, Mr Rhea,' he admitted. 'I'm being honest with you now — I owe lots and lots, to umpteen different tradesmen. The butcher, the garage, the farrier, the chap who delivers food for my cattle and horses, the bank of course . . . You see, I can't afford to let this groom go, and he will, if there's no accommodation and no room in the house. Besides, my wife won't have him in the house, being just a groom, you understand . . . '

I could see he was in dire trouble, but that was not our concern. I made a list of those to whom he owed money and decided I would interview them all to see if any of them admitted removal of the caravan. One obvious starting-point was anyone on his list who had a car or Landrover fitted with a towbar. But when I discreetly inspected the vehicles owned by Farrell's nominees, at least eight of them had towbars . . .

It took a few days to trace and interview each of these suspects. I found them all, asked about the money that was owed to them by Farrell and then questioned them about the caravan. None admitted anything. In spite of our circulations, there was no news of its whereabouts, and it seemed it was going to be lost forever, adding one more undetected crime to our statistics.

Then, some five or six weeks afterwards, I got another call which, on the face of it, had nothing to do with this case.

'It's Hull City Police,' said a voice. 'D/C Casson speaking.'

'D/C Rhea at this end,' I replied. 'How can I help?'

'We've had a spate of housebreakings and shopbreakings in and around Hull,' he said. 'We've got a suspect in, a good 'un, I might add, and he's implicated a mate of his. The mate is thought to be in possession of some of the nicked goods, household things. Among the identifiable stuff is a Bush radio — we've got the serial number; he's got away with some tinned foods and crockery, and other odds and ends from houses. Apart from nicking cash, he's also got himself kitted out for his holiday by pinching everything he needs.'

'And you think he's on holiday with his ill-gotten gains on our patch?'

'We're sure he is, him and his girlfriend. He's called Mills, Peter Henry Mills, and his girl is Susan Dunn. We don't think she's implicated, but if you bring her in, she might be able to tell us something useful.'

I took details of the couple, and a description of their physical appearance, and then he said,

'They're holidaying in a caravan. The address we have is Mill Close, Pattington. Is that on your patch?'

'It's in this sub-division,' I confirmed. 'What do you want us to do, precisely?'

'Arrest them both on suspicion of committing our crimes, seal the caravan in case it's full of stolen goods and detain them in your cells till I get there.'

'Right, I'll have words with my D/S, but I can see no problem. Shall we ring to let you know when they're inside?'

'I'd appreciate that.'

Gerry Connolly and I drove to Pattington, which is a pretty village between Ashfordly and York. Brick-built houses line an interesting street, and we had no difficulty finding Mill Close in a small valley behind the church. It was a disused flour-mill on the banks of a stream, and the old millwheel was still in working condition. Tucked into a corner of a field behind the mill were half a dozen caravans, most of which appeared to be occupied by visitors. Cars stood beside each one, so I looked for a car bearing a Hull registration plate, i.e. one with a sequence of letters ending in either AT, KH or RH. There had been no mention of a car by the Hull CID, but Mills would need one to reach here — besides, he might have borrowed one, hired one or even bought one, or his girl might have done likewise. This was not a cast-iron method of locating him, for he could have got his car from anywhere, but such checks often produced a good starting-point. And in this case, it did. We found a Morris Minor beside a caravan, and it bore the Hull registration letters AKH.

As Gerry and I approached the caravan, I noticed it was a Nomad but at that stage had no reason to connect it with the one missing from Farrell's farm. It was just one of many on this site, and it had been backed into a hedgerow, which meant we did not notice its number plate. And we never thought of looking.

The couple inside, who admitted being Peter Henry Mills and Susan Dunn, offered no resistance, although he protested his innocence at the accusations we levelled at him, and she stood up for him, in her innocence. We took the caravan keys and those of the car, which had been hired for the week, and locked both before we drove the couple to the police station pending the arrival of officers from Hull.

On the way into the office, Gerry was quietly quizzing them.

'Your caravan, is it?' he asked. 'Do you rent the space all the year?'

'It's not mine,' said Mills affably. 'I saw this advert in the *Hull Daily Mail*; I rent it from a chap who lives up here; he's got all those you saw just now. Chap called Crossley, a builder, he is.'

And then the warning bells rang in my head. I began to wonder if that caravan belonged to Andrew Farrell. Crossley was owed money, he did have a vehicle capable of towing such a caravan away, and here it was, anonymous among lots of others and now being rented out to holidaymakers.

I spoke nothing of my suspicions at this stage, but when we had placed Mills and Dunn in separate cells, having secured the services of a policewoman from Strensford to look after the woman, I voiced my suspicions to Gerry Connolly.

'Seems you'd better have words with our friend Crossley, then,' he beamed.

I found David Crossley at home that evening, and he welcomed me indoors; at my request, we went into the room which served as his office, away from his wife and family.

'David,' I said, 'you might know why I am here.'

'Still chasing Farrell's caravan, are you?' He was pleasant enough.

'I think I've found it,' I said. 'On your little holiday site at Pattington, at the old mill. You let it to a wanted housebreaker from Hull, David. He's just been arrested and the caravan has been sealed off.'

He laughed aloud. 'A fair cop, isn't that what they say? But I haven't stolen it, Mr Rhea. I'm not dishonest. I've just removed it temporarily, hidden it from him, until he pays me what he owes. And when he pays me, he can have it back.'

'A court would say that, as you have been making use of it for personal gain, you had every intention of permanently depriving Farrell of it. That makes it theft.'

'Nobody else has used it, Mr Rhea; that couple from Hull, Mills and Dunn, came without booking — they'd seen my adverts in the paper for the other vans, and came on spec.'

He said they were a one-off let, that he'd had no plans to rent this particular vehicle.

I pondered upon his culpability. If he had a claim of right to that caravan, a claim made in good faith, and if he also had no intention of permanently depriving Farrell of his caravan, there was no crime. But that issue was not for the police to decide — it was for a court of law to determine.

I did not arrest Crossley but told him I would have to report all the facts for consideration by my senior officers. When I told Gerry Connolly, he threw his hands into the air in horror, saying, 'Why does life have to be so bloody complicated? I'll tell Farrell what has happened.'

When Farrell heard the tale, he expressed some relief but no surprise, and then said to Gerry, 'Sergeant, I do not wish to press charges. I will not prosecute David Crossley.'

'You've no choice,' said Connolly. 'A crime has been committed.'

But his desire not to prosecute did sway our chief constable, for he read the file because of its curious nature; he sought the advice of the county solicitor before deciding whether or not to send the papers to the Director of Public Prosecutions for his advice. Because of the odd facts, all the recommendations were for no prosecution.

And so Peter Henry Mills was taken to Hull, along with several identifiable stolen goods from the caravan, and Susan Dunn was released without charge. She said she would stand by him for ever and ever and accused us of planting the stolen radio in the caravan.

And when we examined the caravan more closely, we did find that it still bore the registration number of Andrew Farrell's car. This was evidence in support of Crossley's claim that he had removed the caravan as a means of retrieving what was owed to him.

It was three weeks later when I bumped into Andrew Farrell in the street.

'Ah, Mr Rhea,' he said. 'Thanks for sorting out that caravan

job for me. I think your sergeant was very accommodating in
the circumstances, but if I had known it was David Crossley,
I'd never have reported it stolen in the first place. I'm letting
him keep it as a holiday letting caravan for this season, or until
he makes the equivalent of the money I owe him, with a bit
extra, of course, for tax.'

'That's good of you.'

'Yes, well, I don't want to bankrupt him, and it's one way of
helping me and him. I have found accommodation for my
groom — he's in the attic of our house. Angela did agree at
length, and so things are working out now. I am making
money with the horses too, so I will be able to pay my debts —
in time, of course.'

'So all's well that ends well, eh?' I smiled.

'Well, actually, all this might have done me good, given me
a superb idea for making more money.'

'Really?' I asked.

'Yes, a caravan site in our fields, for holidaymakers and
caravan rallies. A site of static vans and touring vans, a large
complex, of course, with toilets and shower facilities, and a
farm shop, all to cater for visitors from overseas and even
people in permanent residence . . . I think that is my next
project, Mr Rhea, subject to planning permission, of course.'

I wished him every success but did wonder what Angela
would think of masses of tourists and caravans defacing the
views from her magnificent home.

I rather felt Andrew would have another fight ahead, but he
was a trier. And for that, he deserved credit.

8

Riddle of destiny, who can show
What thy short visit meant?

Charles Lamb (1775-1834)

Sneak thieves are among the most loathsome of creatures.
Through their personal greed and odious behaviour, they not
only deprive people of their valuables but also cast a dark and
depressing cloud of suspicion over many innocent people. In
some cases, where the thief is not identified and caught, that
suspicion can endure for a long, long time. For this reason
alone, a sneak thief is one of the most repulsive of criminals.
Sometimes, I think the word 'sneak' is an anagram of snake,
snakes being the most lowly and despised of creatures, while
'a snake in the grass' is the term applied to a hidden enemy
and a disguised danger. Those feelings may well apply to the
sneak thieves who operate in any establishment.

It is a sad fact that these vermin are found in many places
where numbers of people congregate. They frequent dance
halls, sports centres, swimming-pools, offices, factories and
other places of work, private parties and even social gatherings
of all sizes. Much of their evil trade never reaches the official
ears of the police service because the organization which
harbours them prefers not to create even more alarm by
encouraging an investigation. The result is that many sneak-
thieves, having created an atmosphere of distrust, continue to
operate.

The police see an arrest as highly beneficial to all honest

citizens and a release by many from suspicion. That is one of
the real strengths of true liberty, the feeling of being free
within the law. There is no civil liberty when innocent people
remain under suspicion of being thieves while the real thief,
for whatever reason, is allowed to continue his or her nefarious
activities.

Thefts by sneak thieves range from the goods which they
help to manufacture via the office supplies which help to keep
the business in operation to cash and valuables taken from
coats and bags left in cloakrooms. Some regard their thieving
as a perk of the job and justify it accordingly, especially if they
are on low wages, but police records are full of the names of
people caught stealing from their place of work. This is theft,
and today it carries a maximum penalty of ten years' imprisonment, even if the thief only gets away with a piece of cheese, a
brick or the contents of a charity collecting-box. Clearly,
sentences of that magnitude are not given for minor transgressions, but it remains the case that ten years is the maximum
possible sentence for stealing.

It is a sad fact that some people cannot help stealing. There
are kleptomaniacs everywhere – they steal cups and saucers
from cafés, towels from hotels, spoons from British Railways,
cash from their friends or families, food from the canteen or
jars of coffee from the stockroom. They will pinch anything
and seem not to care that their activities are crimes or that they
place others under suspicion and, in some cases, put the jobs
and livelihood of their colleagues at risk by pilfering from their
employers' profits.

It follows that, where the police are notified that a sneak
thief is active, they make very serious attempts to arrest or at
least deter the perpetrator. Happily, there are many scientific
aids and modern technological methods which are capable of
trapping persistent sneak thieves.

One aspect of their crimes is that they are usually repeated,
not only once but time and time again. A thief who has
successfully purloined a side of bacon from the firm's canteen
or stolen cash from the till will try to take more, then more,
and yet still more . . . and in this way they generally trap
themselves, with a little help from the police.

I found myself investigating this type of crime soon after I began my attachment to Eltering CID, and it involved the hall which adjoined the Anglican church of St Erasmus. The hall was a busy one and was in use most days of the week, with regular events such as hunt balls, dances, whist drives, evening classes and afternoon classes, craft fairs, private parties and a range of other popular events. It had even hosted a dog show, a model railway exhibition and a ballet-dancing display. It was a fine, spacious building with a superb sprung dance floor of polished wood, a balcony for observers, an ante-room for use as a bar, and two large cloakrooms standing at either side of the impressive entrance hall.

The chairman of the St Erasmus Hall Social Committee was Mr Aaron Eyles, a retired butcher, and he called at the police station one Monday morning.

'Ah've a bit of a delicate matter to discuss,' was his opening remark, 'summat that'll not do with being spread around.'

The station duty constable knew old Aaron very well and managed to elicit the fact that he wished to discuss some crimes at the church hall, crimes of a highly sensitive nature, and so John referred him to the CID. Gerry Connolly invited him into his office and offered him a chair and a cup of coffee. I took in the two coffees, and Gerry said, 'Sit down, Nick. Fetch your coffee in here,' then introduced us. He made it clear to Aaron that I was utterly reliable and would not spread gossip about the town.

'So, Aaron, these crimes,' said Gerry. 'What are they?'

'Sneak thieves, Mr Connolly. Somebody's pinching from t'ladies' cloakrooms at St Erasmus's. Bit o' cash, cosmetics, purses, umbrellas even. Daft things like that − one woman's lost a torch, and somebody else has had a new scarf pinched.'

'Over what sort of period, Aaron?' asked Connolly.

'Six months mebbe. Mebbe a bit longer.'

'And you've not reported any to us, is that right? I can't recall any reports.'

'Nay, we haven't. T'committee thought they could fettle it themselves. Ah think some of them thought them thefts were not really thefts, tha knaws; they thought it was folks forgetting where they'd putten things, you know what folks are.'

'I know what folks are,' agreed Connolly. 'So, when are the things vanishing? I thought you had cloakroom attendants at all your dos.'

'Nearly all, Mr Connolly. Some of t'private hirings don't use attendants; Ah mean, a wedding wouldn't bother with 'em, and they sometimes don't get asked for t'smaller jobs. It costs, you see; they get paid by the hour, and t'hirer has to pay.'

'And are all the things vanishing from the ladies' cloak-room?'

He nodded and there was sadness in his eyes. 'Aye,' he said softly. 'That's t'problem. You see, Ada Clarkson is attendant in the ladies' end. Now she's been doing that job for years, Mr Connolly, with never a hint of owt going wrong. Never a hint. Ah mean, she's churchwarden, she cleans t'church and orga-nizes flower rotas, she's into charitable work in town, helps old folks, the blind, the infirm . . . you couldn't find a more helpful, honest woman.'

'And the stuff is going when Ada is on duty?' I could see Connolly hated to disillusion this old man but he was merely echoing the thoughts that poor old Aaron was entertaining.

'Aye,' he said. 'That's true. At first, folks were reporting the thefts to Ada but they stopped when nowt was done. So they come to me or t'secretary now — that's young Miss McCowey, Alec's lass.'

'And have you mentioned anything to Ada?' asked Gerry.

'Not for t'last month, Mr Connolly. Ah thowt Ah'd give her t'benefit of my doubts, in a manner of speaking, but Ah kept a record of complaints. There's been four late dances, two evening classes and a demonstration of cooking by gas in the evening, and in all cases Ada was working. During each of the four dances, money went from t'ladies' cloakroom, Mr Con-nolly, and Ah don't know what to make of it.'

Connolly was firm with him. 'Aaron, some of the most unlikely people turn to crime for all kinds of reasons. Ada is mebbe going through a crisis . . . is she passing through the menopause, eh? Doing things not in character? That's if it is her. We might be making too many accusations without doing the necessary investigations. We might be making assump-tions that are wrong.'

'Aye, well, Ah've been through it time and time again, trying to tell myself it can't be Ada, never in a million years, but it all points to her, Mr Connolly. Ah daren't face her about it . . . '

'Someone will have to, Aaron.'

'Aye, Ah know. But Ah couldn't. Ah just couldn't. Ah'll be honest with you. Ah couldn't face her, not Ada, not after all t'happy times we've had and the wonderful work she's done for t'church and t'people of Eltering. Ah mean, you couldn't find a better woman, a more honest worker.'

'But in spite of that, you sound convinced of her guilt? If she's as honest as you say, it could be somebody else. What about her companion, the man who operates the gents' cloakroom?'

'Harry Nattrass? Honest as the day is long, he is, an' all. There's nowt gone from his cloakroom, Mr Connolly, not ever.'

'And he's a church worker as well, is he?'

'Not particularly. He does this job as an interest, really. He's got a full-time job. He works in a grocer's shop in town, Major's. Not much of a job, but he's content.'

'Ages? How old are they?'

Connolly was thinking of Ada's possible menopause, for we knew that some women who were going through that difficult phase of their lives were prone to shoplifting.

'Ada? She'll be fiftyish. She's got a grown-up family, both married. Husband's a churchwarden an' all. He works for Langton's Garage, a mechanic.'

'And Harry?'

'Forty mebbe. Married with two bairns, having a struggle to live on his wage — shop assistants aren't well paid, Mr Connolly, and Ah happen to know he's having to take care what he spends. He never has new clothes, can't afford to run a car and hardly ever goes for a drink, so he takes part-time jobs to make ends meet.'

'A suitable candidate for our suspicious minds, eh?' said Connolly. 'He can't make ends meet, his growing family need clothes, shoes, food and so on, so he starts pinching to help him meet his costs. And once he's started, he can't stop. It could be him, Aaron.'

Aaron shook his head. 'Nay, lad nowt's ever gone from his cloakroom. He does a good job for us, allus has.'

'So what are you going to do, Aaron?' asked Connolly, his eyes searching the old man's face as he mischievously put this question.

'T'committee's asked me to report the thefts to t'police, Mr Connolly. We did consider sacking Ada but felt we ought to be sure she was guilty first.'

'So you want us to catch Ada red-handed?'

'Well, aye, if that's what it means, Mr Connolly.'

'Right, we need a record of the crimes already committed; those you have recorded yourself will do for a start. Days, dates and times are what we need, with a list of things that have gone.'

Aaron had a list of those in his pocket, the result of the committee's interest in events. He handed them to Gerry, who scanned them.

'This'll do for us,' he said. 'I have to have evidence of the commission of the crimes before I can take action. Now, Aaron, how about a look around the hall?'

'Aye, any time.'

'Now?' he asked.

'Sure,' agreed Aaron. And so Gerry drove us to St Erasmus's Church Hall and let us in with his key. It was around 11.30 a.m. now, and the building was deserted.

The entrance was via two huge double doors in thick wood. They were painted a dark green and were as solid as those in ancient castles. They swung wide into a deep foyer, where on the left was the ladies' cloakroom, with the gentlemen's on the right. In each wall between the foyer and the cloakrooms was a hatch for handing over coats and other articles in return for tickets, while access to each cloakroom was a separate door leading from the foyer.

'Are the public allowed in at all?' I heard Connolly ask.

'Oh, aye,' acknowledged Aaron. 'Ah mean to say, Mr Connolly, the toilets are in there an' all, behind the coat rails. When a do is in progress, folks come and go all t' time. But Ada and Harry keep an eye on folks moving through. If anyone stopped to pick a pocket or raid a handbag, Ada would see 'em.'

'Even if she was coping with a rush of customers at that hatch? Issuing cloakroom tickets? Taking money?'

In Connolly's professional eyes, this was the first chink in the argument over Ada's probable guilt, but he looked carefully at the toilet, shut away in a cubicle behind the coat rails, and then had a look in the gentlemen's room. It mirrored the ladies' room.

'Now, Aaron,' he said, 'you said the stuff's been going during dances. So why dances, I wonder? What's the procedure at dances — by Ada and Harry, I mean?'

'Well, generally we start at eight or mebbe half-past, and we keep t'doors open till eleven. We never let anybody in after eleven; that's one of t'rules of this hall. After eleven, daft lads get stupid with drink and come causing bother, so we lock those outer doors till the dance ends. Folks can get out, sure, 'cos either Harry or Ada'll unlocks t'doors, but nobody gets in after eleven. It doesn't matter whether it's a Saturday night dance that ends before midnight or a midweek 'un that goes on till one or two.'

Connolly asked, 'So Harry and Ada won't be taking coats after eleven?'

'No, but folks are using the toilets and they are dishing out coats to those who leave early — that's not many, mark you.'

'So what do Harry and Ada do after eleven?' asked Connolly.

'Relax a bit, Ah'd say,' said Aaron. 'Check t'takings, get ready for dishing t'coats out again, that sort o' thing.'

'Hmm,' he said. 'This is a puzzle, Aaron. Right, now I've seen the place, I'm going to put forward a suggestion. I'll need your consent, and I'll need total secrecy from you if you agree.'

Aaron looked at me for guidance, but I did not know what was in Gerry's mind.

'Aye, right, if it'll stop the pinching,' said Aaron.

'It'll tell us what goes on, but nobody must know we're operating here, right? Not even your committee.'

'Right, Mr Connolly.'

Gerry told him that a time-lapse camera would be installed in the ladies' cloakroom, and it would operate throughout the next dance and perhaps the one that followed. It took a picture every two seconds; it operated from a long-life battery and could be fixed to one of the wooden beams high above the cloakroom. It would be focused upon the rails of coats, and it had a wide-angle lens which would take in most of the floor area. If a thief came in to search the coats and handbags or to steal things like umbrellas and scarves, the camera would take a photograph of them in action.

'What about one in t'gents?' asked Aaron.

'We've only the one camera at the moment,' said Gerry. 'And it's in demand, as you can imagine. It's used almost exclusively for this kind of work.'

'So this sort o' thing goes on a lot, eh?' asked Aaron.

'It does, I'm afraid, Aaron. But now I'll need a note of the dates of your next few dances so we can select one when the camera is available. We'll start with the ladies.'

Aaron was in full agreement; for one thing, this would eliminate the necessity for a confrontation with Ada, and if she was guilty, this would provide proof instead of supposition.

Within a fortnight of that meeting, Gerry had obtained permission to make use of the camera, and the experts from Headquarters arrived to fit it. They were dressed in old overalls and came in an old van; if anyone saw them at work in the hall, the explanation was that they were inspecting the wiring on behalf of the council, a fairly routine examination.

Gerry and I went along to tell them exactly what was required of the camera, and a suitable place was determined. Happily, this hall had a lofty beamed ceiling without any form of underdrawing. Its rafters vanished into the darkness of the pointed roof. That applied to the cloakrooms too, and it was an easy task to conceal this small camera. It did make the tiniest of clicking sounds as it took its sequence of snaps, but it was felt the noise would not attract any interest — besides, no one could see into that dark roof void without a good torch, and the camera would be expertly sited and concealed.

The first dance at which our camera was to be a witness was scheduled for a Saturday night. At five o'clock I went to set the camera in motion; it would run for forty-eight hours if necessary, but our scenes-of-crime experts would return to the hall on Sunday morning to retrieve it. They, Gerry Connolly, Aaron and I would then inspect the developed pictures; they should be ready that same afternoon. Aaron's role was to identify any thief pictured on the film, and we knew he was dreading the task of having to identify Ada.

So the trap was set.

On the specific instructions of Sergeant Connolly, no police officers went into the dance hall that evening, although we were on duty in the office to await any call from Aaron. The uniform branch were not told of the reason for keeping away from the hall, but the instructions were issued via the duty sergeant, for we did not want our trap to be wasted by the unscheduled arrival of a crime-beating bobby. The dance progressed without incident until ten minutes to midnight, when a girl reported to Aaron, who was on duty as usual inside the main building, that her purse had been stolen, along with £5.12s.6d and a marcasite brooch worth 15 shillings.

Aaron took particulars, as he always did; in this he played a superb role, for he gave an absolutely normal response. After the dance hall had closed, he rang us with news of the latest theft, and we felt sure we must have captured the thief on film. We were all anxious to solve this one – was it Ada or not?

Although we had continued on duty until the end of the dance, just in case there had been other, unexpected developments, we now had to wait until Sunday to find out the truth about Ada Clarkson. On Sunday morning, the scenes-of-crime officers (SOCO) removed and developed the film. They came to Eltering Office at 3.30 p.m., when Aaron had been asked to attend.

'We've a good set,' beamed D/PC Mitchell as he addressed us. 'We've caught a woman in action, dipping into several pockets and purses, and we've got summat else.'

He spread the little black-and-white photographs along the table in sequence; each bore a date and time imprinted in white along the top edge.

'Right, this is the entrance to the cloakroom.' He indicated the door, standing open. 'These are the rails of coats, this is the chair where Mrs Clarkson sits to take money, and here, in the bottom left-hand corner, is the ladies' toilet with two cubicles. There's a door leading into each one, but we can't see into either because there's a roof over them.'

He began to point to each successive photograph and continued: 'At eleven-o-one and fifteen seconds, she goes out.

That's when she locks the outer door, we believe. Comes back after twenty seconds . . . see her? Leaves the cloakroom door open . . . stands near the rails . . . then, look at this! In comes lover boy . . . '

'That's Harry!' cried poor old Aaron, in shock and some disbelief.

'Right,' said D/PC Mitchell. 'Harry comes into the ladies' cloakroom . . . looks around . . . goes to Ada . . . they get into a clinch, see . . . his hands are all over her . . . and . . . wait for it . . . they go into one of the cubicles of the ladies' toilet and vanish from our sight. Both of 'em. Lock themselves in . . . they were in there twenty bloody minutes . . . '

'My God!' cried Aaron. 'Of all the people, of all the people I would never have said would do this . . . adultery . . . two people like that, two friends . . . married . . . happily . . . '

'Hang on,' said Mitchell. 'Now, here comes your thief.'

A young woman in her twenties came into the cloakroom as Ada and Harry were busy in the cubicle; she made a furtive entry, looked through the hatch to peer across the passage to see if Harry's cloakroom was empty, and then tried one cubicle door. It was locked, and so she tried the other — it was open and the cubicle was empty. At that point she began to rifle the pockets of the hanging coats. She worked through them quickly and expertly, and we could see her slipping items into her own handbag before leaving. In all, her actions took less than one minute, and no one else came in.

'Do you know her?' Connolly asked Aaron.

'Aye, it's that lass of Tomkins'. Jean.' He was still in a state of shock at the revelations about Ada. 'Works at the secondary modern school in the kitchens . . . allus was a worry to her dad . . . she's got a bairn, you know, not married, mind . . . '

'Right, well, it looks as if we have found our thief.' Gerry was happy. 'Nick, you can interview her later today. Take a policewoman with you in case she says you tried to rape her. Get a cough, threaten to search her house for the other missing odds and sods . . . get a voluntary from her.'

'Right, fine.' It would be nice to get several crimes written off as detected.

Connolly thanked Mitchell for the valuable use of the

time-lapse camera and said its merits would be noted in his quarterly report to Headquarters. I was about to leave and interview Jean Tomkins when Aaron asked,

'Mr Connolly, that business between Ada and Harry. Well, I mean, what can I do now?'

'That is not a crime, Aaron. It's not an offence against criminal law, and so we are not interested. I'm afraid it's down to you.'

And so poor old Aaron had another matter about which to confront Ada Clarkson, and this time the police would not do it for him.

When I interviewed Jean Tomkins, she admitted more than twenty crimes she had committed in that cloakroom. And as an excuse, she said, 'I knew what Ada was up to, you see, and she's always at my mum for not going to church . . .'

'You don't mean you did this to get at Ada?' I was astonished.

'I needed money, Mr Rhea, for my bairn. Ada was always pretending to be better than us, holier. Well, she's not, is she? Going into that toilet with Harry Nattrass, the dirty bitch . . .'

It was odd hearing the girl speak like that; she seemed to think she was punishing Ada, whereas in reality she was punishing those from whom she had stolen.

Aaron did mention our findings to Ada and Harry, and they both left their work at the church hall. Ada also stopped going to church, but I don't think she stopped seeing Harry.

On another curious occasion we were asked to solve the problem of the disappearing bacon joints, and in this instance we also resorted to modern technology in our efforts to trace the thief.

The investigation began when we received a visit from a worried man called Brian King, who was manager of the bacon factory in Eltering. It was part of a large group of food wholesalers, and Brian, a local man in his late thirties, had been appointed manager some six months prior to this visit. Whatever the problems he had inherited, this one appeared to worry him deeply.

'I'd like advice,' he began, in what we had come to learn was a familiar opening gambit.

'OK,' smiled Connolly, as charming as ever. 'What can we do for you, Mr King?'

'A member of my staff is thieving, Sergeant. Now, I'm sure you realize that it is putting a strain on me, but it is also throwing suspicion on every member of my work-force — that's almost thirty people, counting the office staff and drivers.'

'So, tell me, Mr King, how is this thief operating?'

'I don't know,' he sighed with the resignation of a defeated man. 'I've wracked my brains without coming to an answer, and I might add that I do have a very volatile work-force. If I make an accusation which I cannot substantiate, they will walk out; that would cost me my job.'

'We are not here to perform the duties of managers of business establishments, Mr King,' said Connolly, with more than a hint of firmness in his voice. 'Our job is to catch thieves, and if you make a formal complaint, we will do our best to achieve that. I'm afraid it might upset your staff if we start asking questions, but we can accept no responsibility for a deterioration in your manager/staff relationships.'

'I am aware of that, Sergeant, which is why I thought long and hard before coming to see you.'

'So long as we both understand that point. So, tell me, what is happening?'

'I did wonder whether some secret method might be employed first; one reads of devices that will photograph a thief or those powders that will leave traces on their hands if they touch an object which has been marked . . . '

'Yes, we do have such facilities,' smiled Connolly, 'but, in fairness, I would guess a factory would be too large an area for our time-lapse camera to be of any use and, well, to paint all your bits of meat with fluorescent powder might not be feasible . . . I've no idea what it would do to the meat, for example . . . '

'But you will help me?'

'If you are making a formal complaint of a series of thefts in your establishment, then, yes, we will come along and sort it out.'

King took a deep breath and nodded fiercely. 'Yes, I will

make a formal complaint, and to hell with the consequences.'

'Good,' beamed Connolly. 'Then let's hear your story.'

King told us that for the past few weeks small joints of top-quality bacon had been spirited out of the factory. At first it was thought the checking system was faulty, but a careful check on the stock did reveal a deficiency over each week. Five or six joints were being taken each week. It was not a lot, he stressed. It was not as if drivers or delivery men were filching lorry loads of meat or the workers somehow fiddling massive sides of bacon, hams or half-pigs. The stolen objects were joints of dressed bacon, small enough to hide under an overall or even in a cycle saddlebag. They weighed two or three pounds and were highly popular with people living alone, and with pensioners.

'When are they disappearing?' I asked, for I was involved with this enquiry in my capacity as Aide.

'At night, almost every night,' he said, wringing his hands. 'We prepare the meat each morning, freshly killed, of course, and a lot goes out the same day. But some we dress during the afternoons, then place it in a cool room overnight. Some we freeze, of course, and some we place in chilled accommodation – a refrigerator. But not these joints – there's a high turn-over of them, they're one of our best lines, and so they are laid out ready to be loaded into our vans first thing the next morning. Each morning our vans go out into the town, or into neighbouring towns and villages, to sell those products. There are other small items too – sausages, pork pies, sliced bacon, liver and so on. But only those joints are stolen.'

'So they vanish after you lock up at night and before you open next morning? What times are those?' I asked.

'We close at 4.30 p.m. and we open next morning at 6 a.m.'

'Any sign of forced entry?' asked Connolly.

'No, that's one of my worries. I think the thief has a key; we've thought about changing the locks, but I don't think head office would sanction that expenditure, especially for such a reason.'

'You've asked them?' Connolly put to him.

'Er, no, not yet. It would be a last resort.'

'So, am I right in thinking all your staff are now under suspicion?'

'Yes, I'm afraid so. It's not as if it's a major series of thefts, Sergeant, but, if someone is getting away with those joints at the rate of five or six a week, they are making a useful extra income, at our expense. And my work-force are now beginning to distrust one another . . . '

'You've discussed it with them?'

'Yes, without my suggesting one of them is a thief. But they now wonder which of them is the pilferer . . . they're an honest crowd, you see, Sergeant, but there is a definite air of unease in the factory. I must bring things to a conclusion.'

He told us that several members of staff had keys and that the keys were of the old-fashioned mortise type, so easy to copy and even make. Security seemed very lax, we felt.

'Do any members of staff know of your visit to us?' asked Connolly.

'Only my secretary,' he said. 'And she can be trusted. I asked her not to disclose my whereabouts.'

'Right,' said Connolly. 'Before we can go any further, we need to inspect your factory. When would be suitable?'

'Any evening, Sergeant,' he said.

Gerry Connolly was of the opinion that there was no time like the present, and we agreed to meet Mr King at the factory that night at eight o'clock. At the appointed time, he met us in the car-park, let us in and showed us around. The place was well lit at night, and it comprised a series of large rooms, some used for preparation and some for storage.

At the side of the building was the office block. We toured the entire complex, examining doors and windows, noting that there were several skylights which were kept open, as were several high windows, especially in the factory portion. These were high enough off the ground to be beyond the reach of children. Some around the lower parts of the walls were also kept open, but stoutly barred. No fully grown man or woman could wriggle through.

'A duplicate key job, it seems to me,' said Connolly, partly to me and partly to himself. 'A sneak thief with inside knowledge, one who's prepared to let all his or her colleagues be suspected. We'll have to nail the bastard, Nick.'

The cold room in which the joints of bacon were laid out in readiness for morning had no windows, although it did have a gap where the door should be. There was no door; access was via a corridor, itself kept almost at freezing-point, with fridges and deep-freezes along its way. Once inside the factory, anyone could run along this corridor, snaffle a joint and leave.

'Right,' said Gerry, having seen the premises. 'We'll use a pressure mat.'

'What's that?' asked King.

'It is a pad of rubber which fits beneath a door mat or rug, or even a carpet for that matter. It bleeps when someone stands on it. There is a door mat outside that cold room of yours, so this won't be noticed.'

'Won't it alert the thief if it bleeps?' asked King.

'No,' smiled Gerry. 'We pop the pressure mat under the existing door mat, and it is plugged into the electrical circuit. Inside, there is a bleeper, but it doesn't sound in the premises; it sounds in a police car outside, or in a police station. When it bleeps, we surround the place and arrest the villain because we know he's inside.'

'It sounds perfect,' said King.

'It isn't,' said Connolly. 'Some villains move so fast that they're off the premises before we can get in, but it has had a lot of success.'

'I'd like you to try it, please. You have my approval.'

And so we prepared our trap.

On the first night, the bleeper sounded and we rushed to the factory, but he had gone before we arrived. And so had a joint of bacon. On the second night, the same thing happened, except that in this instance we were waiting outside, only a minute away by car. There was no sign of a break-in during any of these raids. We dare not reveal our presence immediately outside the factory in case we alerted our suspect, but when he escaped on the third night, without even a sighting by the waiting police officers, we decided we must take alternative action. Could someone actually hide in the factory? The timing of each raid did vary slightly, although most were between 10 p.m. and midnight. A two-hour wait in those chilly rooms was not the finest of ways of spending an evening, and yet it seemed the only answer.

We drew straws. I drew the short one.

'Right, Nick. You're first on. Wrap up in your warmest

clothes and wait in that cold room. We'll re-set the pressure mat so that it bleeps the moment someone stands on it; at that sound, switch on your torch to highlight the thief – he'll be in the doorway at that time, and then switch on all the lights in the factory. We'll have men outside all the doors to nab him as he runs out.'

That night, therefore, I wrapped in layers of long johns and sweaters and put on furry boots, the sort we used when on winter patrol, and prepared for my stint. I let myself in with a key provided by Mr King and had no trouble finding my way along the corridor to the cold room. I saw the mat and avoided standing on it as I entered the chill room with its complement of prepared bacon joints. They filled several tables and shelves around the roof. There seemed to be hundreds . . . And then I settled down to a long, cold wait.

Later, in the chilling darkness, I heard a slight noise. It was a noise which I could not identify, and the hair on the nape of my neck prickled and stood erect as I waited. My heart began to thump as I knew someone was approaching, so silently, so carefully . . . I wished I had a colleague with me; I wished someone else had drawn that short straw . . . and then silence. Nothing. I dare not move now. Had I been detected? Had the thief spotted the pressure mat? There was no light, so I assumed he had not.

And then the bleep. It made me jump with fright, it was so sudden, but there it was. The thief was in the room now, there with me, and so I switched on my torch. Immediately the room was filled with light, and I saw the distinct figure of a young fox running off with a bacon joint.

'Hey!' I shouted, giving chase and hitting the first light switch I found. But he galloped along that corridor and leapt onto a window-ledge, squeezed through the bars of the open window with the joint between his teeth and jumped onto the branch of a tree outside. And then he vanished.

The outer door burst open and in charged Sergeant Connolly and a couple of uniformed policemen. 'Where is he?'

'Gone,' I said. 'Got clean away.'

'Nick, you don't mean that . . . ' Gerry sounded more sorry than angry. 'You mean you sat in there and let him get away . . . '

'Sergeant,' I said, 'if you're going to catch this thief, you'll need more than a handful of policemen.'

'Rubbish!' He was still rising to my bait. 'Look, Nick, this is not good enough. I should have put a more experienced detective in here.'

'No, Sarge,' I laughed. 'You should have put a Master of Foxhounds and a pack of good dogs. The thief is a fox. He got away through that window.'

'You're joking,' he smiled.

'I'm not,' I said. 'Sharp as lightning, he was; he knows he can just get a joint between those bars . . .'

'Who's going to tell Mr King?' He looked at us all.

'You are, Sergeant,' we all chanted.

9

For God's sake, look after our people.
Robert Falcon Scott (1868-1912)

Of the variety of events in the police officer's calendar, that of
a visit by a Very Important Person is often the most fraught,
because the personage must be protected against madmen and
terrorists and at the same time proceed along a predestined
route without interruption. To permit the populace to see and
even speak to the personage and at the same time prevent
lunatics shooting them or throwing rotten eggs into their faces
is not the most easy of tasks. But the work of the VIP must be
allowed to continue, and the VIP in question must not allow
the less sane members of society to hinder their freedom and
their communion with ordinary folk.

In understanding the risks that prevail each time a member
of the royal family or a top politician appears in public, I have
the greatest admiration for them. They can never go out alone,
not even into the shops or to an inn for a drink; they are always
surrounded by an army of officials, and they can never drop
their guard for one tiniest moment. They have no privacy, and
their every word and action is scrutinized, criticized and
headlined in the less savoury of our newspapers.

The movements of VIPs are of concern to the police because
a police constable holds office under the sovereign. He or she
is an officer of the Crown and also a public servant, and the
constable's duty includes the protection of life and property,

whether that life and property belong to a VIP or not. That is a wide brief, but it does include the protection of important people as well as the protection of ordinary mortals, amongst whom the constable himself can be numbered. Constables are ordinary people who are charged with extraordinary powers and responsibilities.

But obviously there are occasions when a Very Important Person requires more attention than usual. A visit by HM The Queen to a local town is such an occasion, but does this also include the opening of a new supermarket by a well-known TV personality? Exactly what is a Very Important Person?

A lot of people think themselves important for reasons which are sometimes quite strange. Because some have grown rich or famous, they feel they are important, and because some have become personalities via television, they also feel themselves important. But are they? The snag is that famous singers or entertainers can draw crowds, and so the police must then act to prevent obstructions and danger to the public when these people manifest themselves in public places. The fact that a bunch of scruffy youths can sing in a way that appeals to teenagers does give them some importance, if only because they are an utter nuisance when they move around the globe. It is important that they do not get in the way of others trying to go about their business.

Being a police officer does allow one to work closely with VIPs, if only in a protective sense, and there are many duties which the service must perform when a VIP visits the area. The obvious ones are control of traffic and crowds, and the less obvious ones involve security and planning. When Her Majesty visits, however, there is more planning and more security because there are greater crowds and more traffic, coupled with the continuing risk to her life. Every movement is planned to the minute, every step she takes is arranged in advance and rehearsed, and every possible security measure is taken. A royal visit is a headache to the security services and the police, and when it concludes without incident, there is immense satisfaction and immense relief.

But things can go wrong. There was one famous occasion when Her Majesty's motorcade was cruising through a northern town. All routes had been sealed off, including a tiny back alley which led directly onto the royal route. But at the crucial moment the constable whose duty was to halt traffic at that exit was called to an elderly lady who had collapsed in the crowd. As no traffic was waiting in his alley, he attended the old lady. Any right-minded person would have done likewise.

And then, just as the royal procession was approaching, a dustcart chugged down that alley and emerged directly ahead of the motorcade. Before anyone could prevent it, the dustcart, with grimy men hanging on to it and the effluvium of the town's waste accompanying it, had become part of the procession. It was behind the leading police motor-cycle outriders but in front of the royal limousine. And there was no way off that route for over a mile. To enthusiastic cheers from the townspeople, their dustcart preceded the royal procession until a convenient layby materialized; it was then gently guided out of Her Majesty's way. I'm sure she was amused.

It is that kind of mishap that causes senior police officers to worry about their pensions, for all dread the likelihood of something going wrong, especially during a royal visit.

I remember when Prince Charles came to Strensford as part of the town's 1,300th anniversary celebrations of its abbey's foundation. The great unveiling of a plaque was about to occur. The local brass band was waiting to play. As His Royal Highness and other dignitaries stood by, with Prince Charles waiting to perform the unveiling ceremony, the bishop began his eulogy. His speech was timed to continue for twenty minutes, but he made the mistake of pausing after the first paragraph. Bishops seem to enjoy long, meaningful pauses, but this one was too long for the conductor of the brass band; he thought the bishop had finished. He promptly brought his musicians to life, and their rumbustious music shortened that ceremony by a good quarter of an hour.

Prince Charles was amused and, I think, relieved, for he later said to the conductor, 'You came in there a bit quick, eh?' and chuckled.

But surely the worst experience to have occurred in our force was when I was an Aide to the CID at Strensford. Somehow, a combination of events managed to lose Her Majesty The Queen.

The intelligent reader will ask: how on earth can anyone

lose the Queen?

It happened like this.

Her Majesty had a very important engagement in London one evening, one which could not be cancelled. It was scheduled to finish around 9 p.m. But she also had an equally important engagement in Edinburgh at 10 a.m. the following morning. She therefore decided to travel by royal train, leaving London at 10 p.m. with her entourage. She would sleep on the train, and it was decided that the royal train would break its journey around midnight, when it would be guided into a quiet, peaceful and secure siding until around 7.30 a.m., when it would resume its journey, to arrive in Edinburgh around 9.30 a.m., in good time for Her Majesty's 10 a.m. engagement. Thus the royal train would be parked somewhere for about seven hours. That place had to be secure, private and yet accessible to the main London-Edinburgh route. And what better place than a tiny branch line on the north-eastern edge of the North York Moors?

It was therefore decreed that the royal train would be diverted off the main line and through some scenic country-side which embraced the branch line that led from Thirsk into the hills. The line passed through the villages of Little Cringle, Harksworth and Crossby before regaining the main line some fifteen miles to the north. The Beeching Axe closed this line in 1964, but the tracks were still there, and it was ideal for this purpose.

The royal train would remain overnight in Little Cringle Station, which stood a mile or so from the village after which it was named, and it was the duty of our police force to provide security and protection to the train and its VIP passengers during its stay. I was one of the CID men detailed for that duty, one of several, in fact. My role was to arrive at Little Cringle Station at 11.30 p.m. and remain there on security duties until departure of the train next morning. The royal train was expected to arrive at 12.35 a.m.

Armed with my flask of coffee and a box of sandwiches, I drove through the dark lanes to Little Cringle and reported to the sergeant in charge at the deserted station. I was posted to a bridge overlooking the line, and had to stop anarchists and their ilk from dropping bombs onto the royal train. I had no firearm, only my detective stave and a personal radio. I hoped the anarchists would never know that.

And so, that fine May night, I walked up and down that bridge, waiting for the train to appear. The expected time of arrival passed with no sign of it. Another half an hour passed and still there was no sign, and I could see my colleagues on the station moving around in concern.

Clearly, there was a problem of some kind, for trains with the Queen on board should never be late. I knew I must not leave my post without good reason, and so I walked up and down, puzzled and growing increasingly concerned as time passed without any reports. Then the detective sergeant came to me, walking quickly through the night.

'Nick,' he said, 'we've a problem. Come into the office.'

I followed him into the disused station master's office which had been utilized as a control room for this occasion, and found the others sitting around.

'Right,' said Detective Sergeant Proctor. 'We're all here, and this is the problem. The royal train should have arrived here at 12.35 a.m. and it hasn't. It has Her Majesty on board and members of her entourage, including her private police officer. I have checked with British Rail and our own control room, and they maintain the train is where it should be. They say it is here. Well, I for one know it bloody well isn't. You all know that it isn't here, and you can't just spirit away an engine and several coaches full of VIPs. We have a radio link with the train, of course, and the chap on duty says the train is in its siding, safe and sound, and Her Majesty is sleeping. He reckons he is at Little Cringle as arranged, and he will not accept any other suggestion. And the main line is clear, gentlemen, so the royal train is not on the main line. British Transport police have checked.'

'Then where the hell is it?' asked one of the detectives.

'We don't know. The signalman at Thirsk, whose job was to switch the points for it to enter this line, has gone off duty. We're having a man sent to have words with him, to see if he's diverted it along the wrong bloody line — either by design or by carelessness.'

That this might have been done deliberately presented a chilling scenario and had horrific implications for the effectiveness of the overall security arrangements surrounding Her Majesty.

'But if the chap in charge of the train thinks he's at Little Cringle, or *says* he's at Little Cringle, something is wrong.' I had my little say. 'Could the royal train have got into the wrong hands?'

'Oh, for God's sake don't start thinking like that!' groaned the sergeant. 'It's bad enough losing the bloody train, let's not start thinking somebody's kidnapped the Queen! This isn't a bloody novel, Nick, it's real life!'

'It must have got shunted into the wrong branch line,' concluded Proctor. 'It's the only possible answer. Now, who's got the map?'

Someone produced an Ordnance Survey map of the district which the CID had used to identify which bridges to supervise and which roads to patrol, and Proctor examined it. After a moment, he said,

'Nick, here a minute. This is your patch, isn't it?'

He indicated a branch line which led from just south of Thirsk and through the hills into Ryedale, reaching the villages of Maddleskirk and Elsinby, both on my own beat.

'It's not used by service trains, Sergeant,' I told him. 'But it is used occasionally. Maddleskirk College do have trains visiting Maddleskirk Station to deliver boys to the college. Special trains come at the start of each term and at the end of each term. The line is still open, but there's no public service now, no through trains.'

As he spoke, a radio call came from Headquarters. It was to say that an officer had visited the home of the signalman in question, but he was not there. His mother said he'd only been doing the job for a few weeks and that he'd come home, got changed and gone fishing. He was a keen fisherman and hadn't gone to bed because he now had two days off and wanted to make full use of them. She had no idea where he'd gone; he rarely told her. She did say that he usually went up Swaledale, but he might have gone over into Eskdale looking for salmon, or there again he might have gone to Whitby to do some sea fishing from a boat. The message also said that, whatever line the train had been sent along, its points had now reverted to their original position to cater for main-line expresses, and so no one knew which line had been used. We put an All-Stations message out for all police officers to seek this signalman; he had to be interviewed without delay.

'Right, Nick, I'm going to send you over to Maddleskirk. It'll take you, what? Half-an-hour from here? Check that line, will you, and see if you can find the royal train. I'll have checks made on the other lines — there's lots branch off the main line between York and Darlington. Yours is the one immediately before the one that should have been utilized; that signalman could have pulled the wrong lever.'

And so I went about my mission. But when I got to Maddleskirk Station, which, like the one at Little Cringle, lies a mile out of the village, there was no sign of a train. I motored through the valley to Elsinby and again found no sign of a train, but then, at the tiny halt beyond Elsinby at Ploatby Junction, I could see the dark bulk of a stationary train. Ploatby Junction was not really a station, only a mere halt where, in the past, the line divided. One branch extended from here to Malton, while the other went into Ashfordly. Now it was unmanned and unused; there was not even a sign to announce its name. I drove steadily along the land and parked on the ashen surface which had once been a car-park. There was no one around, although one of the carriages of the still train did bear dim lights.

I went towards that carriage, noting it was now 2.15 a.m. I tapped on the door, hoping to God it did not contain the Queen's apartments, and it was opened by a smart-suited man with close-cropped hair.

'What is it?' he snapped.

'CID,' I said, producing my warrant card. 'D/PC Rhea, local force.'

'Come in, and don't slam the door,' he said.

I went in and found myself in a mobile office; he gave me a mug of steaming coffee and then asked, 'Where the hell have your lot been? We've been here the best part of a couple of hours with never a sign of any liaison . . . talk about security . . . '

'You're in the wrong station,' I said. 'This is not Little Cringle, this is Ploatby Junction.'

'You're not serious? Have we passed Cringle?'

'No. You're not on the right line,' I said. 'You've been sent down the wrong branch line . . . '

'My God! Is this line busy? Hell, if something runs into us . . . '

'No, no problem,' I told him. 'It's disused, it's quite safe, there's no traffic on this line at night,' and I explained things to him.

'My God, trust British Rail! So what do we do now?'

'I suggest you remain here till morning,' I said. 'It's safe, you can be back on the main line within a few minutes, although you'll have to reverse all the way, and you can be on your way on time tomorrow without any problems.' I explained the geography of the district to him with the aid of a map in his mobile office.

'I'll check with BR and suggest that. You know, when your lot said we were on the wrong line, we thought it could be somebody breaking in to your wavelengths, somebody out to harm Her Majesty. From leaving the main line, the time it took us to arrive here was just the same as if we'd gone to Little Cringle. We saw this platform and halted, just as normal. Mind, I did find it odd that no one from the local *gendarmerie* came to liaise with us.'

'I'd better radio Headquarters and tell them where you are,' I said.

And so I did. The detectives from Little Cringle all rushed over to Ploatby Junction, and we adopted our guardian role from that point onwards. At 7.25 a.m. the driver started his engine, and the huge train slowly reversed towards the distant main line, where another signalman had come on duty. Her Majesty and her entourage had had a pleasant night's sleep, totally unaware that they had spent the night in an unscheduled location and blissfully unaware of our alarm.

I arrived home just as Mary was getting up and dressing the family. I stayed out of bed and helped and then had my breakfast with my wife and little family of four children.

'Did you have a busy night?' asked Mary when we had time to chat.

'I was involved in the royal visit to Ploatby,' I said, but I don't think she believed the Queen had slept within sight of our lofty police house.

I wondered how that tiny community of two or three farms and a dozen or so houses at Ploatby would have reacted if they had known that Her Majesty had spent the night among them.

Later the rumours did begin to circulate, and one of the local men said to me, 'Noo then, Mr Rhea, Ah've 'eard tell that Her Majesty had ti sleep on yon station t'other week. Now, there's no fire there, no waiting-room, no toilets, nowhere for a cup o' tea or a sandwich. Nowt. Noo, if Ah'd known that, she could have used my bed for t'night — Ah'd have moved out, tha knows, if they'd come and asked. T'sheets wad have been warmed up and we've allus got eggs and bacon in for breakfast. It's nut right, is it, letting a Queen sleep on a draughty station like that when there's folks here wi' spare beds and spare rooms?'

'I'll pass the word on in case it happens again,' I promised him. In fact, it did happen again, for before the tracks were removed, this line was considered ideal for parking the royal train at night. But I don't think any of its passengers enjoyed bed-and-breakfast in Ploatby.

Another VIP visit caused a bit of a flutter in Aidensfield. I learned of it through a chat with George, the landlord of the Brewers' Arms.

'I'm not sure whether this is a matter for you or not,' he said, 'but we've a famous person coming to the pub for dinner next week. Friday night.'

'Is he staying at the Brewers' Arms?' I asked.

'No. He's just coming for dinner. He's arriving with Sir Eldric and Lady Tippet-Greve, and they have requested total secrecy. They do not want his visit spoiled by sightseers, and they have sworn me to total secrecy.'

'Is it a politician or a member of the royal family?' I asked. 'We don't normally take an interest in visits by those who are not in that category.'

'No, he's a singer,' said George. 'He's staying with Sir Eldric and Lady Tippet-Greve at High Hall for five days. He's doing a spot of grouse-shooting on the moors and wants to see something of North York Moors and the scenery. And he wants to see a typical English pub, to have a pint and a meal there.'

'So they're bringing him to the Brewers' Arms, eh?' I smiled. 'Well, they couldn't find a better example of a village pub, George. You'll feed him well?'

'There's a party of a dozen coming,' said George. 'I'm having the dining-room decorated for the job, but I thought I'd better tell you, just in case we get trouble in the village.'

'If no one knows he's coming, George, I think things will pass peacefully on Friday.'

'Aye, but word gets around, you know; I mean, once he's inside, folks'll recognize him and they'll be ringing their friends and they'll come to the pub, and before we know it, there'll be chaos.'

'I'm on an attachment to CID, George,' I said. 'I'll have to get another uniformed constable to pay a visit.'

'No, no,' he said. 'I don't want that, I don't want anyone outside Aidensfield to know he's coming. If a uniformed bobby hangs about, folks will sense there's something going on. Can't you come in civvies, off duty? Just to be around, just in case? Their tables are booked for eight. They've taken the whole dining-room.'

It was an earnest plea and, as I was not anticipating having to work that evening, I said, 'I'll see what I can do, George, but I really ought to know who's coming. Just in case.'

'You won't tell a soul, will you?' he pleaded. 'I mean, I could get into a load of bother if word gets out.'

'It's our secret, George,' I assured him.

'It's Bing Crosby!' he said. 'Bing Crosby's coming to the Brewers' Arms!'

I knew this would not present the kind of problems one associated with the Beatles or the Rolling Stones, but if word did reach the wider public, there could be a crowd and there could be problems that were associated with crowds. There might be traffic congestion in the village, and if some wilder elements came along, there could be trouble such as minor fights and the kind of bother one expects from silly youths, especially if they resort to drinking on the street. I also knew George wasn't imagining this, for it had been reported that 'The Old Groaner' was in the area on a private visit.

He was not performing at any concerts, and the entire visit was being regarded as a personal and private one. Until now,

I'd had no idea he was acquainted with the Tippet-Greves.

'I'll be there,' I promised George.

In the days that followed, everyone in Aidensfield and district heard the news, and when I arrived at the pub with Mary (in whom I had confided the secret), I found it packed. People who never normally patronized the Brewers' Arms were there, old ladies with glazed eyes were there, youngsters who had heard about Crosby and weren't quite sure what he did were there, and everyone was struggling to buy drinks at the bar and to catch a glimpse of the crooner.

'He got here early,' said George to me in a confidential whisper. 'Sir Eldric's party is in the dining-room. We've drawn the curtains for privacy.'

'Thanks. A good idea,' I agreed, for it was almost dark anyway, being a late September day. By this time, a small crowd had gathered outside, hoping to catch sight of Crosby, but his early arrival had defeated them. It was a pity, I felt, for they were local people who were simply standing there to catch a sight of this world-famous singer. Inside, however, the place was packed. I moved among the crowd, fighting for space as Mary chatted to some friends, fans of Crosby, who had heard the whispered rumours. A couple of hours passed in this way, and then George hailed me.

'There's a coach arrived!' he said. 'In the car-park at the back. I can't cope with a coach-load of fans, Nick. Can you send 'em on their way?'

'I'll have words with them,' I assured him.

I went into the car-park at the rear of the inn and saw a crowd of men descending from a mini-bus, a twelve-seater. Others joined them from a couple of cars parked behind. There'd be twenty men in all. But no coach.

I had to be diplomatic, for I was not wearing uniform, and besides, I could not ban these men from the Brewers' Arms. I had no such power. Besides, a too-forceful attempt to deter them would only result in their determination to find out why.

'It's full, gents!' I said. 'Packed out. You'll never reach the bar.'

'Want a bet, mister?' grinned one of them. 'We don't play rugger for nothing. We can always make a scrum. Thanks, but we'll get our pints. We'll be no trouble if we're left alone.'

And they marched steadfastly across the car-park to the back door of the inn. As they did so, a little man carrying a pork-pie hat emerged and walked towards me. I waited in the car-park, watching the departing rugger team as they filed, one by one, into the packed inn. I hoped they would not cause bother — I could always ring for a duty car if bother was threatened.

The rugger team passed the little man, and he seemed lost as he noticed me standing in the centre of the car-park.

'Say,' he said in that soft and most distinctive voice, 'where's the john?'

'It's a bit primitive,' I said jokingly. 'A relic of the last century.'

'I don't care,' he chuckled. 'Gee, I am enjoying this.'

'It is Mr Crosby, isn't it?' I ventured.

'Sure, but without my toupee, no one knows me; I just walked through that crowd in there, and no one stopped me. You won't tell, will you?'

'No, of course not. I'm the village policeman, by the way, PC Rhea.'

'Glad to know you. I like this village, Mr Rhea, and your countryside. Marvellous, but I must hurry. My hosts'll wonder where I've got to.'

He went into the unlit toilet, a brick-built square which had a urinal channel and a battered water closet in a separate cubicle. But there was no light, and the only ventilation was via the open top of the affair, for it had no roof.

I returned to Mary, and as I was talking, Crosby came back into the hotel, pushed past the crowds and reached me. He recognized me.

'Sure is a quaint john,' he said quietly, chuckling as he moved back into the dining-room without anyone recognizing him.

'Who's that?' asked my pal Malcolm.

'Bing Crosby,' I said.

'Never . . . I don't believe that . . . '

'He's taken his toupee off,' I told him. 'He likes not being recognized, and he looks smaller than he does on screen . . . '

'But I wanted to meet him . . . '

'You nearly did,' I grinned.

And then the rugger team started to sing. Word of our illustrious guest had reached them, and they launched into 'White Christmas' with all the fervour a rugger team can muster. I groaned, and I could see that George was angry and upset at their behaviour.

'Shut up!' I heard him appeal to them. 'We don't want the evening spoilt . . .'

But they continued in fine voice, doing a repertoire of Crosby's songs, and George was growing more and more embarrassed. The more he tried to persuade them to end their singing, the more determined they became to sing, and we felt sure their music would reach the ears of the party in the dining-room. George decided to apologize to Sir Eldric and his party, and went across to the dining-room. At least no one was hanging around outside its door. I watched from the distance, and then George came out, closely followed by Crosby.

Crosby came into the bar and stood behind the counter with George, who rapped for silence.

'Quiet, everybody!' George's loud voice filled the bar, and he rapped it again with an ashtray. Even the rugger team fell silent.

'Ladies and gentlemen,' he shouted, for there was still a babble of excited chatter at the appearance of Crosby at his side, 'Mr Bing Crosby.'

The pub filled with cheers as Crosby said, 'I've enjoyed my visit to your inn.' We all cheered again. 'And so I thought I'd join your choir with a few songs . . .'

And so he did. Led by Bing Crosby, the combined choirs of the Vale of Mowbray 1st XV, the regulars of the Brewers' Arms and a handful of visitors from surrounding villages sang a medley of the best-known Crosby songs led by the maestro himself. And we ended by singing 'White Christmas'.

Crosby had to leave with his party but he had given us a fine concert, and George bought drinks for everyone that night, even for the visiting rugger team. Two or three weeks later a signed photograph of Crosby arrived, and it was placed in a position of distinction behind the bar.

But perhaps the best news of all came a month or two later. George showed me the letter he had received from the brewery which owned the premises.

It announced that new indoor toilets for ladies and gents were to be installed.

People who consider themselves important, but who are probably not in the least meritorious, often find themselves in situations which are embarrassing. A lot of this is due to their opinion of themselves, some believing they are God's gift to the world and that, as a consequence, nothing they do is wrong, while others blithely jog along in the erroneous view that they are indispensable to the nation which has nurtured them. To be very well known is indeed a severe handicap. That became evident in this next tale.

Such a person was a Very Famous TV Personality. I am not allowed to name him here, nor even to create a fictitious name which might, with some astute detective work, lead to his identification. And so I will call him VFTVP – Very Famous TV Personality.

That he was talented, handsome and popular was never in doubt, but it was known to those closely associated with him that his desirability and attractiveness concealed a person who was not very nice at all. The police in whose area he lived knew of his peccadilloes and of his more serious wrongdoings, one of which was a conviction for rape when he was a teenage lout.

His appearances on the screens of our national television network had made him a modern household name, and those of us who knew of his background and of his seedy private life sometimes wondered how the public would react if they knew the truth about him. But we, as police officers, could never reveal a confidence of that kind. We knew about his past, and we respected his efforts to forge a new future.

As part of his new image, he had married a delightful young actress, and the publicity shots of them together in their current bliss did seem to suggest he had reformed. Certainly, it made the old ladies and the middle-aged ladies who were his chief fans think he was wonderful, kind, considerate and generally quite charming. But we knew he was an out-and-out bastard, a womanizing drunkard, and that he beat his wife without mercy. Time and time again our men had been called to the cottage he rented on the Moors to quell the violent disputes he created at his home. And then, next morning, he would be his usual charming self.

Oddly enough, one of his fans was D/PC Wharton, with whom I worked in Eltering CID. He had seen the programmes that featured the VFTVP, and we knew that he modelled himself on the man. The clothes, the hair-do and even some of the jargon he used had come from the screen image of that appalling man. He knew of the rape conviction but reckoned that the worst of men could be reformed and redeemed. And that is what he felt about our VFTVP. It required a murder investigation to change his mind.

The body of a woman had been found in woodland close to Eltering, and she had been strangled. Her clothes had been scattered around the area, she had been savagely raped and her life had ended with her own tights being tied around her neck. She was twenty-four years old and the daughter of a local racehorse trainer.

The body was found at four o'clock one August afternoon, and we managed to keep the news of the discovery out of the regional TV and news programmes; it would be released at nine o'clock in readiness for blanket coverage in the following day's newspapers. Our aim was not to deny news to the public but to try to trap her killer.

We reckoned that lack of news that evening would compel the killer to return to the scene, just to see if his handiwork had been discovered. Several of us were therefore detailed to keep observations in that forest. I found myself doing the 8-10 p.m. stint with Paul Wharton. Our mission was simple — we had to conceal ourselves in the forest so that we could overlook the patch of land where the body had been discovered. As a forest track passed between that patch and our hiding-place, we had also to note the registration numbers and descriptions of cars which passed along that route.

There were no incidents of major interest until at almost 9.30 p.m., a Rover 2000 eased to a halt outside our patch of forest. We could see it contained two people, a man and a woman. Then it reversed into the trees. It moved along a wide track covered with pine needles, and we could see the two people talking for a few minutes, and then they climbed out and got into the rear seat. There were further animated movements of arms, lots of kissing and passion and then, with a scream, the woman flung open the car door and ran into the trees, her clothing torn and flying behind.

The man ran after her, shouting obscenities which rang through the woodland as the girl was calling, 'No, don't, no . . . '

'Time for Sir Galahad to rescue a fair maid, you think?' said Wharton.

'You take the girl, I'll get him,' I said, more in hope than expectation.

Wharton ran. We did not need torches in the half-light, and as I galloped to head off the chasing man, he called after the girl, 'It's all right, it's the police . . . '

I was closing on the man with great speed, for it was clear that he was physically out of condition. When I was behind him, I called for him to halt, but he refused. He was clearly terrified of me and Paul Wharton, not knowing what he had let himself in for.

'Police!' I shouted as I closed in. 'Halt . . . '

He replied with a stream of abuse, and so I accelerated over those closing yards and brought him down with a flying rugby tackle. We crashed head first into the soft carpet of pine needles, his body acting as a cushion for mine as I knocked the wind out of him. I picked him up and snapped my handcuffs on him before he could do any more harm, then held his manacled arms as I steered him back to his own Rover. He never spoke during that walk. As I approached the car, I saw that Paul had caught the girl and they were walking back together, Paul supporting her with his arms.

'So,' said Paul as my man sank against the car for support, 'what's all this?'

'He tried to rape me, that's what! I know I agreed to a cuddle and a spot of music on the radio, but he went berserk.'

'She led me on, I thought she was game . . . ' and the face turned around to reveal his identity. It was our VFTVP.

'I did no such thing, you evil bastard . . . ' she bellowed at him. 'You are filthy, you are evil, you want locking up . . . '

Paul, his dreams shattered, was horrified. 'But it's . . . you are . . . '

'Sod off, you stupid copper!' snapped the VFTVP. 'I want

my solicitor. This cow is a prostitute . . . I've paid her to come here tonight . . . I'll ruin her in court, so help me . . . '

'I'm not, I'm not, I thought you loved me!' wept the girl.

'You are under arrest for attempted rape,' said Paul, his face as grim as the granite rocks which surrounded us. 'You are not obliged to say anything unless you wish to do so, but what you say may be taken down in writing and given in evidence.'

'That bitch is a slut, a cow and a pro. Put that in your notebooks and see if I care.'

We radioed our control room to report this arrest and, in view of the fame of our prisoner, were told to take him to the Divisional Headquarters, where a detective chief inspector would interview him.

For Paul Wharton, there had been the shattering of an illusion, and he no longer believed in the truth of screen images. For me, there was disappointment too. In spite of what we had witnessed, we could not proceed against the VFTVP because the girl refused to make a formal complaint and declined to be a witness. This case occurred many years before the anonymity procedures which now protect victims and suspects alike, and the girl did not want her name dragging through the courts and newpapers. She did not want to be regarded as a loose woman, a slag, a prostitute or a rich man's plaything. And so we could not prosecute him — besides, it was a very doubtful case of attempted rape anyway. We might have secured a conviction for indecent assault — but we got nothing.

For the general public and all his thousands of adoring fans, the VFTVP continued to charm those who saw him in action on their screens. None knew of his darker side but I did learn, two or three years later, that some of the tabloid press were quietly investigating his life-style and were compiling a dossier. One day, I felt, all would be revealed.

And for the detective chief inspector, there was hope.

'I think he killed that lass,' he said to me many days later. 'That story told by your girl, about him ripping off her clothes and so on, well, it all fits with the murdered lass.'

'Did you ask him about his whereabouts at the time of her death,' I asked.

'We did. He said he was in London, reading scripts at his

flat. Alone. He won't say anything else without his solicitor present. I'd love to nail him for that job, you know. I'm sure as hell he's guilty.'

'But what a way to return to the scene of a crime, sir, to bring another woman and have a go at her . . . '

'Exactly, young Nick. Exactly what I thought. By doing it like that, no one would suspect his part in the first crime, would they? Except experienced CID men . . . What a clever sod, what a cunning bastard he really is . . . How he can come over in such a charming way on screen beats me, it really does . . . '

'So what are you going to do now, sir?'

'Wait,' he said. 'Wait with my eyes open and with that file never closed.'

And that file is still open.

10

A brief reflection solves the mystery.

Bishop William Stubbs (1825-1901)

As I mentioned earlier in this book, I'm sure most young constables have ambitions to arrest a suspected murderer. Certainly, many fostered this dream when I joined the service, so when I started work within the CID, I looked forward to such an occasion.

I knew that if another murder was reported, I would be drafted onto the enquiry as a member of a team. For those purposes, a team comprises two detectives. They are either two detective constables or a detective sergeant with a detective constable. They are based at the incident room, which is an office established for the duration of the investigation. Each team is allocated specific tasks which are called 'actions', and in this way each team investigates a particular aspect of the crime until that aspect has been totally exhausted and, if possible, clarified. The outcome of this action is made known to those in charge of the incident room, so that the result can be filed and recorded. The result of one team's enquiries may have relevance to another action being dealt with by another team — collation of such links is the work of the clerical staff within the incident room.

The incident room can be established in a police station, perhaps by using a recreation room or even a games room — anything will suffice so long as it is large enough to accommodate all the stationery and paraphernalia of a big investigation, in addition to some forty or more detectives working in teams of two. In remote situations, the incident room may even be based in a village hall, community centre, schoolroom or any other suitable accommodation. A detective sergeant runs the administrative side of the work in this room, while overall charge of the work of the incident room, and allocation of actions, is in the hands of an experienced detective inspector or chief inspector. In charge of the overall enquiry will be a detective superintendent or perhaps a detective chief superintendent, depending upon the size of the police force involved or, of course, the nature of the investigation.

I knew that all detectives felt the thrill of the chase when instructed to attend a briefing following the report of a murder; it meant working a twelve-hour day, usually from 9 a.m. until 9 p.m., until the killer was caught or the enquiry ended. But the camaraderie and excitement of this vital aspect of crime investigation are never exhausted, even in the most experienced of detectives. And, fortunately for the expansion of my police experience, albeit with the utmost sympathy for the victim, we did receive a report of a murder whilst I was an Aide.

It came at 8.45 a.m. one Monday morning, just as we were all arriving for the day's work. PC John Rogers took the call.

I heard him say, 'Just a moment, Mr Flint. I think you ought to speak to the CID.'

Detective Sergeant Gerry Connolly heard this interchange, nodded his understanding of its nature and went through to his office to take the call. He came back a few seconds later and said to us,

'I think we've got a murder on our hands, lads. I'm going round to have a look — No. 16 Driffield Terrace. Nick, you come with me. John, send a car round to that address, will you? With a uniformed man to seal off the house. Tell him to liaise with me there. Don't do anything further until you hear from me, and don't tell the press, not at this stage. And John, call the doctor; ask him to meet me there urgently.'

He asked me to go with him because I happened to be the only other CID man present on duty; Paul Wharton was working a late shift, and it was Ian Shackleton's day off. On the way to the house, which was a five-minute drive, Gerry told me that the first thing was to examine the body without touching it and without touching anything else in the house. The doctor would be required to certify death, however, and as the local police doctor, he would be advised on the need to touch as little as possible and not to move the body. It was vital that the scene of a murder be interfered with as little as possible.

We arrived to find a youth standing in the doorway of the terrace cottage. He looked pale and ghastly, and I guessed he was suffering from shock. He came to meet us, recognizing Connolly.

'In there,' he said, almost sobbing the words. 'In the kitchen . . . '

'You're Mr Flint, are you?' asked Connolly.

'Yes, I'm . . . '

'Wait here,' Gerry said to the youth. 'Nick, follow me and don't touch a thing; in fact, put your hands in your pockets.'

The front door led directly off the street into a narrow passage, and I noticed a *Daily Mail* stuck in the letter-box. Inside, I was tempted to pull it from the letter-box but resisted in time. I could see the date — it was that morning's edition. Inside, the stairs ascended to the left while the passage continued through the building. On the right was the front room, with a door opening into it from that passage; further along was a dining-room, also with the door standing open. The passage was carpeted with a long, dark maroon runner and bore one or two pictures along its walls; there was a mirror, too, and a small stand for walking-sticks.

At the end of the passage was the kitchen. This was at the back of the house, and as I peered beyond Gerry's bulky shape, I could see the legs of an elderly lady who lay on the floor.

'I'll have to go in,' he said gently. 'You stand at the door and look into the kitchen; keep your hands in your pockets and just look around. Note things in your memory, the position of everyday things . . . Has she washed up? Used the kitchen table? Had a meal? Is there anything odd about the scene?'

As Gerry entered the kitchen with all the caution of his years in CID work, I stood and watched. The dead lady was in

her nightdress and was laid with her head touching the outer
door and her neck at an awkward angle, twisted savagely to
the left. Blood covered the tiled floor in the region of her head;
it was dark and congealed. She wore slippers but her legs were
bare and her hair was covered with an old-fashioned hair-net.
Gerry stood at her side, mentally noting a hundred and one
tiny details before he carefully leaned forward to touch her
forehead.

'Cold as ice,' he said gently. 'She's dead all right, been dead
a while by the look of it.'

As he visually examined the body, I looked around the
kitchen. The window over the sink was broken, and I could
see slivers of glass in the sink. The catch was unfastened and
the window, of the transom type, was open, but not wide
enough to admit the average-sized person. I saw a torch on the
floor too, not far from her right hand, and her walking-stick
lay under the table. The table was set for breakfast with a
packet of cornflakes and a bowl, a jar of marmalade and some
butter, with a sugar bowl standing near a large mug.

On the mantelpiece, a tea caddy was standing with its lid
off, and a corner cupboard had its door standing wide open,
with the lids off several tins and jars.

'What do you make of it, Nick?' Gerry turned to me, not
moving from his position.

'It looks as though somebody's broken in during the night,
Sergeant. The glass in the sink shows the window was
smashed from the outside. The villain opens it and climbs in
through that window — it's large enough, then he closes it
slightly once he's in. He begins looking for money, I think —
all those lids off jars — and she hears him. She's in bed but
gets her torch, comes downstairs, collects a walking-stick on
the way, possibly from that stand in the passage, and comes in
here to investigate. She's a brave lady. He goes for her — hits
her with something, or she falls and smashes her head against
the door or something else. A forensic pathologist will help
determine that. And having done the foul deed, chummy
leaves, by either the front door or the kitchen door.'

'Not the kitchen door, Nick. She's lying against it. It
wouldn't open, so he couldn't leave that way. It would be the
front door, then. Is the key in?'

I went to have a look. It was hanging on a string behind the letter-box. So many people made their keys available in this trusting manner, but with only one key to a household's front door, this was often the only convenient method of letting more than one person use it.

I then wondered if this lady lived alone, or whether she had a family, or even lodgers. That would have to be established very soon.

Gerry Connolly was saying, 'That seems to be the sequence of events, but we've a lot of work to do before we can definitely establish that. Now, we need our scenes-of-crime men, official photographer, two uniform constables to seal the rear and front entrances to everyone except investigators. The doctor's been called. I'll have to inform the D/C/I, get the official wheels in motion. And now what, Nick?'

I was puzzled for a moment, but recovered to say,

'Interview that youth, Mr Flint. It seems he found her.'

'Right, that's vital — and Nick, always remember that the person who finds the body, or the person who was last to see the victim alive, is the prime suspect. Lots of killers seem to think suspicion is removed from them if they report finding the body. Never forget that likelihood. So I will interview Mr Flint, but you can sit in; it'll be good experience.'

'Thanks, Sarge.'

'And what else must we do immediately?'

I thought we had covered most of the immediate actions, and he smiled.

'We need to search the house, Nick, in case the killer's still here, hiding, sleeping off a drunken stupor . . . villains do that, you know. And don't forget there could be another body in the house . . . '

Together, without touching the areas that might bear fingerprints, we searched every room, every wardrobe, cupboard and hiding-place, under beds, in the toilet, in the loft and then outside in the coalhouse and outside loo. No one was hiding there, and there was not another dead body in the house.

'Won't be a moment, Mr Flint,' Gerry called as he caught sight of the anxious youth who was still waiting outside. 'We'll have a word with you in a second.'

Using the official radio in his car, he called the office and said, 'It's a murder investigation; address 16 Driffield Terrace, Eltering. Elderly lady found dead in suspicious circumstances after the house has been broken into. Please notify all departments and ask them to liaise with me at the scene. Call D/S Barber and ask him to establish an incident room; we can use the billiard room at Eltering nick. And I want immediate house-to-house enquiries – get Barber to recruit some teams straight away.'

In the force control room, there was a pre-arranged list of experts who had to be called to the scene of a suspected murder, and they would now be summoned. An incident room would be established and the whole drama surrounding a murder would now be set in motion.

Dr Stamford, who served as police doctor for Eltering, arrived and was shown the body. He was prepared to certify death but not the cause; that would be determined later that day by a post-mortem examination.

'Right,' said Connolly when Dr Stamford had gone. 'We'll talk to that man Flint now, Nick. Let's get him seen and on his way before the cavalry arrive.'

This meant an interview about the circumstances of his discovery of the body, followed by a written statement from him in which all the essential points were incorporated. That would be filed in a statement file, and all the relevant facts extracted for inclusion in a file index system. No detail was too insignificant in such an enquiry, and the interrogation of any witness would inevitably be dramatic for them, sometimes giving them the feeling that they were under suspicion. If they could not appreciate the lengths to which the police had to go to catch a murderer, then it was unfortunate.

Sitting in the front passenger seat of the CID car, with me in the rear, Connolly interviewed Nigel Flint. He was twenty-two years old and lived alone in a flat at No. 14A Market House, Market Place, Eltering. He was a clerk with a large-scale haulage contractor who operated from spacious premises on the outskirts of Eltering. He told us that the dead lady was Miss Edith Holt, who was in her seventies, and said he would be prepared to make the formal identification.

'I know, er, knew, her as Aunty Edie,' he told us. 'She was

a close friend of my mother's. My mother lives on that new estate off Strensford Road, St Hilda's Way, Number 3. Anyway, she isn't a real aunt, she's not related to us, Mr Connolly, but ever since I was tiny, I've called her Aunt Edie.'

'That establishes your links with her,' said Connolly. 'So tell us about finding her this morning.'

I could see that this was going to be a traumatic time for Flint, but he took a deep breath and said, 'I always pop in to see her on my way to work. Every morning. Mum asked me to do it, to see if Aunt Edie wanted anything. Groceries, rent paid, bits and pieces for the house. Last week, she was on about getting a new toaster, that sort of thing.'

'So you called this morning. What time?'

'Just before quarter to nine. Twenty to, or thereabouts.'

'And what did you find?'

'Well, the first thing was the paper. It was still in the letter-box, so I thought she must still be in bed. She did lie in late sometimes.'

'Was the door shut?'

'Yes, closed, but not locked. I tried it. I don't have a key, but she leaves one on a string behind the letter-box, so I can let myself in if I have to. Anyway, it was open, Mr Connolly, which I thought was funny, seeing the paper was still there. When I got inside, I shouted upstairs but there was no reply, so I went through to the kitchen . . . she always had her breakfast in the kitchen . . . and, well, there she was.'

'You didn't see her before you got to the kitchen?'

Flint was puzzled at this, so Connolly elaborated.

'Was the kitchen door closed or open as you approached it?'

'Oh, closed – well, not latched, if you know what I mean. Closed almost completely. I hadn't to turn the handle to open it, I just pushed it open and . . . saw her.'

'Look, Nigel, I know this is painful, but what exactly did you do next?'

'I could see she was dead, all that blood . . . I just ran out and called you from the kiosk.'

'Which kiosk?'

'At the end of this street, on the corner.'

'Did you touch her? Speak to her? Look upstairs to see if there was an intruder about? Anything like that?'

'No, nothing. I just panicked and ran.'

Having recorded Nigel Flint's account, Gerry let him go; he had the awesome task of informing his own mother of this because, until now, he had not spoken to anyone save ourselves. But already a crowd of interested onlookers was gathering outside Edith Holt's little home, and by this time the cavalry — the mass of police and scientific investigators — was beginning to assemble.

'Right, Nick, you go back to the office and join the staff of the incident room. A typist will be allocated, so get her to type up this statement and distribute copies to all key personnel. Make sure the D/C/I gets one. We'll need to interview Flint again, I'm sure, about Aunt Edie's life-style, whether she encouraged visitors or whether she was rumoured to have money around the house, that sort of thing.'

I nodded my understanding as he went on, 'And make a statement yourself, get it typed up and entered into the system. Detail the facts you noticed in the house — the *Daily Mail*, the state of the kitchen, the window and so on.'

When I returned to Eltering Police Station, it was almost eleven o'clock and a detective inspector, detective sergeant and detective constable had already arrived in a large van from Headquarters to begin the setting-up of the incident room. Two GPO engineers were installing outside lines for the public to use, and Barbara, a strikingly beautiful typist, had been drafted in. The CID had brought a massive box of stationery, statement forms, pens and pencils and all the requirements of an office. They had produced a blackboard, two typewriters, a photocopying machine, a duplicating machine and even a couple of desks. I introduced myself and they gave me a statement form so that I could begin to compile my own statement. Barbara was already installed at a desk and had boiled a kettle, also brought by the CID, along with coffee, tea and two bottles of milk. Teams of detectives from all over the county had been drafted in, and they had been instructed to report at Eltering for the first conference at 2 p.m.

As this was happening, the body was being photographed, as was the house and especially the kitchen and its broken window; fingerprint experts were examining the house too, and a forensic scientist was studying the corpse in its position before moving it to a mortuary for a post-mortem. The coroner had been informed, and the press had now heard of the death and were clamouring for news.

The next two or three hours were a whirlwind of activity, and I found myself heavily involved in helping to set up the incident room. Having been to the house and seen the body, I wrote the facts on the blackboard so that all the incoming CID officers could see it. It said: 8.45 a.m., Monday, 18 April. Body of Miss Edith Holt, 72 years, spinster, found at No. 16 Driffield Terrace. 5'4" tall, slim build, grey hair with hair-net, blue eyes. Dressed in white nightdress and pink slippers, and found lying in kitchen. Death believed from a head wound. Intruder had entered via kitchen window by breaking in; not known if anything stolen. Scene visited by doctor, forensic pathologist, SOCO, photographers, detective super-intendent and assistant chief constable.' (In fact, the ACC had travelled all the way from Northallerton to pay his visit.) The notes on the blackboard also included Nigel Flint's name and address, and a brief physical description of him. As he was the finder of the body, we needed to know if other residents had seen him entering or leaving the house, or whether someone of a different description had been observed.

'Nick,' said Connolly a few minutes before two o'clock, 'pop round to the murder house in the car, see if any of our lads are still there; if so, tell 'em to get themselves round here to the CID conference. It starts at 2 p.m.

I drove round to Miss Holt's house, now the scene of immense public interest, and the constable on duty recognized me and allowed me inside. The front door was closed to prevent peeping in by ghouls; ghouls always gather at the scene of a dramatic death, a fire, traffic accident, air crash and similar event. I went to the kitchen where the scenes-of crime officers were still working and told them of the conference; one would attend while the other two worked. The volunteer said he would come back with me in the car. The body had now been removed, and there was no one else in the house.

On the way out, I halted, for I had noticed a trilby hat hanging behind the front door. It looked fairly new. With the door standing open, it had not been noticed, and I could not recall seeing it that morning when I had noticed the *Daily*

Mail. But I could not say for sure whether or not it had been there, for the door had been standing open all the time I had been in the house on that first occasion.

'That hat,' I said to my SOCO companion. 'It's odd, eh? In a spinster's home . . . '

'We'll need to have it identified,' he said with no more ado. 'Find out whom it belongs to, how it came to be here. We can trace its sale through the manufacturer, and you might even trace the buyer through its retail outlet.' He lifted the grey felt trilby from the hook at the back of the door, popped it into a large plastic bag and labelled it as an exhibit. We took it back to the incident room.

The first conference was conducted by Connolly, who outlined the facts. He read out Flint's statement, and then mine, and said that the preliminary opinion of the pathologist was that Miss Holt had died from several blows to the head with a blunt instrument of some kind. That afternoon's post-mortem would confirm or refute that, but no murder weapon had been found. The assembled detectives, thirty in all, were divided into teams of two, and each team was given a specific action. Many were already involved in house-to-house enquiries in the area; one 'action' was to find out Miss Holt's financial position, another was to interview night people, such as bakers, other policemen, early-morning travellers in lorries that passed through, to see if anyone had been seen in suspicious circumstances. Another team had to make discreet enquiries into the background and character of Nigel Flint.

I then mentioned the trilby hat.

'Right, Nick. Action for you. Trace the owner. Right?'

'Right,' I said.

And so the murder investigation got underway.

I began my action by noting the manufacturer's name and address from the label inside the hatband; the hat was size 6½, and it was in almost new condition. The scenes-of-crime people took a photograph of it, but the felt texture would not reveal any fingerprints. I found it had been made in Bradford, and so I rang the CID of Bradford City Police and asked them to visit the factory to determine its history since manufacture. This could be done by a code number I discovered inside the leather headband.

'I'm going to ask Flint if he saw it this morning,' I told Gerry Connolly. 'It might belong to somebody who called regularly on the old lady.'

'Good idea,' he said. I went to his home address, but there was no reply, so I went to the office where he worked. He was at his desk, pale and quiet, and the manager had no objection to my speaking with him. I showed him the trilby, still in its plastic bag.

'It was hanging behind the front door,' I explained. 'Do you know if it belongs to any of your aunt's visitors?'

'Are you saying the killer left it behind?' he asked.

'It's possible,' I said. 'I'm trying to find out more about it — who put it there, for example, whether it was there when you went in this morning.'

He thought hard and then said, 'Yes, it was there. It doesn't belong to her and I've never seen a friend wearing it. When I walked in, I pushed the door open, but the draught blowing from the kitchen blew it shut. When I ran out to phone, I had to open that door — and I saw the hat . . . it didn't mean anything then, Mr Rhea, but, well, is it the killer's?'

'Let's say it might lead us to a suspect,' I said. I got him to make a written statement confirming the presence of that hat and he signed it, asking, 'But can you honestly find out who it belongs to?'

'It won't be easy,' I admitted. 'In fact, it might be impossible, but we'll do our best.'

'They say every murderer leaves a clue behind,' he said.

'It's often the case,' I agreed, leaving him to his work.

When I returned to the incident room, Connolly hailed me.

'Ah, Nick, old son. Just the chap. That bloody trilby of yours. We've found the owner — or rather he's found us.'

'Oh?' This sounded interesting.

'It belongs to the assistant chief,' he laughed. 'He came to visit the scene of the crime at lunch-time and, being the gentleman he is, he took his hat off and hung it behind the door. Then he forgot it! It's his, Nick, so cancel that action. If that had been any of us doing such a daft thing, we'd have been bollocked up hill and down dale!'

I looked at the hat in my hand, and I remembered the words of Nigel Flint.

'Sergeant,' I said, 'I think Nigel Flint is our killer. He's just stated to me that he saw this hat behind the door this morning, when he found Edith dead. He can't have, because it wasn't there then. He's lying. Is he trying to throw suspicion onto the owner of the hat?'

'I think we'd better have another word with Nigel Flint,' he said.

I did not go to that interview, for it required the skills of a very experienced detective, and so Gerry Connolly went to see Nigel once more.

Nigel admitted killing her. Desperately short of cash, he knew Aunt Edith had cash hidden all over the house and had broken in to steal some of it, intending to make it look like a burglary. He'd broken in during the night hours, around two o'clock in the morning, but she had caught him – in his panic to avoid discovery, he'd picked up the electric iron which had been on the draining-board and had repeatedly struck her with it. She never knew it was him, he was sure, and that gave him some relief, but he had run off, taking the iron with him. He'd thrown it in the river to get rid of it. He wept as he gave his statement to Gerry Connolly, saying over and over again that he'd had no intention of killing Aunt Edie . . .

We recovered the iron from the river, and the forensic experts found strands of her hair and blood upon it. I did not arrest or charge Nigel with his crime – that was done by Sergeant Connolly, but I did feel I had done my bit towards arresting a killer. He pleaded guilty to burglary but not guilty to the charge of murder. The court accepted a plea of guilty to manslaughter, however, and he was given five years imprisonment for the manslaughter, and two for the burglary, the sentences to run concurrently. He'd stolen £23 from her house.

He is now out of prison and living in Lancashire.

Another case remains a puzzle, at least in my mind if not in the official records.

One December morning, when drizzle and fog made the countryside damp and miserable, a farmer's wife called Irene Sheldon came into the police station. She reported that her husband, William, was missing from home. He was seventy-two years old and rather frail, and she was worried about him.

Ian Shackleton interviewed her. She was a very attractive woman, well dressed in green clothes which highlighted her long auburn hair and her pale skin. There was an aura of power about her, the sort of woman who was dominant and capable, the kind who could run any successful business, ranging from a farm to a restaurant. She was also capable of undertaking manual tasks about the farm, shearing the sheep or loading bales of hay, although she usually got others to perform such labouring tasks.

'So why would he go missing?' Ian asked her.

She hung her handsome head. 'He found out I was having an *affaire*,' she readily admitted. 'I've been seeing another man – but that's not a criminal offence, is it?' She stuck out her chin defiantly.

'You are much younger than him?' commented Ian.

'Yes, I'm forty-five. I'm his second wife. His first died eight years ago, and I used to be his housekeeper. He married me five years ago. He's too old. There's too much of an age-gap between us. I should have known better, really, but he is a charming old man, really charming . . . '

'So what precisely prompted him to run off?'

'We had a row. He found out I was seeing Bernard – my feller – at weekends and evenings. We'd been away, you see, me and Bernard, to the Royal Show and to other events. I mean, I do need a younger man . . . '

'This row,' Ian quizzed her, 'was it violent?'

She shook her head. 'No, he's not a violent man, not at all. He sometimes sulks a lot, gets very depressed and moody, and when I said I could not stop seeing Bernard, well, he just went absolutely quiet. That was last night. He went to bed early, soon after nine, and was very quiet. When I took him his tea up this morning, his bed was empty. We slept in separate rooms, by the way, His outdoor clothes have gone, the ones he works in, but he's taken no money or anything. His car's still there.'

'Shotguns? Has he taken any guns? Gone shooting maybe?'

'No, I looked. The gun's still there, the one he uses for rabbiting.'

'Was he suicidal at all, during the time you've known him?'

'Yes, often,' she said. 'He can be very jealous; if he took me to the hunt ball and I was asked by someone else to dance, he would go into a huff and sulk all night. Several times, he's threatened to end it all because he thought I'd stopped loving him. He's odd, like that, very dark at times, very moody and deep.'

'Normally, when an adult goes missing, we are not too interested,' said Ian. 'Adults are free to leave home whenever they wish. So unless there is a suggestion of a crime either by them, or against them, we take little action. But I think in this case there is real concern for his safety. We'll circulate details and a description of him.'

'What about a search? Don't you make a search?' she asked.

'Not unless we have good cause, and at this stage there is no cause for a search — besides, where do we start? No, we will circulate the surrounding police officers in the hope they might find him wandering or that he is seen somewhere so that we have an indication of his whereabouts. Old folks do wander, you know. They get on buses, go for long walks, ride bikes, spend time in pubs and cafés . . .'

Ian talked to her for a long time, eliciting from her what amounted to a most frank confession of her *affaires* with other men, the current one being Bernard Balcombe, who was a salesman for cattle feeds. Some she had managed to conceal from poor old William, but this one had come to a head in this terrible manner. Ian asked if there was a likelihood that William had known of the previous ones, even if he had not said so. She thought it was possible, but unlikely. He also learned that, by his first wife, William had two sons, and so Ian said he would ask them if they had seen their father. She gave us their addresses, thanked us for our interest and left.

'What do you make of her?' Ian asked when she had gone.

'She comes over as a cold and calculating woman,' I said. ' "Chilling" is the word I'd use.'

'The sort who would drive a fellow to suicide to get her hands on his money, eh?' He floated his thoughts in this way.

'I wouldn't put it past her.' My own views were that she was a calculating sort of woman.

'I'm off for a word with his sons,' he decided.

He returned two hours later. The old man had not gone to

either of his sons during his anguish, something they both found odd. Each said that in the past old William had gone to one or other of his sons to complain about his new wife: that she was getting through too much money, that she was not caring for him, that she was spending time away from the farm, meeting other men . . .

'So he did know she was being unfaithful, long before this *affaire*.'

'Yes, he knew, all right. He was moody, they both agreed with that, but he was never suicidal. They think he might have gone for a long walk, to think things over. But they will ask around their relatives and go out and look for him. They know his haunts.'

'Is the farm his own?' I asked.

'Yes, he owns it outright; it's worth a fortune. He's changed his will, by the way, only in the last month; Irene does not know he's done that.'

'So who benefits?' I wondered.

'The farm and all the stock are willed to both lads. He's cut her out completely; he reckons if she goes with other men now, she can find some other mug to look after her in old age. He's had enough of her.'

'So Irene thinks she will get the farm if he dies, eh?' I asked Ian.

'So the sons tell me.'

We heard nothing of William Sheldon for the next two days, in spite of searches by his wife, his sons and friends of the family and in spite of our own wide circulation. Then we got a 999 call from a fisherman.

'There's a body in the beck,' he said. 'The River Elter, about a mile downstream from Warren Bridge. It looks like a man.'

I went with the uniformed police constable, and we drove to the area known as Warren Ings. It lay some three miles from the town centre, and the River Elter wove a deep and winding course through the flat countryside. For well over two miles, the river skirted Sheldon's land, where it formed a formidable barrier to the south of the extensive farm, I guided the constable to Warren Bridge, where we found the fisherman waiting for us.

'It's a fair walk down here.' He showed us a footpath along the edge of the river, and we followed him through the hazels and alders that lined the banks.

We came eventually to a long, wide curve in the river where, on the bank which formed the outer rim of that curve, there were many thick alder trees whose roots formed a curious array of stems which protruded from the water. The flow of the river had gradually washed away the earth at this point, leaving the roots exposed, but the trees had not been weakened by it. They grew as strong and as firm as ever.

'In that pool,' said the fisherman, whose name we had learned was Frederick Shearman and who lived at Thirsk. He indicated a deep pool at the far side of those alders, and we approached to see the distinctive shape of a body submerged in the clear water. It looked very deep here, and the body was below the surface, being washed gently by the movement of the flow on this wide curve.

I studied its position for a few moments, noting that the bank over the position of the body was high and sheer. It was sandy in appearance, and there were sand martins' nest holes at intervals along the miniature cliff. It was about six or seven feet high, with a sheer drop into the water. A tangle of alder roots was some six or seven feet upstream, but directly below the sheer bank the water looked very deep indeed. I asked the constable to go and radio for assistance; I needed to have the attendance of Gerry Connolly and the police underwater search unit, whose task would be to recover the corpse. In addition, I needed the inevitable doctor to certify death.

There was no need for heroics at this late stage. No one dived in to effect a dramatic rescue, for that this person was dead was never in doubt. As we waited for the next stage of this development, I wondered if I was looking at the remains of poor old William Sheldon.

With the eventual arrival of our experts, the body was recovered but, as it came out of the water with the aid of two police frogmen, there was a shock for us all. A cement block had been tied to its neck on the end of a length of rope, and that had kept the body anchored to the bottom of the river.

The body was that of William Sheldon; his eldest son, Stanley, later had the unpleasant job of making a formal identification of the remains. The post-mortem revealed that death had been due to drowning, which meant he was alive when he had entered the water, and there was a large abrasion to the back of his head. The pathologist could not say what had produced that — it might have been caused by the cement block striking him as it dragged him down, or contact with rocks under the surface, or he might have been knocked unconscious before entering the water.

At the inquest which followed, the coroner asked the pathologist the questions that we had all been asking ourselves and which, indeed, we had also put to him.

'Doctor,' he said, 'tell me this. In your expert opinion, could Mr Sheldon have committed suicide? Could he have walked to the banks of that river, tied the block around his own neck and then jumped in, to be weighted down until he drowned?'

'Yes, sir, he could. He was a frail man but, being a farmer, he could easily have carried that block. It is one of many that are still around the farm buildings. He used them for securing stack sheets against high winds.'

'So a determined man could have committed suicide in this way?'

'Yes, sir.'

'Now, tell me, Doctor. The abrasion on his skull. Was that sufficient to render him unconscious?'

'Yes, in my opinion it was.'

'And can you say whether that was inflicted before or after he entered the water?'

'I can say it was inflicted when he was alive, sir, and we know he was alive when he entered the water. It is possible that someone knocked him unconscious with a heavy blow to the head, tied the weight around his neck and threw him into the river. That is not impossible but I cannot state with any certainty that that is what actually happened. We can only speculate upon what actually occurred, and I cannot speculate further upon the available evidence.'

'But you can confirm that he died from drowning?'

'I can. If he had been dead when he entered the water, there would not have been water in his lungs. I have tested the water found in his lungs and confirm it is the same as that which flows in the River Elter.'

'And that is significant?' asked the coroner.

The pathologist continued: 'Yes, sir. This means he was not drowned elsewhere and brought here for disposal. I confirm that he died from drowning, sir. But whether he was thrown in or threw himself in is something I cannot say. Nor can I say whether or not he was conscious when he entered the river.'

Having listened to this evidence, the coroner summed up.

'We are told by the second Mrs Sheldon that her husband was suicidal, but no note has been found; we are also told by his sons that, although he was moody and upset at his wife's self-confessed unfaithfulness, he was not suicidal. So there is a conflict of evidence here. However, I must place on record that his body was found in the River Elter and that he was alive when he entered the water, in a state of either consciousness or unconsciousness. His death is due to drowning, and there was an abrasion on his head which was sufficient to render him unconscious. I am not prepared to accept that William Sheldon took his own life; there is no evidence of that. Nor can I speculate under what precise circumstances his body came to be in the river – it is possible that a third party or parties knocked him unconscious and threw him into the river, his head weighted down so that he drowned. I therefore record an open verdict.'

This caused a buzz of interest in the court, for such a verdict was rather unusual, and the following day's newspapers bore headlines such as 'Mystery of Farmer's Final Hours'.

Mrs Sheldon, with enormous suspicion hanging over her, left the farm to live in Wales, and the two sons moved back. Bernard Balcombe also moved on, having taken a job with another animal feeds firm in the Midlands.

So the facts surrounding the death of William Sheldon remain a mystery, and it was only three weeks after the inquest that I came to the end of my period as an Aide to CID. I left with happy memories and with this puzzle in my mind. Even now I still ponder over William's death, wondering whether it was murder or suicide.

We shall never know until someone confesses.

That case was the last in which I was involved as a Constable in Disguise. I wondered if, over those interesting months, I had sufficiently impressed those faceless Powers-that-Be who decide the progress of one's career and whether, at some distant time, I would join the CID. Gerry Connolly did say I'd fulfilled his expectations and that he hoped one day I would be selected for a detective training course as a prelude to joining the CID. But I knew that such a transfer could not be immediate — even if I had been successful in my recent work, I would have to await a vacancy and there were many ambitious young officers queueing for very few CID posts.

In the meantime, I returned to my beat at Aidensfield, there to continue my work as a rural constable in the stunning countryside of North Yorkshire.

Constable
Among the
Heather

1   Daffodil Duty

In nature, there are neither rewards nor punishments – there are consequences.
Robert Green Ingersoll (1833–99)

High on the moors above Aidensfield there is a lonely farmstead. A farmer and his wife worked its upland fields all their married life; it was a tough, never-ending task with little monetary reward but they raised a family and saw their small heather-encircled property increase in value. When retirement beckoned, the couple sold their farm to settle in a cottage at Elsinby.

During their working life, they had never had a holiday, but twice a month or so the husband had enjoyed a day at the cattle mart, while occasionally his wife had gone shopping to York or joined a WI outing to Scarborough. So far as a longer holiday was concerned, neither had had any wish to go away and, besides, someone had to care for the livestock for twenty-four hours a day, 365 days a year.

As a retirement present, their children decided to send the couple overseas. They selected a trip to Switzerland which would include all the excitement of flying and the sheer joy of exploring a foreign country. On the first night, when their parents would be in their room, the children rang them at the hotel to see how they were coping.

From the discussion that followed, it was evident they were thoroughly enjoying themselves, and then their son asked, 'Dad, what's the view like from your bedroom window?'

'There isn't one,' said the old man. 'But there would be, if it wasn't for all these mountains.'

I mention this yarn because the people who live on the heights of the North York Moors are so accustomed to dramatic and

long-distance views that vistas from other places are often
disappointing. It is claimed that upon the moors you don't
have to go seeking views; they offer themselves to be enjoyed.
Such visitors as William Wordsworth and John Wesley have
admired some of our views, modern tourists now come and
attempt to identify distant towns and hills from the many
vantage-points, and there is even a claim that the towers of
Lincoln Cathedral can be seen from one particular place – and
that cathedral stands over one hundred miles to the south.
Certainly there are views which extend for fifty miles or so,
and without doubt many are stunning in their range. Examples
include the famous vista from Sutton Bank Top on the A170,
the broad expanse around Chimney Bank Top at Rosedale, the
view of Eskdale from Lealholm Bank Top, and the panorama
of Whitby from the summit of Blue Bank near Sleights. From
Ralph Cross between Castleton and Hutton-le-Hole, there is
a view of almost 360 degrees, and from Ampleforth Beacon
you can see the North York Moors National Park towards the
coast, the Dales National Park towards the Pennines and even
the Wolds to the south.

There are many more, some well known and others which can
be found only by leisurely exploration. These viewpoints draw
visitors to the moors, and when people arrive in large numbers,
they often cause problems for many people, including village
constables.

In the mind of a constable, it is a constant source of
amazement that ordinary people can generate so much extraordinary work or create so many complexities as they occupy
themselves upon this fair earth. In our quiet moorland villages
during those peaceful days in the mid-1960s, we knew that,
when the summer season began, usually around Whitsuntide,
it would, for a few short months, change the pace of our gentle
life. There would be an influx of people, cars and litter. There
would be an increase of lost and found property, outbreaks of
petty violence and drunkenness, and misadventures by the daft
and unprepared, as well as many unforeseen problems. Rarely
a week would pass without a blemish of some kind.

These problems have led the moor folk to question the merit
of sharing their inheritance with others who care so little for it,

and there are times when one wonders if we should attempt to deter those who spoil the blessed tranquillity and beauty of nature's finest places. Perhaps we should increase our efforts to convince outsiders that the whole of Yorkshire is a land of pit-heaps, back-to-back streets and factory chimneys. It's an image we managed to cultivate in the past, and it might prevent the thoughtless and careless from plaguing our landscape.

Such thoughts often occurred to me as I patrolled the more popular parts of the southern aspect of the moors. It was on such a tour of duty, one bright and sunny Sunday in early March, that I was experiencing a cool breeze that brought goosepimples to the flesh and a threat of rain or even snow on the higher ground. It was not the sort of day when you'd expect an influx of tourists but, with Easter close at hand and with some workers using the last of their annual holidays before 31 March, I found that the honeypots of the moors were busier than expected. I think the bright sunshine was responsible – people loved to drive onto the moors in such conditions.

An added bonus was that, after a shower of rain, the clarity of long-distance views was remarkable. Some seemed to stretch almost into infinity, and picnickers would sit in their cars to admire distant places. It gave them the feeling of being on top of the world.

In my official mini-van with its blue light on top, I was enjoying a 9 a.m.–5 p.m. shift, and it didn't escape my notice that I was getting paid to tour the moors while others were having to do so in their own time. During the first few hours, I found little to harass me. I had spent time report-writing in the office at Ashfordly, followed by an hour in Brantsford, where I patrolled the market town on foot as the church bells rang. After this, I decided to drive onto the heights above Lairsbeck, with its scattering of cottages around the tiny chapel. There was a Forestry Commission plantation nearby and, over the months, we had received occasional reports of damage to several units of fire-fighting equipment. These were left unattended around the perimeter of the trees, and we wondered at the mentality of those who destroy or damage life-saving equipment – I would inspect them during my visit. I would also eat my sandwich lunch on the moors. Just like a tourist, I'd find a view of my

very own! My decision made, I drove to the top of Bracken
Hill. I would park there and enjoy a walk along the heathery
ridge with its own fine views of Lairsdale.

Once I was out of the sheltering fabric of the van, the wind
was chilling and more than fresh in spite of the sun; a brisk
moorland walk would be an excellent appetizer.

And so it was. A leisurely ramble around the plantation
showed that the fire-fighting equipment had not been interfered
with; this pleased me, and I decided upon a short diversion from
the route back to my van. This took me across the open moor,
where a skylark was singing and black-faced sheep roamed
without hindrance. Up here, there are no fences to contain
the sheep: they live almost as wild animals, each instinctively
remaining within its own patch of heather or 'heeaf'. 'Heeafed
yows' (ewes) are those which are mature enough to remain
within their own territory and, at that time of the year, many
were carrying unborn lambs. Others had already given birth to
delightful black-faced infants, and the tiny lambs were tough
enough to survive the bleak conditions which prevailed.

I enjoyed the brisk walk and found myself upon a little-used
track which led back to the car-park. As I strode across the
heather, moving rapidly to keep warm, I became aware of a
Bedford personnel-carrier which was parked on a nab top.
A nab is a protruding piece of land. This one overlooked
Lairsdale, and the vehicle was positioned so that its passengers
could enjoy the views on all sides. Someone had selected the
ideal place for a picnic.

As I approached, a large brown-and-white mongrel, the size
of a greyhound, leapt from the rear doors. It was fussing about
in a state of some excitement and was immediately followed
by three laughing children. Dog and children galloped away
in a frenzy of barking and shouting, and there seemed to be
a large family with the vehicle. As it stood with its rear doors
wide open, I could see the wooden seats which ran along
each side, with three seats in the front, one of which was
the driver's. The driver, a tall man in his fifties, with greying
hair, was laughing and calling encouragement to the children
and the dog, and at that moment I felt happiness for the family
in their exuberance.

But almost immediately that happiness turned to disbelief and shock. The dog began to chase some sheep and lambs. The children encouraged it, laughing and shouting as the frightened animals galloped through the bracken and heather. The mongrel raced in pursuit, clearly enjoying the 'game'.

I expected the grey-haired man to call it off, to make the children stop. But he didn't. He was laughing too. He was curiously enjoying the panic generated in the sheep.

The distressed animals did not know which way to run to escape from the barking dog or the shouting children. Tiny lambs bleated in terror and became separated from their mothers, while panic caused the pregnant ewes to be in danger of aborting. If they did, it would be a costly business for the farmer who owned them, and a traumatic time for the animals. Within moments, the flock had been scattered, and I knew that if this daft dog managed to bite one and taste blood, it could turn into a sheep-killer.

'Hey!' I shouted and ran towards the van. 'Hey, stop that! Call that dog off!'

The grey-haired man turned and saw me. No one had been aware of my presence until that moment. The whole family was clearly surprised and embarrassed at my unexpected arrival. As I shouted in my anger and horror at their stupidity, I noticed another man climb from the van. He was younger than the first and was followed by two women. One was about his own age, and the other might have been his mother or mother-in-law.

'Bonnie, heel!' He looked at me, then at the frenzied dog and immediately appraised the situation. 'John, call Bonnie off, stop him . . .'

But the dog had other ideas. It ignored the calls to heel and bounded through the clumps of heather, seeking more sheep to chase, more lambs to harass. The three children were a long way behind it, too far away to seize it, and so the shouting man had to rely on the authority in his voice.

'Bonnie, heel! Heel, I say! Damn you, heel!'

'I'm sorry, Constable . . .' the older man was at my side. 'I had no idea it would do that . . . I must . . .'

'That dog should be shot!' I snapped at him. 'Of all the crazy things to do, letting it loose like that . . .'

'Bonnie, heel!' the younger man was having some success now. His powerful voice had penetrated the dog's consciousness and halted its mad gallop; it stood with tail wagging and looked at its master, then once more regarded the sheep. At this stage, they had come to a standstill and had assembled at a safe distance to stare stupidly at the dog. It was on the point of repeating its game when its master called again.

'Heel!' he shouted, 'Heel, Bonnie, heel!'

The three children, a boy and two girls in their early teens, now came to the side of the man. The dog came too, wagging its tail and panting in joy.

'Sorry, Dad,' said the boy. 'I thought it was a bit of fun.'

'All right, no harm done,' said the man as the mongrel arrived at his side, its tail wagging half in happiness but half in expectation of trouble. It had recognized the anger in his voice. 'Heel, Bonnie! Sit!'

The dog sat and looked up at him, eyes wide and trusting. Its tongue lolled as it panted heavily from the exercise, and its tail thumped the ground. I was now at the younger man's side, the children hovering at a discreet distance. The older man had been lingering just out of my sight, close to the two women, but now made as if to speak to me . . .

'Er, Constable . . .' He stepped forward, but I was in no mood for excuses. I ignored his interruption.

'Who is the owner of this dog?' I demanded.

'Er, it's mine,' said the younger man.

'For a start, it's not wearing a collar,' I said. 'And that is an offence. The collar should bear your name and address. And it is also an offence to allow a dog to worry livestock – and chasing them is classed as worrying. It means the owner of these sheep could have shot your dog if he'd caught it just now. It also means I can summon you to court for you to give reasons why your dog shouldn't be destroyed at the worst or at the very least kept under control, and it means that, if any damage or injury is done to these sheep, the farmer can claim compensation from you.'

One of the girls started to cry.

'Look, the children would have no idea of the consequences. We're townspeople, we don't understand the seriousness . . . I mean, the dog was just playing . . .'

'The dog was not just playing!' I retorted. 'You people were encouraging it. It was chasing sheep. Some are heavy with unborn lambs and they might have aborted – they still might abort – and that will cost the farmer a lot of money. He might come to you for compensation. This might cost you a lot of money. Now, your name, please.'

'Look, I'm sorry. I'll make sure it never happens again.'

The older man came forward again. 'Look, er, Constable, this is my son-in-law, and he meant no harm. Now, I think . . .'

'Are you the owner of the dog?' I put to the older man.

'No, officer, I am not.'

'Then kindly allow me to speak to the owner. This is *his* responsibility. So,' I continued to address the younger man, 'your name and address, please?'

My notebook was ready. He said his name was John Horwell and gave an address in Wakefield; he was thirty-eight years old and a schoolmaster. I gave him a lecture about general behaviour in the countryside and suggested he make an effort to learn more about rural matters; I said he would be capable of passing his knowledge to the children, both his own and those he taught at school.

I then told him, in very official tones and by invoking the correct procedures, that I was going to report him for: (a) allowing a dog to be in a public place while not wearing a collar bearing the owner's name and address; (b) being the owner of a dog which worried livestock on agricultural land, i.e. the moor. I said that I was going to summon him to appear at court to show cause why an order should not be made for the dog to be kept under proper control.

Whilst I was at it, I also asked for his driving licence and insurance, but as he had none with him, I issued him with the standard form HO/RT/1, which meant he had five clear days to produce them at a police office of his choice. He chose Wakefield. I told him to take his dog licence too.

In throwing the book at Mr Horwell, I was fairly certain that the chief constable would not authorize prosecution on any of these charges; instead, he would probably issue a formal written caution, but it would be a a valuable lesson to the family. I took all their names as possible witnesses.

My concern was that incidents of this kind had to be halted. They were becoming increasingly frequent as more people took their leisure on the moors. I now felt that this family would be more careful, and they would relate their story to friends and neighbours. The long-term deterrent effect would be of some modest benefit to country folk and their livestock.

Having cast gloom and despondency upon their outing, I noted the registration number of the vehicle just in case I had been given a false name and address. Then I departed towards my own vehicle, making a mental note to provide the farmer with details of this incident, should he wish to pursue the matter privately. I was not in any mood to sit near that location for my picnic lunch, so I drove to another viewpoint, there to calm down over my coffee and sandwiches.

When I returned to Ashfordly police office later that afternoon, I completed my paperwork and rang the West Riding Constabulary control room to ask them to check ownership of the Bedford carrier. When I provided the registration number, the girl immediately said, 'It's in our records. It belongs to Mr Laurence Nelson,' and she gave me his address.

'Nelson?' the name triggered some kind of memory deep in my mind, but its significance eluded me.

'Yes,' she said. 'He's the chief constable of Holbeck County Borough Force.'

I groaned. A chief constable! I had almost booked a chief constable! But he should have known better! Nonetheless, I wondered how he would view my behaviour during those fraught moments. I wondered if he would be critical of my actions, whether I had done everything according to the book or whether I had exceeded my authority. And I wondered what Sergeant Blaketon would do with my report when I concluded it with the sentence, 'Mr Horwell is the son-in-law of Mr Laurence Nelson, chief constable of Holbeck County Borough Police Force. Mr Nelson was present during my interview of the defendant.'

I was to learn later that Horwell was given a written caution for each of his transgressions, which I felt was quite adequate.

I heard nothing from Mr Laurence Nelson and don't know whether he ever contacted any of my superiors.

As a matter of historical record, some years later his tiny police force was absorbed into the surrounding county constabulary as a result of boundary changes, and it no longer exists.

While the splendid heights attracted the multitudes, so did the lush green dales and the pretty stone-built villages. They drew an increasingly mobile public from the humdrum existence of dingy city streets and the conformity of semi-detached suburbia. Quite suddenly, the splendour of the Yorkshire landscape was available to all. The influx surprised those of us who lived and worked in the more remote and attractive districts.

This was in direct contrast to pre-war days. Then, the occasional visitor would pass through a village, perhaps halting for a drink and a chat at the village inn, but by the mid-1960s they were coming in their thousands. Some came by coachload, others came on foot or by bicycle, but mostly they came by car. I think it is fair comment that our villages, and even the charming market towns, were unprepared for this onslaught upon their amenities. There were few car-parking facilities, no public toilets, a definite shortage of places to halt for a soft drink or cup of tea, and a dearth of information directed specifically at visitors.

Many had no idea how to behave in the countryside – they left gates open, which caused cattle and horses to stray, sometimes with fatal consequences; they regarded all fields, whether crop-bearing or not, as common land; they left their rubbish and litter; they picked wild flowers to the point of rarity, and some even chopped up wooden fences to light fires or demolished dry stone walls in their determination to take home a piece of moorland granite to start a rockery. There was ingratitude, ignorance and vandalism on a scale hitherto unknown.

But the people of the moors learned to cope. Some saw the financial advantages of this perpetual influx and opened cafés, caravan sites and bed-and-breakfast establishments, while those in authority were forced to plan for this expanding tourist industry. Car-parks appeared, direction signs proliferated, information packs were compiled and byelaws created, all to regulate the increasing flow of visitors and protect the countryside and its inhabitants.

One pretty dale received more than its fair share; tens of thousands of visitors swarmed along its narrow, hilly lanes. The snag was that most of them arrived at the same time. They were not spread out across the year or even the summer season as were other places – they were compressed into a couple of weekends every year, usually around Easter.

The outcome was that the police were duty-bound to sort out the traffic confusion created by thousands of cars on lanes far too narrow, winding and steep to accommodate the width or length of a bus. It was a recipe for chaos. Just add a stubborn tractor-driver or shepherd with his flock, and the mixture could become volatile. The result could be a traffic jam several miles long – and this was in the days long before the M1 or the M25 and their notorious blockages.

The short-lived attraction was wild daffodils. There were hundreds of thousands of them, even millions, and they grew (and still grow) in splendid and colourful profusion along the banks of the River Dove in Farndale. There are miles of them, and they add a unique charm to this delightful moorland dale. The dale is also known for its thatched cottages and cruck houses, as well as its remoteness and splendid upland views, but it was the wild daffodils which first attracted the crowds.

Topographical books published before the turn of this century omitted references to these flowers, but once news of their presence did circulate, it brought in the thieves and vandals. They all wanted summat for nowt.

Greedy visitors came with scissors, scythes, sickles, trowels, spades and wheelbarrows and began to dig up the bulbs or cut barrowloads of flowers to sell in local city markets. Such was the threat from these looters that in 1953 the dale was made a local nature reserve, with a byelaw to protect the flowers.

And so the police officers whose duty took them to Farndale had two prime tasks – one was to control traffic, and the other was to protect the flowers, although there were also such ancillary tasks as first aid, lost and found property, missing children and wandering old ladies, thefts, vehicle breakdowns, lost dogs, litter and that host of other problems that are generated when crowds assemble.

Daffodil Duty, as we termed it, was one of my regular tasks, although Farndale was not on my own beat. Like the other officers in the area, I was diverted to Farndale from time to time, and it was a busy, if enjoyable task. Five or six constables, a sergeant and some special constables were drafted in when the daffodils bloomed. Our brief was simple – it was to keep the traffic moving.

Fortunately, although the roads were narrow, steep and winding, they did have one advantage: they formed a figure 8 as they wove around the dale. There was a tiny car-park near the central length of that figure 8, and if a one-way traffic system was instituted around the loops, it would prevent blockages. But only half the figure 8 (the lower half) was wide enough to cope with buses – and buses came by the score. On the main approach roads, signs were erected to guide coaches along one specific route: they must drive up the right-hand side of the lower dale, turn left along the link road and disgorge their passengers, and then park on the return leg of the bottom of the figure 8. That lane was wide enough to permit coaches to park, and when their passengers regained them, they could drive out of the dale without problems. Coaches had not to enter the top half of the figure 8.

Private cars, on the other hand, could cope with the steep, narrow lanes around the top half of that figure 8 (even if some of their drivers couldn't!). However, this could operate only on a one-way system. There was no space for large numbers of cars to pass or overtake each other. We created a system whereby they entered the dale via the same route as the coaches and were directed by a policeman on traffic duty across to the left of the dale. They then drove up the left of the top of the figure 8 and circled the dale to return to the centre, where they encountered the same policeman. There they were fed into the incoming stream of cars to cross the 8 in the middle, and then they could leave the dale down the left hand leg. (They could not leave via the right-hand leg because the incoming buses filled the roads.) And with good nature from all, and a capable policeman on that central road of the figure 8, it worked. Traffic on that central stretch must be kept moving.

Understandably, some of the local residents and farmers did not relish a full tour of the dale to post a letter or gain access to their own premises. In time, we got to know them and their foibles and so would halt the traffic to allow a local person to go against the flow.

This was not always a success, however, because inevitably some obstreperous motorist would demand to go the same way, having seen us treat the locals with some sympathy. Initially, we explained our actions to those who grumbled, but too many wanted special treatment. After a time our patience was exhausted, so we never explained or argued with such drivers – if they were very awkward, they found themselves doing a longer than usual tour. The total round trip was in the region of eleven miles, but with a spot of collusion from other constables, awkward and inconsiderate drivers could find themselves doing a long second trip.

The truly tricky bit, from a traffic-control point of view, was the central part of that figure 8. All traffic used that short stretch of road whether entering or leaving the dale. Traffic new to the dale, both buses and cars, was channelled along it, but cars which had toured the top of the dale were also channelled along it as they were guided to their exit route. So long as everyone kept moving, knew where they were heading and did as they were told, there was no trouble. Even so, it required a good and patient constable to cope with the never-ending problems at that very important point. A blockage there would halt the entire dale, something of no great consequence to tourists but of very serious consideration if it prevented access by emergency vehicles, such as ambulances, fire appliances and doctors' cars.

I recall one such problem. A coach had overshot the junction by about ten yards and needed to reverse in order to get around the bend into its correct route. But in those few moments other cars had arrived and were now queuing behind it. If each one reversed a short distance, the problem would be solved – the coach could move backwards, giving it space to turn the corner and then be on its way. But when I put this to the lady driving the car immediately behind it, she said haughtily, 'Officer, I never reverse!'

'But, madam,' I replied, 'if you don't, the entire dale will be blocked. All I'm asking is for you to move back to that gate . . . a few yards . . . then the bus can proceed.'

'I have told you, Constable. I never reverse. Never!'

I could have argued all day and threatened her with prosecution for obstructing the highway, but none of that would solve the immediate crisis. Already more cars were heading this way – if we didn't get her moving soon, there would be a massive blockage.

'Would you mind if I moved it for you?' I asked.

'Not at all.' She was a picture of charm and, I suspect, some relief as I reversed her little Austin for the necessary distance.

That hiccup was of little consequence in comparison with the traffic jam created there one Easter Sunday afternoon at the peak of the influx of vehicles.

We had a new constable with us. He had transferred from Leeds City Police because his wife hated town life, and he had been posted to Eltering. His name was David Parry; he had about eight years service and was soon trying to impress us with stories of his daring exploits in policing a city, especially around the Saturday night trouble-spots as the pubs turned out. We got the impression he had controlled the entire centre of Leeds single-handed, and he adapted his boasting to the situation when he was earmarked for Daffodil Duty in Farndale. As we assembled in the village hall for briefing and allocation of points, he boasted that this traffic duty was nothing compared with rush hour on The Headrow at Leeds, one of the busiest thoroughfares in the city.

'I can do the Headrow with my eyes shut,' he said that Easter Sunday morning. 'Multiple lanes, traffic lights, junctions to cope with . . . crowds . . . lorries and buses . . . that was a piece of cake. What have you here, then? A few buses and cars – mebbe a tractor or two? All on the same road? It's a country lane – it'll be a doddle.'

'I'm delighted that we have such an expert amongst us,' beamed Sergeant Bairstow with his customary good nature. 'So, David, maybe you'd do the central stretch? That bit definitely needs the skills of an expert point-duty man.'

Bairstow explained the requirements and the likely problems, then showed PC Parry the link road at the junction of the figure 8.

'Nothing to it, Sarge!' beamed Parry as he warmed to the task of showing us country cousins how to do a proper job.

'Nick.' The sergeant turned to me. 'You've done this before; you take this car-park. Stop 'em parking here except for disgorging passengers. And relieve David as and when necessary. Explain your job to him before you hand over. OK?'

'Fine, Sarge,' I smiled.

After a cup of coffee, we went to our posts. It was a dull April morning, with clouds threatening rain, and we wondered if the weather would deter the visitors. We felt it would not. Many would already have made plans or even left home by now. For the first hour or so, however, very few vehicles arrived, and I knew that PC Parry would find this boring in the extreme. But as lunch time approached, the clouds evaporated, a warm breeze appeared from the west, and the April sun beamed upon the dale. And the daffodils opened their trumpet-shaped blooms to welcome the incoming visitors as they began to arrive by the hundred and even the thousand.

Quite suddenly, the dale was transformed. From my vantage-point on the car-park, I could see the procession of oncoming buses and cars. It stretched way out of sight. The constable at the first junction was feeding them across to PC Parry, who in turn was dividing the buses and cars. The cars were being sent towards me; some disgorged their passengers and went on to park higher in the dale. Others completed a circular tour before returning later for their passengers.

By two o'clock the dale was filled with moving vehicles, but I began to realize that their progress was slowing. Quite suddenly, things went wrong. Within minutes traffic in the dale was grinding to a halt. The queue of buses waiting to disgorge passengers was growing, and then, as I looked across the dale to the junction at the far side, I could see that the traffic was stationary for a long way back. Nothing was moving. No cars were passing my point. They were backed for miles down the far side . . . and there was a queue from both the upper and lower dale . . . outgoing cars had been brought to a halt and so had incoming vehicles. The entire dale, miles and miles of it, was at a standstill and the air was was beginning to fill with the ghastly music of the great British motoring public – they were tooting their car horns. It sounded like the centre of Paris . . .

The blockage could only be at PC Parry's point. Sergeant Bairstow was up the dale, so I decided to investigate. After all, Parry's point was only a few yards from mine, although beyond my line of vision. When I arrived, I found mayhem. Cars and buses were jammed at his point; a bus was stuck across the road, there was a tractor and trailer trying to manœuvre past them, and cars were queuing patiently to get past them all. Some drivers were out of their cars, arguing, others were blowing their horns, and some bus passengers had disembarked to march steadfastly towards the daffodils. And in the middle of the road there was PC Parry.

He was on his knees. His hands were covering his head, which was bare. His cap was lying a few yards away, and he held his head close to the surface of the road. I could see by the movements of his body that he was in great distress and appeared to be weeping. I ran to help him, assisting him to his feet and placing him momentarily in a house doorway as uncontrollable tears flowed down his face. Then, with the aid of two bus-drivers, I organized some shunting of buses and cars, a telling-off for the tractor-driver, and after some ten minutes and a lot of shouting, we got things moving again. Eventually the cars filtered towards the higher dale, and the buses went to their parking spaces. The horn-honking faded away as the traffic began to move.

But I had David Parry to deal with. I asked one level-headed motorist to give PC Parry a lift to the village hall, and as he did so, I radioed for Sergeant Bairstow to come and look at his ailing constable.

'I think he needs treatment, Sarge,' I said into my radio. 'But I'm not sure what his problem is.'

'I'll see to him, Nick,' came the response.

I stood on the busy road, guiding buses and cars to their correct destinations, and then an ambulance arrived. It manœuvred itself through the throng of incoming traffic and eventually rushed off to Brantsford Cottage Hospital with PC Parry inside.

That Daffodil Duty became a very busy one, and as we ended our duty at six o'clock that evening, Sergeant Bairstow thanked us all. It had been a record turn-out, so he thought – but tomorrow was still to come.

'Same again tomorrow, lads,' he smiled. 'Same points. Easter Monday will be busy – the weather forecast says it'll be fine and sunny, like today.'

'What about PC Parry, Sarge?' I asked. 'How is he?'

'He's fine now, thanks, Nick,' smiled Bairstow. 'They've sent him home. But we're replacing him for tomorrow's duties. We shan't be using him again for Daffodil Duty.'

'Are our country drivers too much for him?' asked one of the constables.

'No, it's the daffodils,' laughed Bairstow. 'It seems he's allergic to them. The pollen got to him . . . he sneezed himself silly . . .'

'That's flower power,' chuckled some wag as we prepared to leave.

2 Life's Little Mysteries

> Like one that on a lonesome road
> Doth walk in fear and dread,
> And having once turned round walks on,
> And turns no more his head.
> Samuel Taylor Coleridge (1772–1834)

It requires the knowledge of a local person to make full use of the interconnecting network of minor roads which pattern the heights and dales of the North York Moors. Businessfolk and visitors tend to use the A- or B-class routes, even though only one A-class road runs north to south across the moors. That is the A169 from Whitby to Pickering. The A171 crosses the northern moors from west to east as it runs from Guisborough to Scarborough; it visits Whitby, then hugs the picturesque coastline as it turns towards the Queen of Watering Places. Another main road, the A174, touches the very northernmost part of the moors between Staithes and Whitby, while the A172/173 lie over to the west. There are no other A-class roads, although the B1257, with its panoramic views, runs down Bilsdale from Stokesley to Helmsley. This is the only B-class road completely to traverse the heights.

This dearth of main roads is compensated by a bewildering network of unclassified routes. They run down the dales or snake across the moors to link dale with dale or village with village. In addition, there are hundreds of miles of ancient tracks, green lanes, disused roads and bridleways, and these do tend to be well used by the moorfolk, especially when the main roads are busy with summer traffic.

A large-scale map will help identify these, but in general terms they are beyond the sights of the casual visitor. However, one moorland road is centuries older than any of these, and it has been discovered by the tourists.

It is the Roman road which crosses Wheeldale Moor near Goathland. Alternatively known as 'T'Aud Wife's Trod' or 'Wade's Causeway', ancient legend said it was built by the giant Wade and his wife Bell who had to cross the moors between Mulgrave Castle and Pickering Castle. More professional examination proved it to be of great historical importance and antiquity, because it was found to be a genuine Roman road and not the work of a legendary giant. It is the only Roman road known to have entered this part of North Yorkshire and is the finest example of its type in Britain. Six hundred feet above sea-level, the uncovered portion extends about a mile and a quarter, and it is a remarkable feat of construction. Sixteen feet wide and made up of flat stones on a bed of gravel, it is raised in the centre to facilitate drainage and even has side gutters and culverts.

It is even more remarkable when we realize that some of our own roads were little more than mud tracks even into this century. It required a man like John MacAdam (1756–1836) to emulate this style many centuries later. The Roman road has survived almost twenty centuries on this bleak and windswept moorland, and it is sad to record that some of it has been ploughed up, and some stones have been plundered for house-building, while others have been utilized in the construction of the present road from Stape to Egton Bridge. Fortunately, this fine stretch has survived.

In my routine patrols as the village constable of Aidensfield, I had little cause to visit the Roman road, but my wife and I had taken the children to see it during one of my days off duty. It was not on my patch, although it did lie on the boundaries of the division in which I was stationed. For this reason, it was perfectly feasible that sooner or later I should have to deal with an incident up there. It happened one miserable, wet and foggy day in June and was to prove a most interesting and curious day's work.

Even the initial inquiry contained a certain air of mystery. I was instructed to visit Ravenstone Farm on the edge of Wheeldale Moor, and there examine a tractor being used by the tenant farmer, a Mr Stanley Bayley. As the farm was very remote, I was provided with a map reference and was told that it overlooked Wheeldale Gill and that the road to it was rather rough.

'Understood,' I responded. 'But what is the purpose of this vehicle-examination?'

'We have received an anonymous call,' Control informed me. 'It suggests we examine the tractor being used at that address. No further details were given. The caller rang off. Over.'

'Ten four.' I gave the formal acknowledgement of the message and set about my task. This meant a rough drive along forest tracks, and it would be around noon when I reached the edge of Wheeldale Moor.

By now, the entire landscape was obliterated by a thick moorland fog, a 'roak' as it was locally known. Damp, wet and clinging, it deadened all the sounds of the moors as it eerily enveloped my little van. With headlights blazing, I chugged and bounced along the track. It was slow progress, for the road was rutted with deep holes and puddles; huge, bare stones protruded at intervals and threatened to tear off my exhaust system, and at times I had to drive onto the turf to circumnavigate a particularly rough stretch. I passed the southern tip of the Roman road and began to wonder if I was approaching the right place but a check on the map proved I was right. By 12.15, therefore, in clinging fog, I turned along a farm track, crossed a cattle grid and found myself in a farmyard which appeared to be full of brown hens, broken-down farm waggons and derelict implements.

There was no sign of human habitation.

In the clinging mist, the entire premises looked like a deserted homestead from a Gothic novel. A zinc bath full of water stood in the yard, with a goose on guard – it honked at my approach, but no one appeared; a rusting reaper stood abandoned in one corner, and several old ploughs and iron tractor wheels littered the yard. A thin, dirty cat peered at me from beneath a wooden trough, then scuttled away into an outbuilding, frightened when my foot kicked an empty tin. As I surveyed this desolate spot, I began to wonder if I was the victim of some kind of prank. Determined to find an answer, I made for the door of the house. It needed a few coats of paint, and there was no lock; it was held shut with a piece of string. There was a hole where the knob should be.

I rapped as loudly as I could, and shouted, 'Anybody there?'

With some surprise and relief, I did get a response. Inside the house, I heard a door open and soon a man opened the door. In his late thirties and about my height, he was dressed in work clothes and smelled of cows; he had not shaved for days, his fair hair was matted and dank, and his hands were ingrained with the filth of months.

'Oh,' he said. 'The law.'

'Mr Bayley?'

'Aye,' he said, not inviting me in.

'Can I see your tractor?' I asked.

'What for?' he put to me.

I laughed. 'Look, I don't know. I've been instructed to examine it.' I hoped my own puzzlement would soften him. 'Our office got an anonymous call . . .'

'There's some nosey buggers about. It'll be some o' them hikers we get in. They get lost, they come here looking for help . . . Come on, then, follow me. It's in t'shed. It *is* taxed, thoo knows.'

He led me across the untidy yard into a dry building which was open on one side. The interior of the shed was even more untidy than the exterior, being filled with empty sacks and oil drums, but a small tractor was parked in one of the bays.

'There she is,' he said, with a certain pride in his voice. 'Grand little lass is yon.'

It was. It was a lovely little Fergie, as these tiny Ferguson tractors were called. Painted a pleasing grey, it was surprisingly clean and well maintained. I guessed it was of the 1950s era. It had an exhaust which rose from the engine like a chimney, which meant it could operate in deep water. Huge semi-circular mudguards covered the giant rear wheels. I found the tax disc and noted it was up-to-date, so I still wondered why I was staring at this delightful machine. And then, as I walked to the rear of it, I knew.

The seat was wrong. I remembered these tractors having a metal seat which was shaped to accommodate the backside of an average farmworker; with holes for ventilation, each seat was mounted on a tough horseshoe-shaped spring of steel. This gave some comfort to the roughest ride. But this tractor had no such seat. Instead, it bore an enormous and totally strange contraption with coloured wires and plastic pipes. It took only seconds for me to recognize it as a pilot's ejector seat from a jet aircraft. As I stared at it, I recalled a crash on these moors several months ago. The pilot had been killed . . . wreckage had been strewn for miles.

'This seat?' I asked him.

'Aye, Ah kem across it ower t'moor,' he said. 'Frev yon jet that crashed a while back . . . doon in t'gill, t'seat was, it had flown hundreds o' yards from t'plane. Them RAF fellers never found it, so Ah thought it would be grand for me.'

And so, with some skilful adaptations and a spot of home welding, he had secured it to his tractor.

When I took a closer look, I was horrified.

'Good God, Mr Bayley!' I exclaimed as I scrutinized his very grand tractor seat. 'This one is alive!'

'Alive?' he looked puzzled.

'It's an ejector seat,' I explained. 'When a pilot is crashing, he pulls a lever which detonates an explosive charge under this seat. That shoots off the canopy and propels the seat from the plane – with the pilot in it. Then he's supposed to separate from it and parachute to safety. But this pilot didn't manage that, did he? He didn't eject. He was thrown out and killed, remember?'

'Aye.'

'So when the plane crashed, this seat must have been flung far enough . . . and it's still full of explosive! See . . . the firing pin's not been used. Now, whatever you do, don't touch it. I'll make it safe.'

'Dis thoo mean ti say Ah've been sittin' on yon pack o' gunpowder and Ah could have been blown sky high?'

'That's exactly what I'm saying, Mr Bayley.'

The expression on his face was a joy to behold. Fortunately, police officers are instructed on the safe methods of dealing with ejector seats, and I knew exactly how to secure this one. I found the safety pin with its red label tucked into a side pocket and slipped it into position. Now the seat was safe; it would not explode. I found it amazing that it had survived intact like this.

'What would really 'ave 'appened if yon thing 'ad gone off wi' me sitting on it?' he asked, still brooding over my initial comments.

'I meant what I said,' I told him. 'It would have sent you hundreds of feet into the sky.' I had to laugh now. 'But with no parachute, you'd have come down with one hell of a bump – and the chances are you would have broken your back on landing, or maybe your neck in the process of being launched. In short, you could have been killed, Mr Bayley. Pilots are trained to use those seats – tractor-drivers aren't.'

'But thoo'll not be arresting me for pinching it?'

'No,' I said. 'I've received no complaint about a theft. Besides, it was lost. But I think I'd better call the RAF to come and remove the explosive charges, to make it safe. They might let you keep the seat.'

'Thanks,' he said with feeling, that feeling being one of relief.

'It's thanks to the anonymous caller,' I reminded him. 'Mebbe hikers aren't such a nuisance?'

'Mebbe not,' he grinned suddenly. 'Ah might let 'em sleep in my barn from now on. Now, is thoo coming in for a drink, then?'

'Aye,' I said.

I first called the office on my radio and explained the problem. The duty sergeant said he would request the RAF to deal with the seat. I was then accompanied into the house and, in the custom of the moors, was invited to sit down for dinner, as lunch is called hereabouts. In spite of the state of the exterior, the kitchen was a model of cleanliness, thanks to the busy Mrs Bayley, and the meal was superb.

I left the farm an hour later, having sampled a tiny drop of the Bayley's home-made beer. As I drove, I did wonder what on earth would have happened it that seat had launched Mr Bayley from his little Fergie. If nothing else, it would have surprised the grouse population, and I did wonder if Mr Bayley had ever flown . . .

But my day's duty was not over. As I was returning along the pot-holed track beyond the farm, a middle-aged man hailed me. Clad in overalls and sporting a flat cap, he appeared out of the mist, which was now thinning but still of considerable density, and he waved me to a halt.

'Ah saw you go up Ravenstone way,' he said as I climbed out. 'Ah thought Ah'd better wait and catch you on t'way back.'

'Summat wrong?' I asked.

'Aye,' he said. He explained that his name was Ernie Smallwood and that he was the warden for the Roman road, employed by the Ministry of Works. His job was to maintain the ancient road and keep it safe from modern predators. Then he told me, 'There's a chap sitting in my 'ut. Ah can't get a word o' sense out of 'im.'

'Who is he?' I asked. 'One of your workmen?'

'Nay, lad, there's only me works this road. Ah think 'e's a 'iker got lost. Ah reckon 'e doesn't know where 'e is. 'E sounds a bit daft to me.'

'Is he injured?' I was contemplating the need for an ambulance and could call one via the radio before venturing along this ancient highway.

'No, 'e doesn't seem 'urt, just dazed.'

'Right, I'll come and have a look at him.'

Ernie led me along the uneven surface of this amazing road; perhaps it had once been smooth enough for chariots, but the ravages of centuries had rendered it rough and undulating. Nonetheless, the craftsmanship in its construction was evident, and I was very conscious that I was walking along a road built for the use of Roman soldiers about a century after Christ. The sense of history was almost overwhelming.

Ernie took me to his hut, which was a small wooden building like a garden shed. Perched on the moor beside the Roman road and overlooking one of the streams which trickled into Wheeldale Beck, it was painted dark green to blend with the moors. Behind it was a partition which contained a basic toilet, but the hut had no electricity or water, although it did provide a modicum of shelter and rest during Ernie's lonely working hours. His bike was propped against the outside, and inside was a pair of old armchairs, a Calor-gas ring, kettle and tea-making equipment, along with a few other comforts such as paperbacks, magazines and tins of sweets. I also noticed some little carved stone animals. I was to learn that Ernie whiled away his time by sculpting animals from pieces of moorland stone – but he never used any from the road in his care! I spotted a realistic badger and squirrel among them.

Sitting in one of the armchairs was a pale, haggard man in his early thirties. A rucksack stood on the floor at his side; I saw it had a rolled-up sleeping-bag secured to the top. He was clad in hiking gear – large, well-oiled boots, thick socks and adequate sweaters completed his outfit, and he wore a white woolly hat. I could see strands of fair hair sticking from beneath it, around his ears and neck, and his pale blue eyes looked frightened and nervous. He sat almost as if he was in a stupor, and his hands were clasped on his lap. He had the typical appearance of a man in a state of shock.

'Hello.' I stood before him. 'I'm PC Rhea, one of the local policemen. Can I help you?'

There was no response; it was as if he had not heard my voice. I tried again, but the outcome was the same.

'E's been like that since 'e got here,' said Ernie, who stood at the door. 'Not a word 'as 'e said. Nowt.'

I knew that one good remedy for shock was a cup of hot, sweet tea, so I asked Ernie if he would brew one. He smiled and agreed, going down to the beck to fill his kettle with pure moorland water. Soon it was singing on his gas ring. Although I repeatedly tried to make contact with the hiker, I got no response. Eventually I thrust a mug of tea into his hands and was pleased when he accepted it. He began to sip. I felt we had achieved a breakthrough!

'Was he here when you got to work, Ernie?'

'Not then,' he said. 'Ah got 'ere at eight, and there was no sign of 'im. Then Ah went along t'road, towards t'south end; it was my morning check, like Ah do every morning. Ah got back only a short while ago, for my dinner break. 'E was here then. Ah never lock t'doors, t'shed's allus available in a storm. This lad was sitting there, just like 'e is now.'

I joined Ernie and the silent visitor in this most traditional of English rituals and was pleased to see that the fellow did lift the mug to his lips and drink. Ernie allowed me to use the other chair, and as we waited for the lad to recover, Ernie told me about his lonely task. I thought it must be the most curious job in Great Britain, being the lengthman on a Roman road. During this chat, I did not address the youth but did notice that he drank every drop of tea and that our calm chatter in his presence did seem to have created a new awareness in him.

'Thanks,' he said suddenly and without warning. He placed the empty mug on Ernie's shelf. 'Look, I'm sorry . . .'

'That's OK, so long as you're safe and well,' I said. 'Can I give you a lift anywhere? I'm heading back through Brantsford and Ashfordly.'

'Where am I now?' The lad blinked and took several deep breaths, exhaling long, loud rushes of air. It was as if he'd emerged from a coma.

'Wheeldale Moor,' I said.

'I got lost last night, in the fog,' he volunteered. 'I was terrified . . . I must have walked all night . . . It was near dawn when I lay down near one of those streams but it was too cold . . . Then I found this old track and guessed it must lead somewhere. I walked along it, but was worn out, so I sat down for a rest, up there somewhere,' and he waved his hands to indicate a distant part of the old road.

After a pause, he continued: 'And then I went to sleep, I think; I had a funny dream . . . it frightened me. Then, this morning, after I woke up, I found this little shed and came in for a rest . . . I was shattered, really shattered . . . I hadn't a clue where I was, out here . . .'

'There's a youth hostel further across the moor,' I told him.

'I wasn't looking for hostels. I thought I could walk up here and find somewhere to sleep overnight, somewhere in the open, then make my way back today. Anyway, I'm safe.'

'Will anyone be looking for you?' I asked, wondering whether a search had already been instigated.

He shook his head. 'I doubt it. Look, could I have another cup of tea? I'm as dry as a bone . . .'

Ernie obliged. The lad went on to say he lived in Essex but was working on the railways, helping to plan the removal of the tracks along those lines which were to be closed following the 1963 Beeching Report. He had always wanted to see the moors but had had no idea they were so vast and that they could be so inhospitable in the middle of summer.

Now he was chattering quite amiably to Ernie and expressed surprise when Ernie said he'd never been on a train. I knew that was quite feasible – there were people on these moors who had never been out of their own dale, let alone on a train journey.

'Look, I'm sorry,' he went on. 'You must have thought I was odd . . . but, well, I was absolutely whacked, shocked rigid after last night. That tea worked wonders.'

'I'd better have you checked at a hospital,' I suggested. 'Shock is a funny thing.'

'No, it's not the fact I got lost,' he said quietly. 'It was my dream . . . well, I don't think it was a dream. I still can't believe it. Something woke me up, a noise I think, at dawn, and I remember sitting on this old track . . .'

'What happened?' I asked.

'Well, you might think I've been drinking or something, but I swear I haven't. I've got to tell somebody. I can't stop thinking about it. I'd been asleep, literally where I lay, even without my sleeping-bag, and this noise woke me. It was just breaking daylight, and it was misty, not as thick as it was later on, but quite hazy. I heard the noise. It was horses and carts, I thought . . .'

He paused and I could see perspiration on his pale forehead. This was clearly an effort. I wondered what kind of experience could have put him into such a state of shock. Then Ernie winked at me – I had no idea why, but we did not actively persuade the youth to continue. We allowed him to proceed at his own pace as he sipped the second mug of tea. Then he went on with his tale.

'Well, I sat up. I was still on that old road, near the edge, and very tired. I'm sure I was awake . . . anyway, I looked into the mist, thinking it was a local farmer coming along but there were these two chariots . . . racing . . . four horses on each one . . . a man driving each, one with a red tunic and one with a green one . . . they had helmets on and were whipping the horses towards me. Well, I dived out of the way and they came swishing past. I could hear a crowd cheering somewhere in the mist. The noise of the chariot wheels was amazing, rattling along those rough stones on that track out there, and the men, cursing in a language I couldn't understand . . . the horses panting, harness rattling . . .'

'And they disappeared into t'roak?' suggested Ernie.

'Roak?' the lad was puzzled.

'Fog, the morning mist.'

'Yes, they did. I mean, I know I wasn't asleep, I know I was awake, but they don't have chariot races up here, do they?'

'Now and again,' said Ernie slowly. 'Ah've seen 'em, and others has, who live up here. Just like you said.'

'Really?' The lad's eyes brightened. 'Then I wasn't dreaming?'

'No, you saw a chariot race,' said Ernie. 'They used to 'ave 'em along this road – there's a slope just a bit further along. T'spectators used to stand there and cheer. They did 'ave four horses, sometimes six, yoked up in their chariot races, but two as a rule, in war and in normal manœuvres . . .'

'But who are they?'

'The Romans,' said Ernie with all seriousness. 'This is a Roman road, tha knows.'

The lad looked horrified. 'You're joking?'

'No,' said Ernie, lifting a Ministry of Works leaflet from a shelf and passing it to him. 'It's my job to tend it. You saw t'chariot race. Ah've seen it and so have others, but nobody talks about it.'

'But I don't believe in ghosts . . .'

'Me neither,' said Ernie. 'At least, not till I saw yon race.'

'If I tell my mates about this, they'll think I'm crackers,' said the youth, now laughing with the relief that came from the fact that someone did believe him. 'I mean, ghosts don't exist, do they? They can't . . . But those chariots? Surely it would be some local lads doing it for a laugh? I mean, I heard the noise, the rattling, the horses panting, the cheering, I saw the men cursing and whipping their horses . . . I had to dive out of their way . . .'

'You 'ave a look in t'soft bits of ground between them stones out there and try and find t'wheel marks,' challenged Ernie. We all knew there would be none.

Ernie's account of the chariot race was identical with that of the lad, whose name was Ian Jarvis, and he told it in a most practical manner. He said the race usually heralded a time of peril for England – they'd appeared in 1805 before Nelson's death at Trafalgar. They'd also appeared before each of the two world wars – and shortly after Ian's sighting, a Labour government was elected! By the time Ernie had finished his story, Ian Jarvis accepted he had seen a Roman chariot race, but he did not try to understand how or why.

I gave him a lift into Brantsford, and he now seemed fully recovered; he caught a bus back to Malton.

Several weeks later, I learned he had invited Ernie on a train ride from Malton to the Brontë country, which Ernie had always wanted to visit. They were two men who had shared a curious experience – or was it merely a dream? No one talks of the chariots any more, but I often wonder whether they still race across Wheeldale Moor at the crack of dawn.

On another occasion, I had to deal with a lengthman who cared for a stretch of modern moorland road. His name was Rodney James Featherstonehaugh, and he had been the Aidensfield roadman for some twenty years. During my time there, he was nearing retirement, and although others of his kind were being detailed to work in road gangs, Rodney was left alone to end his career around the village he loved. And he did a good job. He was responsible for the lanes around Aidensfield, Elsinby, Briggsby, Ploatby, Waindale, Lairsbeck, Maddleskirk and Crampton. He worked completely alone, although he was answerable to some distant and anonymous boss in the local Highways Department.

I was never sure how Rodney received his instructions or list of duties for the week, or whether any of his superiors ever came to visit him or inspect his work. But his work was immaculate. Without supervision, Rodney kept our lanes and byways in a state of near perfection. He gritted and sanded them in winter, dug out snow drifts or cleared gutters; he weeded the edges, trimmed the verges, clipped overgrown hedges and made sure all the road signs were maintained in a clean and legible state. Nothing seemed to be too much trouble. He was at his best during the winter, when he had an uncanny knack of anticipating frost and snow. Then he would be out at dawn, digging a route through the drifts or scattering salt on the icy stretches which caused the most difficulties.

The snag with a man like Rodney is that no one really appreciates him until he's gone. When he retired, he was missed – in fact, with oceans of goodwill, he would sometimes turn out in his own time, merely to clear a drain or salt a hill which was causing problems. He was that sort of man. His work was his life, and he loved the roads for which he had cared for so long. He knew every inch of them, their history, their weak points, the places liable to frost pockets or flooding. In short, Rodney was irreplaceable.

When he retired, no one took his place. The villages, through private individuals and formal representations by the parish councils, appealed for a replacement, but their pleas were ignored. The council said its team of highway operatives would maintain the roads with just the same care and to the same standard, but of course they could not and did not. Floods developed, drains were blocked, weeds grew apace, the verges thrived until they obstructed corners and blocked views. Rodney had made his mark on our locality.

I came across him quite frequently during my patrols, and I would always stop for a chat. We had a good understanding of one another's duties and areas of responsibility, and if I spotted something which needed his attention, such as a pot hole, damage to a direction sign or the emergence of a spring through the middle of the road, I would inform Rodney and he would do something about it. Similarly, if he knew there were to be roadworks in the area, such as occurred when laying a new surface or digging up a road to lay water mains or telephone lines, he would tell me. I felt that between us we provided a useful public service.

Rodney was very recognizable, even at a great distance. At times, I parked on some of our loftier ridges and saw his dark figure busy with his brush and shovel some miles down the dale. For some reason, he always wore black, which was surprisingly visible in daylight; he had a long black coat, like an army greatcoat, which he wore both summer and winter. His headgear was like a baseball player's cap, and in winter he wore black leather leggings over his stout and studded leather boots.

He pushed a council barrow around too. It was on two wheels, as the dustcarts of our cities used to be, and was really a dustbin on a pair of old car wheels. I think he had made it himself. He used it to contain the rubbish he collected, and it carried his tools – his huge, stiff brush, the shovel, a rod for clearing drains, a hammer and other essentials.

It was some time before I realized what he looked like beneath all that gear. Once I saw him in the Hopbind Inn at Elsinby, and it was a while before I realized that the swarthy, smart man at the bar was Rodney. Like his clothing, he was dark. He had a head of rich black hair with just a hint of grey; his eyebrows were black too, and so were his eyes. He had a black moustache and was swarthy and dark skinned, not through a suntan but through his ancestors. I sometimes wondered if he had gypsy blood in his veins, or whether some of his ancestors came from Spain or Italy.

I liked him. I found him totally honest and reliable, meticulous in his work and always good-humoured and willing in both his private and professional duties. Oddly enough, I never did discover whether he was married or had a family, for he never spoke about his home interests.

But of all the facets of Rodney Featherstonehaugh, the one which most intrigued me was his devotion to time-keeping.

From time to time when I was on patrol, I would see him sitting in the hedge bottom or in the entrance to a field, with his wheeled dustbin on hand, and on such occasions I would stop for a chat. In time I realized that these occasions were his official breaks. He started work at 7.30, with a ten-minute ''lowance' break mid-morning, a dinner break of half an hour at noon and a tea break of ten minutes during the afternoon, before finishing at 4.30 p.m. When I realized that these were his break time, I avoided chatting to him then – after all, a man is entitled to some time free from the cares of office – and I tried to talk to him when he was actually on his feet and going about his daily routine. He did not mind such interruptions, but I felt he should have some privacy. My own job had taught me the value of a meal which is uninterrupted by public demands.

Through regularly patrolling those self-same lanes, I became accustomed to Rodney's break times. I began to realize that when he was sweeping the grit of winter from the roads, to gather it and replace it in nice heaps by the roadside, he would take his first break at 10 a.m., with dinner at noon and his tea break at 2.30 p.m., all being serviced from the flasks, sandwiches, cakes and fruit he carried with him.

Then one bright and sunny June morning, at 9.30 a.m., I noticed him sitting in the entrance to a field just beyond Crampton Lane End. It was a junction where the lane from Crampton emerged onto the busier Malton to Ashfordly road. The road sloped quite steeply down to that junction, and Rodney's chosen gateway was right on the corner. It gave him long views along the road and up the hill. I could see him for some time before I arrived. His bin was nearby as usual, but this was half an hour earlier than his normal time and, knowing Rodney's meticulous time-keeping, I wondered if something was wrong. Maybe he was ill?

I drew up and parked, then clambered out to meet him.

'Morning, Rodney,' I greeted him. 'All right?'

'Aye, Mr Rhea.' He was munching a piece of fruitcake and had a flask of coffee at his side. 'It's 'lowance time.'

'You're early,' I said. 'I thought you might be ill.'

'Nay, Ah'm fine. They've changed my times.'

I presumed 'they' were the council.

'Oh, well, I won't trouble you . . .'

'We've changed areas,' he added, as if in explanation. 'Ah was under Ashfordly, now Ah'm under Brantsford, so they've changed my 'lowance time. Half-nine instead of ten.'

'But does it really matter?' I asked in all innocence.

'Aye, well, if they say half-nine, then half-nine it is. Ah mean, it *is* a bit early, if you ask me, but, well, Ah'm not in a position to argue.'

'No,' I smiled. 'We must all do as we're told, Rodney. Well, I must be off. I'm meeting the sergeant at Ashfordly, and I'd better not keep him waiting.'

'It's a nuisance, all this chopping and changing,' he grumbled as I prepared to leave. 'Ah can't see why they must keep on changing. Progress is all right so long as it doesn't change anything. That's how Ah sees it.'

I could sympathize with him. I have a theory that council managers and their white-collar staff, including their counterparts in other public bodies, regularly reorganize things in order to keep themselves in a job. Much work is generated by any reorganization, and at times it means that more staff are recruited to cope with the increase in paperwork. Reorganizations are wonderful job-creation schemes, even if they never achieve an improvement in efficiency or cost.

'You'll be on half-nine 'lowance for a while then?'

'Aye,' he said. 'And here, for all this week. I'm on this length, cutting hedges, trimming verges, guttering and the like.'

'I'll see you around then!' I smiled and drove away.

Sure enough, for the next couple of days, he was sitting in that same gateway from precisely 9.30 a.m. until 9.40 a.m.

And then, on the Thursday, I had an awful shock. I was on an early patrol, having started at 6 a.m., and my own breakfast break was scheduled for 10 a.m. at my own police house in Aidensfield. But a few minutes after 9.30 a.m. I received a radio call from Control to the effect that a lorry had run off the road and had gone through the hedge into a field at Crampton Lane End. There were injuries; an ambulance had been called, and a man who lived in a cottage at the lane end had witnessed the accident. He'd called the police with the news that somebody had been hurt. There were no further details. Switching on my blue light, I dashed to the scene. As I approached, I found myself worrying about Rodney. He had his break at Crampton Lane End at half past nine, and I knew the gateway was directly in the line of a runaway lorry . . . I pressed the accelerator.

I was relieved when I could not see his wheeled dustbin, but as I parked and hurried to the crashed lorry, I realized it had

run away down the hill, over the verge and then through the
very gateway that Rodney occupied. And it must have gone
through as near 9.30 a.m. as made no difference. So where
was he?

The lorry had run into the field beyond, then nose-dived
into a hollow; its load of rubble had not shifted, but the driver
was trapped in his cab. I found him groaning in agony; his
leg appeared to be trapped somewhere near the foot pedals.
He was alone. Jim Lewis from the cottage was on hand and
helped me give comfort to the driver. I radioed for the fire
brigade, saying we would need cutting gear, and in the busy
time which followed, I forgot about Rodney. He was nowhere
to be seen. In time, we released the driver and rushed him
off to hospital with a suspected broken leg, chest injuries and
concussion, then a breakdown truck was contacted to remove
the damaged lorry.

I now had an accident report to compile, and my day would
be fully occupied. I gave no further thought to Rodney's near-
brush with death until I had to fill in the accident report later
that day. I was working in the office which is attached to the
police house, using my faithful little typewriter. In the space
for 'Time of Accident', I wrote '9.30 a.m.', the time given to
me by Jim Lewis. He was sure about that – he'd tuned into
the radio news just as the lorry crashed. As I entered the time,
I wondered where Rodney had got to. But even as I worked,
there was a knock on the office door. I opened it to find Rodney
standing there, accompanied by his faithful bin.

'Oh, hello, Rodney. Come in.'

'Nay, Ah shan't stay, Mr Rhea. Ah just wondered if Ah
could ask a favour.'

'Of course. What is it?'

'That wagon this morning, it went through yon gateway
. . .'

'And I was very worried that you could have been injured,'
I said. 'It went right through that gate you've been using – and
spot on half past nine too!'

'Aye, Ah know, but, you see, Mr Rhea, Ah didn't have
my 'lowance till ten this morning. I wasn't there when she
crashed.'

'You could have been killed if you had been there!' I cried.

'Aye, t'reason Ah came was, well, if anybody from t'council asks, Ah'd not want 'em to know Ah took my 'lowance break late.'

'I can't imagine anybody checking on that, Rodney!'

'Well, you never can tell, Mr Rhea. Ah mean, Ah'm supposed to take 'lowance at half-nine, not ten. And today Ah didn't. Ah took it late, you see . . . contrary to instructions.'

'And saved your own life in the process, eh?' I smiled.

'But you will back me up, won't you?'

'Of course I will, Rodney. If anybody asks, I'll say you were in that next gateway, eh? At half past nine.'

'Aye,' he relaxed now. 'Thanks, Ah'll say t' same.'

'As a matter of interest, Rodney, why did you take a late 'lowance?'

'My old cart got a flat tyre. I took her to t'garage to get it fixed and took my 'lowance there, while they fixed it. It took me half an hour to get there, you see . . .'

'I see,' I smiled. 'Never fear, Rodney, your secret is safe with me.'

And off he went, very pleased at his own piece of subterfuge. I don't think he realized he owed his life to that flat tyre, but I did wonder what went through his mind each day as he worried about his unseen bosses. If I knew them, they wouldn't know of his existence. Poor old Rodney, he was a slave to his own conscience, a lovely chap.

•

3 'Sup That!'

Mid pleasures and palaces though we may roam,
Be it ever so humble, there's no place like home.
J.H. Payne (1791-1852)

One aspect of rural life which continues to fascinate me is the
wealth of differing styles in the cottages and houses found in
most small villages. In some cases, they are in very isolated
locations. They represent the entire range of social classes and
aspirations, but in a village community most of their owners
live happily together. Millionaires and professional people live
next door to labourers and lorry-drivers. You cannot reproduce
that social mix in modern housing estates – they tend to be
limited to people of one kind or class, and the houses are all
too similar.

Most of us know of stockbrokers' ghettos, professional
parades, executive avenues and council towerblocks, but
these communities lack the character of a true village whose
community spirit has matured over centuries. I believe that in
modern times no one is capable of designing or constructing
a genuine village with all its charm, benefits and close-knit
atmosphere. A village needs time to mature; it must evolve
over many generations and contain many generations. A true
village is a splendid place in which to live and bring up one's
children.

So far as the houses are concerned, the lack of planning
control in times past has produced a fascinating mixture of
good and bad, of ugly and beautiful, of large and small. At
one end of the scale, there is the grandeur of the Big House
where His Lordship or the squire used to live (and in many
cases continues to live), and at the other there is the rustic
simplicity of tiny cottages which serve the basic needs of

their occupants. Between these extremes is a range of other homes, sometimes in terraces, sometimes semi-detached, but very frequently standing alone in a much-loved piece of well-tended ground. All are rich in contrast and full of interest.

Perhaps that is over-simplifying the position, especially as it affects the moorland and dales around Aidensfield. For example, the word 'hall' can indicate something as massive as Castle Howard, which achieved fame as 'Brideshead' on television, or it could refer to a small farm deep in the hills. One famous hall on the edge of my beat had a cricket field on the lawn where the Yorkshire first team would sometimes play. In direct contrast, I have visited halls which were smaller than a semi-detached house.

Similarly, the name 'castle' appears in the names of some houses. Danby Castle in Eskdale is a small working farm, although in Henry VIII's time it *was* a castle. Indeed, one of his wives, Catherine Parr, lived here. There are other occupied homes around the moors which bear the suffix 'castle' and are very handsome and well-maintained; these are not open to the public because they are private houses. Of several Bumper Castles, one is a farm, while another is a pub. Slingsby Castle, for example, is not a true castle. It is a fine example of an Elizabethan type of house, although it dates from the time of Charles II. Now in ruins, it was never completed and has never been occupied – but it is massive and imposing, even though it was built for a dwarf, Sir Charles Cavendish. He was clearly a little man with big ideas.

Contradictions can also be found in the word 'house'. A dwelling with this common name can be very substantial or it might be a tiny cottage nestling in the quieter part of a moorland village. For the patrolling constable, it all means that one cannot gain a true impression of a person's home merely from its name.

One example was Bracken Hill Farm at Gelderslack. Believing its name has some rapport with the moors, I expected a small hill farm of the kind that had survived for generations, but to my surprise I found a massive spread of whitewashed buildings, with a hacienda that might have come from Spain, a range of satellite extensions that reminded me of a Californian ranch, and views that reminded me of the Loire Valley in France. Even the vehicles in the farmyard might have come from either Texas or the Motor Show.

Another surprise occurred when I was called by a lady who looked after Meadow Cottage, Crampton, while its owners were away.

As I motored to the address, I sought a pretty cottage sitting on the edge of a field replete with colourful wild flowers. Instead, I found a massive establishment with a courtyard surrounded by stables and looseboxes, complete with fabulous gardens overlooked by a house that occupied the space of half a dozen semi-detached dwellings. The gardens were spread along the banks of the river, and a small boat was moored at the edge of the lawn. It was probably the most unlikely 'cottage' I have ever encountered.

The reason for the lady's call is worthy of inclusion. She was housekeeper to Mr and Mrs Rudolph Faulkner. He was a top executive for a Yorkshire brewing company and was regularly away on business, often overseas. His wife, Felicity, sometimes accompanied him, and this was such an occasion. They had left the housekeeper, Mrs Winnie Hilton, in charge of their home for a couple of weeks. Winnie lived nearby and was the widow of a retired farmworker.

Just before lunch one Sunday, as she gazed across her garden fence, she noticed two coaches halt outside Meadow Cottage. This was not unusual, for the village did attract tourists. On this occasion, she watched a gaggle of almost a hundred people climb out. It was a warm, sunny day in June, and they were all armed with picnic equipment. At this point Winnie became horrified, because they all trooped through the gates of the Faulkners' home and into the splendid gardens before ambling across the lawns towards the river bank. Each was seeking a good place to enjoy a picnic. In this part of the country, it is a sad fact that some dopey visitors do wander into private gardens, but this was a mass invasion. Surely they had not mistaken Meadow Cottage for Castle Howard or Crampton Hall?

Winnie rushed outside to remonstrate with the bus-drivers, but they replied that they had been told to stop here for a picnic lunch. They had no idea who had given the orders to their firm; their order had come from their head office. She knew that if such a visit had been sanctioned by the Faulkners, she would have been informed. In the absence of such consent, she rang me to complain about the trespassers.

I was in the middle of my lunch and, as this was not an emergency, I spent another five minutes finishing my meal before driving the few miles to Crampton. This pretty village stands on the banks of the River Rye and is a delight; it is virtually unspoilt and presents a continuing aura of rustic calm. But things were not very calm that day because Winnie was stalking up and down in her pinny, her face as black as thunder.

'Now, Winnie,' I said, 'what's this all about?'

She repeated her story, pointing to the hordes of people on the Faulkners' lawn. They were enjoying their meal, for it was a splendid situation.

For my part, I knew my official limitations so far as trespass was concerned – simple trespass is not a criminal offence, nor is it a police matter. It could enter the realms of criminal law if certain other factors were incorporated, such as the pursuit of game or when committing malicious damage. But if these people did not have the Faulkners' authority, I felt I should at least try to remove them. I might be justified in so doing on the grounds that I was preventing a breach of the peace by Winnie!

As she fussed and grumbled, I spoke to the bus-drivers, who said they were simply obeying orders, and I then asked who was in charge of the party. They said it was a Mr Williamson, who was among the crowd by the river. With Winnie at my side, I set about locating him. My uniformed arrival caused something of a stir as I marched around and called for Mr Williamson. Eventually a nervous-looking individual with thin, light hair and rimmed spectacles disentangled himself from the crowd. In his early forties, he wore a green blazer and lighter green trousers, and I saw that most of the others in the party wore the same uniform. I now realized that the party comprised adults and young people mainly in their late teens. He faced me with a show of bravery and said, 'I'm Stanley Williamson.'

After introducing myself, I explained the problem as I understood it, but he looked puzzled.

'No, Mr Rhea, we have permission, I assure you. I got it from the headmaster.'

'But it's not his house. He can't give permission.' I pointed out. 'The Faulkners are away, and I'm assured they have not agreed to this.'

'They'd 'ave told me,' chipped in Winnie Hilton at my side.

My chat with Mr Williamson revealed that this was a party of choristers and musicians from a Yorkshire public school. They were on their way to give a concert at Keldford Hall, which lay about an hour's drive beyond Crampton. They were due there around 2.30 p.m. for rehearsals, and the concert was to begin at 6.30 p.m. after an early evening meal. The headmaster had suggested a break on the journey, hence the picnic lunch in the grounds of Meadow Cottage.

''E once came to stay here,' announced Winnie.

'Who did?' I asked her.

'That headmaster. He came for a weekend.'

'So he knows the house and the Faulkners?'

'Aye,' she said. 'Tim's at school there.'

I now began to see the proverbial dim light at the end of the proverbial long tunnel. 'Tim?' I asked.

'Their son, Timothy, 'e's in the sixth form.'

'That's right,' chipped in Mr Williamson. 'He should have been here today, he plays the violin, but he couldn't make it. He's broken his finger, playing cricket . . .'

'I think we'd better have words with the headmaster,' I suggested. 'Can we do it from the house?' I put to Winnie.

With Williamson and Winnie at my side, I entered the splendid lounge, courtesy of Winnie's key, and rang the school. Since it was a boarding school, the headmaster was available.

Upon my explaining the problem, he told me that when this concert had been first proposed, several months ago, he had asked Timothy Faulkner whether it would be agreeable if the choristers and orchestra halted at his parents' house. Knowing the house and its grounds, the head felt it was the ideal point for a break in the long journey. Tim had said it would be fine. The head had expected him to clear this proposal with his parents – clearly, Tim had not bothered.

To give due credit to the headmaster, two or three days before finalizing his arrangements he had called Tim to his study to check that his parents had approved the proposal. Tim, not admitting he had forgotten to ask and wishing to keep faith with the head, and also knowing that his parents would be out of the country on the day, had confirmed the plans.

'Obviously, Mr Rhea, there has been a breakdown in communication,' he said, and I could sense his embarrassment.

'So I've got a hundred trespassers in the grounds of an empty house,' I told him and, with him still on the line, I relayed the explanation to Winnie.

'That's just t'sort o' trick young Mr Tim would do,' she sighed. ''E really is the limit . . .'

'Can I suggest we allow these people to remain, provided they leave no mess?' I put to her.

'Aye,' she nodded. 'Seeing Mr Tim's said so.'

And so the crisis was over.

As Winnie locked the house, I walked away with Mr Williamson, who said, 'Thanks for sorting that out, Mr Rhea. The lady was upset.'

'She was just doing her job – and so was I. So you go back and enjoy the picnic – but please make sure your people leave things tidy, eh?'

'I will – and, look, by way of apologizing for the trouble we've caused, I've two complimentary tickets,' he dug into his pocket. 'Maybe you and Mrs Rhea would like to join us?'

'I'd love to,' I said. 'But how about Winnie and a friend? She's had more hassle than me! She has no transport, so it would mean taking her with you on one of these buses and then bringing her back again.'

'I think, under the circumstances, we could fix that,' he smiled.

And so Winnie Hilton and her friend Alice saw the rehearsals, had a meal with the group and had a look around Keldford Hall before going to the concert.

'By gum, Mr Rhea,' she said when I saw her a few days later in the village, 'I did enjoy yon concert. It's t'first time I've been to a posh affair like that.'

'What about Mr Faulkner? Was he upset about those picnickers?' I asked eventually.

'I never told him,' she said slyly. And neither did I.

Because the Faulkners' cottage was so splendid, I expected a similar spread at Thorngill Grange, a dwelling high on the moors above Gelderslack.

The reason for my call involved a missing hiker. A middle-aged man called Simon Milner had decided to tackle the long-distance Blackamoor Walk and had not arrived home at the expected time. He had been due back at tea time the day before my enquiries. Sensibly, Mr Milner junior had allowed time for his father to turn up or make contact before raising the alarm, but as neither had happened by breakfast time next morning, he decided to inform us.

Sergeant Charlie Bairstow took the call when I was in the office at Ashfordly.

'Right, Mr Milner, we'll circulate a description – I don't intend instituting a full search just yet. Perhaps he's called at a pub somewhere and stayed overnight?'

'A pub!' Milner junior had apparently been horrified at the suggestion. 'My father does not go into public houses, Sergeant. He is a Methodist lay preacher . . . a teetotaller . . . a man of strong principles and high morals!'

'It's just a thought, Mr Milner. No offence meant. I mean, our moorland inns are havens of refuge, you know, not dens of iniquity. You'll be sure to call us if he does turn up?'

He said he would keep us informed.

We circulated a physical description of the hiker, but at this early stage there was no real cause for alarm. Mr Milner, in his middle fifties, was an experienced rambler and was not known to be suffering from any illness or disease. Searching for hikers who had become overdue was a regular feature of our work. Many simply strayed from their chosen path or took longer than they had planned; more often than not, they found temporary accommodation in barns, inns and boarding houses, or even in friendly farms and cottages. In the case of Mr Milner, however, it seemed we could ignore the hospitality of the moorland inns.

Sadly, some hikers are a nuisance. Those who walk alone seldom bother to tell anyone of their route or intention, nor do they advise us of any enforced delay. As a consequence, at the behest of anxious friends or relatives, we often find ourselves searching for them, albeit in a very perfunctory manner in the early stages. But if they do not turn up, genuine concern develops and the longer the delay, the greater the concern and the more intensified the search, But, realistically, where does one begin to search 553 square miles of elevated and open moorland?

It was a curious fact that, in the months before Mr Milner's case, we had experienced an increasing number of problems with hikers. This had been especially noticeable among those attempting the long-distance Blackamoor Walk, a trek of around seventy miles across the loftier parts of the moors. It had become quite commonplace for some to stroll into Ashfordly market-place in the early hours of the morning, singing and shouting, having consumed bottles of strong liquor along their way. In some cases, there was a definite party atmosphere, and it seemed that parties of hikers were making whoopee somewhere on the hills. Their overdue return to civilization had not seemed to bother them, even if it had created anxiety among their friends and families.

As there were no pubs on the actual route of the Walk, these people must have diverted a considerable distance to get supplies – and that would cause delays and ultimately some worries among loved-ones waiting at home or at checkpoints. But there was another problem – in their happiness at reaching civilization, their singing and exuberance awoke the residents of Ashfordly; furthermore, they left their litter all over the place and in many cases became noisy, unpleasant and unwanted. It is fair to add that some who became too abusive or obnoxious ended their trip in our cells and even in court.

Some would sleep off the booze in barns or even in the open fields, but even in these cases, anyone who was overdue was likely to become the focus of an expensive search by the police or Moorland Rescue Search Party. Clearly, the upright and sober Mr Milner was not in this category. I could not imagine him rolling home in full voice after a session in a moorland pub.

It was ten o'clock that morning when I left Ashfordly police station to resume my patrol, and in the absence of more urgent work I decided to carry out a limited search for Mr Milner. I selected the area around Thorngill Grange. In that vicinity, a section of the Blackamoor Walk passed through the north-western corner of my beat before terminating at Ashfordly.

Having determined that Mr Milner was expected to conclude his hike along this stretch, I decided upon a modest search of the surrounding moor. A check on the map showed that Thorngill Grange stood on the edge of the heathered heights, close to where the Walk dipped from the more remote sections before entering a wooded glen for its final three miles or so. Until now, I had never had any reason to visit Thorngill Grange, but a check on the Electoral Register showed me that it was occupied by Albert and Dorothy Potter. I had no more information about the place or its inhabitants.

It did not take long to discover that it was even more remote than the map had suggested. I reached the end of a rough, unmade track some time before catching sight of the house. The track deteriorated into a primitive footpath across the heather before dropping into the dale beyond. When I parked at the brow of the ridge, I could see the house sitting at the head of the dale. It would require a considerable hike to reach it. But this was neither a mansion, a gentleman's residence nor even a farm. It was a tiny thatched cottage, one end of which was derelict while the other seemed barely suitable for anyone to occupy. A dry stone wall surrounded the cottage, but there was no name on the small wooden gate which opened into the paddock and nothing to indicate that this was Thorngill Grange. There was no other building nearby. The house stood utterly alone.

Beyond, on the heights above the other side of this tiny dale, was the open moor, treeless, flat and awe-inspiring. The wild expanse of heather was within a few days of bursting into the gorgeous purple which is so beautiful and dramatic. Running

from the heights was a moorland stream, the Thorn Gill which
gave its name to this cottage, and it flowed down a narrow cleft
in the hills, eventually to reach the River Rye near Rievaulx
Abbey. Black-faced sheep roamed these moors without the
benefit of fencing, and the paths they had created over the
centuries criss-crossed among the heather, some being utilized
by an increasing number of ramblers and hikers.

The Blackamoor Walk traversed these high and lonely
moors, and indeed there was a primitive stone footbridge
across the gill. It led from the main route of the Walk towards
Thorngill Grange, and I guessed the Potters made use of it to
check their sheep and lambs if indeed they farmed the moor.
But the bridge was not part of the Walk – the route passed the
end of it.

The views from this point were staggering in their range
and beauty, and as a perfect hideaway, Thorngill Grange must
surely be a dream. Perhaps the Potters used it only as a country
cottage? I would soon know the answer.

I opened the gate, which squeaked a little, and was greeted
by a black-and-white Border collie who fussed around my legs
as I made for the unpainted oak door. It opened even before I
reached it, and a very short, very fat woman in her late sixties
stood before me. Her greying hair was pulled back in a tight
bun, and she was wiping her hands on her apron; they were
covered in flour, I noted.

'By gum,' she smiled through gums which contained about
a third of their complement of teeth, 'it's a policeman!'

'Hello,' I greeted her. 'I'm PC Rhea from Aidensfield.'

'Well then, you'd better come in and sit down. Ah've a kettle
on t'hob. You'll have a cup o' tea and a bun?'

This was not an invitation – it was a statement of fact,
because it was customary for the moorland folk to entertain
visitors in this way, and I had arrived at ''lowance time'.

I ducked under the low beam above the doorway, the straw
thatching brushing my head as I removed my cap, and found
myself stepping back a century or even further. The low roof
was heavily beamed in dark oak. Some polished horse brasses,
genuine ones, plus a few horseshoes, were crudely nailed to
some cross timbers. The floor was of smooth sandstone, and

it bore a clip rug before the fireplace. The fireplace was a massive hole in the thick stone wall; in the right of the gap was a black oven with a brass handle and an ornate design on the door, while to the right was the hot water boiler, identified by the tap under which was a ladling can, a white enamel mug with a handle; it caught the drips from the tap. A peat fire was smouldering between them, and above it was a smoke hood, a relic of bygone times. Above the smouldering peat, hanging on a large hook which in turn dangled from an adjustable rail, was a large black kettle. It was singing all the time. In spite of the bright sunshine outside, the room was dark and cool.

Before asking the purpose of my visit, the little fat lady busied herself with warming the tea-pot, then disappeared into the pantry, where she piled a plate full of cakes, buns and cheese. She set it all before me on the plain, scrubbed wooden table, one end of which she was utilizing for her baking. She produced some milk in a metal can and poured it into a mug. Only then did she pour the water onto the tea leaves, and as the tea brewed, she continued with her baking as she talked to me. She was in fact making a 'tatie and onion pie, which she thrust into the oven. Then she settled beside me.

'That's for his dinner. Now then, what can I do for you?' Her smile revealed those awful gaps in her teeth. 'It's nice to 'ave a visitor, Mr Rhea.'

'Are you Mrs Potter?' I asked.

'Aye, that's me. Our Albert's out at work. Was it him you wanted?'

'Not particularly,' I answered, and then explained the purpose of my call, giving her a brief description of the missing Mr Milner. She listened, nodding from time to time.

'Aye, a chap like yon did pop in last night. He was fit and well, and we sent him on his way. They do come wandering this way,' she said slowly. 'They see yon bridge over t'gill and think it's part of t'main route. Some are that tired, they're walking in their sleep and just need an hour or two's rest. Ah've slept 'em in 'ere on bad nights, but yon middle-aged feller didn't stay. We gave him a drink and off he went. Singing tiv himself, he was. 'The Old Rugged Cross', I reckon it was supposed to be. He was in good fettle, Mr Rhea, I'll say that, and said he was heading for Ashfordly.'

'Thanks. I can check further down the dale. But if he does come back, ask him to get in touch with his son or the police at Ashfordly. He's overdue and we are just a bit worried about him.'

'Some daft folks treat these moors as if they're parks and gardens,' she said. 'They need respect, these moors, eh?'

'They do,' I agreed, and now she was pouring my mug of tea. She pushed the plate of cakes towards me.

I stayed longer than I should have, for she provided me with a fascinating account of her life at this remote place.

Her husband, Albert, had once farmed this patch of land, rearing sheep and Highland cattle, but as he was now nearing sixty-five, with no pension in sight, he had turned his hand to freelance gardening. This morning he was working for Sir William Ashdale and would be home for his dinner just after twelve. I decided to stay and meet him, for it was now almost twelve, and besides, that pie smelt wonderful . . .

Mrs Potter showed me around the little house, which they owned – they had paid £120 for it a few years earlier. The derelict portion had turf walls, parts of which were still standing, while its roof, once thatched with heather, had collapsed. There had been no attempt to repair it. That was where Albert had once kept his cattle or shorn his sheep. A cross passage separated that part from the living-accommodation, all of which was on the ground floor. There were two tiny bedrooms, each with a stone floor and beamed ceiling, but no bathroom or running water. They obtained their water from the gill; the toilet was a shed behind the cottage, and for electricity they had installed a generator which was petrol-driven – that was their only modern contraption.

By the time this tour ended, Albert had arrived. He used a pedal cycle of considerable size and vintage. His shovel, rake, hoe and gripe were tied to the crossbar. He placed his bike in a shed, then came towards me.

'Now then,' he said in the local manner of greeting.

'Now then.' I shook his hand. 'I'm PC Rhea.'

'Albert Potter,' he introduced himself. 'Thoo'll be coming in for thi dinner then?'

'No thanks. I had my 'lowance here not long since.'

'But it's dinner time now, and Ah shall be having mine, so you might as well join me.'

And so I did; I was not expected to refuse.

He was a tall and lanky fellow with arms and legs that seemed too long for his thin body. He wore a thick blue-and-white striped shirt with the sleeves rolled up, but with no collar. The neck was open, and a collar stud occupied one of the buttonholes. Heavy brown boots and thick brown trousers with braces completed his outfit. Fit and bronzed, he looked remarkably strong for a man in his middle sixties, but he was a man of few words. He sat and ate in silence, and I did likewise, savouring the potato and onion pie, then the apple pie and custard that followed. Then, without speaking, he went to a cupboard and opened it to reveal shelves full of bottles without labels. They contained fluids – red, yellow, brown, dark brown, dark blue, orange and other variations. He selected one which was full of a purplish liquid, removed the cork with a corkscrew, then poured me a glass full.

'Sup that,' he said. 'It'll put hairs on your chest.'

'What is it?' I asked, tentatively sniffing at the potion.

'Bilberry wine, good stuff. Eight years old if it's a day. Our Dot makes it,' and he drank deeply.

Wary of the fact that I was on duty and that I had to drive back, I took a sip. It was lethal. I had but a thimbleful and even with that tiny amount could sense its power – but it was really beautiful, smooth and full, rich with the flavour of the moors. But for all its beauty and delectability, it was powerful stuff.

'Good year for bilberries that year,' he said. 'Have some more, lad. See whether you can tell me whether them berries came from Sutton Bank Top or Bransdale or Fryup Dale.'

'You mean they all taste different?'

'They do that! Once you know 'em, they're as easy to tell apart as French grapes.'

I tried a little more, hoping for some indication of its source
. . .

Weakening, I tried still more, encouraged by this sombre character.

'I think it's Bransdale,' I said, but in truth I had no idea.

'No, this 'un's Bransdale,' and he produced another bottle from somewhere. 'Now, just you see t'difference.'

'I shouldn't,' I said. 'I mean, I am on duty . . .'

'Rubbish, it's good for your arteries, cleans 'em out, gets rid o' clots . . . here.'

He poured a huge helping and, in order to satisfy myself that there was a difference between Sutton Bank bilberries and Bransdale bilberries, I took a sip. Then I took a little more, just to make sure I was receiving the full flavour.

As I was doing my best to identify any distinctions, Dorothy came in.

'There's a couple of hikers at the door,' she said to her husband. 'They're asking for two bottles of Rievaulx rhubarb, two Ashfordly elderberry, two Egton Bridge gooseberry, two Rannockdale raspberry and a couple of Bransdale bramble.'

'There's enough, I reckon,' said Albert.

And as I became aware that I was slightly fuddled by the strong liquor, he poured me another helping, saying this was Fryup bilberries and maybe I'd like to compare it with the Fryup brambles or perhaps the Hollin Wood sloes. I was vaguely aware of Mrs Potter returning to put some money in a tin and of her husband saying, 'Think on and fetch a few bottles up from t'cellar. Dot . . .'

'Er,' – I sensed that my brain was no longer operating my voice in an efficient constabulary manner, but hoped I did not sound too stupid. 'Er, Albert, when that man called last night, the hiker we're looking for, er, well, did he sample your wine?'

'Aye,' said Albert. 'He said he never drank alcohol, so Ah said this wasn't alcohol. Ah told him it was home-made wine, full o' fruit and flavour. So he had a few, and that made him happier, so he bought a few bottles before he set off. Six, I think; all he could fit in his rucksack. He reckoned our Bilsdale bramble was like nectar and couldn't get enough of the Hambleton haw wine.'

'I'd better go for a walk,' I said, rising somewhat uncertainly from the chair.

'It's worst when you've had nowt to eat,' said Albert. 'But give it an hour and you'll be as right as rain.'

I thanked them, and they presented me with a bottle of Byland potato and Ashfordly redcurrant, which I placed in the van. The radio was burbling but I could not decipher the words – it wouldn't be a message for me. With legs feeling distinctly wobbly, I set off towards that little stone bridge; I could see two or three little stone bridges, so I aimed for the middle one, doused my head in the cool waters of that gill and then walked briskly in the fresh air. I walked for a long time, blissfully unaware of the hours that passed, but I did find a barn.

Quite suddenly, as Albert had indicated, I felt fine. It was almost as if a miracle had happened: the fuzziness cleared like a fog lifting, and I was sure I was no longer under the influence of Potter wine. I realized that the barn offered sanctuary for hikers – or constables who were sweating profusely and perhaps, if the truth was admitted, still just a little unsteady on their feet. And there, in the cool of the afternoon, I found the missing Mr Simon Milner. He was sitting on a bale of hay, singing softly to himself, with two empty bottles at his side.

'Mr Milner?' I managed to say.

'After goodnoon, Oshiffer.' He made a clumsy attempt at saluting me. 'I say, you should neck this sampler . . . sample this nectar . . . er . . . dog of the drigs . . . drink of the gods . . . God is a funderful wellow, eh? Giving us the earths of the fruit . . . providing us with the greed . . . the . . . ingredients . . .'

By now, I was reasonably in command of my own senses. 'Come along, Mr Milner, it's time to go home.'

He started to sing 'Time to go home' in the manner of television's Andy Pandy programme and waved his hand like that little puppet. I wished his son could see him now. With something of a struggle, I managed to get him back to the van and plonked him in the passenger seat.

I decided to tell Mr and Mrs Potter that I'd found him. As I went to their door, four more hikers were leaving with bottles of the potent Potter potion, and I now knew why we had so many very merry and excitable hikers in Ashfordly. They had no need of a pub with a supply of this kind available.

I thanked the Potters for their hospitality and left, driving Mr Milner down to the youth hostel in case his son had alerted them. As I drove away, I heard the radio calling me – and with horror I realized I had been off the air and out of contact for hours. The sergeant knew I was heading for the heights, and in all probability their inability to contact me since eleven that morning would mean I had been posted lost on the moors . . .

'Echo Seven,' called Control in a voice that rang with exasperation and worry. 'Echo Seven, receiving? Over.'

'Echo Seven receiving,' I responded in what I hoped was a matter-of-fact, calm manner. My head was clear. I was horrified to see it was nearly 4.30!

There was a long silence, and then another voice said, 'Echo Seven. Location please.'

'Echo Seven, Thorngill Moor, near the Blackamoor Walk route. I have just located the missing man, Mr Simon Milner. He is with me in the vehicle; he is fit and well, no injuries. My intended destination is Ashfordly youth hostel. Over.'

I could explain my long absence by saying I had obtained several differing clues and conflicting sightings about the hiker's whereabouts and, due to the uncertainty, it had taken me several hours to locate my quarry. The fact that I had found him would undoubtedly save me from a mammoth bollocking.

'Echo Seven. Upon your return, report to the duty inspector. He wishes to give you advice. A search party has been organized to look for you – you never booked off the air and there has been great concern . . .

I groaned as Control gave me a well-deserved reprimand over the air. I knew I had been guilty of the self-same thoughtlessness as the many hikers and, like them, I had imbibed the powerful juices of the Potters. I did not try to excuse myself over the radio, but sighed as I turned for home.

Mr Milner sighed at my side, but he was asleep; he was now in his own world of bucolic and alcoholic bliss; a nice

story for his chapel friends when he recovered. But I suppose
he could be honest because, after all, even though he had
strayed from his ways like a lost sheep, he had not entered a
pub.

As I drove through acres of maturing heather, a very
official thought occurred to me. If the Potters were selling
intoxicating liquor, they would require a justices' licence
and an excise licence, and they would have to abide by
the licensing hours. Or would they need an off-licence,
seeing their customers did not drink inside the premises?
If customers did enter to drink, the premises could be
classified as public house, and in addition there were certain
requirements applicable to the brewing of wines and spirits
. . .

I groaned. It all threatened to become very complicated.

I felt that a word of warning about the laws of selling
intoxicants would be my first task, rather than a heavy-
handed prosecution which involved the Customs and Excise
and the Liquor Licensing laws. But I did not know whether
I dare return, because if I did, old Albert would probably
ask me to test his Rannockdale turnip, Lairsbeck parsnip
or Thackerston carrot. I wasn't sure I would be able to
resist.

I decided it might be best to overlook this particular episode,
due to my own involuntary involvement and, to be precise, I
had no direct proof of their sale to customers. Hints yes, but
not proof.

But I could not shirk my duty. I decided that I must return
to advise Dot and Albert on the illegality of selling their wine,
if only to give Ashfordly and its people a break from merry
ramblers.

I did learn afterwards that news of this establishment had
reached the rambling clubs that passed this way and that most
of their members made a point of calling for refreshment.
Perhaps if the Potters opened a licensed restaurant, they
would be able to make some money? I might put that idea
to them.

Because they were not at that time licensed, it did mean that
Mr Milner had not disgraced himself by frequenting a pub. But

right now I had to get Mr Milner home and prepare myself for a telling-off by the inspector.

'Come on, Mr Milner,' I said to the inert figure in my passenger seat. 'It's time to go home . . .'

'Time to go home, time to go home.' In his fuddled state, he started to sing and wave ta-ta.

4 *April Fool!*

A joke's a very serious thing.
  Charles Churchill (1731–64)

When our eldest child, Elizabeth, started at the village school, we felt sure she would quickly learn all that was necessary to equip her for the future. Each afternoon, we would ask what she had learned that day, and it seemed that she was progressing very satisfactorily. Then one day she announced she had learned about April Fool jokes. I could not ascertain whether this gem of wisdom had come from the teachers or her classmates, but with the solemnity that only a 5-year-old can muster, she did say that the jokes must end at noon on 1 April and that nobody must be hurt by the pranks. This suggested a sense of responsibility.

Because this fruitful portion of learning had come to my notice in mid-March, I had forgotten about it by 1 April. Like almost everyone else, though, I was aware of April Fool jokes – indeed, police officers throughout the country play jokes upon each other or their bosses, taking care never to harm or disrupt the public peace in so doing. I have recounted several of these in earlier *Constable* books (see *Constable through the Meadow*).

For example, one mild joke involved an alteration of a list of telephone numbers in the police station – the superintendent's private number was listed as the 'new' number for the speaking clock. When an unsuspecting constable checked the time at 3 a.m., his enquiry was not well received.

Another constable had his private car number placed on the stolen vehicle index and as a result got stopped countless times by officers of other forces while on his way to a fishing match. Some constables have been told to check mortuaries for security, only to see 'corpses' sit up in the darkness. Another was confronted by a road-sweeper who was cleaning the town's street at 3 a.m. This rookie constable, having been told to stop and interview all suspicious people seen around at night, spoke to this character. The sweeper said he liked cleaning the streets at this time of day because it was quiet and they didn't get messed up again before he finished. In fact, the heavily disguised road-sweeper was one of his colleagues whom, as he was new to the town, the rookie did not recognize.

I have been guilty of some jokes too, several of which have appeared in print, such as the reported discovery of a gold mine in the grounds of Coultersdale Abbey, a North Yorkshire ruin, the appearance of the legendary boves in England from which we get the saying 'Heaven's a bove', and the location of a colony of miniature blind sabre-toothed tigers in an ancient Yorkshire caving system.

In addition to these pranks, there have been offers of lead-free pencils, UFO sightings, cars with self-repairing punctures, and the stone-by-stone removal of Whitby Abbey to a new site.

I liked John Blashford-Snell's account of a tribe of natives who carried their heads under their arms, and Richard Dimbleby's famous television documentary about the spaghetti harvest. And there are many others that have appealed to my sense of humour.

But I did not like 5-year-old Elizabeth's April Fool joke.

It began one Saturday morning, when she was off school. She was out of bed rather early, and I should have expected something of a mischievous nature from the knowing grin on her face. But, like a lamb going to slaughter, the significance of the date had temporarily escaped me as I concentrated on lots of paperwork which I had to complete before going on duty. I ignored the danger signs exhibited by Elizabeth, one of which involved her hanging around my office while looking distinctly pleased with herself.

I was working mornings, which was especially pleasing on a Saturday, and I now had a four-hour route to perform. This had been pre-determined by the sergeant. I had to begin at 9 a.m., patrol to Elsinby for a 10 a.m. point at the telephone kiosk, followed by points at Crampton kiosk at 11 a.m., Briggsby at noon and then back home to book off duty precisely at 1 p.m. 'Point' was the name we used to indicate the time and place we had to be for a possible rendezvous with the sergeant or other senior officer. During this patrol, I would visit a few outlying farms to check some stock registers and discuss the renewal of one or two firearms certificates.

At ten minutes to nine, I went into my little office which adjoined the police house at Aidensfield and telephoned the police station at Ashfordly. This was a daily ritual to see whether any messages awaited me. I was given a list of stolen vehicles, details of a couple of overnight crimes, and the description of a missing woman. It was a very routine start to my day.

I had to depart from my house at nine o'clock precisely. All my supervisory officers, and Sergeant Blaketon in particular, were keen on precise timing. Nine o'clock meant exactly that, not a minute past nine nor even a minute *to* nine. And I knew Sergeant Blaketon was on duty this morning; that meant he could be sitting outside my house in his official car, checking on whether or not I had managed to climb out of bed following my 1 a.m. finish this same morning. In his mind, punctuality was of paramount importance, and I do believe we sacrificed many fruitful enquiries and duties in order to be at a specific place at a specific time, just in case Oscar Blaketon was checking.

But on this fine spring morning things were going to plan. I had my cap on, my notebook was up to date and everything was in order by two minutes to nine. I kissed Mary and the children goodbye, still not comprehending the menace of Elizabeth's knowing grin. I went into the office for my van keys – I kept them on a hook under the counter.

They weren't there. They were not hanging in their usual place. I was sure I'd put them there last night when coming off duty. It was where I always hung them. I checked my uniform pockets without success, then rushed upstairs to see if they were on the bedside cabinet. They weren't. I checked my pockets again . . . then the bedroom floor, the bathroom floor . . . downstairs into the kitchen, into the downstairs loo, back to the office again . . .

'Have you seen the van keys?' I shouted to Mary as the clock struck nine. She was busy in the kitchen, washing the breakfast pots.

'You always put them on that hook in your office.'

'I know, but they're not there.'

'They must have fallen off. You're so careful with your keys, especially official ones,' came the voice from the kitchen.

'Then you haven't seen them?'

'No, I never do! I have no need to.'

'I haven't put them down on the draining-board or the breakfast table, have I?'

'No, I've cleared the table, I'd have seen them.'

I groaned. I decided to peep outside to see if Sergeant Blaketon had arrived. Fortunately, he had not. The coast was clear, which allowed me a few more minutes to continue my frantic search. I retraced my routine procedures, checking all the likely places again and again, and it was then that I realized that Elizabeth was following me around and scrutinizing all my actions – grinning the whole time.

'Elizabeth,' I asked, halting a moment in my anguish, 'have you seen daddy's keys? The keys for the police van?'

She clenched her lips and smiled in her silence. Mary had come through to my office at this stage and witnessed this behaviour. Elizabeth's grin was rather like that of the Mona Lisa with teeth.

'Elizabeth?' Mary recognized the mischief in that smile. 'Have you got daddy's keys?'

The response was a more firmly clenched mouth and fixed smile, with her tiny, round face going red with the effort of containing herself.

'Look, Elizabeth,' I said, 'Daddy's got to go to work and he must have the van keys. He can't get into the van without them – he can't switch the radio on and can't go to work.'

There was a spare set of keys, but they were kept on a board in the sergeants' office at Ashfordly police station, and I had no wish to allow Oscar Blaketon to learn of my dilemma by requesting them.

'Elizabeth,' Mary now took up the challenge, 'if you have got daddy's van keys, you must say so. He has to go to work, and the sergeant will be very cross if he doesn't go out in the van. Now, where are they?'

'April Fool, Daddy!' she grinned, her tight little mouth now opening as she could contain herself no longer. 'Daddy's an April Foo-hool!' she chanted.

I should have realized; I should have connected her wicked grins with the arrival of All Fool's Day, but I had not. I had to laugh at my own stupidity. I'd been well and truly caught.

'All right, Elizabeth, you made daddy an April Fool. Now, can I have the keys?'

'I have to keep them hidden till twelve o'clock,' she said solemnly. 'You're not a real April Fool if you get them back before twelve o'clock, and I know when twelve o'clock is. It's when both pointers are on twelve.'

'No, Elizabeth, you mustn't,' I tried to reason with her. 'You have made an April Fool out of daddy because he could not find the keys, so you've won. Now, I'd like my keys.'

'They said at school to wait till twelve o'clock,' she announced, that resolute line appearing on her face. 'And I'm not telling you where the keys are, Daddy.'

'Elizabeth . . .'

'You're an April Fool if you can't find them!' she began to chant.

Then the telephone rang.

'You answer it,' I entreated Mary. 'If it's the office, tell them I'm on patrol. Say I went out at nine.'

Mary did so. I heard her announcing that to whoever was calling, and she came back to say, 'It was Eltering office. You haven't booked on the air. They were checking.'

'They've booked me on now, have they?'

'They said it must be bad reception. Come on, Elizabeth, don't be silly . . .'

'I am not being silly!' she stamped her feet. 'April Fooling daddy is not silly. Everybody will be doing it.'

It became very evident that Elizabeth was not going to reveal her hiding-place. It was no good wasting time arguing – time was pressing and I had to do something positive. I did consider making all the clocks and watches show the time as twelve o'clock but I didn't think that would fool her. My only option was to go on patrol, otherwise I could be in serious trouble from Sergeant Blaketon and, because the van was now out of commission, I needed some alternative transport. I decided to use my own car, hiding it where necessary. I could make those hourly points, and if any senior officer challenged me, I could claim either that the radio reception was poor or that my van would not start. Both were correct! And then, after twelve noon, I could return home when, hopefully, Elizabeth would return my keys.

As Elizabeth stood with a grin of triumph upon her face, I knew I should remonstrate with her, and yet it seemed such a cruel thing to do when she was flushed with triumph. I could not be angry with her, not now. My own frustration had evaporated, and so I decided I would regard her triumph as a genuine victory. I praised her for her cleverness and headed for my car.

Fortunately, she had not hidden its keys, and so I made my way to the first point. I must admit I did so with some trepidation because, if the office had been trying to raise me on the radio, I would be subjected to a form of inquisition. But as I stood beside the telephone box at Elsinby there was no phone call and no visit from the ever-vigilant Sergeant Blaketon. From ten o'clock until eleven, I continued to visit outlying farms in my own car, the change in my transport not causing a flicker of interest in the farmers upon whom I called. At eleven, there was no telephone call at Crampton kiosk and I decided that, immediately after my noon point at Briggsby, I would drive home, hopefully to retrieve the keys from Elizabeth so that I could complete my tour of duty in official transport. Looking back upon the events of that morning, I suppose I had a charmed existence, because there were no official calls at the telephone kiosks, which in turn meant no one had been endeavouring to raise me on the radio.

Having completed my noon point, therefore, again with no calls from the office, I rushed home. Upon my return, Elizabeth was waiting with a triumphant smirk on her little face, and I admitted to her that I was an April Fool of the very best kind. I had not been able to prevent her trick from enduring until noon, and I knew I should be the subject of some discussion at school on Monday.

'So, Elizabeth,' I smiled, 'where are my van keys, please?'

'I was a very good hider, wasn't I?' she smiled at me.

'Yes, you were,' I had to agree. 'A very good hider indeed. Now, I must finish my tour of duty, Elizabeth, so can you get daddy's keys, please?'

'I've forgotten where I put them.' She stuck a finger in her mouth as she stared at me.

'But you can't . . . Mary!' I shouted. 'Mary, now she can't remember where she's hidden my keys!'

'Never mind, darling,' Mary patted me on the shoulder. 'You go and finish this patrol, and I'm sure Elizabeth and I can find your silly old keys.'

So I completed that patrol in my own car, and it was with some relief that I eased into my drive prompt at one o'clock to book off duty. I went into my office, happy that I'd been able to check a great many outstanding stock registers. Before lunch, I settled down to finalize my notebook with entries of my day's duties.

As I worked, Mary came in, albeit a little sheepishly.

'Darling,' she began, and I knew from the tone of her voice that there was a problem. 'Darling, I'm afraid Elizabeth genuinely can't remember where she's hidden your keys.'

As I groaned, the telephone rang. It was Sergeant Blaketon.

'Rhea?' he bellowed into the telephone. 'Where the devil have you been? We've been trying to raise you on the radio for the last twenty minutes. You are the only patrol on duty in the section. I need assistance.'

'Sorry, Sergeant,' I said. 'There was bad atmospherics . . . reception was poor all morning . . .'

'Yes, I guessed that. So get yourself down to Brantsford immediately. I need assistance, urgently.'

'Right, Sergeant,' I acknowledged. 'What is your location in Brantsford?'

'The police office, Rhea. Rendezvous there.'

I puzzled over his problem and had no alternative but to forgo my lunch and rush off in my own car. This morning's episode was costing me a fortune in petrol. Fifteen minutes later I parked on the hardstanding outside Brantsford police station and went in to meet the sergeant. He had heard my arrival, but his own problems were such that he apparently did not notice I was not in the official van.

'Sergeant?' I rushed into the office where he was waiting for me.

'Ah Rhea, sorry to drag you from your lunch, but I'm the victim of an April Fool's joke. Some idiot has let all my tyres down. I need help to change the wheels. The jack won't go under the car . . . and I need assistance to get them all blown up.'

Had I been in the mini-van, I knew that its jack would have been useless for this task, but I did have my own hydraulic jack. It was in the boot of my car. It was not issued with the vehicle but was my own property, a most useful present from my father. And so, my using that piece of equipment, I helped him raise the official car off the ground, first removing the two rear wheels, which we had inflated by a local garage, then the front ones and finally the spare, which was softer than it should have been. It was a long job.

'Thank you, Rhea,' he said when it was all over. 'I do hate being the subject of such pranks. Perhaps we can forget this ever happened, eh? As colleagues? As man to man?'

'I'm sure we can, Sergeant,' I agreed, wondering how long it would take me to recover my own official keys from Elizabeth's hiding-place. If that took a long time, I would need his co-operation. One good April Fool's joke deserved another, I felt.

But I needn't have worried. Mary found the keys after lunch. Elizabeth had hidden them in the ironing-board. There was a small hole in the cover, just large enough to slide in the keys from a mini van. Elizabeth, having remembered that Mary had once lost a brooch in there, had considered it a perfect hiding-place for the mini-van keys. Mary had found them as she'd lifted the ironing-board from its parking place – the keys had jingled in their secret nest.

I put them in my pocket and made a resolution not to leave them on the hook on All Fool's Day next year, and to cut myself a spare copy of them, just in case.

My short involvement with Sergeant Blaketon that day did have its merits. That night, he told me to finish an hour earlier than usual on my second tour, a 10 p.m. to 2 a.m. shift. He would cover the extra hour, he said, so my 1 a.m. finish was a thank-you from him.

It was highly appreciated as I curled up in bed against Mary's warm body for an extra hour on a cool spring morning. I thought Elizabeth had done me a good turn after all.

Practical jokes, were not, however, restricted to April Fool's Day. Although some were fun, others could be malicious. In reflecting upon Sergeant Blaketon's four flat tyres, I did wonder whether they were the result of a real joke or whether they were an act of malice. I had a sneaking suspicion they were the latter.

From time to time, reports of acts of a malicious but supposedly jocular nature were received at our offices. Quite often, they were perpetrated by one neighbour upon another usually from spite or revenge. We dealt with damaged cars, paint sprayed on doors or gates, damaged garden plants or greenhouses, broken windows and a host of petty nuisances. The perpetrators regarded them as jokes, the victims regarded them as menacing, and the police regarded them as a crime of malicious damage. Some perpetrators were never prosecuted because there was insufficient evidence to support a court appearance, even though the villain was known.

One such troublesome series of pranks occurred at Elsinby; it caused me a lot of work before I eventually traced and dealt with the culprit. During my enquiries, I was to learn that a lot of incidents had happened at the Hopbind Inn before I was made aware of them. For example, one trick was to lash the bumpers of parked cars to benches outside the pub. When a driver set off home at closing time, he would find himself towing a bench along the High street – which did not do much good to the bench. Then the pranks grew more serious. One car bumper was lashed to that of a car parked behind it, and so a tug-of-war developed between the two vehicles, sometimes resulting in the separation of the said bumper from the car.

It was at this stage that the landlord, George Ward, told me of these occurrences. He stressed that this was not an official complaint. Indeed, he was not the victim; his customers were the victims. He was merely making me aware of the on-going series of pranks because of their nuisance value.

Strictly speaking, it was no concern of mine unless and until I received a formal complaint from one of the 'injured persons', as we termed all victims of crime whether or not they suffered physically. After this unofficial notification, though, whenever I paid a visit to the Hopbind Inn, whether on duty or not, I would discreetly ask whether further pranks had been played. It seemed they came in short bursts and always under cover of darkness. Weeks would pass without anything happening, and then there would be a series of related incidents all within, say, a week. Then there would be another lull until a further outbreak occurred.

It seemed almost as if the joker was producing new ideas which he would use for a few days before turning to something else – when the lashed bumper-bar idea had run its course, he spent a week smearing windscreens with grease. After that, he switched on the cars' headlights so that the batteries became exhausted. Flat tyres were deployed, as were eggs broken upon roofs, or dustbin lids roped to the rear wheels – the clatter they made as the wheels turned was unbelievable.

From my point of view, there was one interesting feature: none of the pranks was truly malicious. For example, the tyres were not slashed, the cars' paintwork was not dented or scraped with coins, their petrol tanks were not filled with sugar, and their engines not interfered with. In other words, these were fairly harmless pranks which did not result in permanent damage. They were little more than a nuisance.

I patrolled the area whenever I was on duty, sometimes concealing myself in the churchyard or among shrubs and trees which allowed me to observe the pub and its car-park. Like the villain, I operated under cover of darkness, but I never saw any of these acts committed. Neither did anyone else – the prankster was never seen. This was odd. He seemed to know when he was able to operate. If only I could catch him in the act, I could threaten him with prosecution, and that would surely halt this silly behaviour.

Over the duration of these pranks, I never received any official complaint from the victims, and I regarded this as an acceptance of their minor nature. But they did become more serious as time went by. On one occasion, the door handle of a small van was lashed to the wooden framework of the porch of the inn – and when the van set off, down came the porch. Another time, one end of a rope was tied around one of the fence posts of the railings outside the inn, the other end being tied to a pick-up truck. And when the pick-up moved off, the railings were demolished. But even so, I never received any formal complaint, even though the regulars were aware of my interest. I did encourage them to make a report, but none did and I began to wonder why there persisted this apparent group reticence.

As the pranks continued, I received details through local gossip, and it was noteworthy that every incident occurred outside the Hopbind Inn. Nothing of this kind happened inside the pub, nor did the pranks extend into other areas of the village. From time to time, I discussed them with George, the landlord, and he accepted they were a nuisance but that no one seemed unduly bothered.

Then there was a fairly serious event. Outside the pub, on its extensive forecourt, were two petrol pumps. In addition to filling his customers with ale, George would also fill their cars with petrol, and the prankster chose to lash a tractor to one of those pumps. He had used a strong rope which he'd found on the tractor, and when the machine set off, it almost dragged the petrol pump to the ground and nearly fractured the pipes inside. This time, George decided to report it to me and to make it official.

'If you'd reported it earlier, George, I could have arranged long-term observations with my colleagues. We might have stopped these goings-on by now. There's a limit to the time I can spend sitting in bushes.'

'We don't want official action taking, Mr Rhea,' he said. 'We want it dealt with without any court appearances or owt like that.'

'But I can't taken an official report from you on those terms, George. Once I've made it formal, I will have to take the culprit to court, if we track him down.'

'Then I withdraw my official complaint, Mr Rhea. Look,

you are our local bobby, surely you can stop this carry-on before it gets out of hand, before real damage is done or somebody gets hurt?'

'I can't stop it, George, if I don't know who's involved. I must catch him in the act if I am to stop him. I've kept observations out there for weeks now, I've asked questions around the village, but no one tells me who's doing these things. We all know it's going on and has been going on for weeks, but no one will tell me who's behind it. I suspect you all know . . .'

He regarded me steadily. 'Aye,' he said. 'We all know but we don't want the lad taken to court.'

'Then if you know, you'll have had words with him yourselves?'

'Aye, lots of us have spoken to him, but it only makes him worse.'

'I think you and I had better have a long talk, George,' I said.

'Then you'd better come in, Mr Rhea.'

Over a coffee in his private lounge, George told me the story. His first statement confirmed something I had suspected for a while – that all the victims were related.

'They're all cousins, half-cousins and even quarter-cousins,' he said. 'Except me. Those whose cars were tied up or messed up are all related.'

'A local family?' I asked.

'Aye, all living hereabouts. They're all Pattons, but some have different names through marrying.'

'So is the culprit a Patton or from another family who's got some grudge against them?' I asked.

'He's one of the Pattons,' he said, clearly expecting me to know which one. But there was a huge family whose members were spread right across the dale and the moors beyond. I knew several of them, albeit not very well, but could not guess which was the phantom prankster.

'I'm sorry, George. I don't know all the Pattons, and I have no idea which is the troublemaker.'

'It's young Noel,' he said. 'We all know it's him; mind, nobody's caught him at it, nor even seen him.'

'So how do they know?' I asked.

'It's common knowledge in the family.' George poured me a second coffee. 'The lad's not all there, if you know what I mean. He's not daft enough to be certified or sent into a mental institution, but he was at the back of the queue when God was dishing brains out. He's about eleven pence to the shilling. He works on one of the family farms, Dykegate Farm, labouring, doing basic jobs, and he bikes there every day.'

'That's off my patch.' I knew the farm, but it was on the beat of a neighbouring constable. 'So where's he live?'

'Pattington, in Long Row, number eight. With his mum. She's a Patton – not married, by the way.'

'So he's got no dad?'

'It's worse than that, Mr Rhea. They reckon Noel's dad was her own brother.'

'So he's the product of incest!'

I could now understand why the family did not want this lad prosecuted. If he appeared before a court, his family history would have to be presented to the magistrates, and no one wanted to open up old secrets or have the family's shame discussed in the pages of the local press. As Pattington was off my patch and in a different police division, I had never visited the village on duty, and this explained why I did not know the lad or his family.

'Aye, it was a sad thing, but the father is now married and working not far away. He's one of the Pattons, well respected, a chapel-goer an' all,' said George. 'His wife doesn't know Noel's his son; outsiders all think he's a nephew.'

'Well, he is!' I put to George. 'He's the fellow's nephew as well as his son!'

'You wouldn't think he was any relation, the way some of the Pattons treat him. They treat him like a dog at times, they tolerate him around, no one really loves him. Even his mother tries to ignore him.'

This chat enabled me to understand the motive behind Noel's actions. He seemed to be getting at his family for their attitude towards him, and I could also understand the desire for family unity and secrecy. In spite of all this, I knew, for the sake of all, that Noel's silly behaviour must be halted. If he was allowed to continue his pranks, they would grow more daring and more serious until one day there would be a serious accident or injury.

'Does he come into your pub?' I asked George, for I wanted to have a look at this youth, so that I'd know him in the future.

He shook his head. 'His mother's a strict chapel woman,' he told me. 'Alcohol and pubs are not regarded as proper, so she's brought Noel up to believe drink is evil – mebbe she was drunk when he was conceived . . . or his dad might have been. His real dad won't go into a pub but drinks whisky at home, gallons of it. He buys it from me, telephones his order in and the shop delivers it with the groceries. He thinks it's all a secret. Anyroad, Noel never comes in either. I think that might be a motive for his tricks as well. Mebbe he's getting at those of his clan who do indulge in evil spirits!'

I thanked George for his wealth of knowledge and told him I appreciated his confiding in me. Now that I was aware of the background, it explained a lot and was helpful – but how could I halt Noel's silly behaviour?

In the weeks that followed, he played more tricks: balloons appeared on one car, another's windows were painted with white emulsion, and a chunk of wallpaper was glued to the door of yet another. I attributed all this to Noel, even though I had never set eyes on the lad, for all the cars belonged to members of the Patton family.

I kept observation on the pub forecourt without ever catching sight of Noel, and I did have words with the village constable for Pattington and explained the situation to him. He knew Noel but said the lad never caused any trouble on his patch. I learned he was in his early twenties, fairly tall and slim, with long blond hair, and he rode a red bike with dropped handlebars.

Then, quite by chance, I was off duty in Ashfordly and doing some shopping in Thompson's hardware shop when I became aware of the presence of a young man of that description. He was selecting various objects from the shelves and popping them into a basket – they were things like shelf-brackets, wall plugs, screws and other DIY items. I peeped outside the large window and saw a red racing bike propped against the wall. So this was young Patton, I guessed. Then he went to the counter and asked for a box of 200 rounds of .22 ammunition.

'Have you your certificate?' the shopkeeper asked.

It is illegal to sell such ammunition to anyone who is not the holder of a firearms certificate, and the seller must endorse the certificate with the amount and type he sells. This does not apply to shotgun ammunition, nor pellets for air weapons, but it does strictly apply for ammunition – i.e. bullets – for use with rifles and such handguns as revolvers and pistols. Clearly, this lad had such a weapon.

I hovered behind a tall display stand and listened. This knowledge would be of use to me.

'I haven't a certificate,' said the youth. 'I allus uses my uncle's bullets. He lets me.'

'Who's rifle is it?' asked the shopkeeper.

'Mine,' said Noel. 'Me grandad gave me it.'

'Well, you must have a certificate for the rifle, so fetch that in and I can let you have the bullets.'

'No,' said the lad. 'I've no certificate for t'gun, never 'ave had. I just have it and borrow bullets. But I thought I'd try to buy some for myself. I am over seventeen, so how can I get this certificate?'

'You'll have to apply to the police,' said the shopkeeper. 'And if they think you are a fit and proper person to possess such a firearm, you will be granted a certificate.'

'Aye, right,' said Noel, paying for his odds and ends.

When he left the shop, I followed. I could not let this opportunity pass without making use of it.

As he placed his purchases in the pannier behind the saddle, I said, 'Hello, are you Noel Patton?'

'Aye.' He stood up and looked at me, a puzzled expression on his face. I was not wearing uniform.

'I'm PC Rhea from Aidensfield,' I introduced myself. 'Part of my responsibility is the Hopbind Inn at Elsinby.'

'Oh aye.' He looked me up and down but gave nothing away.

'I have reason to believe you have been making a nuisance of yourself there, playing tricks on cars and things.'

He said nothing. Simple though he might be, he was shrewd and cunning, I realized.

'All I want to say, Noel, is that it must stop. No more pranks, no more jokes on your family or their cars when they're at the pub. No more ropes tied to bumpers, petrol pumps and the like.'

'Who said it were me?' he suddenly shouted.

'It doesn't matter who said it was. I know it was. All I'm saying is that it must stop. Right now, as from today. No more pranks, right?'

'Nobody's seen me, nobody knows . . .'

'I know it's you, Noel, and so do lots of other folks. Now, I happen to know you have a rifle without a certificate. I could get you sent to prison for that.'

'Grandad gave it to me. It's from the big war.'

'No matter, you must have a certificate. Now, as I said, I'm the policeman at Aidensfield, and if there are any more pranks outside the Hopbind, I'll take you to court for having that gun without a certificate. Do you understand?'

'Prison?' he gasped.

'If you misbehave,' I said grimly. I had over-emphasized the penalties but felt it justified if it stopped his antics.

'No more pranks then, Mr Policeman. I'm sorry. It's just they keep getting at me.'

'I'm sorry, but you mustn't take it out on them like that, Noel.'

'OK, I won't,' and he sat astride his bike, ready to ride off. 'So what about the gun then?'

I did wonder whether I should arrange for it to be confiscated but said, 'You apply for a certificate, and your local bobby will send it to our headquarters. Then you'll be able to keep that gun.' I knew that by this procedure he would be carefully vetted by his local policeman.

'Right,' and off he rode.

A couple of months passed without incident and then, when I was standing outside the telephone kiosk at Elsinby, awaiting any call that might come, Noel rode up on his red bike. He halted at my side.

'Mr Rhea,' he said, surprising me because he remembered my name, 'that gun o' mine. Me mum wouldn't let me apply for a certificate, nor would my Uncle Jack. They said I had no need, I could use the farm guns for killing rabbits and pigeons . . .'

'So you'll have handed in your rifle, have you? To your local policeman?'

'No, I've buried it.'

'Buried it? Where?'

'There's a deep bog in Ferrers Wood. I pushed it right down, used a rake handle to make sure it went real deep, then all t'watter covered it up. Nobody'll find it there, Mr Rhea, nobody.'

I knew he was telling the truth.

'Thanks for telling me, Noel. Maybe that was the wisest thing to do.'

'Mum said it was.' He smiled and rode off towards Pattington.

And there was no more pranks on the Patton cars when they parked outside the Hopbind Inn at Elsinby.

5 The Storeman Syndrome

I question if keeping it does much good.
Revd Richard Harris Barham (1788–1845)

In the middle years of this century, there existed within the police service – and probably within many other organizations – a philosophy that, if you wanted something which would improve your conditions or make your work easier or more efficient, you should not be allowed to have it.

I am sure that notion still persists, although there has been an improvement in many aspects of the police administration. Once it was believed that those who funded the police service would love and cherish officers who could spend the least. Now the idea is that you spend as much as possible in order to convince the authorities that more money is always needed if efficiency is to be maintained or improved.

I think the logic behind the earlier financially repressive thinking was simply that it saved money. Certainly lots of people asked lots of questions if official money was freely spent; few seemed to realize that a police force has all the financial needs and expenditure of any other large organization. A lot of the blame must rest upon those senior officers who, unlike Oliver Twist, were afraid to ask for more. They were allocated a budget and constantly struggled to function within its limitations. What they should have done is spent more to prove that the funds were inadequate for their needs. But they would never ask for more, because they thought it was an admission of failure, which meant that those of us lower down the scale had to make do and improvise.

One glaring example presented to us immediately upon joining the force was that we were issued with second-hand uniforms. I think the force tailor thought that all police officers were six foot six inches high, sixteen-stone giants with chests like barrels. Certainly all the second-hand uniforms seemed tailored for men of that ilk, and all recruits were issued with them. It was thought they would never dare complain.

If, for example, your uniform jacket was large enough to accommodate a pregnant hippopotamus, you had to tolerate its shapelessness and size because the effort of exchanging it for one more comfortable involved much expense and paperwork. To point out its defects labelled you a rebel; it also suggested that the man in charge of issuing uniforms (usually a sergeant) had been inefficient in giving you something that did not fit, and such overt criticism could ruin one's prospects. Original thinkers were considered subversives who had no part in the police service, and such outrageous requests or ideas were not tolerated. The result was that we never complained about our appearance because we dare not.

As a consequence, many police officers plodded around the streets in badly fitting, second-hand uniforms that gave the wearer's rear end the appearance of a sauntering elephant with an overweight problem. Those who wonder why uniformed policemen suddenly bend their knees and flex their legs to give the appearance of a diamond-shaped ballet pose, while quothing 'Hello, Hello', may now appreciate that it has something to do with ill-fitting trousers.

Proud wives, mothers or girlfriends with needlework skills did sometimes try to improve this baggy frippery, but some policemen did not benefit from such caring love. They walked around like pantalooned scarecrows in the belief that the secret of smartness was to cut your hair, clean your boots and press your trousers from time to time; any other aspects of dress were not important. There was, however, an implication that, if your uniform fitted perfectly, you were deformed.

Having been nurtured to this philosophy, it was with some surprise that I once entered the camphor-scented uniform store at force headquarters to find it stocked to the ceiling with brand-new uniforms in a range of interesting and even useful sizes. But I was to learn that these were never issued – they were stored, and I then discovered that that is precisely the function of stores and storemen. Their mission in life is to store things, not to issue them, and the Storeman Syndrome exists at all levels of the service, and in all departments. This is true in many other large organizations storemen and storewomen make it very difficult to draw items from their cherished stock. They produce a mass of schemes and procedures which are designed to prevent the staff's having the necessities of their calling.

I recall one police officer who was in charge of stores when ballpoint pens became fashionable. It was deemed by someone in authority that all officers should be issued with an official ballpoint pen. Progress had at last arrived within the service, because ballpoints would write in the rain without smudging the page – and that was a massive step forward for the busy outdoor constable. Making a neat and legible fountain pen entry in one's notebook on a rainy day was, until then, almost impossible, and so ballpoints revolutionized police work. But this giant stride towards the twentieth century had not reckoned with the Storeman Syndrome. Our storemen did not believe that ballpoints could run dry without warning when out in the town – it seemed they were always supposed to run dry when you were in the office, because you were not allowed a refill until the old one actually ceased to function. How one was supposed to take statements and make notes when on town duty with a pen devoid of ink was never decided, but the storeman said you could have a replacement refill only when the first one became exhausted – and application for that refill had to be made in writing.

'But, Sergeant,' I said when I was a mere 16-year-old cadet, 'how can I apply in writing if the pen's run dry?'

'We'll have none of that clever stuff here, young Rhea,' he said.

I went out and bought my own supply of ballpoints – which, on reflection, is precisely what the Storeman Syndrome seeks to achieve. If everyone behaved like that, many pens would be stored and never issued. In the older police stations of this kingdom, there must be mountains of unused ballpoint pens of a most ancient style, memorials to past and diligent storemen.

Upon being transferred to Aidensfield, I thought I would experience an end of the Storeman Syndrome, for our local section station was Ashfordly. Surely the sergeants in such a small and friendly station would look after their men and be willing to issue them with all their routine necessities?

But I hadn't bargained for Sergeant Blaketon.

When I first arrived, I did not require any stores, because my predecessor had stocked my office shelves – a kind touch, I felt. I had a plentiful supply of official forms, envelopes, a rubber, a few ballpoints, chalk (for marking the road at the scene of a traffic accident), a ruler and other office and operational essentials. Looking back, I have no idea how the previous Aidensfield constable had managed to stockpile such quantities – he must have raided the store while Sergeant Blaketon was on holiday.

I was soon to learn that Sergeant Blaketon took his storeman duties most seriously. He alone kept the key to the stores; it could be used by others only after signing for it in 'the Store Key Book', and such signings had to be witnessed in writing by another officer. It had then to be recorded in that book precisely what had been removed from the store, each person present witnessing the honesty of the transaction. Inside the store, there was another book. This one listed every single object in the stores, and the entries created a series of running totals. On one occasion, I saw he had four gross tins of Vim and 250 floor-cloths – I reckoned these would keep our cells scoured well into the twenty-first century. These ponderous procedures were to counteract any suggestion of pilfering by the local constables.

On one occasion I was privileged to sneak a rare peep into Sergeant Blaketon's store. That was when I realized it was there – what I had originally thought to be a small cupboard in the wall of his office was in reality a spacious storeroom. When the door was opened, it led into a type of cupboard-under-the-stairs. It ran the length of the sergeant's office wall and was about six feet wide, extending under his private accommodation at Ashfordly police station. It was a veritable Aladdin's Cave, stocked with everything from mop handles to pencil-sharpeners, by way of ink wells, toilet rolls and tins of furniture polish. A quick appraisal of the contents showed that some stock had been there since the foundation of the North Riding Constabulary in 1856 and were now museum pieces. Examples included acetylene cycle lamps, pen-holders and nibs, two spare whistle chains, a tin of black lead and other assorted gems.

The only reason I managed to see these cherished stocks was that, at the precise moment Sergeant Blaketon opened the door, his telephone rang. Thus I had a few brief moments of ecstasy as with a worried frown on his face, he watched my antics. My only purpose in being there was to obtain a new notebook, which I did after signing for it. I'm sure he thought I was scheming to pilfer something.

I recall two supreme examples of Sergeant Blaketon's own individual flair in storemanship. The first involved an electric light bulb.

Those of us with office accommodation adjoining our private houses were instructed to obtain official bulbs for the office. I think this was to prevent some of us making an application for an office bulb allowance. I would have been quite happy to furnish a bulb from my own funds, but orders are orders. Consequently, when my office bulb began to flicker, I thought it was time for a new one. When I was next in Ashfordly police station, I made my request.

'I need a new bulb for the office, Sergeant,' I began.

'Size?' asked Sergeant Blaketon.

'100 watt.'

'We don't stock hundreds. You'll have to make do with a 60 watt,' he said.

'That's not very bright if I'm working at night,' I said.

'Economy, Rhea, economy. We can't go around dishing out big bulbs when smaller wattages will do. Now, you've brought your old one in?'

'No, Sergeant. It's not finished yet, it's flickering. I think it might go out soon. I want to be prepared.'

'But if your present one is still working, why do you want a replacement?'

I groaned inwardly. Here was the Storeman Syndrome in all its perfection.

'It's nearly done, Sergeant. It's been used ever since I came to Aidensfield, and it's flickering, like they do just before they pack up. I thought I'd be prepared for when it does fizzle out.

I don't want to be caught out at night with no bulb if you're not around to issue one.'

'You know I can't issue a new bulb without taking in the old one,' he said. 'That is my system. New for old.'

I knew his system. He thought that if he issued something new without inspecting the expired old equivalent, the new thing would be purloined for the private use of the officer, who would later return for another new one. And so production of the old was an indication of total honesty. Men like Oscar Blaketon don't even trust themselves.

'So what happens if it goes out when I'm in the middle of an urgent report?'

'You've got bulbs at home, haven't you? In the house? Borrow one of those until you get the official one replaced.'

'That'll mean my family might have to cope with the dark!'

'But that is not my problem, Rhea,' he smirked. 'I have no interest in your domestic problems. So that's it – when your bulb blows, come to me for a new one, and fetch the old one in, as proof.'

And having said that, he refused to change his tactics.

The next example involved No. 1 cell. There were two cells at Ashfordly police station, No. 1 being the male cell and No. 2 the female cell. They were rarely, if ever, used by prisoners, because we seldom arrested anyone at Ashfordly, but we did make use of the toilet in No. 1, because the cell toilets were the only ones in the police station. While on duty one day, I had occasion to visit the loo in No. 1 and noticed that the toilet roll was almost exhausted.

'Sergeant,' I later announced to Sergeant Blaketon, 'we need a new toilet roll in No. 1 cell.'

'Is it finished?' he asked.

'No, there's about three sheets left.'

'Then I'll issue one when it's exhausted. When it runs out, fetch me the cardboard tube from the roll.'

'But if you get a prisoner in who needs more than three sheets, he's going to be in a bit of a pickle, Sergeant,' I said. 'Or it could be one of us, alone in the station. If we put one out now, in reserve, like they do in hotels . . .'

'This is not an hotel, Rhea. This is a police station, and I issue new toilet rolls only on production of the used tube. Otherwise everybody would be asking for them.'

'Do you think we'd take them home or something, Sergeant?' In my exasperation I was cheeky to him.

'It has been known, Rhea,' was his cold reply. 'Just ask British Rail or any of your hotels . . .'

'I can't imagine any of our men wanting to make private use of this paper,' I laughed. 'It's nearly as bad as cutting up squares of the *Daily Mirror*.'

'I care not for your opinions or sarcasm, Rhea. My job is to maintain stocks of equipment and to issue it when needed. It is not my intention to squander official supplies. A new toilet roll is not needed yet.'

And that was that.

Ten minutes later I returned to the loo, used the three sheets and beamed at him as I held out the cardboard tube.

'I do trust you have not wasted official toilet paper, Rhea, in order to make your point,' he said as he handed me a new roll and booked it out.

'No, I've thrown it down the toilet, Sergeant,' I assured him. 'But before I left the cell, it did serve a useful purpose.'

For me, and indeed all the other constables in Ashfordly section, it became something of an ongoing challenge to persuade Sergeant Blaketon to part with any official stores. We used all sorts of devices and excuses in our attempts to win our deserved odds and ends, but his system reigned unconquered.

And then, to our delight, one market day, his stores were superbly raided.

I was on duty and was patrolling among the colourful stalls, savouring the atmosphere that is generated by this weekly conglomeration of fish, fruit and fancy goods, when a uniformed police constable hailed me.

I recognized him as the deputy chief constable's official driver but did not know his name.

'Ah,' he said. 'Caught you. I'm PC Hughes, David Hughes. DCC's driver.'

'PC Rhea, Nicholas; Nick.' We shook hands.

'The boss spotted you as we drove past,' said Hughes. 'He asked me to take you back to the car.'

'Something wrong?' I wondered why on earth the deputy chief constable would want to talk to me. He wasn't in the habit of calling on constables like this.

'No. He wants to visit your office. There's no one in just now.'

I approached the gleaming black Humber Snipe, flung up a smart salute and said, 'Good morning, sir,' as he lowered his window.

'Hop in, Constable,' he invited, and so I did. As we cruised away, he said, 'I'm in the area and thought I'd give the station an official visit. It's locked.'

'Sergeant Bairstow is on day off, sir,' I told him. 'And Sergeant Blaketon went over to Brantsford.'

'And you are PC Rhea, eh?'

'Yes, sir,' I replied, wondering how he knew my name. I was later to learn he had an amazing memory for numbers – he'd seen the numerals on my shoulders. He was a charming man, easy-going but efficient.

When we arrived at the station, I unlocked the door and escorted him inside. PC Hughes waited outside in the official car. The DCC examined the cells, the books, the general state of the place and the daily occurrence book. In keeping with the procedures for such a visit, he would then make an entry in the occurrence book to record the event.

'Well, your sergeants and colleagues keep the place in good order, PC Rhea,' he said. 'I wish all our stations were so efficiently kept. Now, I'll just sign your occurrence book and then I'll be on my way.' And he began to tap his pockets as he sought a pen. 'Damn,' he said. 'I must have left my pen in the office.'

'You can borrow mine, sir,' and I produced my ballpoint.

'I'll need one for the rest of the day,' he said. 'Can you issue me with one from your stock?'

I explained Sergeant Blaketon's book procedures, and the DCC smiled. 'I'll witness your signature for the issue of one ballpoint to me,' he said, with just a trace of humour in his eyes. But when I opened the cupboard door and stepped inside, he followed and exclaimed, 'Well, I'll be damned! This is like a museum!'

He went inside and picked things off the shelves to examine them, chuckling and shaking his head as he found treasures from a bygone age. There was even an old-fashioned stalk telephone, a copper kettle, a leather-bound book with no entries at all, a Victorian pen-holder and stacks of old files.

'PC Rhea,' he said suddenly, 'am I right in thinking there was a charity stall on your market-place today as I came past?'

'Yes, sir. It's for the parish church. They're raising funds to repair the bell tower.'

'Then all this surplus stuff must go. Have it taken to the stall now and get rid of it. It is no use here; in fact, I issued an instruction several months ago for all such clutter to be cleared out. This lot will help a deserving cause.'

'I'll inform Sergeant Blaketon, sir.'

'It's no good relying on old Oscar, PC Rhea. I served with him at Scarborough years ago. I know him too well. No, we'll do it now, you, me and PC Hughes.'

And so we did. We loaded the rear seat and the boot of the DCC's official car with what amounted to a cache of antiques and surplus but unused domestic goods of ages past, such as old tins of polish and brush-heads. The stallholder was delighted. The DCC left a note for Sergeant Blaketon to explain what he'd done, and I resumed my patrol.

Later Sergeant Blaketon said nothing to me, and when I did next peer into his cupboard, I saw he'd used the space to accommodate more stocks. Among the boxes, I noticed three gross of toilet rolls. The one in No. 1 cell had just five sheets left, but even with such a colossal supply, I wasn't going to ask him for a replacement just yet.

When patrolling the moors around Aidensfield, I soon discovered that the Storeman Syndrome is not confined to those employed in formal organizations. It exists among individuals too. There are many examples of those who simply cannot throw anything away, in case it might come in useful for some obscure future purpose.

I have heard it said that everything comes in useful once every seven years. On one of my moves to another house, I found a coiled and lengthy piece of wire in an outbuilding. In its prime, it had been an old-fashioned television aerial. Following the belief that it might be useful one day, I kept it – and some ten years later found it ideal for cleaning out drains. Policemen do tend to keep things 'just in case'. Storerooms and cupboards throughout the land are full of things which are kept 'just in case'. It is true, of course, that, if one disposes of any one of these items, it will be required two or three days after the dustman has carted it away. That might explain why my garage is full of odd bits of apparently useless paraphernalia, all of which I believe have some potential destiny.

But scattered about the moors and dales are people who keep things for best, who reserve rooms for special events which seldom seem to happen, who keep drawers full of linen which is never used, and crockery which has never been sullied with food or drink. The front doors of such homes are rarely opened, and visitors are invariably welcomed in the kitchen. Even now, I find myself in this category – our callers come to the kitchen door. It's a matter of custom, not discrimination. In my tours of duty I had occasion to visit many such places and came to realize that it was not an unusual aspect of moorland life. In fact, it was very much a part of the prevailing practice.

The typical situation was like this. A householder or family living on a farm, or in a country house or cottage, would live in the kitchen. This was a plain, functional place, often with a bare stone floor, but with a couple of Windsor chairs for comfort and with a bare wooden table for all meals. There was rarely a dining-room – all meals were taken in the kitchen. Elsewhere in the house would be a sitting-room; this was more comfortable, perhaps with rugs or even a carpet on the floor, settees and easy chairs and a welcoming fire. There would be sideboards too and pictures on the wall.

But in addition to these there was the best room, sometimes knows as 'the house' or in some areas as 'the parlour'. This was often at the front of the house, close to the seldom-used front door. Judging from those I have seen, they were dark and airless and always smelt of mothballs. The window was never opened, the rooms usually faced north and so attracted little sunshine or light, and they were full of 'best' things which were to be used only on special occasions and which had, in many cases, been passed down from one generation to the next. Wonderful old antique furnishings, a firescreen, cushions, rugs, the carpet, easy chairs, crockery, drawers full of unopened linen such as pillowcases, sheets and serviettes, smart cutlery, a selection of ancient books, some antique ornaments, a piano, the family Bible and the inevitable, well-thumbed album of family photographs. Most rooms of this type that I had occasion to visit reeked of Victoriana and must have been an antique-collector's dream – in some there was even an aspidistra in a heavy brown pot. Throughout the life of the contents, they had seldom been used, having always been kept for best.

'Best' seemed to imply family gatherings such as christenings, weddings and funerals (especially funerals), although if an important visitor called, the room might be put into use. It would have to be someone very important indeed to justify preparation of that room, for the status of the visitor had to be substantial before the fire was lit and the room made welcoming. Routine calls by vicars, vets, van-drivers, valuers and visiting relations did not quality – there had to be something special about the call and the caller.

The degree of high importance was generally something associated with the family. I doubt whether the Queen, if she called without warning, would be shown into that room, and the same might be said of the lord of the manor, although if cousin Freda came all the way from Canada to trace the family tree, the lady of the house might get her duster out and 'do' that room.

If the room was maintained for very important family occasions, its contents were likewise separated from the rigours of the daily routine. Gifts given to the husband and wife at their wedding, for birthdays, at Christmas and anniversaries were seldom used – they were put away for a special occasion. Drawers in such rooms and indeed in bedrooms and other parts of the house contained unopened parcels dating from the wedding day of the occupiers. I found this an intriguing practice. Things needed from day to day, such as household crockery, were used with alacrity, but special things, such as presents, were never used – they were always put away. I was never quite sure why, although it happened with such regularity.

Having once been put away for a special occasion, such an item rarely saw service, because there was never an occasion special enough to justify unwrapping it or opening it. Whatever occurred never quite seemed to qualify for the ceremonial use of Aunt Emily's gift of china, Uncle Jasper's white sheets or Cousin Ermintrude's canteen of cutlery.

In contemplating this logic, I doubt if that predetermined visit by Her Majesty would be of sufficient importance to bring out such treasures. She'd probably be given a drink of tea in a mug bearing a picture of her grandmother, but she might be allowed to sit on the best sofa in the best room to sip it; if she came to a family funeral, however, the best room would be available.

Probably the most upsetting incident which involved such a room happened one hot July day. It was just after 10 a.m. and I was prepared to patrol Aidensfield and district in my little van when Dr Archie McGee from Elsinby knocked at the door. He was dressed in his plus-fours as usual, and I never knew whether he was doing his rounds or going shooting.

'Ah, Nick,' he beamed in his affable way. 'I've just driven past Mrs Gregory's place and there's a light on. I thought I'd mention it – she's away, you know. She's gone to her sister's funeral in Bradford.'

'It must be something serious to get her away from home,' I smiled. 'But how long's she been away?'

'Day before yesterday,' he said. 'I came past last night and there was no light.'

'Me too,' I said. 'I came past at half-past eleven last night, and it was all in darkness. Thanks, Doctor, I'll have a look. Did you stop at the house?'

'No,' he said. 'I've an appointment at Malton Hospital. Got to be going,' and off he went.

Mrs Gregory's house, known as Southview, was only a few hundred yards from my own police house, but I took the van because of its radio capability. I parked outside. It was a magnificent house, a stone-built double-fronted building with a tiled roof and oak windowframes. It stood in its own grounds and was tucked deep into the hillside midway down Aidensfield Bank, with expansive views to the south.

I knew Mrs Gregory by sight. She was a lady in her mid seventies, I guessed, and she had been a widow for years. She had no children, but I did know she had sisters in various parts of Yorkshire. The house revealed something of her status – although she was a Yorkshirewoman from a simple background, she had married well, because her house was what is often described as 'a gentleman's residence' or even 'a gentry house'. I knew little of her husband, for he had died long before my arrival in the village.

Upon leaving my van, I could see the light burning in one of the front rooms, so I knocked on the front door, and when there was no reply, I tried the back. Again there was no response, so I examined the windows. Those at the front and rear were secure but as I went around the side, where the house wall was literally a yard from the limestone cliff face near where it had been built, my heart sank. A small pantry window had been smashed and was standing open. I knew better than to climb in that way, for evidence of forensic interest might be adhering to the framework.

I returned to the doors and tried the knobs. The back door opened easily – the key was in the lock on the inside, and chummy had used this route as his exit. As I entered, aware of the need to proceed with great care, I knew the house had been burgled. My heart sank. This was probably the first time for years that Mrs Gregory had been away, and I could only feel deep sorrow on her behalf. But it was time to set in motion the official procedures and then to trace Mrs Gregory.

I did make a quick tour of the stricken house, just to ensure that the villain was not still hiding, and then closed the doors as I set in motion the investigation. I called the CID in Eltering, who said Detective Sergeant Gerry Connolly and Detective PC Paul Wharton would attend within the half hour. In the meantime, I left the van outside the house and walked down to the post office-cum-shop to ask Joe Steel if he knew how I could contact Mrs Gregory. He did; he gave me her sister's home number. I returned to the van and radioed Force Control, asking them to contact Mrs Gregory with the sad news and ask her to ring me before coming home. Then I stood outside the house to await the might of the local CID.

Connolly and Wharton came and commenced their investigation. The curious thing was the state of one room. The entire floor was covered with masses of wrapping paper and screwed-up newspaper. It covered the tops of flat surfaces, such as the table and sideboard, and even filled the spaces beneath chairs and bookcases. The room looked like an expanded version of our children's bedrooms on Christmas morning.

'What's all this, Nick?' asked Detective Sergeant Connolly, showing me the rubbish.

'No idea,' I had to admit. 'I've not been in the house until today.'

'It's neat and tidy otherwise, but we can't tell what's gone until she returns. Certainly the place has been done over, and it looks like an expert job. We've not found any marks.'

By that, he meant there were no fingerprints, which suggested the work of a professional thief rather than a local lad who had broken in for kicks.

'We'll be off, Nick,' said Connolly. 'Lock the house and then call us when she gets back – we'll find out what's gone then.'

When I got home, Mary said there'd already been a call from Mrs Gregory, and she would be home that evening around seven o'clock; in view of the awful news, her nephew was driving her home and would stay a day or two. I made sure I was at the house to meet them.

Mrs Gregory arrived in her nephew's Hillman Husky and headed straight for the front door. She was a sturdy woman of moorland stock, with iron-grey hair peeping from beneath a tight-fitting purple hat. She walked like a farm labourer, her stout legs carrying her quickly across the ground. She almost waddled into the house after nodding briefly to me. I followed her in, leaving her nephew to see to her luggage and the car.

'I'm sorry this has happened, Mrs Gregory.' I tried to reassure her but she seemed not to care. 'The CID have been. They've done their work but will have to visit you when you can tell them what's been taken.'

She buzzed from room to room, saying, 'Nowt from here, nowt from this 'un . . .' until she arrived at the room with all the waste paper on the floor.

'This is how we found it, Mrs Gregory. We've not touched anything.'

'They've had a right do in 'ere, eh?' she said. 'They've opened stuff I've had parcelled up since I was wed.'

She picked up one piece of ancient silver-coloured wrapping paper. 'Egg cups, I think,' she said. 'From his lot.'

I stood back as she examined the mess, and when her nephew came in, I suggested he make a cup of tea for us all. I learned his name was Robert Atkinson. Gradually she moved every piece of paper, and when she had finished, she led me into the kitchen, where Robert had prepared a cup of tea and some biscuits. It was an old-fashioned kitchen with a black-leaded fireside and beams overhead.

'It's all my wedding presents,' she said eventually. 'That's what he's got. Crockery, silverware, pots and pans, linen, glassware . . .'

'You mean you never used any of it, Mrs Gregory?'

'Never had the need,' she said. 'Allus had enough stuff without opening presents. Besides, my Alexander died two days after our wedding, so I never had the heart to open anything.'

'Oh, dear, I am sorry.'

'It was a long time ago,' she said. 'Long before you saw t'light of day, young man. He went off t'war, First World War that was, and got himself killed. Married for two days, I was. And so I never opened any of them presents. He left me well provided for.'

'What did he do? For a living?' I asked her as Robert poured the tea.

'He was in business, ironmongery. His family have a chain of shops in t'West Riding; they're still there. I get a pension from 'em, and I've shares. I'm all right for cash, Mr Rhea, and that stuff is all insured.'

'If I might say so, Mrs Gregory, you are taking this remarkable well.'

'It's no good doing any other,' she said. 'You can't make things better by worrying. I've never used any of that stuff, so

I shan't miss it. In fact, Mr Rhea, it's mebbe solved a problem. All them nephews and nieces o' mine might have fought over those things. Well, they can't now.'

'I'll need a list,' I said. 'To circulate through our channels, to other police forces and antique-dealers.'

'I'll have my wedding "thank-you" list somewhere,' she said. 'I can get a full list in a while.'

'We'll need a description of the objects,' I said. 'You know, any distinguishing marks, unusual designs, that sort of thing.'

I rang Gerry Connolly from her house and explained it would take a while for her to compile the list, but he was happy that she was able to do so at all; many in this situation might not know exactly what had been taken. I kept her company for about an hour and was delighted that she had been such a tower of strength in her loss.

As I got up to leave, she stooped and picked up a black-lead brush from the hearth.

'See this brush, Mr Rhea?'

'My granny had one like that,' I said.

'That was a wedding present,' she smiled. 'I use it every day. I'm right glad he never took that. You can't get good black-lead brushes like that nowadays.'

I left, marvelling that she had never had any use or joy from her wedding presents, save the black-lead brush.

As a postscript, we did recover several of her silver items, because they had been monogrammed by her late husband's family. They began to turn up in second-hand salerooms and antique shops in various parts of the country, but the thief was never arrested.

I think that, if he had stolen her black-lead brush, she would have been very upset. But we might not have recovered that – it didn't bear the family monogram.

6 Kittens Among the Phobias

Our antagonist is our helper.
Edmund Burke (1729–97)

There is no doubt that some people are truly afraid of police officers, and there are also some who dislike or even hate them. The reasons are many and varied.

From my own experiences, I found that political propaganda of the more sinister type is responsible for a large amount of fear and distrust, this often being based on one solitary act by a less-than-perfect officer or through well-chosen photographs of highly publicized confrontations. There is certainly a wealth of anti-police myth in some political circles through which gullible idealists grow to believe those who preach poison rather than those who are better equipped to reveal the truth. The trouble is that it is easy to accept the ravings of those who profess to know more than oneself. Enlightenment can come later, sometimes much later and sometimes too late, and it is often achieved when the disaffected one has been subjected to some experience which starkly reveals the falsehoods upon which past beliefs have been based.

But there are some who are afraid of the police for other reasons, such as those which have deep-rooted origins in one's childhood or upbringing. Sometimes a belief imposed upon a child's mind will never be eradicated. A lot of children grow up in fear of the police because their parents have regularly threatened to 'tell the policeman' if they are naughty. And, for a child, it is naughty to spill one's dinner or wet one's pants. I believe children should be brought up with a healthy respect for the police, because the service exists for the benefit of all society and not just a portion of it, but I do not believe youngsters should be taught to fear the office of constable.

Having said that, there are those who nurse an irrational fear of the police, and over the years while patrolling from Aidensfield, I came to know such a woman in Ashfordly. The strange thing was that she was not frightened of *policemen* – she was frightened of police *stations*. Maybe she was a member of that group of people who fear or hate official places such as banks, dentists' surgeries, council chambers, income tax offices or DHSS departments. Whatever the root cause of her fear, she knew it was irrational and even silly, and yet she could do nothing to overcome it. She had no fear of police officers, however, and was quite happy to chat with them in the street or mingle with them socially. I grew to know her from my irregular but frequent patrols in Ashfordly, our local market town.

Being the village constable of Aidensfield, I had to patrol Ashfordly's streets from time to time, usually twice a week during a selected morning or afternoon, each time being a four-hour stint. We rural constables undertook such duties when the town was short of officers due to other commitments, such as court appearances, courses, annual leave and so on, and in time I came to know several Ashfordly residents.

One of them was a busy little woman who seemed to trot everywhere. She was in her middle forties, I estimated, with rimless spectacles and a hair-do that kept her dark brown locks firmly in place. She was always smartly dressed but she scarcely reached five feet in height. She had the tiniest of features – little feet, little hands, a little body, and she drove a little car, a Morris Mini, in fact. She was like a petite and pretty china doll and at times looked almost as fragile.

I first became aware of her as I patrolled the market-place. Periodically during the day she would rush in, park her tiny car and then trot into a succession of shops, offices and cottages, her tiny feet twinkling across the cobbles. Occasionally the face of a Yorkshire terrier would peer from the rear seat of her car, and sometimes there would be a poodle or a tiny terrier of some sort. More often that not, she was accompanied by a small dog, and if I was hovering anywhere nearby, she would smile and bid me good morning or good afternoon before rushing about her business.

There was no official reason for me to wonder who she was or what she was doing, but it is a feature of police work that one acquires local knowledge, often without realizing. And in time I learned that this was Mrs Delia Ballentine. She lived near the castle, and her husband, Geoff, worked for an agricultural implements dealer in Ashfordly. She did not have a job, but she was heavily engaged in work for local charities and organizations – she was secretary of the Ashfordly WI, for example, and she did voluntary work for the Red Cross, the parish church, the RSPCA and a host of other groups, which explained why she was always rushing.

The first time we spoke was when she was collecting for the Spastics Society. I was in the market-place in uniform when she asked if I'd care to make a donation, I did and was rewarded with a badge which I pinned to my tunic. I commented on the state of the weather, as English folk tend to do, and she said she had to hurry home to prepare Geoff's dinner, as Yorkshire people call their lunch. On several occasions thereafter she persuaded me to part with small sums of money for an amazing variety of charities and worthwhile causes, and in every case she had to rush off to attend to some other task.

Then one Friday morning, when the market was a riot of colour with its fascinating range of stalls, vehicles and crowds, I saw her collecting for a local school for handicapped children.

I slipped some money into her collecting box and said, 'You should get around to the police station. There's a conference there; it starts in twenty minutes. There's eight traffic officers just dying to support worthy causes. You might get a few bob, with a bit of luck.'

She shuddered. It was a visible shudder, and it surprised me. 'Oh, no.' She tried to shrug off the moment. 'I couldn't.'

'They wouldn't mind . . .' I began.

'No, it's not that.' She hesitated and I waited for her to continue. She added, 'I'm terrified of police stations.'

'Police stations?' I must have sounded sceptical, because she laughed at me.

'Silly, isn't it?' she chuckled at her own absurdity. 'I just don't like going inside police stations. I don't know why.'

'I can understand folks not wanting to go into a prison or even a lift, but I've never come across this before,' I said. 'But you're not frightened of policemen?'

'No, not at all,' she told me. 'That makes it all the dafter, doesn't it?'

'Well, if you ever go around to our station and I'm there, just shout and I'll come outside to see what you want!'

'Thanks, I will! Well, I must be off. I've other calls to make . . .' and she twinkled away towards her little car. A dachshund barked from the front passenger seat, and I wondered how many dogs she kept.

As she disappeared, I pondered upon her odd phobia and tried to work out whether there was a word for it. I knew that the fear of a particular place was known as topophobia, the fear of night was nyctophobia, and a fear of streets or crossing places was dromophobia. There were others, such as ergasiophobia, which is a fear of surgeries, brontophobia, which is a fear of thunder, and thalassophobia, which is a fear of the sea. A fear of confined spaces is claustrophobia, a fear of deep places is bathophobia, and a fear of dry places is xerophobia, with dipsophobia being a fear of drinking or drunkenness, and hydrophobia a fear of water or wet places. Thinking along these lines, I wondered if fear of police stations was nickophobia, cellophobia, custophobia or mere constabularophobia. Whatever its name, it was a curious and somewhat unsettling fear, but one with which she could live without too many problems. After all, many people live and die without ever entering a police station. I felt sure Delia could survive without having to face that challenge.

But I was wrong.

I was performing another tour of duty in Ashfordly one July afternoon and was in the police station when a youth came in. About seventeen years old, he was carrying a hessian sack which was dripping wet and squirming with some form of life.

'Now, what have got?' I asked him.

'Kittens,' he said. 'Somebody threw 'em into t'beck but they landed in some rushes, tied up in this sack. They didn't go right into t'water. I found 'em when I was fishing. They're all alive.'

He opened the top of the sack to reveal three beautiful black-and-white kittens, several weeks old. Their eyes were open and they were quite capable of walking. Within seconds, they were crawling all over the counter, and I asked him if he was prepared to keep them.

'No chance,' he said. 'I live with my granny, we've no space, that's why I fetched 'em here. I thought you'd know what to do.'

'Right, we'll see to them,' I assured him. 'Thanks for saving their lives. It was a rotten trick, eh? Throwing them in the beck like that.'

'If I'd seen who'd chucked 'em in, I'd have chucked him in an' all,' said the youth, whose name was Ian Trueman. I took details for our records, and off he went.

I was now left with the problem of three active and interesting kittens which had to be fed and housed, but we did have procedures for dealing with stray dogs and lost and found pets of every kind. Because these three active chaps were literally crawling into everything, threatening to overturn filing trays, clog the typewriter and send the telephone crashing to the floor, I decided to pop them into No. 2 cell until I could deal with them. A dish of milk would keep them happy as they explored its delights.

I began to prepare the cell for their stay. I went into the garage to find a cat tray and some litter or earth, found a saucer in the sergeant's office and used some of my own milk from a bottle I carried for my break periods. As I fussed over the kittens in their prison-like home, I heard someone enter the enquiry office, and so I called 'I won't be a moment'. I then tried to close the cell door without the kittens rushing out at my heels, for one of them seemed determined to escape from custody. I had to sit him on the cell bed as I rushed out. But in time I got them all safely behind the proverbial bars and returned to the enquiry office to dispose of the wet and ruined sack.

And there, to my astonishment, was Delia Ballentine. She was standing at the counter, holding on to the front edge of the top surface as she shook with fear and anxiety. I could see the perspiration standing out on her brow and could appreciate

Kittens Among the Phobias

the sheer willpower that had driven her to enter this feared place.

'Hello,' I said, with the sack dangling from my hand. She could not speak for a moment. 'Let's go outside,' I suggested.

She shook her head. 'No, I must try to beat this silly fear.'

'There's no need.' I threw the sack into the rubbish bin and said, 'Look, Mrs Ballentine, I'll see you out there. It's no problem . . .'

She did not reply but stood with her hands gripping the edge of the counter until her knuckles turned white. Then I could hear the kittens mewing pitifully . . . she heard them too.

'What's that?' she asked, the fear vanishing from her face in an instant as she concentrated upon the distinctive distress cries.

'There's three kittens in our cell,' and I explained how they came to be here.

'Oh, the poor things! Can I take them? I mean, if no one wants them . . .'

'That would solve a lot of our problems,' I said. 'If no one claims them, we'd have to find a good home or have them put to sleep,' I told her.

During this conversation, it was fascinating to notice the apparent evaporation of her fear, and she even followed me into the cell as I went to retrieve the kittens. When I gave them to her, she seemed to be totally in control, her entire concentration being upon the tiny animals. As she petted them, I searched under the counter and found a cardboard box big enough to accommodate all three. I sat the box on the counter as I talked to her. But as I tried to elicit the reason for her visit, those tremblings and overt nervous tics returned, all heralded by the perspiration on her face. I found myself admiring her courage in making such a determined effort to enter this dreaded building.

Once I had the kittens safely inside the box, I took her outside and placed them on the back seat of her car as I tried to interview her. Now free from her trauma, she told me she had just discovered she had lost a precious brooch. It was in the shape of a swan and was made of 22 carat gold; it was antique, a present from her husband's grandmother, and she felt she had to come to report it. Losing it had been of sufficient worry to compel her to overcome her resistance to police stations.

So I recorded particulars, saying that if it came to our notice, it would be restored to her. In fact, it was later returned to her, albeit not through our assistance – someone had found it in the back room of the town hall and had recognized it. Apparently, Delia had been to a WI meeting there a couple of days earlier and the brooch had become detached from her dress. She hailed me in the street shortly after its return; I said I was delighted and would delete it from our records.

'You didn't come to the station to report its recovery?' I asked, wondering if she had made such an attempt.

'No, I couldn't, I really couldn't. I thought because I'd done it once, I could do it again but I just couldn't, Mr Rhea. I really did try. That first time, I think I was so worried about what Geoff would say about my losing the brooch that I managed to force myself to go into the station.'

'But those cats, Mrs Ballentine, when you saw those kittens, you lost all your fears, if only for a few moments.'

'I know, and I thought I could do it again without the cats, but I couldn't. I know it's so silly, but it must be something deep inside that makes me frightened, mustn't it?'

'I'm no medical expert, but it does seem to be a psychological problem!' I smiled. 'Anyway, you've got your precious brooch back and I'm delighted. Now, those kittens? Did you get them a good home?'

'We're still looking after them, until they're a wee bit older, but I've got some people interested in them. Look, Mr Rhea, if ever you get any more kittens or other animals in, I'll take them off your hands. I'd rather do that than let you have them put down.'

'We'd welcome that sort of arrangement.' I was delighted to hear this. 'Found animals can be a problem to us. But you'd not be able to call and collect them?'

'You or your men would have to deliver them to the house or bring them out to the car, I'm afraid.' She looked slightly embarrassed at her own frailty.

'That is no problem,' I said. 'I'll have a word with Sergeant Bairstow or Sergeant Blaketon and see that your name goes in our records. I'm sure we can arrange a cat and mouse delivery service when it's necessary.'

And so it came to pass.

This explains why, from time to time in Ashfordly, a police van can be seen motoring through the town with passengers which vary from cats and dogs to budgerigars, parrots and canaries, via hamsters, pet mice, white rabbits and even iguanas or ferrets. In all cases, they showed far less fear of our police station and its cells than did Mrs Delia Ballentine.

While Delia Ballentine had a genuine fear of police stations, Daniel Joseph Price hated police officers. Indeed, he hated everything connected with the service – its uniform, its members, its offices and its duties. There was absolutely nothing he liked about us. He made no secret of this loathing. Whenever he spotted me, he would make a point of approaching me, vociferously to broadcast aspects of his lifelong hatred.

'I hate coppers,' he would say as he glared at me. 'I really do hate coppers. I'll never help the police, you know that? Never.'

When he first made this attitude known to me, I tried to elicit some reason for his hatred, but he would never explain. I tried asking other people, but they did not know either, and so the deep-seated cause of Daniel's continuing malice remained a mystery. In time, I grew to accept his verbal outbursts, whether in the street or in the pub, and I didn't feel too concerned about his attitude. After a while, I never tried to reason with him or to make any response.

Following months of listening to him, I adopted a new tactic. Whenever he approached me to announce his persistent hatred, I would simply say, 'Thanks, Dan, I know. You've told me many times.'

But this served only to compel him to emphasize his vitriol. 'But I really do hate policemen, Mr Rhea. Do you understand what I'm saying?'

'Yes, I do, and I accept it,' I would say, wondering whether he expected some kind of violent reaction or official response from me.

Once I said, 'If you hate policemen, it's your own problem, not mine. I can do nothing about it. If it's any consolation, I don't hate you. I don't hate anyone, Daniel. And if you were in trouble, I would help you, either when I'm off duty or on.'

'But I'll never help you, Mr Rhea. Can't you understand that? I'll never give you information about crimes, I'll never warn you of trouble, I'll never come to your help if you are in bother, I'll never be a witness for you . . .'

In an effort to create some kind of positive reply to his ramblings, I tried to explain that helping the police was not merely of benefit to the officers concerned – helping the police was a way of helping society. Police officers gained nothing from such aid, other than the satisfaction of helping the public to deal with wrongdoers, whether the wrongdoers were criminals or merely those in need of professional help. But Daniel could not see it in that way. He seemed to think that helping the police was against his religion or that there was something grossly anti-social in volunteering to provide information or assistance to us.

I did wonder to what extent he would continue his one-man campaign. I came to realize that he did not hate me in person; indeed, he would sometimes buy me a drink if I was off duty. The odd thing was that, while buying me the drink, he would announce that he really did hate policemen, although he had nothing against me personally.

This peculiar relationship endured for a long time, and I must admit I took little heed of his words. In some ways, I quite liked Daniel. He was honest, if nothing else, and he did spend a lot of time helping the old folk in Aidensfield, doing their shopping for them or bits of decorating and cleaning. He had a wonderful manner with children too, being a bundle of fun during the village sports days, church fêtes and the like. He worked as a labourer on building sites, always managing to find local employment, and he lived with his mother in one of the council houses. He was never troublesome from my point of view, he never came rolling home drunk or abusive. He did not run a car but used an old black pedal cycle to get around the lanes. In his mid forties, he was a solidly built man who was a shade overweight, and his round, somewhat flabby face usually bore a contented smile. He did seem to be a very contented person – until he saw me.

During his leisure moments, he wore a well-tailored black suit. I never saw him in a sports jacket or casual wear of any kind; even when cycling to the pub or romping around at a garden fête, he would wear his black suit, and the result of this continual wear was that it had become extremely shabby. At close quarters, I could see that the suit was made of quality material, and sometimes I wondered whether he was descended from a sophisticated family who had fallen on hard times, the suit having perhaps belonged to some long-dead and wealthy male ancestor.

Alternatively, he might have bought it at a jumble sale. It was certainly from a bygone era. When new, it would have been beyond his financial limits and perhaps his social horizons, but it never seemed to wear out and was an undoubted bargain. I'm sure he regarded it as a worthwhile acquisition, and I'm equally sure he cherished it, but a visit to the cleaners would have worked miracles.

In my daily patrols, I had a feeling that, sooner or later in my professional life, I would encounter Daniel's bigotry. It was almost inevitable in a village the size of Aidensfield, where one's neighbours and fellow residents live so close to each other. From time to time, I tried to anticipate the kind of problems it would present, and then I endeavoured to work out a series of feasible responses. And, sure enough, that day did arrive – but it brought a curious problem that I had not foreseen.

At five o'clock one evening, which was in fact my day off, there was a knock at the door, and I opened it to find Daniel standing there in his crumpled, greasy suit. He looked far from happy, and I realized that something pretty awful must have happened to persuade him to call voluntarily at the police house.

'Come in, Daniel.' I stood back and held open the door.

'No,' he said. 'I'll say my piece here.'

'As you wish.' I had no intention of antagonizing him.

'Somebody's pinched our silver tray!' He rushed out the words as if he was talking treason. 'T'insurance man says I've got to tell t'police, so I'm telling you.'

'I'll have to take details,' I began. 'You are reporting a crime to me.'

'T'insurance said I had to tell t'police. I've told you, so that's it.'

'No, it isn't it,' I said. 'It's not as simple as that, Daniel. I've got official forms to compile if you are reporting a crime. The insurance will expect a full report from us, and I can't do that without doing my job properly. So either you come in and help me fill in those forms, or I will not be able to complete the necessary details.'

He stared at his feet for a few moments, and I knew he was wrestling with his conscience. I made no comment about his previous antagonism and simply waited with the door held open. With a massive sigh, he stepped over the threshold, and I led him into my office. I must admit I experienced a feeling of success. I seated him beside the desk, drew the necessary crime report forms from the drawer and explained the formalities involved. But he was most reluctant to provide me with all the facts; he saw this as helping the police. In carrying out this interview, I had to drag every piece of information from him.

Through persistent questioning, I did learn that two men had visited his mother that morning, ostensibly to see if she had any old junk or ornaments to sell. They had told a good story and, while one had kept her talking, the other had explored the house. Only after they'd gone had the old lady realized the tray was missing. Daniel was clearly upset, especially at the evil way his elderly mother had been treated by these rogues.

I could see that he was battling with his conscience – he wanted the tray found and the rogues caught, but he did not want to break his lifelong embargo by helping the police. As a consequence, I did succeed in abstracting sufficient information for completion of my official form but not enough upon which to base a thorough investigation. For example, he would not or could not give me a detailed description of the missing tray, save to say it was roughly oval in shape with a handle at each end and legs underneath. It was a large one, some two feet long by twelve inches wide. It sounded more like a piece of silverware from a stately home than a tray from a Yorkshire council house. He offered no description of the two men, nor did he provide me with any of the *modus operandi* they had utilized.

I decided I would have to talk to Mrs Price but made a mental note to do so tomorrow – and then a thought struck me. Daniel would not have come to seek my official help without some kind of pressure, so did this tray belong to him or his mother? I had assumed it was his property, but now I began to suspect it was very important to her and that that could be the reason for his uncharacteristic visit. I became even more determined to talk to her and would do so when Daniel was at work. In the meantime, I could enter the crime into the official channels with an assurance that further enquiries would be made. Having made this uncharacteristic visit, Daniel rushed away.

At ten o'clock next morning, I paid a visit to Mrs Price and found her at home and quite composed. She was slightly stooped with age, but her hair still bore signs of its original auburn, and her brown eyes were alert and full of life. Upon recognizing me, she bade me enter her smart, clean home and settled me on the settee, insisting that I have a cup of tea.

'I've come about the missing tray, Mrs Price,' I said.

'Daniel did not want to bother you,' she smiled, 'but I insisted. The insurance company said it must be reported stolen, you see, but, well, Daniel is a bit silly when it comes to dealing with policemen.'

'I need a detailed description of the tray, Mrs Price, one that we can circulate among antique-dealers and salerooms.'

'Oh, Daniel said it would not be necessary. He said you'd never do anything to trace it, you'd just record it so the insurance company could be sure it was a crime.'

'Then Daniel is wrong, Mrs Price. We will circulate a full description to every police force in the United Kingdom, to Interpol and to all antique-dealers, salerooms, silversmiths and others who might be offered it. And, of course, our CID will make local enquiries about the men who took it.'

'Then a photograph would be useful?' she smiled. I found her to be an amazingly alert and wise old woman, with a keen brain and a wry sense of humour.

'It would be ideal.'

'Then I have one or two.'

She ferreted about in a cupboard near the fireplace and produced an old leather-bound album which she opened. Inside were lots of old prints, some secured in the book and others loosely assembled. But in time her bent old fingers found the ones she sought, and she passed them to me. I found myself looking at a silver salver. It was exquisitely ornate and bore a coat of arms in the centre.

'Daniel could not put a value upon it, Mrs Price,' I told her, 'but this seems to be a very valuable piece of silver.'

'It is, Mr Rhea, in terms of both money and sentimentality. Now Daniel could not put a value upon it simply because I have never given him any idea of its worth.'

'I put it down as £10,' I confessed to her.

'I'd put it much closer to twenty times that, Mr Rhea. Now listen. When Daniel was a youth, he was rather impetuous and liable to do silly things, and so I have never revealed the full nature of that salver to him. He knew it was a family heirloom but thought it was just an old tray I had inherited. In fact, it is the only thing I have which can be traced through my family – the tray was made in 1779; it bears that date. The coat of arms is my family crest.'

I did not ask about the circumstances of the family, but she did say her grandfather had tried to sell the family silver, hence the photographs were intended for the catalogue, but her own mother had rescued this salver. It had been withdrawn and given to her mother, and now it was hers; when she died, it should have passed to Daniel. She had sent Daniel to report the theft, not realizing how much detail I would require and not appreciating his own lack of knowledge of what should have been a fascinating inheritance. My mind now flashed to the old suit that Daniel habitually wore – had that also come from grandad? It seemed that Daniel was of noble ancestry, but just how far back in history I could not guess. It might be a subject for some genealogical research – even by Daniel, if he so wished.

Thanks to my visit and the alertness of Mrs Price, I did walk away with a detailed description of the salver, a far better idea of its value and a very useful photograph. I also managed to obtain reasonable descriptions of the two thieves – apparently, one of them had said he'd like to go to the toilet, and she'd allowed him upstairs to the bathroom. The salver had been kept on a dressing-table in the spare bedroom – the thief had seen it and had somehow smuggled it out of the house, probably stuffed up his jacket. Nothing else was missing.

When I informed Detective Sergeant Gerry Connolly, he was pleased the matter had been recorded – and he was delighted with the photograph. He told me that in recent weeks a team of two supposed antique-dealers had been operating in the area, and Mrs Price had been their most recent victim. Their MO was simple: they entered houses occupied by elderly folks under the pretext of inspecting and valuing goods, and while one kept the householder occupied, the other would find an excuse for exploring the house. They removed anything that took their fancy. And now, thanks to her, a fairly comprehensive description of the men was available – she had been able to fill gaps left by other old folks. But, more important to the Prices, the salver was identifiable. The coat of arms in the centre made it unique, and so copies of the photo were made for the widest possible distribution.

Two nights later I popped into the Brewers Arms at Aidensfield while on a late evening patrol and saw Daniel in his usual corner at the bar. He saw me, smiled briefly and nodded, but on this occasion there was no bravado about his refusing to co-operate with the police. I did not mention the theft before his pals – if he wished to do so, that was his privilege, and after checking the ages of some youngsters in the lounge, I left.

It was five days later when I got a call from Detective Sergeant Connolly.

'Ah, Nick, glad to have caught you. We've some good news – that silver salver of Mrs Price's. It's been recovered.'

'Really? Where?' I was delighted, more for Mrs Price than for myself.

'Birmingham. Birmingham City Police have done wonders for us – they've set up an Antiques Squad, and one of their lads spotted the salver in an antique shop. The dealer paid £850 for it – so whoever sold it to him knew it was worth a bob or two. But the even better news is that it has a set of fingerprints on it, and we're hoping they match those of our suspects. That'll take a day or two.'

'So when can Mrs Price have it back?' I asked.

'It'll take a while. If we get the villains, we'll need the salver for evidence, so we're talking of a couple of months or so at the least. But at least it's safe, and she will get it back eventually.'

'Thanks, Sergeant, that's great news. I'll go and tell her.'

But when I knocked on the door, Daniel opened it.

'What do you want?' he asked bluntly.

'I'd like to talk to your mother,' I said.

'Mother? What for?'

'About the stolen salver. I understand it is her property, Daniel, not yours.'

His face showed I had scored a point over him. Then Mrs Price came to see who was at the door and beckoned me to enter. 'Come in, Mr Rhea.'

With Daniel following me into the front room, she showed me the settee and smiled. 'Well, Mr Rhea, you have some news?'

'Yes.' I was so pleased for her as I explained the developments. Daniel listened too, but when I'd finished, he said, 'You mean you came here to quiz my mother after I'd given you all that help?'

'There were certain things to clarify, Daniel, and a more detailed description to obtain; you were at work. Your mother was most helpful . . .'

'I didn't tell you of Mr Rhea's visit, Daniel, because I knew how you'd react, you silly man. Anyway, it has paid dividends – the salver is safe again. Safe for you, I might add, although I'm not sure that you deserve it!'

'But I gave all the information to him, then he comes sneaking into my house asking question, snooping behind my back, poking his nose into my private life . . .'

'Daniel!' said Mrs Price. 'You are a silly fool.'

'I'll go.' I stood up to leave. 'I'll be in touch when we've more news, Mrs Price.'

'I hate the police,' said Daniel, standing up to follow me to the door. 'They're so untrustworthy, so devious . . .'

Mrs Price just smiled.

7 Private Lives

> The only trouble is, we do not understand what is
> happening to our neighbours.
>   Joseph Chamberlain (1836–1914)

Each of us feels entitled to a private life in which we may do as we please within the confines of our own home. If that statement sounds eminently just, the reality is not quite like that, because our private life and behaviour are regulated. For example, we must be careful not to disturb or upset the neighbours in a way that infringes the law.

The truth is that we cannot do exactly as we wish, even within our own home. Instead, there are many rules to restrict the use to which we can put our home. For example, it cannot legally become a brothel or a place for taking drugs, nor can it become a slaughter-house, public house, pawnbroker's shop, firearms dealer's premises, nursing home, gaming house, pet shop, theatre or hotel without some official intervention. Furthermore, we cannot do exactly as we wish within our own home, because we might antagonize one of the many official agencies. Running a scrap-metal business from the back yard, a horse-racing establishment from the front lawn, a cats' home in the garden shed, or rock concerts in the attic might not receive universal approval.

In spite of many restrictions, though, it may still be said that an Englishman's home is his castle, because we can enjoy a high degree of privacy within its confines. This reassuring old saying comes from the famous lawyer, statesman and jurist Sir Edward Coke (1552–1634): 'The house of everyone is to him as his castle and fortress, as well for his defence against injury or violence as for his repose.' The trouble with most of us is that we respect that notion up to a point, for, if we are honest, we still like to know what the neighbours are doing, and then we might object if their behaviour annoys us.

The snag is that the actions of one's neighbours can often extend beyond the immediate boundaries of their home, at times affecting the entire community. Simple and acceptable examples might include weddings and funerals which, although based on one's home, do in varying degrees affect the state of prevailing calm in a village community. Lots of people arrive, traffic is generated, crowds of spectators assemble, curiosity is aroused and the movement of ordinary people is sometimes restricted to permit the procession to pass. We do not object to that, nor do we normally object when something other than a wedding or funeral occurs, particularly when there is a positive increase in the interest shown by a healthy community.

Examples in Aidensfield included a visit by Her Majesty The Queen to nearby Hovingham on the occasion of the wedding of the Duke and Duchess of Kent, the visit of Sophia Loren to Castle Howard, along with Peter Ustinov and other famous faces, while filming *Lady L*, followed by several other camera crews who came later to film sequences for James Herriot's books.

During my constableship, Aidensfield itself was host to a surprising number of very famous people, ranging from British prime ministers to one of Charlie Chaplin's daughters, via cousins of the American president and several foreign princes and princesses. All were highly identifiable in a village of fewer than 200 souls. Nonetheless, in the midst of all this excitement, the village people afforded these guests a welcome degree of privacy. Word of their presence rarely reached anyone outside the community, the press never got to hear of their visits, and these famous folk could pop into the Brewers Arms or walk across the local moors without fear of being accosted by admirers, photographers and hangers-on.

As the village constable, I was often privy to these occasions, being asked by the hosts to ward off any unwelcome attention should it arise. I think it is fair to say that the people of Aidensfield became accustomed to having the famous and wealthy as guests in their pretty village.

Their discretion and loyalty to such a visitor were tested during one long, hot summer.

The story, which involves the private lives to two people, centres upon the old blacksmith's workshop. When the last blacksmith of Aidensfield ended his craft, an enterprising young man called Kevin Bell purchased the premises and turned it into a craftsman woodworker's shop. He began to produce handmade goods of every kind, from large items of furniture to such small objects as serviette rings, ashtrays, egg cups and three-legged stools.

Like so many local woodworkers, he carved an emblem upon his work. Hereabouts we have the Mouseman of Kilburn who carves everything in oak and then adorns it with his famous mouse trademark; there are those who identify their handicraft with acorns, lizards, owls and other distinctive marks. Kevin chose his own name for his logo and carved a bell upon his products. His work was good, his furniture was sound, and his application implied a determination to succeed. And so he did. He would never become a millionaire but he would and did become a respected craftsman.

But there was a mystery about Kevin.

He came to live and work in Aidensfield some months after my own arrival, but he was not a local man. He came from York, having nurtured a dream of becoming a rural craftsman, and I respected him for having the nerve to put his ambition to the test. He was a tall man, around thirty years old, with a slightly balding head of light brown hair; slim and powerful, he played cricket and squash.

Everyone liked Kevin – he became a welcome and important asset to Aidensfield. He made his home in the limestone cottage adjoining the old blacksmith's shop. This had been the home of a succession of blacksmiths, many of whom had been content to live in rather primitive conditions, but Kevin's woodworking skills and DIY ability turned it into a dream house.

The mystery which puzzled the local people involved his family.

An older woman came to live there, a Mrs Marie Bell, and we discovered she was Kevin's mother. She was in her mid fifties, we estimated, for her blonde hair was turning grey. She became a part of the village community by joining the Women's Institute and helping with parish church matters. In time, I learned that her husband had died, and so she had come to live with her unmarried son in Aidensfield. The arrangement seemed a good one, for it meant that Kevin had someone to look after his precious house, to ensure he was adequately fed and his clothes were washed. Mum and son appeared to have none of the problems that can accrue when different generations live together.

There was also a small boy, about seven years old. He came at the same time as Mrs Bell and was called Robert. As he was of a build and colouring similar to Kevin's, everyone assumed he was a late arrival in the family. Without asking or prying, they assumed that Mrs Bell had produced him just prior to her menopause, a time when many women are likely to conceive. The Bells did nothing to change that assumption.

Young Robert joined the local school, accompanied Mrs Bell to the shop or upon bus rides in Ashfordly, went to other children's houses for parties and invited them back, and took part in most of the village's events. Everyone called him Robert Bell, he called Mrs Bell 'mummy', and he related to Kevin as if the latter was an elder brother.

But I was to learn the truth.

As with so many of these family secrets, the truth came out quite accidentally and, having learned it in that way, I had no intention of making anyone else aware of young Robert's ancestry. The names I am now using are, of course, not the family's real ones, but I have been allowed to reveal that secret in this book – not that it is of earth-shattering consequence.

It seemed that some years earlier Kevin and a girl called Teresa Craven had had a long and enjoyable relationship whose result was Robert. Because Teresa had been eighteen at the time and on the threshold of a major career, Kevin said he would bring up the boy in the hope that perhaps she would one day marry him and settle down to motherhood. The caring Kevin had no wish to prevent Teresa's following her career – it was a most noble gesture, I felt. Then, when Kevin's father died, Mrs Bell took over the responsibility for the little lad;

it was a voluntary offer from a family which, I had already learned, was thoroughly nice and decent.

A bonus was that Teresa was now making a name in her chosen career, and she did visit her son from time to time. And she remained on good terms with Kevin – he seemed quite content to give her all the freedom she desired until she decided to settle down, marry him and raise their son.

This gem of local knowledge came to me through a colleague who served in York City Police. I learned this piece of news when he and I performed duty together at York Races – officers from the North Riding of Yorkshire were drafted in to perform duty at the races, and I found myself working with Tim Lewis. We chatted and he told me that a friend of his had moved to Aidensfield – that friend was Kevin Bell. And so, in this manner, I learned something of Kevin's past. It was during this chat that Tim told me about Teresa's career.

'Does the name Terry Craven mean anything to you?' he asked.

'No,' I admitted. 'Should it?'

'Not unless you're a tennis buff,' he said. 'She's our great white hope for Wimbledon.'

'Oh, *that* Terry Craven!' I had heard the name; in fact, she had been featured only recently in the national newspapers.

Tim went on to say she had been born in York but had moved away with her parents, returning from time to time to visit relatives. She was a talented and highly promising tennis player and had been offered a scholarship at an American university. There she would be coached in the very best of techniques by some of the world's finest exponents. Shortly before going to the USA she had come to York for a holiday, where she had met Kevin and become pregnant. And, Kevin being Kevin, he had promised to bring up the child so that Teresa could follow her career.

In my time at Aidensfield, she had completed her American course and was now part of the world tennis circuit, playing in tournaments at all the major venues – and she was winning. She was high in the list of British seeded women players, being one of our top exponents. From my friend Tim, I understood that when her tennis career was over and her world tours ended, she would marry Kevin and settle down to being a mum for Robert. It was a remarkable tale.

Terry did visit Aidensfield on a regular basis. When her hectic lifestyle permitted her to take time off, she would come to stay quietly in Aidensfield. She stayed with Kevin and his mother and would go for long walks with young Robert. I think he thought she was an aunt – certainly, the other children referred to her as 'Aunt Teresa'. I'm sure most of the village thought so too, although I suspect many did realize the true relationships within that happy family. Her other role, as a leading British ladies tennis-player, was hardly mentioned; those who did not follow tennis would never know of her, for she had not yet become what is termed a 'household name', nor was she universally recognized in airports and public places.

Then things began to go wrong.

I was in the bar of the Brewers Arms one Friday lunchtime in early May, making one of my routine uniformed visits, when a long-haired young man burst in. He rushed across to the bar, ordered a pint and started to chatter to the locals. He sat at one of the tables with some regulars and bought them all a drink, a bonus to their usual lunchtime pint. At first I paid no heed to his behaviour, thinking it was someone known to these characters. Then he came over to me.

'Ah, the village constable, the fountain of all knowledge, the man with everyone's secret tucked in his notebook. Constable,' he smiled at me, 'can I get you a drink?'

'No thanks. I'm on duty,' I said.

'Well, you might be able to help me. The name's Craig.' And he said he was a reporter for one of the less savoury of the Sunday national newspapers. As he talked, I caught the eye of one of the men at the table he'd just left – the man shook his head slowly from side to side. I knew they had not co-operated.

'It depends,' I said cautiously. 'If it's anything to do with the force, we do have an official spokesman.'

'It's nothing to do with the force, Constable,' he said, sipping his pint. 'It's local knowledge I'm after. You'll know of Terry Craven?' I shook my head. 'But you must, the tennis player . . . the next great British Wimbledon champion . . .'

'Sorry, I don't follow tennis.' I pretended to be ignorant. 'I've never heard of him.'

'Look, you can't be much of a village guardian if you don't know her; it's not a him, it's a her, Terry as in Teresa, not Terence. She comes here a lot. Stays in the village, according to my sources . . .'

'Really? We get lots of very famous people here,' I said. 'A tennis-player doesn't make a lot of impact, I'm afraid. Are you sure you haven't got this village confused with Aidensford in Surrey? Some do, you know.'

'No, I have not. Aidensfield is the place. She comes here for quiet holidays. Somebody must know her . . . it's the tiniest bloody village I've ever been in . . . everybody must know everybody else's business . . .'

'If they do know, they respect each other,' I said. 'Now, do you lads know her?' I asked the men at the table and also the barman whose name was Sid. They all shook their heads and muttered their denials. It was a convincing act on their part.

'Why do you want to know?' I asked.

'There's a tale doing the rounds saying she's got a bairn, an illegitimate kid, farmed out. I'm onto the story, I'm after an exclusive . . .'

'You've got the wrong spot here, mate,' said Sid. 'As Mr Rhea says, you must be thinking of Aidensford down south.'

It was evident that the reporter realized there was a conspiracy of silence, and he stormed out. The moment he'd gone, Sid put into operation the unofficial but highly effective Early Warning System we had created. This served all the businesses in the village and surrounding areas. If one received a visit from, say, a con man or someone trying to pass dud cheques, that business would ring another three, who in turn would ring another three and so on, thus warning everyone within a very short time. This useful system was now being operated for the benefit of Teresa Craven.

'Thanks, Sid,' I said. 'I'll go and warn Kevin and Mrs Bell.'

'That bastard! Why do those bloody awful Sunday papers dig up dirt like that? And who buys them anyway?'

As I warned a grateful Kevin of the man's visit, so Sid's system alerted the other places of public resort in Aidensfield and beyond. I was to learn later that the reporter had received absolutely no information from the village, and I was pleased, if only that young Robert's life was being protected from sensational and scandalous journalism.

But it did not end there. On the following Sunday the pub was inundated with journalists – all the muckraking papers were represented and there were a few reputable ones there too. News of a possible indiscretion in Terry Craven's life had permeated the newsrooms and canteens of many papers.

The heavy-spending reporters were buying drinks for all the regulars, hoping that tongues would be freed and news would flow. But Sid had done his duty. No one was prepared to speak, and young Robert's 'Bell' surname and his home at the blacksmith's shop saved his family from investigation. More drink was purchased and more questions were asked, but no answers were given.

Then, without warning to anyone, the local ne'er-do-well, who had the curious name of Claude Jeremiah Greengrass, came into the Brewers Arms. This was not his usual pub – he tended to haunt the Hopbind Inn at Elsinby – but he must have sensed that something important was happening in Aidensfield and that free drinks were available, along with the chance to earn a few bob. He had turned up like the proverbial bad penny. Claude was a pest. Small, pinched and totally untrustworthy, he was always in trouble of some kind; his offences were usually of a minor nature and he lived on his wits. As he materialized in that bar, I scented danger. He was the one man who might reveal the truth, and the others were not in a fit state to warn him by now. They could hardly talk – the reporters had virtually defeated themselves in getting everyone paralytic. But I knew that Claude would know Terry's secret – he knew everyone's secrets . . .

'Ah!' A *News of the World* reporter spotted him before I could reach him through the crowd. 'A newcomer! You, here! Can I get you a drink?'

'I allus has a rum before my Sunday dinner.' He beamed at the journalist, his wizened face crinkling in a leathery smile.

A rum was duly bought.

'Claude,' I said. 'I'd like a word . . .'

'Later, Mr Rhea, I've got drink in my hand, and I never interrupts that, not for you, nor for anybody.'

'But before you talk to these men . . .'

'What men?' asked Claude, and he winked at me. I knew what he meant. He sipped his first rum, savouring the taste as the journalist waited. I left him with the journalist.

'Er, what's your name?'

'Greengrass.'

'Mr Greengrass, we are interested in a young lady called Craven . . .'

'My glass is empty. I allus likes a rum before my Sunday dinner,' said Claude, and I watched the twinkle in his eye. His glass was refilled, and he sipped it slowly. When it was empty, the journalist began, 'Mr Greengrass . . .'

'I do like a rum before my Sunday dinner,' repeated Claude.

The regulars lost count of Claude Jeremiah's rums, because they had also lost count of their own beers, whiskies and brandies. The outcome of that visit by the press was heavy expenditure for the press, a hefty Sunday lunchtime trading session by the Brewers Arms, a lot of late meals in the farms and cottages of the area, and several thumping headaches.

But no one revealed any information about Terry. The reporters had wasted a fortune. Afterwards I thanked Claude Jeremiah.

'It's not often I congratulate you,' I said, 'but you did real well.'

'I do like a rum before my Sunday dinner, Mr Rhea, so when I heard about Terry and that the press were there doling out free booze, I thought they owed me drink or two. I mean to say, they've printed enough scandalous tales about me.'

And so they had. He'd earned his rums.

I think that incident convinced the gutter press that they'd never succeed in getting a story of Terry Craven's private life from the villagers of Aidensfield. The people had, without exception, closed ranks to protect her and her child. I was proud of them.

But the story did not end there. That year, Terry reached the quarter-finals before being knocked out of Wimbledon.

We were all proud of her. In the autumn she returned to Aidensfield for a few weeks rest. She had been told of the village's response to the press enquiries and, in her gratitude, decided to throw a party for everyone in the Brewers Arms. She would pay for all the drinks and a buffet supper. I went along with Mary, for I was off duty, and it was a wonderful occasion. Even Claude Jeremiah had been invited. Everyone was happy for Terry and very proud of her achievements as they sang and drank her health. She made a little speech too. She said that, once her tennis-playing days were over, she would come to live permanently in Aidensfield with her son and husband. She told us that, in fact, she and Kevin were engaged to be married – that was another secret which no one knew.

Five or six years later, she did return and now lives happily in the area as Mrs Kevin Bell. She never won Wimbledon, but she did once reach the semi-finals.

But even now, if you enter the Brewers Arms on a Sunday lunchtime, you might encounter an elf-like man with a wizened and sun-tanned face. If you are unwise enough to ask him a question, it could become an expensive exercise, because, with expectation in his voice, he will respond with, 'I do enjoy a rum before my Sunday dinner.'

Some older maps of the North York Moors show an isolated house known as Owlet Hall. But a search will fail to locate it, because it no longer stands proud in its moorland setting. Sadly, it was demolished, and this is the story.

For many generations, it had been occupied by the Barr family, the last being Jason and Sarah Barr. They had scraped a tough living from the surrounding moorland, chiefly by farming sheep, and they had eked out their existence by undertaking other jobs. They would help their neighbours at harvest, for example, or give assistance at sheep sales, fairs and haytime.

Jason and Sarah had one son called William. He was himself retired, an ex-farmworker, and lived quietly in a council house at Aidensfield. Born at Owlet Hall, he had left the lonely spot in his teens to seek work in the dales, recognizing that his primitive family home, which boasted no water, drains or electricity, could never support him or any family. His parents had lived there until shortly before their deaths, when the house had passed to him. But there was nothing he could do with it. To bring it up to modern standards would have cost him more money than he had earned in a lifetime. No one wanted to buy it, due to its remote position and increasingly dilapidated condition, and no one seemed willing to undertake the expense of 'doing it up'.

The result was that the once-proud house was allowed to fall down, piece by piece. The woodwork of the windows was rotting, parts of the roof were collapsing, and when the back door rotted from its hinges, the ground floor became a shelter for sheep, moorland birds and the occasional hiker. However, upon my appointment as village constable at Aidensfield, the house was still standing and, in spite of its condition, was remarkably dry and cosy inside. It had been built to withstand the rigours of the moorland weather, and I always felt it looked charming in its patch of green. I often wished I had had the enormous sums necessary to renovate it.

Then one day, as I was patrolling the lonely road which ran past Owlet Hall, I noticed a couple of old cars parked outside. They were battered and rusting and painted in what became known as psychedelic colours, all a jumble of bright reds, oranges, blacks, blues, greens and more besides. I parked my van on the moor and walked over to them. Neither was taxed, I noted, but as they were not on public roads, I could not instigate proceedings. Then a long-haired youth with a colourful band around his head and small rimless glasses perched on the end of his nose appeared at the broken door.

'Want something?' he asked.

'I'm checking these cars,' I said. 'Are they yours?'

'They are,' and he offered no more information.

'They're not taxed.' I had to make the point.

'They're not on the road,' he said.

'But if they do go on the road, you'll make sure they are taxed and insured?' He just smiled, a gentle but cheeky smile. 'I'll be watching for them,' I said, smiling back at him. 'Are you staying long?'

'As long as need be,' he said. 'There's eight of us. We're no trouble, we just want to live our lives as we want, with no hassle, no authoritarian oppression, no rules, just happiness and freedom . . .'

'Flower power, communal living and free love?' I had heard these phrases in recent months and had seen reports about the people who had adopted these new ideals. They were hippies.

'That's about it,' he said.

'You've got permission to live here?' I asked.

'No, but we don't need it. We're squatting. We can squat in empty houses and no one can throw us out. I'm sure you know that,' he smiled. 'Besides, this old spot is derelict, falling down, full of holes and no doors. We'll fix it for ourselves.'

I stayed a few moments chatting to this man without seeing any of his friends, and decided they were harmless out here. Indeed, they might make some repairs to William's old house.

It was a further two or three days before I came across William Barr. He was collecting his pension from the post office/shop at Aidensfield and I took the opportunity to chat to him.

'Bill,' I said, 'that old house of yours, Owlet Hall. I was driving past earlier this week and see you've got visitors. A bunch of flower-power people, by the look of it. Your old home's been turned into a hippie commune.'

I explained what I had seen, and he thought for a while.

'They'll not be harming anybody?' he said.

'No, I think not,' I had to admit. 'They're supposed to be a friendly lot, a bit weird by our standards, but they're not likely to plan bank raids or kill moorland sheep for meat.'

'Then they can stay,' he said. 'T'awd spot might as well be useful to somebody.'

And so he allowed them to remain. In fact, it wouldn't have been easy get rid of them for, if pressed, they would surely claim squatters' rights, but because I was aware of their presence, I recorded the matter in my files.

I told the CID, with a special note to the Drugs Squad, for it was known that similar communes had cultivated cannabis plants, and I made a mental note to call at the house every three months or so, with a view to enforcing whichever of our laws they might be breaking. I would let them know of my continuing official interest, for I had no wish for the local youngsters to experiment with drugs of any kind.

By the time of my next visit, things had changed. The old cars were still there, still untaxed and still in their gaudy colours, but there was much more. That extra stuff was rubbish. It was everywhere. The exterior of the hitherto tidy old house was cluttered with every conceivable item of junk – old prams, bedsteads, chairs, a rusty oven, bikes, bottles, lengths of timber, flower pots – it looked like an itinerant trader's encampment of the very worst kind. I picked my way through the miasma to peep at the cars, and the man I'd first met appeared once again.

'Hi, Constable,' he beamed. 'You're back.'

'Yes, and I'll keep coming. This is part of my patch.'

'We're not criminals, man, we're friends to everyone.'

'Is this rubbish all yours?'

'Sure. The council doesn't collect it, so it stays.'

'You might try to remove it, or even burn some.'

'No hassle, man, no hassle. It's ours; we'll deal with it if we want; if we don't want, we won't. So who cares?'

'The people who live round here don't like their area looking like a council tip,' I said. 'They're proud of their countryside and don't like it to be desecrated.'

'Dr Johnson said that fine clothes are good only as they supply the want of other means of procuring respect,' said the fellow. 'External appearances don't matter. It's the soul that matters, man. So what's a bit of rubbish? Superficial, that's all. Unimportant in the real world . . .'

'You should try to keep the place neat, tidy and clean,' I tried again.

'Why, Constable, why? To get respect? False respect? People must take us as we are or not at all. Why pretend? We mean no harm, we just want to live our lives in peace.'

'And so do the villagers,' I said. 'Their rights and opinions are as valid as yours.'

'Sure they are.' He beamed and vanished indoors.

I was powerless to prosecute them under the Litter Act, because this was not a public place – it was private land. And the Civic Amenities Act was not then in force.

Over the following months, the hippies made themselves increasingly unwelcome. With no known form of income, they did require certain commodities, and one general store, not in Aidensfield but in Ashfordly, made the mistake of trusting them by supplying them with groceries on credit. The commune members took full advantage of that generosity – they never paid, although they did offer to perform some work in lieu. One of their plans was to offer to deliver groceries to the surrounding villages, but timely advice by one of our constables soon alerted the grocer to that risk. For every delivery they made, they would probably help themselves to a few items.

The great British public would find itself supporting these parasites. In addition to their known activities, they were suspected of helping themselves to the occasional bottle of milk from doorsteps, they had filled their cars' tanks with petrol at local garages and not paid their bills, they had persuaded the coal merchant to deliver a ton into their coal house and had not paid him . . . and so the problems began to multiply.

Within a year, every small business in the area found itself involuntarily supporting the commune. As one businessman said to me, 'If they'd come and asked for a basket of apples, I'd have given them one, but to pretend to buy one and then not pay – well, that's dishonest.'

His words did sum up the general attitude of the villagers. If the commune had genuinely wished to establish itself with the good will of the local people, that good will was available, but these hippies had abused it. They had resorted to cheating, and that was unforgiveable. Had they pleaded they were honest but poor, voluntary support would have been forthcoming, perhaps with a request for some kind of return assistance in and around the village.

A secondary aspect was their suspected involvement in drugs. We did receive information that some of the hippies were involved with soft drugs, cannabis being named. We heard rumours of parties at which the cannabis was smoked, these being weekend affairs when dozens of like-minded people flocked to Owlet Hall to take advantage of its remote location. Our drugs officer did raid the place from time to time, but no drugs were ever found. We never did know with any certainty whether or not drugs were being used, but the rumours persisted, and so our drugs officers continued with their raids. This did make the public uneasy, many of the local parents being concerned that their children might be tempted to try the drugs at discos or in the pubs and cafés of the district.

The combination of unsettling rumour and established facts meant that poor old William Barr found himself very unpopular. Several villagers blamed him for their problems, claiming, in their ignorance, that he should never have let the property to them. But William was helpless. There was nothing he could do to remove them; few seemed to understand that. There was nothing in criminal law to make their occupation illegal, and therefore nothing I could do to help him. The hippies knew their rights – William could never force them to leave. But they must have sensed that he was contemplating some kind of action, because they succeeded in boarding up the windows and fixing their own locks to the doors. The house was never left empty – one of them was always present.

Eventually, poor old William came to see me.

'Mr Rhea,' – he looked weary and worried – 'them hippies 'ave been in Owlet for more than a year now, and 'ave you seen t'state of it? Terrible! You'd think they'd 'ave a bit o' respect for other folks's property. My pigs never made sike a mess. Isn't there owt you can do?'

'Sorry, Bill, I can't. They know I can't, which makes it worse! Tenancy problems are not a police matter. I don't think you'd get a court order to evict them either, because if you claimed they'd damaged the place, they'd say they'd improved and repaired it, which in some ways they have. Have you got a solicitor who might advise you?'

'No, but the NFU gives advice. They said t'same as you.'

He stood behind the counter of my tiny office, and I felt sorry for him. I wished there was something someone could do, but at that time there was a gap in the law which permitted squatters to take over empty houses and live in them rent-free and to the detriment of the owners. The Labour government then in power refused to change the law, and by the 1970s this was a very common problem for property-owners. Poor old Bill was a victim of this uncaring attitude.

'Folks is blaming me,' he said. 'They owe money here, there and everywhere, they're pinching things, they've turned the house into a rubbish dump . . . now, t'locals is saying it's all my fault.'

And then, as he spoke, I remembered reading of a similar case in a village in some remote part of England. I could not remember precisely which village or even the date, but I did remember the story.

'Bill,' I said, 'I remember a similar case, a few years back. This farmer had squatters in his hand's cottage, down a lane. They took it over, just like yours.'

'And what did 'e do, Mr Rhea?'

'He put a swarm of bees through their kitchen window,' I said. 'And then, when the squatters all rushed out of the place, he put his bull in. He made the house into a home for his prize bull. That cleared 'em out,' I chuckled.

'I 'aven't got a bull,' he said seriously, then added wickedly, 'but I 'ave a useful awd tup.' A tup is the local name for a ram. And off he went, chuckling to himself. As he reached the gate, he turned and called, 'Awd Robbie Mullen owes me a favour.'

Robbie Mullen was a retired railway man who lived at Elsinby, and I knew he kept bees; I'd called upon his services from time to time when a local swarm had required attention.

I awaited developments, but nothing happened until the following May, which, I was to learn, was the time most swarms of bees occur. When a young queen bee is ready to leave the hive, half the resident workers swarm around her, and as she leaves, they cluster about her, going wherever she goes. The others remain with the resident queen. After leaving, the new queen settles on a tree or a fence to wait while several of the workers find her a new home, whereupon she joins them to establish a colony.

Awd Robbie, being an expert, waited until his bees were swarming. As luck would have it, he captured two swarms. He and Bill, with the ram in his pick-up truck, drove out to Owlet Hall early one morning and thrust the two buzzing swarms into the open windows of the house. The result was pandemonium. Eight o r ten hippies, with angry bees buzzing around their long hair, bolted nude from the house, whereupon a huge ram, seeing the open door, bolted inside.

Quite suddenly, and with a minimum of legal bantering, Owlet Hall had a different family of squatters.

Bill was on hand too and swiftly replaced the locks, later throwing from the windows the tatty belongings of his un-wanted guests. I did not turn up that day, for I had no wish to delay their departure by having to deal with two untaxed cars on the road – I wanted to see no psychedelic cars at all and no long-haired alternative members of society. I just wanted rid of them.

And so they vanished, to inflict their unwelcome presence upon someone else. Bill recovered his ram, which, it seemed, had a propensity for rushing headlong into open doorways, but Robbie left his two swarms of bees in the old house. They did not stay.

'I reckon t'smell put 'em off,' he said with all seriousness.

All the belongings left behind were burned, and Bill sold the house to a builder who wanted to demolish it so that he could acquire the stone. And so, within a further year, Owlet Hall disappeared without trace.

In gratitude for my unofficial advice, Bill gave me a pot of honey which, according to Awd Robbie, was made by the very bees who did such a good job on those flower people.

8   Grave Problems

> I love to lose myself in a mystery.
> Sir Thomas Browne (1605–82)

Many police officers conclude their careers without ever having been involved in a murder investigation. I'm sure that some never cherish the desire for that experience, but because murder is constantly regarded as the worst of all crimes, there persists within many officers an ambition to arrest a murderer. If the satisfaction of making that arrest is never achieved, they wish to be a small part of the investigation; there is a certain pride at being part of a murder inquiry team, especially a successful one.

During my time as the village constable at Aidensfield, I never achieved that distinction. If murder had been committed on my patch, the mighty CID would have been called in. Many experienced detectives would have descended upon the locality to take over the investigation, and I might have been co-opted because of my local knowledge, but my role would not have been a primary one, only one of support.

Nonetheless, from time to time murders committed in distant parts did involve me. Occasionally a death in a far-off town would have links with my patch and, for example, I might have to interview the driver of a car who had driven past the scene of the killing at or about the material time.

One infamous crime which involved me on its fringes was the notorious 'Moors Murders' case. Although these crimes are forever associated with the Yorkshire moors, the moors in question are about a hundred miles to the west of those upon which I worked. They were spread across the borders of Lancashire and the West Riding of Yorkshire, while I served in the North Riding of Yorkshire. These 'Yorkshires' were two distinct counties, each with its own county police force; Lancashire was regarded as foreign territory.

The victims of Ian Brady and Myra Hindley had been buried high on those Pennine moors and there seemed little or no connection with my quiet part of Yorkshire. After the couple's conviction, however, I found myself involved in the aftermath. A man and wife whom I shall call Matt and Peggy Copeland had been watching television when a programme about the Moors Murders was shown. One of the photographs was the highly publicized full-face portrait of Myra Hindley, taken when she was looking at her most gaunt and ghastly. Upon seeing that photograph, Peggy Copeland felt sure she had seen that woman accompanied by a man; she was utterly convinced she had seen Myra Hindley digging somewhere upon the North York Moors at least a year prior to her arrest. She could not swear that the man on the moors was Ian Brady, but she never doubted she had seen Hindley.

The time had been early October, the day had been a Sunday, and the Copelands had been alone. As they had parked their car beside a lonely moorland road to enjoy a picnic, so the haunting face of a woman had appeared above a slight hillock. It was swiftly followed by a man's, and both of them stared briefly at the parked car, then vanished down the other side of the moorland mound. The man had had a spade in his hands and appeared to have been digging.

Mrs Copeland thought nothing more about this curious incident until much later, when that face of Myra Hindley had stared from her television screen. She was convinced it was the face of the woman she'd seen on the moors. She discussed her worries with her husband, and for a few days the couple lived with the awesome suspicion that they might have been parked near a murder victim's grave on the North York Moors. Uncertain what to do next, they read as much as they could about the case, to see if there were any known links with the North York Moors, but none was mentioned. Eventually they decided to visit their local police station to air their concern; this was at Peterlee in County Durham.

After exhaustive interviews, the detectives in Durham were sufficiently convinced by Peggy's story to launch an investigation. The snag was that, by this time, many months had elapsed since Peggy's sighting, and furthermore, neither she nor her husband was sufficiently knowledgeable about the North York Moors to pinpoint the precise location. They had toured the moors that Sunday without any pre-arranged plan; they did not really know their way round; neither could recall any particular village or view-point. Following a meeting about the situation, Durham CID decided that the Copelands should revisit the moors in an attempt to find both the place where they had halted for their picnic, and the mound behind which the suspicious man and woman had disappeared.

But the point of search was within Britain's largest area of open heather: there are 553 square miles inside the national park boundaries, with hundreds of miles of roads and an enormous variety of view-points. It was therefore decided that the Copelands should describe, as best they could, the route they had taken and the sights which remained in their memories. From that, an officer who was familiar with the moors would attempt, with their co-operation, to trace their picnic site.

I was selected for that job. In an unmarked police car, I had to tour the moors with the Copelands, and we had to do all within our power to locate that place. It sounded easy, but I knew it wasn't going to be. I suggested that we select a weekend which corresponded to their first visit, i.e. during early October, because the colours, the contours and even the sunlight would make conditions almost identical to that first visit. This was agreed.

At dawn one Sunday morning in October, therefore, Durham CID ferried the Copelands to Guisborough, a market town on the northern tip of the moors. I drove there to meet them.

I had been allowed to use Sergeant Blaketon's official car, immaculate in its black livery. He had checked the milometer, the tyres, the water and oil, and he had also noted there was not a scratch or patch of dirt on his vehicle.

'I want my car back in this condition, Rhea,' he reminded me as I drove off.

Armed with maps, books and photographs of the moors, I

met my companions for the day and, over a coffee in a small café, we tried to identify their route. They had enjoyed a coffee in this very café on that other visit, which made it a perfect starting-point. As a rare treat, I could pay for their coffee from official funds, because I had been issued with a small sum of money towards our subsistence for the day.

Having met this sincere couple, I was looking forward to the task. The Copelands were in their late thirties or early forties and were a genuine, down-to-earth man and woman who had found themselves in a curious situation. I did my best to assure them that they were not wasting their time or mine, for that worry seemed uppermost in their minds. I'm sure I convinced them that we considered a reconstruction of their experience meritworthy, otherwise we should not have agreed to undertake this journey.

Having thoroughly discussed our plans, we sallied forth across the splendid moors. There is no need to repeat all the details of that long and somewhat arduous trip, save to say that we covered every mile of main road within the moors and a good many leagues upon minor roads. We examined every picnic site and halting-place that I knew; we stopped, we reversed, we retraced our steps, we motored down lanes and byways and we examined mounds and bumps from every conceivable angle. We explored every possible site from every possible position. We lunched at a lovely pub and enjoyed coffees, ice-creams and soft drinks as, from time to time, we needed a break and refreshment.

As darkness fell we had not positively identified the location. We had found several 'possibles' which we marked on the Ordnance Survey map, but none proved, without doubt, to be the place where Peggy believed she had set eyes on Myra Hindley. Because darkness prevented any further exploration, I now had the task of driving my charges back to Peterlee, and it was with some sadness at our lack of success that I left the moors for that journey half-way through County Durham.

Upon arrival at the Copelands' neat little house, I was invited in; we organized some fish and chips for ourselves. I met their 15-year-old son, Paul, as we shared the table over our succulent meal. Never have fish and chips tasted so good. We discussed our trip, always trying just one more avenue in the hope we would produce an answer, but we did not. I assured them that, in my own future journeys over the moors, I would forever be alert to any possible location.

After I'd eaten, Peggy and Matt insisted I visit their son's pride and joy. I went through the back door of the house and found myself in a long, narrow extension which reeked of mice. There were hundreds of them – white mice galore, large ones, little ones, old ones and young ones, grey ones and pure white ones, mottled ones and spotty ones . . . I had never seen so many mice in one place. They were all in cages with wire fronts, all gnawing at titbits and all seeming content. Having dutifully admired them, I prepared to say my farewells and thank-yous. But as I hovered in the doorway, Peggy bade me a fond goodbye and handed me a memento of my day's duty – a small wooden cage containing two white mice! It had a glass front and two compartments, one filled with hay for sleeping upon and the other equipped with a treadmill for exercise. A tiny hole separated the two. My new friends were sniffing at me from their bedroom.

'No, really, I can't . . .' I said, thinking of Mary's reaction when I returned home.

'We'd like you to have them,' she said with the utmost sincerity. 'It's a small way of thanking you for your patience and time today. We really did enjoy the outing, even if we didn't find the place.'

I did not have the heart to refuse this gift, and so I placed my two mice on the floor of the police car, bade the Copelands farewell and set about the sixty-mile drive home. The mice squeaked from time to time but I returned to Ashfordly police station with car and mice intact. Sergeant Blaketon was waiting for me. His first task was to stalk around the car to examine it for dents, damage and dirt.

'Rhea, this car is like a midden! Look at it! Mud from fore to aft, mud as high as the roof, and mud thick enough to plant potatoes in. Where the hell have you been?'

'The moors, Sergeant, searching for evidence of a serious crime. The moorland tracks can be dirty, you know . . .'

He grumbled at length about the mud but found no damage. I followed him into the office to make my report. He listened with deep interest as I outlined every mile of my journey, with a glowing account of what we had discovered and a factual account of what we had not traced. From time to time, he quizzed me on portions of the trek which I might have omitted or forgotten, but I gained the impression he was satisfied with the outcome. He concluded the interview by saying I would have to clean the car in the morning. I assured him I would come to Ashfordly first thing – and conveniently forget to remind him that tomorrow was my day off. If he insisted I wash the car *tomorrow*, he'd have to authorize my overtime.

On this strange day, our duty had been done – we had examined the claim put forward by the Copelands, but it had proved of no value to the detectives engaged on the Moors Murder inquiry.

Before I left the office, Blaketon, in an uncharacteristic show of gratitude, said, 'Well done, Rhea. Submit a detailed written report as soon as you can. Include everything. I'll authorize overtime payment for today's duty. You've put in some long hours and I trust they were worthwhile.'

'I think so, Sergeant.'

'So, having spent an entire day with the Copelands, what do you make of them?'

'They were genuine in their belief,' I said. 'I like them, they were good people.'

'Are you saying we've some murder victims buried on our patch?' he put to me.

'No,' I said. 'I'm saying I believe Mr and Mrs Copeland were honest in their actions. I truly believe Mrs Copeland thought she had seen Myra Hindley. Whether she did is another matter; that's something I can't answer.'

'We'll send your report to Durham CID, and they'll get in touch with the murder team. You realize you might have to do the whole thing again?'

'I'll do it, if it's necessary,' I assured him, adding that it might have to wait until next year in the same season, due to the appearance of the landscape and the light.

'Good man. Well, young Rhea, let's get you home to Aidensfield. It's late.'

As he settled in the driving-seat to ferry me home, I climbed into the passenger side of his official car and lifted the mouse cage onto my lap.

'What the hell have you got there, Rhea? It pongs a good deal, I might say.'

'A pair of white mice, Sergeant,' I said inanely.

'You mean this is the result of your day's duty on a major murder investigation? You mean that you've nothing more to show for it than a pair of white mice?'

He was staring straight ahead in the darkness as he started the engine, so I could not see the expression on his face. Was he angry or was he winding me up?

'It is one outcome,' I had to stand my corner. 'A bit of light relief after a hard day. Mr and Mrs Copeland thought the children would like them.'

'I should imagine they would.' Then he chuckled. 'But what's your wife going to think? Who's going to clean them out? Who's going to feed them, Rhea? And are they male and female? If they are, my lad, you'll have millions of mice before you have time to find a cat . . .'

He went on and on about the drawbacks of keeping pet mice as he drove me back to Aidensfield.

When I arrived, the house was in darkness. Mary and the children were in bed, and all were fast asleep. I crept in, clutching the cage and its two cheerful inhabitants, and placed them on a shelf in the kitchen. I fed them supper from the mixture of grains and nuts given to me by Paul Copeland, covered the cage with a duster to keep out the draughts and crawled upstairs to bed. I was exhausted and fell into a deep sleep within seconds.

Next morning Mary awoke before me and trotted downstairs. Her loud shrieks soon aroused me.

Half asleep, I rushed down, forgetting the mice and thinking something awful had happened. I found Mary in the kitchen with the duster in her hands as she stared in astonishment at the two bright-eyed mice.

'What on earth are these?' she demanded.

'Presents,' I said. 'For the children.'

'Oh no, they're not,' she retorted. 'Just you get rid of those this very morning!'

She went on at some length, but the children had heard the commotion and came downstairs to see what was happening. All of them fell heavily and immediately in love with the mice. Amid much persuasion, Mary allowed us to keep them and soon grew fond of their presence, even if they did become a wee bit pungent at times. Happily, they were of the same sex, although I'm not sure which, so they did not reproduce. They lived on that shelf for many years, growing gracefully old, as pet mice do, while enjoying the occasional romp around the house. I did not think that naming them Ian and Myra was at all correct, neither was Matt and Peggy, and so, for reasons which escape me, we called them Ebb and Flo.

But we never undertook a further search of the North York Moors, nor did I ever learn whether the murder team had examined any of the possible sites we had identified. The mystery of Peggy Copeland's unusual sighting remains unresolved.

Another murder mystery was even more curious.

The date was 8 June when a postman hurried into Ashfordly police station; it was around 10 a.m., and by chance I was in the office.

He told me that that morning, while on his rounds, he'd been driving past a clump of pine trees on the moors behind Ashfordly when he'd noticed a small wooden cross planted in the earth. It had not been there before that day. It was adorned with ribbons, and the turf and soil beside it had been newly dug over. I asked him for a precise location and he showed me on an Ordnance Survey map. The clump of trees was beside a lonely moorland road which led through Lairsbeck to serve a few isolated farms before petering out upon the heights of the moors.

I thanked him and decided to have a look at the scene before taking any further action. I found it just as he had described. The cross stood about two feet high and had been fashioned from two hazel twigs. White ribbons dangled from the arms, and it stood within a circle of some two dozen pine trees, with not a cottage or farm in sight. The cross was firmly upright in a thick grassy patch, and immediately in front of it was a small area of recently dug earth. My own guess was that the earth was very fresh – it might even have been dug over that morning; certainly it was not more than a day or two old. It was the size of a human grave, not one small enough for a cat or a dog. Remaining at the site, I radioed the control room at Eltering and outlined the situation. Sergeant Bairstow said he would liaise with me at the scene, his estimated time of arrival being half an hour. I was instructed to wait and not touch anything.

When Charlie Bairstow arrived, he stood and looked for a long time at that odd sight, occasionally scratching his head while walking in a circle around the trees.

'What do you make of it, Nick?' he asked.

'No idea,' I said. 'Could it be a horse, a pony perhaps? A pet cow or calf? Goat? It looks as though something's been buried and commemorated, doesn't it?'

'But would anybody commemorate an animal with a cross?' he asked.

'It wouldn't surprise me,' I said, recalling that some Americans arranged weddings for dogs and birthday parties for cats. 'But who'd bury a person here and then mark the grave like that?'

'There's only one way to find out. We'll have to call in the cavalry.'

By that, he meant he'd call in the CID and their experts, for they would surely examine the grave by digging it up.

From his car radio, he summoned divisional headquarters, whereupon Detective Sergeant Gerry Connolly said he would come immediately; we had to wait yet again and not touch anything. He arrived within three-quarters of an hour and examined the lonely site.

'We'll have to dig it up,' he pronounced. 'I'll get my lads to do it – I'll need a photographer standing by. I'll radio them now while we tape off the area.'

'Anything I can do?' I asked.

'Yes, Nick, get the yellow tape from my car boot. Circle those trees with it and watch where you put your feet. If you find anything there – anything at all, leave it where it is, then tell me.'

Thus the formalities began. One or two cars passed as we worked, but at this stage we did not ask any questions, nor did we interview the few householders whose cottages occupied these remote moors. The nearest was almost half a mile away. Detective Constables Ian Shackleton and Paul Wharton arrived with spades, picks and wheelbarrow, and Detective Sergeant Marks, the photographer, arrived to record progress. The scene was now one of activity and interest, with no fewer than five police cars, lots of police officers and yellow tape, all laced with a high degree of anticipated drama.

Ian Shackleton lost no time in commencing his dig. As the earth was soft, he found it a comparatively easy task, and very soon he had a broad and deep hole. But apart from the soil and a few surprised worms, there was nothing buried there. Joined by Paul Wharton and his pick-axe, they expanded the area of digging until they covered an area of about twelve feet by six in rough terms. Having stretched beyond the boundaries of the original grave without finding anything, they dug several shallow trenches without encountering anything remotely suspicious, and then concentrated upon digging deeper into the original grave and also below the cross. Soon they came to the sub-soil, which was undisturbed. It wasn't long before we had a hole large enough to contain a small swimming-pool, and nothing to show for it but a huge pile of earth. The forlorn little wooden cross lay on one side.

'Nothing,' said Connolly eventually. 'Sod all, in fact. Nowt. Nil.'

'Does it suggest the ground's been prepared for a grave?' suggested Ian Shackleton.

'Well, we're not going to fill it in! If somebody else cares to bury summat here, let 'em!' laughed Connolly. 'Leave the earth as it is, but replace the cross. Charlie,' he addressed Sergeant Bairstow, 'get your lads to visit this place regularly, will you? Summat's being going on, but I've no idea what. See what you can turn up.'

'It's a good task for young Rhea,' beamed Sergeant Bairstow. 'How about it, Nick? See if you can find out just what's been happening here.'

'I'll do my best,' I promised.

And so we dispersed, leaving the earth around the edge of the massive hole, and the cross in its original position, albeit now in bare, upturned earth. I decided to do my best to find answers to the puzzles. Who had place the cross there and why? And who had turned over this earth, and why?

When the others had gone, I drove to the nearest cottage. It was occupied by a farm labourer and his wife who were having their afternoon tea break when I arrived. I was invited in, offered a seat at their kitchen table and given a mug of tea with a piece of fruitcake. I learned that the couple, in their fifties, were Mr and Mrs Byworth, George and Ada. I explained our actions, and George smiled. 'Aye, Mr Rhea, Ah spotted yon police cars and reckoned they'd be digging.'

'You know what's been happening there?'

'A murder, Mr Rhea. Yon trees are called Grave Wood, there's a circle of 'em. They were planted around a grave.'

'When was this?' I interrupted him.

'1895,' he said. 'My dad told me all about it. He lived here before me. It was a farmhand called John Appleton. He killed his wife and little lass and buried 'em right where you were digging. Nasty case, it was. He had no other woman, nowt like that, but he was a bit daft, only in his twenties, and he led his wife and bairn out to look at that grave. He'd dug it ready, and as they stood looking into it, wondering what it was, he killed 'em both, shot 'em. They fell into that grave and he buried 'em. He was found out, mind, and they hanged him.'

'What happened to the bodies? Do you know?'

'Aye,' he said. 'The woman and her bairn were reburied in Ashfordly churchyard. It was a funny do. They had a funny vicar then: 'e wouldn't allow the bodies to come in through t'lychgate for some reason. They had to pass t'coffins over t'church wall. T'graves are still there.'

'And somebody planted those pines in memory of them?'

'They 'ad no relations hereabouts; they came from away when Appleton got work here as a farmhand. I know because he worked on t'same farm as my dad. But they found no relations for the lass and her bairn. Nobody. So the local folks planted them trees, Mr Rhea. In memory.'

Then another aspect occurred to me.

'When was the murder in 1895?' I asked.

'8 June,' he said. '8 June 1895.'

'That's seventy years ago today,' I whispered. 'Today is 8 June.'

'Aye,' he said.

'So the digging out there? The digging before we came, and that cross? What do you know about that, Mr Byworth?'

'Nowt,' he said. 'But awd Horace Baines might know.'

'Horace Baines?' I didn't know the man.

'Used to be our roadman, retired a few years back. He lives in Ashfordly, not far from t'front gate of t'castle.'

'So why should he know?'

'He was up here at six this morning,' smiled George.

'Out for a long walk, was he?'

'No, he was digging, in Grave Wood,' he smiled almost wickedly.

I realized that if we'd asked a few questions before commencing our own digging operation, we might have saved ourselves a lot of work. But I decided the exercise had been good for those CID lads!

'So why would he be digging there?' I asked.

'You'd better ask him, Mr Rhea, cos I don't know.'

'And you don't know who put that little cross there?'

'No idea,' he said, and his wife concurred.

I thanked them for their wonderful co-operation and drove back into Ashfordly, where I had no trouble locating Horace Baines. He was in his pretty stone cottage, a truly picturesque place with honeysuckle over the front door and roses climbing over an outhouse. He led me into his garden, where I admired his flowers and vegetables.

'I'm not in trouble, am I?' he asked.

'No,' I assured him. 'It's curiosity, that's all,' and I explained my purpose.

'You'll know about the murder then?' he put to me.

'I do now,' I said. 'But I didn't know until today.'

'Well, after that lass and her bairn were killed, somebody erected a memorial stone. It stood for years, until the Second World War. Then these moors were used as tank training grounds.'

'Was this before the pines were planted?'

'Aye,' he said briefly. 'Well, I was the roadman; that length was my responsibility. I used to see that little stone every time I came this way. But when the tanks started to train here, they drove straight over it. It got pressed into the earth, Mr Rhea, and in time it got lost, overgrown mebbe.'

'I see.' I could guess what he was going to tell me.

'Well, I kept thinking I would rescue it, but you know how it was, tanks and soldiers everywhere. I never did get it rescued, so this morning, because I woke early, I thought I'd have a look for it and erect it somewhere proper. After the war, when the tanks had gone, somebody planted those trees where the grave was, so I dug in there. But I never found it. Mebbe it is still there, or mebbe somebody else has got it.'

'Our lads dug it over pretty well this morning,' I assured him. 'We dug much more than you, but we never found even a fragment.'

'It'll be somewhere about.' He sounded confident. 'Mebbe it's in a farm shed somewhere, or being used as a paving stone in a footpath or in somebody's rockery . . .'

'Is there a special reason for wanting to recover it?' I asked.

'It was my dad helped the police catch Appleton,' he said. 'He came past one day and saw Appleton digging there. When the lass and kiddie disappeared, he told the police what he'd seen – and they found the bodies. Dad would have wanted me to find that stone, you see.'

'And why did you make the effort today?' I asked him. 'You know it's seventy years today since the murder?'

'Is it? No, I hadn't realized that. I just decided to go all of a sudden. I'd been thinking about it for a week or two. Fancy me picking today of all days!'

'Thanks, it is a strange coincidence, but you have solved one mystery,' I said. 'Now, the little cross of hazel twigs. Did you put that there?'

'No,' he said. 'That wasn't me.'

'Was it there when you were digging?'

'Aye,' he said. 'It was. I moved it while I dug, but I never put it there.'

'Any idea who might have?' I pressed him. 'I'm curious, that's all. There's no official police inquiry about all this, not after all this time!'

'No idea,' he smiled. 'But you might find Mrs Gowland who lives beside the butcher's can help.'

And so I continued my enquiries by calling on Mrs Gladys Gowland, a lady of almost eighty. The uniform helped me to gain her confidence, for she was shy and cautious, but when I explained my interest, she smiled and invited me to sit down. She produced a cup of tea and a scone, then a large wooden box full of newspaper cuttings and faded photographs.

'I don't want any of this published or copied,' she said guardedly. 'I have built my collection of news cuttings about Ashfordly for many, many years, and it is my personal collection, you see.'

I had to convince her that I had no intention of removing any of her documents or of copying anything. She showed me yellowed cuttings about the murder, the trial and the funeral of the victims, a fascinating piece of local history. But apart from a lot of local colour and somewhat exaggerated drama, the cuttings did not tell me much more than Horace Baines had revealed. They shed no light at all on the mysterious little wooden cross, although a later cutting did say that the local people had planted the trees after the Second World War because the grave had been obliterated by the actions of the tanks in training.

I asked her outright: 'Mrs Gowland, when we arrived today, there was a little wooden cross near the grave. Did you put it there?'

'No,' she said, and I believed her, for how could she have trekked in secret to that location?

And so the mystery remained, and it remains to this day. I have no idea who placed that cross on the grave to two murder victims who died during the last century, without relations but with some enduring friends.

However, I did later learn that a cross was traditionally placed at the scene of a murder to prevent the ghost of the victim returning to haunt the area. That cross had to be renewed upon each anniversary of the death. In days gone by, some policemen would scratch a cross in the dust or earth near a murder victim, or sometimes it would be marked on a post or door. So was this the reason for that little wooden cross? Had it been placed there every year since the crime in order to keep at bay the ghosts of the victims? It is a fascinating thought. *It became even more fascinating when the cross reappeared on 8 June 1989!*

As a last act in this piece of unofficial research, I decided to seek the graves in Ashfordly churchyard. I ignored the modern stones as I sought an old tombstone, possibly bearing two names. It took me a long time, but I did find it.

The tombstone bore the name of Anne Appleton and her daughter Marie, who had died tragically on 8 June 1895.

The grave also bore a vase of freshly cut flowers.

9 The Goldfish and the Goat

Accidents will occur in the best regulated families.
Charles Dickens (1812–70)

Traffic accidents have always occupied a lot of police time and effort. As the volume and diversity of traffic have increased, so the range and number of accidents have multiplied. In the good old days before the Second World War, a serious traffic accident was unusual. Today it is common-place and can involve anything from a road roller to a bicycle, by way of articulated lorry, mobile crane, tank, car or caravan. I have included some tales of accidents in previous *Constable* volumes.

Because traffic accidents are so frequent, police officers tend to regard them as routine, but for the unfortunate victims they are anything but routine. They are hurtful, traumatic, expensive, time-wasting, annoying, upsetting and horrible. In many cases, I'm sure that a driver suffers only one serious accident in his or her lifetime, or maybe none at all. Not every minor bump is recorded, but an accident at which the police officiate is something of a rarity for most drivers.

One such driver was 70-year-old Alf Partridge. I had known him for years, for he had been a friend of my family for as long as I could remember, and he was a wonderful character. Rather short in height, he was plump and balding, with a ready smile and an easy manner which charmed everyone. No one had a bad word to say about Alf: he was everyone's friend. He ran a small garage-cum-filling-station in a moorland village called Milthorpe, which was not within my own area of patrol, although from time to time he did cross the moors into my patch. In those cases, he was generally performing a taxi run, his taxi being one part of his village business.

He was also a peat-cutter, for he owned rights to one of the moorland peat bogs from which he supplied a small range of customers. For this, he would drive onto the moors in the spring with his special peat-cutting tools to cut a portion from the bog. After a 'dess' was cut and the face was 'sliped' to deter the rain, the peat sods were stacked or 'rickled' on the 'ligging' or lying ground. Here it was left to dry in the moorland breezes before delivery or use. Special hicking (hand) barrows were used for transporting the peat at the site. The entire operation was fascinating to observe. I don't think Alf undertook his peat-cutting for any real commercial reason – he found it a relaxing change from his garage and taxi business, although he did burn peat in his delightful cottage.

But the things I most vividly remember were the scrupulously tidy and completely efficient cars which he used. They were immaculate inside and out, their engines ticked over like silken watches, and every part was meticulously maintained and cared for.

From time to time when we were children, we would be taxied to various places because our parents did not own a car, and indeed, when I joined the police service at the age of sixteen, I was driven to my interview at force headquarters by Alf in one of his magnificent taxis. Although the car was not pretentious in any way, I can still recall its sheer magic, its smooth drive, its aura of total reliability and efficiency.

Everything about Alf was clean and pleasant; even his garage premises were tidy and neat, for he had trained his men to respect his own high standards. It was like walking into an exhibition rather than a working country garage. Every tool not in use was returned to its allocated space; every piece of scrap metal or other waste was collected and removed, every mess was cleared up and the floor kept clean. Even the window, which overlooked the street, was a joy. It displayed spares, such as tyres, plugs and wash leathers, and he took the trouble to decorate them seasonally with Christmas crackers, Easter eggs or whatever was topical. And no one ever saw Alf lose his temper or become flustered – his whole existence was so well planned that his passage through life was calm, smooth and trouble-free.

It was a matter of pride for Alf that he had never been involved in a traffic accident. In all his years of motoring, he had never once had a scrape with another vehicle, nor even a scratch from nature's defences. The bodies of his cars were immaculate, not even the thorns of the hedgerows or the horns of moorland sheep daring to mark his polished paintwork and glistening chrome.

But one sunny morning in April, on one of the moorland's most remote highways, Alf felt that his reputation had been shattered. His legendary calm was decidedly ruffled, because he was involved in an accident, or perhaps it was a near-miss?

He was driving his black, shining and immaculate Humber Snipe towards his peat bog; he towed a trailer he had built, and it contained his specially angled peat spade, a gripe, his hicking barrow and assorted tools. It was a fine, dry morning and the roads were empty. Indeed, the rough roads across these heights were nearly always empty, their only traffic being the local moorland farmers and peat-cutters who came this way from time to time. Not many outsiders found their way over these heights then, although that situation has now changed. Today that narrow moorland road is surfaced and, because it is shown on tourist maps, it now suffers regular passage of traffic. Alf, had he been alive today, would have been horrified.

But on that spring morning in the mid-1960s Alf had no thoughts of meeting other vehicles. He had traversed these moors for years without seeing another motor along his route. The regular passage of horse-drawn vehicles and coaches had ended, and major, well-surfaced roads had been built through the dales. They coped with visitors, buses and routine traffic.

And so year after year Alf had driven to his peat bog at dawn to cut the required number of sods, and year after year he had driven home contented and happy with his unpressurized life. There were no cars, no traffic lights, no roundabouts, no signposts, no bollards and no houses – there was nothing but a rough track for use by the likes of Alf Partridge.

But one morning another car dared to use the primitive road. At one point the track dips down a gentle slope where it crosses a moorland beck before rising at the other side. Midway down the first slope, in the direction in which Alf was driving that morning, a minor track enters the highway from the right. It was originally a drovers' road and, as cars were becoming more numerous, some daring drivers occasionally made use of it to cross the moors from the northernmost parts of Eskdale. It was proving to be a useful short-cut. At its junction with Alf's road, however, it was not readily visible. It emerged from between high banks of heather; indeed, a stranger would not even realize there was a junction until arriving, for there was no road sign to announce the fact.

As Alf had chugged along his regular route, so a young man in a bright yellow Austin Healey Sprite sports car was hurtling along the drovers' road. In his low-slung car, he was concealed by the high banks of heather and did not see Alf, and Alf did not see him. As Alf approached the junction, so the yellow flash bolted across his route, apparently from nowhere. From his right, it passed directly into Alf's path.

Alf reacted with remarkable speed. He swung his steering wheel savagely to the left, as a result of which he found himself bouncing across the open moorland with his trailer of tools clanking behind. The incident so unnerved him that, for the briefest of moments, he forgot to brake, and so his lovely car cruised for some distance across the smooth grassy patch between the heather patches, then came to an ignominious halt in a bog of sphagnum moss. The engine stalled.

It pitched Alf forward, and within a very few moments the car began to sink. Alf was still inside, but not injured. He was able to observe the yellow sports car disappearing up the slope opposite but had not the time to take its registration number. He was alone to his fate as his car sank slowly into the mire, and so he decided to abandon his precious vehicle. Happily, the bog was not too deep, so when Alf stepped out, he found himself on a firm base, albeit up to the thighs in peat-coloured water and thick yellow mud as his precious Humber sank at his side. It halted when the mire was half-way up its doors.

The problem was what to do next.

Unknown to Alf, the young man in the yellow sports car had halted in Rannockdale to ring the police. Without giving his name, he said he'd seen a car run off the road at Bluestone Beck. The call was received at Eltering police station, and a map revealed that the location was literally yards inside our patch.

I was in Sergeant Blaketon's car at the time. With him acting as driver, we were undertaking an early morning inspection of quarries which had explosives stores and were using the occasion to check the accuracy of our Explosives Register. Then we were diverted to Bluestone Beck.

As we drove down the slope towards Alf's bogged-down car, I recognized him. I said, 'Good Lord, it's Alf!'

'Do you know the driver, Rhea?' asked Sergeant Blaketon.

'Yes, he's been a family friend for years,' I said, and then explained my childhood knowledge of Alf, reinforcing the fact that he had never had an accident or suffered damage to his precious cars.

'In that case, Rhea,' Sergeant Blaketon said formally, 'I had better deal with this accident. If there is a question of prosecuting him for careless driving or something more serious, we can't have a family friend involved in the legal processes.'

'I'd do a fair job on the report, Sergeant.'

'I will deal with it, Rhea,' he said with an air of finality.

As we halted near the scene, I could see Alf furiously digging with his peat-cutting spade. He was throwing masses of muck around as he tried to find some solid ground for his rear wheels – in this mess, they only spun uselessly as he tried to force his car out of the bog. And he was in a terrible state. He was smothered in grime; his clothes, hair and face were dripping with wet sphagnum moss.

It was evident that he did not recognize me when our police car halted a few yards away. In his present highly charged condition, he might not have recognized his own mother, but he had not seen me for years and had no idea I was concealed within that uniform. Sergeant Blaketon strode across the sound piece of moorland to speak to him, as I waited with the car. And I must admit I was amazed at Alf's angry and belligerent response.

'There's no need for you buggers to come here snooping,' were his first words. 'I can get myself out of this . . . I don't need you lot laughing at me . . .'

'We received a report of an accident . . .' began Oscar Blaketon.

'Accident? What accident? There's been no accident. I haven't hit anybody. There's been no crash. No injuries. I was forced off the road, that's what. If I hadn't run down here, I'd have hit him . . . I avoided an accident . . . the silly bugger . . . look at this . . . what a bloody mess . . . I want none of this in the bloody papers and you can keep me out of court if that's what's in your mind . . . so how am I going to get out of here, eh? Just you answer me that!'

'There has been an accident,' chanted Blaketon, adopting a rather formal attitude. 'If, owing to the presence of a motor vehicle on a road, an accident occurs whereby damage is caused to a motor vehicle other than that vehicle, then so far as the law is concerned, it is an accident.

'It conforms to the definition in the Road Traffic Act,' Blaketon went on. 'If another car's driver forced you off the road, then he caused the accident – and the fact that you are sitting up to your eyebrows in plother means there has been an accident, an untoward incident, an unwanted event.'

'Then get after that yellow car and book him for not stopping, Sergeant,' bellowed Alf. 'And what about towing me out of here?'

'You'll need a breakdown truck for that.'

'Well, I can't do much about getting one from here, can I? Can't you blokes radio somebody? Get my mate, Eddie Brookes, Milthorpe 253. He'll come for me. And what about that other idiot, eh? Why aren't you chasing him and his yellow peril? Running folks off the road like this . . .'

'Is there any damage?' shouted Blaketon.

'How should I know?' snapped Alf. 'Look at it! How can I say what harm's done under all this muck? God knows what my underside's hit under this moss . . . I could have knocked the sump off, broken an axle, but I'm stuck solid, I am . . .'

As Alf chuntered and cursed, Blaketon came across to me and sat in the car. He was in a surprisingly gentle mood, and I must admit I was not accustomed to seeing him like this.

'Rhea,' he said, 'you know this character. He sounds a bit irate to me. Now, the way I see it is that there might be a dangerous driving case against the chap in the sports car, if we can find him.'

'And if we can prove it,' I chipped in. 'It's Alf's word against his; Alf might have been half asleep. I know he's an old friend of my parents, but, well, he is getting on a bit.'

'True, very true. But if this Alf's car is not damaged, it is doubtful if there is a reportable accident, eh? In other words, we are not wanted here. We are not duty-bound to deal with this, unless he complains about the other driver.'

'I'd like to get him out of his mess,' I said.

'Then radio them at Eltering and ask them to call his friend, Rhea.'

As Blaketon sat at my side, oddly reluctant to exercise his awesome authority over poor old Alf, I did this small favour. Our Eltering office contacted Eddie Brookes with the story, and he said he'd come immediately with his breakdown truck to tow Alf from the bog.

'I think, under the circumstances, we should depart, Rhea,' said Blaketon. 'I agree this is one driver's word against another, and if this man is a friend of yours, he might talk himself into a careless driving charge if I quiz him too much. You must admit he's a bit irate, he's not thinking straight, he might say too much and drop himself further into the mire.' And he glanced at the bog as he chuckled at his own joke.

'He has good reason,' I said.

'He had no reason to talk to me like that,' said Blaketon. 'I'm only doing my duty. I'm not responsible for his accident.'

'Sergeant,' I said, 'this is his first accident in more than fifty years of driving. I'm not surprised he's a bit angry, especially as it's not his fault. I'm sure you would be the same. I know you have a clean driving record . . .'

'Then let's leave him,' he said quickly. 'If I stay until the breakdown truck arrives, Rhea, I might see the damage on his car, and I might make it an official traffic accident, which means he could be the subject of a report for alleged careless driving.'

'Thanks, Sergeant,' I said. 'Can I have a word with him before we leave?'

'Right ho,' he said, not offering to accompany me. This was not the normal Blaketon, I realized, and I could not understand why he was so gentle with Alf.

I wandered over to Alf, who, upon seeing my approach, launched into a tirade of abuse against everyone, especially drivers of yellow sports cars. But when I removed my cap, he recognized me.

'God! It's young Nick!'

'Hello, Mr Partridge.' I used the name I'd called him in my youth. 'You've got yourself into a bit of pickle, eh?'

That set him off again, but I calmed him down by saying we were leaving, and explained the reasons, adding that Eddie's truck was on his way.

'This'll ruin my record, Nick,' said poor old Alf. 'All these years without a scratch and now this . . .'

'It won't ruin it,' I said. 'There'll be no official entry in our files, especially if you don't make a formal complaint about that yellow car.'

'But my car'll be ruined. Look at it, up to the doorposts in muck and plother . . .'

But we left it at that. He decided not to prosecute the yellow peril. If he had made a formal complaint, it would have been difficult, if not impossible, to prove the case, and Alf would have been called as a witness. That alone would have destroyed his own long record. I felt we had achieved a diplomatic result.

As I drove Blaketon back to the office, I suddenly realized why he had been such a wonderful help to poor old Alf. A few months earlier, during the snowfalls of that winter, there'd been a rumour about Sergeant Blaketon's driving into a ploughed field somewhere in these dales. He'd been off duty at the time, but it had required a farmer and his tractor to drag him out; no official report had been made and there'd been no damage to his car. We had heard through gossip, but Blaketon himself had never said a word about it. I wondered if Alf or Eddie had been involved in that. Obviously Alf didn't remember it, but it did help me to understand why Blaketon was sympathetic to poor old Alf's predicament.

Several months later I saw Alf in Eltering. He was driving the same car, and it looked immaculate.

'Hello, Mr Partridge,' I greeted him, then added, 'The car looks great!'

'There wasn't a mark on it,' he said. 'It was mucky and wet, but there wasn't a scratch. That sphagnum made a soft landing for it.'

'So your record's clean, eh?'

'Aye,' he said. 'Thanks to that sergeant of yours.'

Another harrowing tale involved a serious accident to a caravan unit. A couple from Norfolk, where real hills are a rarity, came to the North York Moors for a caravanning holiday. They decided to tour an area where there are numerous hills of 1-in-3 gradient (33 per cent) and where anything up to a gradient 1-in-10 (10 per cent) rarely warrants a 'Steep Hill' warning notice. For the local people, these gradients present no problem; for the tourist, they can be terrifying, and most certainly they do sift the good drivers from the bad or hopeless.

We call these hills 'banks'. There is the White Horse Bank near Kilburn whose gradient was not, in my time at Aidensfield, mentioned, in case no one believed it. There's the fascinating, winding Chimney Bank at Rosedale, which even the locals admit is 'brant'. That means 'steep' in the dialect of the region, i.e. about 1-in-3 (33 per cent). There are many others, especially in Eskdale, but one which causes a certain amount of angst among dithering drivers is Sutton Bank near Thirsk. It is not particularly steep, but it is a mile long with three gradients, the first being 1-in-4, the second 1-in-5 and the final one 1-in-4.

Until recently, tourists would examine their maps to see that this A-class road led to Scarborough from the A1 and would head towards it. Even if the tourist maps do include a 'Steep Hill' symbol at these locations, few of these dreamy visitors realize what it means, and so, during a typical English summer, these banks are often blocked by motorists for whom the normal occasions for selection of first gear are as common as their birth or funeral. In the case of Sutton Bank, it was frequently blocked by little men in Morris Minors who tried to tow caravans to the summit. The failure rate was high, even when the towing car was a powerful one such as a Volvo or a Mercedes, and a local farmer with a powerful tractor made a fortune from towing such incompetents to safety on the plateau above. Happily, caravans are now banned from this hill – but the hills are not to blame; it is the drivers who are the problem. The local people have no trouble with the hill – even our ancient lady drivers can cope.

Unfortunately for Mr John Plumpton, he was one of those hapless drivers. Utterly hopeless, he braked on every corner, even on level roads; he could not reverse into a parking space and had never previously towed a caravan. His wife, Sally, wasn't much help either, because she couldn't drive at all and was nervous at anything faster than 25 mph. For a man of his calibre to venture into our hilly moors and dales with a heavy load forever on his tail was an act of sheer stupidity. It is like climbing Everest in plimsolls.

It is times like these when police officers ponder upon their role in society, for so often we spend time clearing up the mess left by the nation's hopeless and incompetents. In this case, John Plumpton's lack of skill almost had fatal consequences.

For reasons which are not clear, he decided to take his caravan down Sorrel Bank, which descends from the moors into Maddleskirk. Almost a mile long, it is a narrow, twisting bank with gradients of around 1-in-4 (25 per cent), which is not particularly steep for this area. At the foot, the bank emerges onto a well-used road which leads into the village via the floor of the dale. The latter is not a classified road, so at that time there were no junction markings, and in fact there was no 'Steep Hill' sign on Sorrel Bank. The road is very narrow, being only the width of one vehicle, and the approach along the top skirts a pine forest as it affords superb views across the Vale of York. When it reaches Sorrel Brow Farm, the road suddenly dips as it begins its rapid descent towards the western end of Maddleskirk.

John and Sally Plumpton sailed majestically into this dip, and before John realized what was happening, his unit was gathering speed. Very quickly, the combined weight of car and caravan urged the wheels to turn at an ever-increasing

pace. With no places to run off the road, it was like descending
one of those fairground chutes, each corner bending so sharply
and dropping ever downwards that the road beyond was out
of sight. I don't think John actually steered his car down that
hill. I think the camber of the road and the high verges guided
the front wheels along the road surface without any effort by
him. In fact, I don't think John had any control at all; when I
interviewed him some time later, he could not remember even
having changed to a lower gear.

In simple terms, he panicked. As the car and its caravan
bolted down Sorrel Bank, he simply let it run free, and it
knew where to go. In his panic, he either missed his brake
pedal or omitted to use it; he utterly failed to make use of his
gears for additional control, and it was a classic case of driving
at its very worst. Men of this calibre ought to be severely
tested every few years – they are a liability to themselves and
to others. The outcome of Plumpton's panic was that this huge
moving combination of run-away vehicles careered down that
long, winding hill totally out of control. By the grace of God,
nothing was travelling the other way. The road was empty at
the time. Fortunately the road which formed the junction at
the bottom was also empty, and so the car and caravan hurtled
across but came to an ignominious end at that point.

Opposite the exit from Sorrel Bank, the verge was high but
wide, and there was a hedge containing a solid sycamore tree,
behind which lay a field. That field also sloped steeply from
the hedge and levelled out some yards below, at which point
it produced a thick clump of hawthorn trees.

John and Sally must have had a good view of this field as it
rose to meet them, but as their car just missed the sycamore,
the leading edge of the caravan hit it. This demolished the
caravan; it disintegrated into a pile of matchwood as the car
separated from it and continued down the field, rolling over
several times until it came to rest among the hawthorns. The
roof was flattened, the car was wrecked and the caravan lay in
exploded pieces around the sycamore.

A villager called the police and ambulance, and I arrived to
find this mayhem. Of the caravan, very little remained, and
the family's belongings were scattered across the verge and

the field, with several pairs of Sally's knickers decorating the hedge, and John's clean socks dangling from some elderberry trees. The couple were trapped in their upturned car, and we had to cut them free, both badly injured.

As I helped Sally into the ambulance, she whispered to me, 'Did you find Oliver?'

'Oliver?' I was horrified. 'No, was he in the car?'

'No,' she said weakly. 'In the caravan.'

My heart sank. 'How old is he?'

'Four,' she said. 'It was his birthday last week. He always travels in the caravan . . .' and she drifted into unconsciousness.

As the ambulance surged away to York Hospital with its casualties, I rushed back to the debris and started my search. Oliver must have been in one of the bunks. He could be trapped anywhere.

Aided by the fire brigade who had come to cut free the Plumptons, we sifted through the wreckage but found no sign of the child. I knew that in some freak accidents children can be flung far from the wreckage, and so we arranged a full-scale search of all the shrubbery, with a more stringent examination of the wrecked car. But there was no sign of Oliver. It took us hours to examine every likely place, but the result was nil.

I radioed my office at Eltering. I explained our problem to PC John Rogers and asked if he would ring the hospital. I wanted a doctor to speak to Mrs Plumpton as soon as she regained consciousness, in an attempt to establish just where Oliver would have been lying or sitting or, indeed, whether she was mistaken. Maybe she had not brought him on this holiday? Maybe the stress of the accident had caused her to believe he was there when in fact he was with relatives? Maybe the husband could throw some light on the matter? I told John that I would remain at the scene, continuing the search, until I heard from them. I would carry out a further search of the wreckage and surrounding vegetation, even to the extent of checking every inch of the route down the bank. Maybe Oliver had been been thrown out during that nightmare descent?

With that thought dominating my mind and aided by the dedicated firemen, I climbed the hill and meticulously checked the verges and hedges, hoping against hope that I would find the boy. I did not.

Dejected, we returned to the wreckage. As I wandered among it, I noticed a movement in a man's shoe which was lying among the miasma. I stooped and found a goldfish; it was still alive. It was flicking its tail and gasping as I lifted the shoe to show the nearest fireman.

'I've some water on board!' he laughed. 'Here, there's a plastic bucket over there!'

And so we filled the bucket with water from the fire tender and plonked in the fish. With a flick of its tail, it began to swim around as if nothing had happened.

'I knew a goldfish that had been buried as dead,' said the fireman. 'Then hours later it poked its head out of the soil. It lived another three years . . .'

As we hunted yet again among the larger items, the radio called me. It was John Rogers.

'We've had words with the hospital, Nick. A doctor has spoken to Mrs Plumpton.'

'Yes?' I wanted to get this matter settled.

'Oliver was definitely in the caravan,' he said. 'We've checked and double-checked with her. She'd adamant about it. He is four, as she said, but . . .' – and he burst into laughter.

'What's the matter?' I asked.

'He's not a child, Nick.'

'Not the dog!' I groaned.

'No, he's a goldfish. Apparently he leads an adventurous life. He always goes caravanning with them; he loves travelling. Last year he jumped out of his bowl and spent the night on the floor but survived. On another occasion he got tipped down the sink by mistake but was found alive. He's a kind of James Bond among goldfish!'

I laughed quietly to myself, then said, 'Then he's done it again. This time I've found him alive and well and living in a shoe. Perhaps you'd inform Mrs Plumpton?'

'You're not serious, Nick?'

'I am. He's swimming in a plastic bucket of fire brigade water right now,' I laughed. 'He was found in a shoe, still alive. He's a lucky soul,' I added. John groaned at my awful pun. 'How are the Plumptons?' I asked.

'They'll survive,' he said. 'They've each got a few broken bones – arms and legs mainly – and lots of bruises, but they'll recover. It'll cheer them up to know that Oliver has survived, but John Plumpton says he'll never drive again.'

'Then some good's come out of this,' I thought, and added, 'I'll visit them soon. I'll need a statement from each of them in due course. And I'll take Oliver with me. He can visit them in hospital.'

'He makes a nice twist to the story,' he said, and at that awful pun I groaned as I turned away to begin the task of clearing up the mess.

I had further trouble with another animal which survived a traffic accident. In this case, a small and very decrepit van was travelling down the main street of Crampton when its steering failed. Fortunately it was not moving very rapidly at the time, a feat it was truly incapable of performing in safety, and so the resultant damage should have been negligible. It wove along the highway as its driver did his best to stop, but the brakes weren't very good either. In those few moments, it wobbled onto the footpath, glanced off a telegraph pole, mounted a low wall and overturned.

By that stage, it had arrived in the gravel driveway of a rather nice house and thus lay on its side while the driver scrambled from the passenger seat. To escape from his small van, he had to climb upwards and then leap from the chassis onto the drive. Other than its almost totally blocking the drive, there was no harm to the house or the garden – yet.

Unfortunately the rear of the van contained a very bad-tempered billy goat, and as the vehicle had overturned, so the rear doors had burst open. The goat had therefore taken the opportunity of leaving its transport, and as the driver walked shakily to the rear of the van to check things, so the goat had strolled towards the front, out of sight of the driver, the bulk of the stricken van separating them. And so, as the driver, whose name was Tony Harris, found himself standing on the footpath outside the gate of the house and staring into his empty van, his goat found itself standing in the garden.

As the goat reached the front of the overturned van, the householder, a Mr Douglas Lynton-Cross, opened his front door to see what had arrived in his garden. The goat, we were to learn in due course, was like Awd Billy Barr's ram – it had a propensity for charging through open doors. As there was no one else around against whom to direct its anger, the upset billy noticed Mr Lynton-Cross in the doorway and was thus presented with two objects of interest – and promptly lowered it head, aimed its horns and charged.

Mr Lynton-Cross, an aged man who found sudden agility, bolted into the house but, in his anxiety to reach safety, left the door partly open. The heavy and hairy goat hurtled indoors in hot pursuit and found itself in the front hall of this splendid house. At this early stage, Tony Harris had no idea where his animal had gone. As he hurried off down the High street to (a) summon help and (b) find his goat, the animal in question was exploring the ground floor of Mr Lynton-Cross's home, while its worried occupant watched from the comparative safety of the landing above. The goat wandered into the front lounge, which was where Mr Lynton-Cross kept his collection of lead soldiers. They were arrayed in their colourful uniforms in regimental order and occupied several glass display cases around the walls and indeed in the centre of the spacious room.

It seems that the goat saw another goat there; this was because some of Mr Lynton-Cross's cabinets had mirrors at the back. The purpose of the mirrors was to provide more light for the displays and to create an aura of spaciousness. But billy goats are not *au fait* with such sophisticated display techniques. The visiting beast saw its adversary and charged it. The first charge smashed that display cabinet into small pieces, bringing down the shelves and scattering soldiers across the floor as the goat sought its foe. Here and there in that room, it spotted its likeness, sometimes here, sometimes there, but always peering at it from behind show cases. It charged again and again in its attempts to defeat the threatening enemy. The devastation, accompanied by the sound of much breaking glass, must have been heart-breaking for Mr Lynton-Cross.

When the angry animal had chased the intruder from that room, it decided to seek elsewhere. It knew there was a goat in the house and hadn't yet dealt with it.

It was at that moment that Mrs Lynton-Cross, upon hearing the awful din at the front of the house, emerged from the kitchen to see what was happening. The goat was thus presented with another open door. It charged at Mrs Lynton-Cross, who bolted out into the garden, slamming the kitchen door behind her to avoid the goat's horns. The goat enjoyed a spell of charging at the washing machine, the cupboard doors and the waste bin before re-emerging to seek its fellow trespasser, then it went into the dining-room. It had an enjoyable time charging the sideboard and the drinks cabinet, which revealed yet another goat, and in its eagerness to deal with it shattered precious glasses and bottles of malt whisky before seeing another open door.

This open door was actually the one by which it had entered the house, and so it bolted out and found itself standing in the garden. It rushed onto the lawn just as Tony Harris was returning through the gate. It saw Tony and promptly charged at him. I was later to receive reports of him galloping along the street with the goat in hot pursuit. I think he led the animal back into his own smallholding, but I was then called in. I examined the van, which was still on its side in the driveway of Mr Lynton-Cross's home, and said,

'I'm sorry, Mr Lynton-Cross, but this is not a matter for the police.'

'Why not, for heaven's sake?' he boomed. 'That animal has caused untold damage!'

'The van has overturned on private premises,' I said. 'No other vehicle is involved; it's not on the public road, and so it's not my responsibility.'

'But this damage? To my house, to my collection . . .'

'You'll have to sort that out with Mr Harris' insurance company,' I said. 'If he's comprehensively insured, they will settle matters with you.'

I did establish that Tony had contacted a garage to recover his van, but the case of the bolting goat was not for me, curious and interesting though it was.

I saw Mr Douglas Lynton-Cross several weeks later and asked if he'd obtained compensation for the damage.

'Yes, I did. My collection was not harmed, fortunately, and the insurance company did replace all my damaged furnishings and show cases. It's odd, when Harris came to see me and apologize, he noticed my collection and brought me some of his grandfather's lead soldiers, a sort of apology gift. They were rare ones. I'm pleased to have them, so some good has come of this incident. You know, Mr Rhea, just before that goat incident I was thinking of getting a goat. Someone I spoke to said they brought good luck.'

'It wasn't Tony Harris, was it?' I laughed.

10 'Hello, Young Lovers (Whoever You Are)'

> So for the mother's sake, the child was dear.
> Samuel Taylor Coleridge (1772–1834)

Surely every family wishes to see its children succeed in life. That success might be in the arts, the sciences, a trade or profession of some kind, a business career or some other vocation or calling. Added to these hopes is romance, for most caring parents also desire their offspring to be happy for ever in love and marriage.

This earnest aim can cause over-keen parents to impose their own ideals upon their children, and the police officer is often in a position to see the ill-effects of this. Fights between a daughter and parents over the former's choice of a boy-friend are common-place, but so are disputes over the son's attempts to woo the girl of his dreams when that girl does not win the approval of his parents.

Wise police officers avoid such conflicts. They regard these traumas as purely domestic and personal and, unless there is some suggestion of law-breaking, they do their utmost to keep a great distance between themselves and the affairs of other people's hearts.

But this is not always possible. Lovesick teenage girls do run away to places like Blackpool or London in search of romance or to get away from unsympathetic parents. In the mid 1960s, moral standards were higher than today, and if these girls were under seventeen, the police would attempt to trace them. The care and protection of juveniles were within our range of duty, and there were two classes of juvenile – anyone under seventeen was called a 'young person', while anyone under fourteen was a 'child' in legal terms. A whole range of offences and crimes could be committed against unprotected juveniles, and the younger they were, the greater the official concern if they ran away from home.

High on the list of our worries were offences against girls. If only because it is an offence for a man to have sexual intercourse with a girl under sixteen, we always sought girls below that age who ran off with 'males', as we termed them (men, youths or boys in ordinary language). If the girl was under thirteen, the penalty for unlawful sex with her was life imprisonment, an indication of society's great concern.

There were several other possible crimes, such as rape, incest, indecent assault, procuring girls for prostitution, abducting them for sex or for their 'estates', as well as cruelty, abandonment, vagrancy and even kidnapping. There were hundreds of evils which might befall a young girl who was tempted away from her home, and so we treated these cases with urgency and compassion.

With this in mind, my head became full of thoughts of horror when I received a telephone call from a Mrs Lavinia Underwood of Newcastle-upon-Tyne.

It was late August, when the moors were quilted with their annual covering of deep purple heather. It was a glorious sight, the rich, aristocratic colouring being enhanced by the greens of the mosses, the blues of the sky and, from time to time, some memorable sunsets.

'Is that the policeman at Aidensfield?' Her voice sounded faint and distant on the line, and I detected a strong Tyneside accent.

'Yes,' I shouted back. 'I'm PC Rhea. How can I help?'

'It's my son,' she said. 'He's been lured away by a young woman.'

'We don't normally get involved in domestic matters.' I interrupted her, wanting to stop her before the story became too involved.

'I know, but I'm so worried. She is not the right sort for him, you see. She's a wrong 'un, Constable. I just wondered if you might trace him and warn him, from me. Find him and tell him to come home, immediately, without her. I don't want him tainted with that hussy.'

'How old is he?' I shouted, for the line was awful. It kept fading and crackling.

'Seventeen,' she said, and upon hearing that troublesome age, I knew I had a problem.

'And the girl?' I called.

'That hussy! She's a good two years younger.'

Now it was a serious matter.

If a girl of fifteen, hussy or not, was missing from home, she had to be found before her experiences gave her adult sensations ahead of her time. I had to know more, and this would mean liaison between our force and Newcastle-upon-Tyne City Police. They might know of the girl's background. I obtained the caller's name and address, but she could not tell me who the girl was. Frank had never said who she was; he'd been very secretive about his romance.

Mrs Underwood described her son as fairly tall, of slim build, with light fair hair and glasses. He had a part-time job in a warehouse, checking the stock. He was wearing a green sports jacket, cavalry twill trousers and brown shoes when he left home, and he'd taken a suitcase of other clothes. He'd left home two days earlier, on the Saturday morning, about 10.30.

'Why do you think he's in this area with her?' I asked.

'He said he was going on a farmhouse holiday near Ashfordly,' she shouted at me. 'He's taken my car, you see. We once stayed there, when he was younger, me and my husband and Frank. He liked the area, he loves the moors, he often goes back, especially when the heather's blooming. And now it's blooming, eh?'

'It is indeed, Mrs Underwood, and it looks wonderful. Now, the car? Can I have a description? Its registration number would be a help.'

She could describe it accurately; it was a Morris Minor, green colour, and she gave me its number. She could not suggest an address for Frank because he'd stayed in different bed-and-breakfast places, ranging from farms to cottages, but all had been in or around Ashfordly to afford him easy access to the moors. He liked walking among the heather in the early autumn, he liked to hear the cry of the grouse and the call of the curlew. He'd be somewhere on those moors, she assured me, with that hussy at his side. I took her phone number so that I could keep in touch, and promised every effort to trace her son. It would not be difficult to check every boarding house or similar establishment.

The truth was, of course, that my determination to find Frank was not for the reasons desired by Mrs Underwood. Her motives might be to save him from an awful marriage – mine were to rescue a very young damsel who might be in official distress. I knew that we had to find the couple to prevent crimes being committed against the girl, even though she might be happy to permit such law-breaking.

After replacing the phone and rubbing my ears to counteract the awful noises the defective line had produced, I rang Newcastle police and asked for the Juvenile Liaison Bureau. A W/PC Collier answered. She listened intently as I explained the situation.

I asked if she had (a) any knowledge of Frank Underwood and (b) any report of a 15-year-old girl's being reported missing from home. She asked me to hang on while she checked her card index. After a few minutes, she said that there was no record of a Frank Underwood in their files – and their files contained the names of all juveniles from that area who might be causing concern, or who might be on the fringes of requiring care or protection, or who had been through the courts. But she would enter his name just in case it cropped up elsewhere.

She did say, however, that six girls were missing from their homes within the city police area, only one of whom was fifteen. She was Margaret Ellison, and W/PC Collier gave me an address in Jesmond, followed by a description of the child. I noted all this down and thanked her, but she did emphasize that Margaret Ellison had been missing for three months. Her parents had received postcards from London and Brighton, saying the girl was all right, but no address had been given. The most recent card had been received only three days earlier, but that still allowed time for Margaret to have met Frank in Ashfordly since Saturday last. It was now Monday.

'It doesn't sound as if he's with Margaret,' she added. 'We have every cause to think she's in the south with a youth called

Gibbons. Taking a country holiday is not her kind of fun. She's not for tramping through the heather with the wind in her hair – she's a city girl, she likes the bright lights, night-clubbing, amusement arcades, fairgrounds and so on.'

'Even so, I'll have to check it out,' I said.

'Keep in touch,' she replied in her strong Tyneside accent, and I rang off.

Next I called Ashfordly police office and spoke to Sergeant Bairstow, explaining the circumstances and saying I now intended to carry out an immediate search of the area. He said he would enter details in our occurrence book so that other officers could also watch out for the little green Morris Minor. It did not escape my attention that, if this couple were staying locally in boarding houses, they would probably give false names and addresses to their hosts, and entries in the guests' registers might also be false. They could be one of the countless Mr and Mrs Smiths who visit such places. But I could try.

It was around 10.30 that Monday morning when I left home in my official van for this tour of the local bed-and-breakfast accommodation. It was not a difficult task to conduct organized visits. We maintained our own lists of these premises simply because so many people asked us for addresses to stay, and so I began my enquiries. I visited each in turn, giving a description of the couple and the car, together with their correct names, emphasizing Frank's name rather than the girl's. But none had a teenaged couple staying with them, and none had entries of a Mr and Mrs Underwood in their registers. I spent the whole of that Monday on that task and failed to locate them.

I knew that my colleagues would do likewise when they came on duty, and so on the Tuesday I checked their visitations to avoid duplication and set off again. By lunchtime I had driven miles and checked eighteen bed-and-breakfast houses, five farms and one private hotel, all without result.

And then, after my packed lunch of cheese sandwiches, fruitcake and coffee from a flask, I crossed the moorland ridge from Lairsdale into Whemmelby. It was there that I saw the little green car. It was parked beside a small plantation of Scots pines and occupied a tiny lay-by where fire-fighting equipment stood in case of emergencies. The registration number confirmed it was the car I sought. I tried the doors; they were locked. Of the couple, there was no sign.

I knew this area well: a footpath ran across the moors at this point, and they could be anywhere along that path, in either direction. If I walked one way, they might have gone the other, and so I decided to wait, at least for an hour or two. I radioed Eltering police office to report my location and decision; they would inform Ashfordly office and Sergeant Bairstow.

And so I sat and waited.

There were some reports I could complete, so my vigil was not wasted. I had several returns, one accident report, a schedule of stock registers and a list of some visits to licensed premises to finalize, so I sat and worked, with the window down and the official radio burbling.

I enjoyed the scent of the heather as it mingled with the strong resin of the pines. I heard skylarks singing high in the heavens somewhere beyond my vision, and the burbling song of the curlew. All around, nature was busy with its own life, and the moorland creatures were preparing for autumn; soon those curlews would head for the coast, the silver birches would lose their leaves but the skylarks would remain to fill the moors with their distinctive song.

As I enjoyed those few hours alone, I saw an elderly couple, a man and woman, heading towards me. They were weaving their way through the high heather, following the sheep track which formed the footpath, and I saw that they were clad in hiking gear. Brightly coloured waterproof leggings and boots, warm kagouls and close-fitting woollen hats completed their outfits, and each carried a small rucksack. Both were using thumbsticks too, and they were moving at a swift pace. They were a couple accustomed to the moors and completely confident on a walk of this kind. I decided to ask if they had seen the teenagers during their rambling.

I waited until they had climbed through the V-shaped stile in the dry-stone wall and then hailed them.

'Excuse me,' I greeted them with a smile, 'I'm looking for a young couple, teenagers, a boy and a girl. I wonder if you've seen anyone during your walk?'

They looked at each other, and in a Tyneside accent the man said, 'Sorry, no. We've not seen a soul, have we, Joyce?'

The woman, in her late sixties, shook her head.

'No, we've been out there all morning, Officer,' she said in that distinctive, lilting accent. 'It's been lovely, mind, not a soul; we've had the whole moor to ourselves. But are they lost or something?'

'Not exactly,' I said, 'but they're from your part of the world.' I referred to their accents. 'The lad's run away and taken the girl with her – she's only fifteen.'

'Oh dear, it happens all the time,' said the woman. 'I used to be a teacher, and you'd be surprised how many fourth-form lasses ran off with sixth-form lads!'

'Are you staying in the area?' I asked.

'Aye,' smiled the man. 'We're at Spout House Farm near Gelderslack, bed-and-breakfast.'

'There's no teenagers there, is there?' I asked hopefully, for I had not yet visited that farm.

'No,' he said. 'Just us. But if we do see them, we'll call you. Ashfordly police, isn't it?'

'That's the nearest police station. We'd be most grateful,' I said. 'Well, thanks anyway.'

As they turned to leave, the man went towards the little green car. He produced a key and opened the door.

'Er, excuse me,' I said, wondering if I was about to make a fool of myself, 'but is that your car?'

'Well, not exactly, Officer. It's my mother's.'

My brain did a very, very rapid mental exercise.

'Is she Mrs Underwood?' I asked very slowly, and I gave her address.

'She is,' said the man.

'And, at the risk of seeming a total fool, are you Frank Underwood?' I was looking at his physical appearance. In spite of his age, he did have strands of fair hair protruding from his hat, and he matched the description of the 'youth' I was seeking.

'I am. You don't mean she's reported me missing? The silly old fool . . .' he laughed. 'Look, what did she say, Constable?'

I did not wish to repeat her description of the lady at his side, so I said she'd called me to say her son had disappeared with a young woman and that she'd given me the impression he was seventeen.

'Seventeen? I'm seventy!' he laughed. 'I'm seventy, officer. I am grown up, you know!'

And now I realized what I'd done. The fault on the line had made me mis-hear that word. I'd thought he was seventeen and had deduced, wrongly, that his girl was fifteen, whereas she was probably sixty-eight. I did not ask!

The couple laughed at my embarrassment. Frank explained how possessive his mother had become since she had been widowed – she was ninety-two now, but remarkably fit. Frank, himself a widower, had for a time lived with his mother, but now he'd met Joyce he had decided to allow himself a bit of romance and freedom. He'd borrowed her car because his own was undergoing a complete service. Amazingly, she was still fit enough to drive and insisted on running her own car.

'I've never told mother where Joyce lives, or who she is or anything about her,' he admitted. 'If that seems selfish, Constable, forgive me, but if I did tell mother, she'd pester the life out of Joyce, trying to get her to end her relationship with me. And so I keep Joyce a secret from mother. She's tried to use you to find out who she is – the crafty old thing!'

'So what are you going to do now?' asked Joyce, smiling in her amusement.

'I'm going to ring Newcastle police Juvenile Liaison Bureau to cancel their records of the 17-year-old Frank Underwood. I'm going to confirm that he has not run away with 15-year-old Margaret Ellison (who is missing from that area) and I'm going to ring Mrs Underwood to say that her son is safe and that his private affairs are nothing to do with the police.'

'You won't say where we are, will you? Or that you've found us?'

'No,' I said. 'I promise.'

We departed on good terms, the couple chuckling at their curious experience, and I returned to Ashfordly to explain this clanger to Sergeant Bairstow. But he took it in good part and said he would cancel the searches going on elsewhere.

He would endorse the record, 'Underwood traced with adult partner. No offences revealed.' That would prevent daft questions from higher authority.

When I returned home, my wife and I laughed at the development, and then the telephone rang. It was Mrs Underwood.

'I'm ringing to see if you have found my son yet,' she said the line still crackling and faint.

'Yes,' I said, without going into details. 'I gave him your message and he thanked me.'

'Well, if you see him again, Officer, tell him I'm not feeling very well. Tell him I've had another of my dizzy turns and I think he should come home – without that hussy of course.'

'Yes, I'll do that, Mrs Underwood,' I said.

To clear myself, I rang Mr and Mrs Jackson, the owners of Spout House Farm at Gelderslack, to ask them to pass on the 'sickness' message to Mr Underwood.

'Underwood?' asked Helen Jackson. 'I'm sorry, Mr Rhea, there's no one called Underwood here. Our only guests at the moment are two pensioners, a Mr and Mrs Smith from Newcastle-on-Tyne.'

A story of comparable mother-love involved Mrs Lucy Haines of Crag Top Farm, Briggsby. A great deal younger than Lavinia Underwood (and much younger even than Lavina's son, Frank), she was the widow of Michael Haines. He was a farmer who had died in his early forties. His sudden and early departure from this life meant that Lucy was left with the farm to run and five sturdy sons to rear. In both challenges, she succeeded admirably, for the farm was well run and profitable, while her sons had all responded to their new responsibilities by working hard on the farm before launching themselves into fresh careers.

As Lucy nudged towards her middle fifties, the eldest four sons had all left home. After their youthful taste of the tough work on the farm, they had decided on easier careers.

Andrew had joined the army, Simon had found work in London, first as a motor mechanic and then as a taxi-driver, Paul was doing well as a quantity surveyor with a building company in the Midlands, while John had opened an electrical goods shop in York. Only Stephen, the youngest, was still at home. Now in his middle twenties, he worked alongside his mother, the pair of them slogging from dawn till dusk to keep the farm viable. It was a busy, non-stop life of hard work, for they had a large dairy herd, pigs, sheep and poultry, as well as many acres of arable land which produced barley, wheat and potatoes. That was what Michael Haines had established before his death – he'd worked so hard to create a profitable farm which he could pass to his sons.

The farm occupied a splendid site. Its buildings formed a kind of defensive cluster around the sturdy, stone-built farm house. In some ways, it was like a castle, because the foldyard was akin to a courtyard, with the buildings arranged around it to form a protection against the bitter weather which could blow across that hill top. The house was like the keep, while the barns and outbuildings formed the battlements. The entire group of buildings stood on the summit of a limestone crag with a winding, unmade road leading down to the dale below. The fields were spread across the lofty plain, and some of the slopes were covered with deciduous trees. I always enjoyed the ride back from Crag Top, if only for the long views one could obtain from the descent.

In his endeavours to carve a working farm from that lonely site, Michael Haines had had some help – an aged farmworker called Ralph had supported him for the whole of his (Michael's) life and most of Ralph's. Ralph had started work here when he was fifteen and had worked for Michael Haines' father. Even though the widowed Lucy was never financially well-off, she would never consider getting rid of Ralph. He was part of the establishment and had, over the years, been largely responsible for creating a working farm around this lofty house. Following Michael's death, however, the bulk of the work fell upon the broad shoulders of Lucy and Stephen, because Ralph was, quite simply, too old to undertake the heavier tasks. The years of toil had taken their toll, and he should really have retired by now. But he did not leave – he stayed on to help and would probably stay there until he dropped dead. Unmarried, he knew no other life and lived in a rented cottage in the village.

Ralph's work was his life – and so it was with Lucy and her son. Neither she nor Stephen went anywhere for social outings or holiday visits – they had never been to any of the other sons' homes, for they never had the time or the money; they never took a day off unless it was to visit a local mart or perhaps the Great Yorkshire Show at Harrogate. For them, their farm was their entire life, even if it was a never-ending routine of near drudgery. Lucy saw no alternative; born of moorland farming stock, her parents had also lived this kind of life.

In spite of living in the middle 1960s, Stephen had found himself emulating his mother's early years. It seemed he was destined to follow his ancestors into a life of hard work and little relaxation. I don't think he'd had a girl-friend since leaving school, and I never saw him pop into the local pub for a drink or join the other lads into the cricket or football teams. He was almost a recluse at the grand old age of twenty-five. The only time I noticed him around the village was when he came down to the garage to purchase spares for the tractor. He spent hours working on the tractor, fixing defects, polishing it, mending broken bits and devising modifications of his own. There were few local lads more keen and knowledgeable about tractors.

I did, of course, see both mother and son during my regular visits to the farm. I had to visit the premises at least once a quarter to check the stock register, and there were other occasions of duty, such as renewal of their firearms and shotgun certificates, or warnings if outbreaks of notifiable diseases of animals were suspected within the county. During my visits, I grew to like Lucy. She was a stocky woman scarcely more than five feet in height and slightly overweight in spite of her hard work. She had a round, ruddy face, very dark and pretty eyes, good white teeth and jet black hair which hinted at Continental or gypsy ancestry, though I don't think she had any foreign blood in her veins, for many moorland girls had these dark good looks.

Her face was weathered and tanned and she usually wore her hair tied back in a bun. Her attire about the farm was generally a heavy frock worn beneath a well-used pinny, with an old cardigan about her shoulders in winter, and black wellingtons on her feet all the year. I had never seen her dressed in smart clothes – even when she visited Ashfordly market on a Friday for her fruit and groceries, she wore that old cardigan and her wellies. But, I often thought, she was a good-looking woman who, with a little care and thought about her appearance, could have attracted a fine man – as indeed she once had.

The villagers, myself included, often wondered why she did not sell the farm to provide herself with an income from the capital it would generate. Oddly enough, she gave me a clue during a visit one September.

I called one misty morning, and Lucy produced a mug of coffee and a scone, asking me to join her, Stephen and old Ralph at the kitchen table. She brushed aside some mountaineering books which were on the table, and then Stephen came in and, blushing slightly, removed them to the sideboard. I wondered if he was taking up a new hobby, for these were colourful books full of photographs and descriptive passages, but I did not embarrass him by asking.

'You look tired,' I said to Lucy as we settled down for a chat over the coffee. Stephen had left us, taking his coffee and Ralph's outside, saying there was work to be done in the foldyard.

'He's very shy,' she said, as if in apology for Stephen's awkwardness in company.

'I know the feeling!' I smiled, knowing that some country lads were painfully shy in company of any kind, especially that of girls. 'But how about you? Are you working too hard?'

'Mebbe I am.' She regarded me with a friendly look. 'It makes me realize I'm getting older, Mr Rhea. I'm past fifty, you know.'

'Well you don't look it.' I hoped I was not being patronizing by merely stating the obvious. 'But you can't go on for ever. You ought to sell up and invest the money, and enjoy the result of all your hard work.'

'There's many times I've thought of doing that.' I thought I detected a note of yearning in her voice. 'But Michael wouldn't

have wanted it. He was building up this farm for the lads –
that's all he worked for.'

'But they've left the farm.' I wondered if I was being
too forward in reminding her of this, but I felt I could be
honest.

'Aye,' she sighed. 'That's summat Michael never foresaw.
He saw all his sons taking over, sharing the work and
expanding the farm. He trained them for that – and then
he died. They stuck it for a while, but they'd had enough of
long hours and hard work with no money to spend. They've
all gone, except our Stephen. Mind, if I go, the farm'll be
theirs, to share. They're all part-owners, even if I do all the
work.'

'And what about Stephen?' I asked. 'Will he stay?'

'I don't know,' she sighed. 'What I would like, Mr Rhea,
is for him to find a good, hard-working and honest lass, one
who's been bred on the moors, one who'll take to this kind of
life. Then he'd stay, he'd produce some bairns, and the farm
could be kept in the family just as Michael wanted, and then
handed down. The others say they don't want it; they've said
I should sell up, and they'll let me have their shares till I die.
But, well, there's Stephen. He needs the work, he'd not find
anything else, you know . . .'

As we chatted, I could see that she was actually working
for Stephen's benefit but I also knew there was no guarantee
he would stay to farm this lonely, hilltop site. She ought to
be thinking of herself now, she should retire and enjoy her
investment, for the farm would bring a high sum on the open
market.

As our conversation continued and I accepted her second
mug of coffee, she smiled and asked me a favour.

'I'd like you to do something for me, Mr Rhea.' Those dark
eyes scanned my face. 'A favour, if you will.'

'I hope I can.' I was cautious, wondering what was to come.

'You remember when I towed you out of that ditch last
winter?' she reminded me.

I remembered the incident. In my police van, I had skidded
into a ditch on the outskirts of Aidensfield, and she had halted
with the tractor. She'd towed me out; there was no damage

to the police van and I had never reported it to anyone. But at the time I'd said, 'Thanks, Mrs Haines, if ever you need a favour, well, you know where to come.' And now she was calling in that favour.

'I remember,' I said. 'And I'm always grateful.'

'Well, now I'm asking a favour in return.'

I wondered what was coming.

'It's our Stephen,' she said quietly. 'He never goes out Mr Rhea, he never goes where he's likely to meet a girl. I wish he'd go to the pub or join something but he spends all day working and won't go out. He thinks of nowt else but tractors, and at night he'll sit in to watch television or read.'

'So how can I help?' I wondered.

'Well, you're out and about all the time, meeting people. I wondered if you knew of any suitable lasses, farm lasses like me, who'd make him a friend. He needs a friend, Mr Rhea, a girl-friend. I thought, well, that if you did know of anybody that might suit him, you'd let me know.'

'I will,' I said. 'Just now, I can't think of anyone, but if I do, I'll get in touch.'

'You won't forget?' I realized she was very serious about this.

'No, I won't forget,' I said, taking my leave.

I never regarded myself as a matchmaker, and furthermore. I knew the dangers that could result from such arrangements, but I did not forget her earnest plea. As I motored around the moors, calling at farms and remote houses, I often recalled Lucy's words, but all the desirable young ladies in those areas were 'spoken for', as we termed it. I never saw anyone I thought would tolerate the harsh life of Crag Top Farm or be strong enough to cope with Stephen's painful shyness.

But then, some eighteen months after that chat with Lucy, I visited Marshlands Hall at Gelderslack at the request of the occupants, a Mr and Mrs Slater. They had come to this old manor house and had turned it into fine private hotel; now, to take advantage of the changes in the licensing laws, they wanted to apply for a table licence which would permit them to sell intoxicants to non-residents who took meals in their dining-room. I went along to discuss this with them, armed with my knowledge of the liquor licensing laws.

Bernard and Olive Slater were practical folks who saw the potential in their idea. As I chattered to them, I noticed a young woman working in the grounds. She was hammering some fence posts into the earth with a huge mallet. The Slaters noticed my interest.

'That's Sylvia,' said Olive Slater. 'Our daughter. She's an outdoor type if ever there was one.'

'Does she work here?' I asked out of interest.

'Sort of,' said her father. 'She spends her time rushing all over the world. Her great-aunt – my aunt Felicity – left her some money, so she is almost independent of us. But she uses this house as her base and earns her keep when she's here by working, sometimes outside like she is now, and sometimes by waiting at table or even decorating. She's a real tomboy and a useful handywoman.'

'She's just come back from a climbing expedition in the Alps,' her mother said. 'And before that, she sailed every lake in the British Isles, and she's trekked to the source of every Yorkshire river . . .'

'She sounds a restless sort of lass!' I laughed.

'She ought to be settling down,' her father joked. 'She's nearly thirty now, and there's no sign of a man in her life. If you know of any young men who could meet her challenge, I'd be grateful – she's always too busy rushing off to meet any local lads.'

At this, I recalled Lucy's plea about her Stephen. Here were two young people, each isolated in their own way, with no hope of meeting one another, and for a fleeting moment I wondered if they had anything in common. As I watched the powerful Sylvia hammering in those fence posts, I thought she might be ideal for Stephen. Where else would a farmer find a girl capable of doing a man's work?

'I might know just the lad,' I said, and told them about Stephen Haines.

'We think she'd do well with a place of her own,' said Olive Slater. 'She needs to settle down and extend some of her energy making it a success – she's got nothing at the moment, you see, except a bit of cash which won't last for ever. She can't go on for ever rushing around the world on her own. This isn't our own premises, we rent it, so we can't pass it on.'

'Well,' I said, 'I'm sure the Haines could use some help from time to time. Whether she and Stephen hit it off remains to be seen.'

'Tell Mrs Haines to give us a call if she does need help about the farm,' invited Bernard Slater, 'and I know our Sylvia will welcome the change – and the bit of cash. If a romance blossoms, well, that's a bonus. We'd rather she became independent instead of using us as a base and, let's face it, a convenience. We do have a permanent staff, and we can't pay any of them off every time our Sylvia decides to come home. We'd never get them back when she left.'

'So something away from here would be an asset?' I said.

'Ideal,' said Bernard Slater. 'I think she could do with some work away from here.'

It was another three months before I revisited Crag Top Farm, and I found Lucy with her arm in plaster. She had fallen off the roof of an outbuilding while replacing some loose tiles and had broken her wrist.

'How are you coping?' I asked. I knew that winter is a quiet time on the farm, but I also knew that much does require attention in winter, especially maintenance work. With one person incapacitated, life would not be easy.

'I'll be honest. I'm not coping,' she said. 'Our Stephen is doing his best, but the cattle take most of his time, and I'm tied to the house now. There's fencing to do, ditching and so on . . . and there's no workers available just now. They won't work for farm wages, and poor old Ralph's getting too slow.'

It was then that I recalled Sylvia Slater and, remembering my earlier conversation with Lucy, I said, 'I know just the person!'

I explained that Sylvia was older than Stephen by a year or two, but that she seemed a capable lass so far as outdoor work was concerned. She might be willing to come along if she wasn't canoeing down the Amazon, hiking through the Grand

Canyon or rebuilding ruined castles. Lucy listened intently and smiled.

'She might be just the sort to jerk our Stephen out of his shyness.'

I gave her the number of Marshlands Hall Hotel before I left.

As I was on holiday at the time of the next quarterly visit to the farm, the stock registers were inspected by a colleague, and so there was a gap of six months before I returned to Crag Top Farm. By then it was summer, and the countryside was looking its best. The hedgerows were in full leaf, buttercups covered the floor of the dale with their golden blooms, and forget-me-nots decorated the woods around Crag Top.

The farm was smart and tidy as I knocked on the kitchen door. It was opened by Stephen, who invited me in as his mother would have. He and old Ralph were having their 'lowance, as the mid-morning break is called, and both were sitting at the scrubbed wooden kitchen table. Blushing slightly, Stephen invited me to join them. He had made some coffee in a pan, and there was a fruitcake on the table. I smiled and accepted.

Stephen produced the necessary books from the bureau without my having to ask and laid them in front of me before joining me over coffee. But of Lucy there was no sign. Ralph said nothing but merely grinned at me as Stephen sat and looked into his coffee mug. Conversation would not be easy. But where *was* Lucy?

'Your mum not around?' I asked eventually.

He shook his head. 'She's gone mountaineering,' he said, then added quickly, 'She allus has had a liking for mountains, and when that lass o' Slater's came to help out, they decided to have a month off. They're gone to Canada, to the Rockies.'

Good for Lucy! I was surprised at this sudden abandonment of the farm, but I smiled at Stephen.

'She's a fine lass, that Sylvia,' I said.

'She's too bossy for me,' he grunted. 'She's as bad as my mother, so I'm off when they get back, Mr Rhea.'

'Off?' I asked. 'Where to?'

'Hull,' he said. 'There's a new tractor distributor opened there. They were advertising for a tractor mechanic. I got the job. I start next week.'

'And the farm? What's going to happen to that?'

'Mum and Sylvia will run it,' he said quietly, getting up to return to his task.

Constable
by the
Stream

1 Nymphs of Still Waters

> And she forgot the stars, the moon, the sun,
> And she forgot the blue above the trees,
> And she forgot the dells where waters run,
> And she forgot the chilly autumn breeze.
>
> John Keats (1795–1821)

After a beautiful and memorable early morning experience, I could add my own lines to Keats's verse; they would read,

> And she forgot she had no bathing suit on.
> And she forgot the masculine eye that sees.

To be strictly accurate, my lines should read 'they' instead of 'she', because my early morning patrol was enlivened and enhanced by the sight of two beautiful maidens, two sylphs, two nubile nymphs bathing in a remote lake. And both were nude.

At first I thought I was dreaming, and then I wondered whether I was experiencing one of those moments that seem to happen only to other people, like seeing fairies or ghosts or experiencing religious visions. Those who cannot see them do not believe or understand those who can.

But those enchanting figures were real enough. Not real enough to touch, of course, but real enough to watch.

I was spellbound as I saw them splashing in the clear waters and heard their laughter ringing bell-like in the powerful silence of that morning.

As I gazed upon the delights before me I was reminded of

the many legends, mainly Grecian but some British, which tell of water nymphs. Those lovely goddess-like creatures have, over the centuries, been inextricably linked with springs and streams and here was I, seeing two dream-like creatures frolicking in a quiet lake before six o'clock one brisk and bright spring morning.

I knew of ancient stories which told of such heavenly sights. Homer wrote of nymphs which were semi-divine maidens; they inhabited waters like seas, lakes, rivers and fountains and there is a verse which says,

> They spring from fountains and from sacred groves,
> And holy streams that flow into the sea.

Here in the north of England, there are similar tales. Some local, but ancient stories continue to associate holy maidens with wells and springs, one of which flows near Giggleswick in the Yorkshire Dales. This is the famous Ebbing and Flowing Well whose origins are so ancient that they have been lost in the passage of time. The creation of this magic spring is said to have occurred long before the foundation of Christianity. The story tells of a maiden who was fleeing for her life; she prayed to the gods that she would escape her pursuer.

When she reached the point where the spring now flows, the gods answered her prayers. She was instantly turned into the magic spring which continues to ebb and flow from a mysterious underground source. Its surface rises and falls in a most curious manner. Its movement is sometimes accompanied by sighs and it is said that these are sighs of relief coming from that hunted nymph.

But in my own pleasure at sighting two nudes by the lake, I realized there was a very practical explanation. These were not sprites or legendary nymphs, but two very real and very beautiful young women. Nonetheless, it must be said that the moment was magical because these were two of the most beautiful of maidens. Furthermore, the ethereal quality of the morning did add enchantment. It was a stunning opening to that day's duty and I was reminded of the wise words of a former chief constable who said, 'Men who do not appreciate the beauty of a naked woman must have something wrong with them!'

However, I had work to do which was why I was in this wood at such an early hour. From time to time, we got reports of escapees from local Borstal institutions or even mental hospitals and on occasions these young men would sleep rough in local woodlands. They'd build shelters among the undergrowth and would light fires to keep themselves warm or to provide hot meals – sometimes the rising smoke was a sign of their presence.

Other indications came with the raiding of isolated farms for food like raw turnips or potatoes, eggs or milk. Some would even break into village houses or shops in their hunt for food or cash, and some had been known to steal a change of clothing or footwear.

In recent days, I had received reports of a suspicious man in these woods and this made me wonder if we had an escapee in the vicinity, even if there had been no other evidence of his presence. From the reports, I felt sure someone was lurking there and checked my own lists of recent escapees and wanted persons. But I found none that would be of direct interest to me as the village constable of Aidensfield. I had not received any reports of stolen food or unlawful entry into premises, nor had I received any reports of gunshots or traps used by poachers in that woodland. In short, the mystery man was something of a puzzle, but in truth he was not of any pressing concern because he did not seem to be engaged upon any unlawful activity. He might be nothing more than a keen ornithologist or a local person taking an early-morning stroll – but, as the village constable, it would be useful to know what he was doing, if only to placate those who worried about him.

I decided not to make any special effort to locate him; instead, I would be aware of his presence and remain alert for further sightings or reports of wrongdoing.

On that lovely morning, therefore, I was patrolling a 'route', as we called the duty. This gave me the opportunity to have a quiet walk among the trees just to see if there was any substance to the mystery-man stories. Reports suggested he'd been lurking among the mixed coniferous and deciduous trees which adorned a hillside to the south-west of Aidensfield. The first report came from a gamekeeper; he'd seen the fellow at a distance shortly before five o'clock one morning but had lost sight of him among the trees. Quite naturally, he suspected poachers. Then, on another day, around 5.30 in the morning, a cowman had spotted the man; his version was that the character was a youngish man with long hair who seemed to be furtively clambering among the hillside shrubs and trees. He seemed to have been hurrying from the lake which lay deep in a small valley within that woodland. The cowman had been unable to pursue the fellow because he was herding his cows into the mistal for milking and lacked the necessary time to locate him. He did say, however, that the man did not appear to be doing anything suspicious and he thought he might be camping in the woods.

I had these reports in mind as I'd started that early morning route at 5 a.m. My scheduled patrol had to include the villages of Elsinby and Maddleskirk; I was to be at each of them at 6 a.m. and 7 a.m. respectively and was to end that patrol at my police house at 8 a.m.

As the stretch of woodland in question lay within that route, and as I had not yet solved the mystery of the man among the trees, I decided I would explore the area. It would add purpose to my solitary walk.

I found myself walking along a deserted cart track which skirted the lower edge of the wood and from there I turned along a smaller path which led to the bottom lake. There are three lakes in these woods; they are all fed by the same stream which rises in the hills above, the top lake overflowing to form the middle one, and the middle one overflowing into the bottom one. The bottom one is the largest of the trio and offers good fishing as well as a wealth of rare and interesting wildlife ranging from plants to birds, via trees, fish and insects. It is, in fact, noted for its dragonflies and damselflies and the entire area, which is on private property, has been designated a nature reserve.

Among the structures around the lakes is a shelter of rough timber built by some local boy scouts to house their canoes and I knew to search there for signs of a secretive presence. I found nothing. During my perambulations, I walked quietly through the trees, avoiding the paths that would give rise to unwelcome noise, avoiding fallen twigs which would crack if I stood on them or thick coverings of leaves which would rustle. If there was anyone living rough hereabouts, I did not want to give warning of my approach by sending birds chattering from me.

A startled pheasant or wood pigeon can create an awful din, while the alarm call of a blackbird is enough to alert any countryman. Thus I moved gingerly and carefully about my business, eyes and ears alert as I emulated generations of gamekeepers in my stealthy prowling. After thoroughly checking the ground around the bottom lake, I moved to the middle one and repeated my search, again with no success. And then, as I climbed through the trees to the top and smallest lake, only marginally larger than a good village pond, I heard sounds. Voices. Light voices. Movements among the undergrowth. Bushes rustling. A chaffinch flying off in noisy alarm. A twig cracking. Laughter. Water splashing ...

So there *was* somebody! I froze. I stood like a statue among the freshly leafed trees, not making a sound as I tried to gauge the precise location of those sounds. I decided they came from the north-eastern corner of the lake, close to the entry point of the stream which fed it. I knew that the forest track ran past that point too ... if there was a vehicle, it would be parked nearby. I could obtain its registration number, if necessary.

It was now that my local knowledge proved valuable because I knew of a large, chair-shaped boulder near the western shore and realized it would provide me with a secure vantage point. I could hide behind it as I watched the activities of the visitors. Moving quickly, silently and confidently through the trees, I gained the big rock and began to scan the water.

It was then that I saw two heads near the centre of the lake.

Two young women were bathing there, neither wearing a
swimming cap but they were keeping their heads above the
surface. One was a light blonde while the other was also blonde
but of a slightly darker shade. They swam with ease, chattering
to each other as they moved gracefully through the smooth
water with the morning sun glinting from the surface. There
was the slightest hint of a haze over the lake, a misty atmosphere
which intensified towards the distant shore. But I could see no
one else nor could I discern any vehicle parked nearby. I
wondered if the man seen earlier had any links with these girls.

I did not recognize either of them and was about to leave
when they emerged from the water. Both were exquisitely
beautiful and splendidly shaped – and they were completely
naked. As they rose from the cool, clear waters I watched with
fascination as their long, slender limbs carried them to the
distant shore; they halted near the edge, turned and scooped
handfuls of clean water with which they washed their lithe
young bodies. They presented a sight to be treasured, a sight to
be captured for ever by a skilled artist. But there was no artist to
observe them – just an appreciative village constable. The water
cascaded between their shapely and ample breasts, down their
flat stomachs, flowing between their legs and around their
thighs as they rinsed away the water-borne particles which
clung to them.

They continued with their ablutions until they had washed
away every piece of surplus mud and greenery which had been
carried from the lake and its floor. Unabashed, uninhibited,
free and beautiful, they cleaned themselves, then suddenly
turned and ran off.

I heard them laughing with joy as they vanished among the
distant trees and shrubs. I waited. I did not want to announce
my intrusive presence in any way, nor did I want them to think I
had been spying on them. Did they visit this lake each morning? Were they camping nearby? Were they visitors? And it was
so early ... I looked at my watch. 5.50. Who would rise for a
swim before six in a chilly fresh-water lake? No one that I
knew....

But they had vanished. I did not see them depart nor did I hear any more voices. They had vanished beyond the thick greenery at the far end of the lake and I waited for a long time, forgetting that I had to be in Elsinby at 6 a.m.! I never made that rendezvous but walked from the wood in something of a daze. I wondered if I had really seen those girls, or was it all a pleasant dream? But I never saw them again.

I was brought back to reality when Sergeant Blaketon met me at my 7 a.m. point, and I wondered if he had driven out to meet me at six. But he said nothing about that missed rendezvous. He did, however, mention my dirty boots and my muddy trouser legs.

'I've been in the woods, sergeant,' I explained. 'I've had reports of a possible poacher or someone living rough,' and I outlined the reports I'd received.

'Good, keep up the good work, Rhea. Anything else to report?'

'No, it's all quiet, sergeant.'

'Good, well enjoy your walk. I'll get myself home for some breakfast. You can't beat an early start to the day – it sets the pulses racing. See you later.'

And that was it – until I chanced to see a girly calendar in a York shop the following Christmas. And there was my rock, the chair-shaped rock by the lake, with a beautiful blonde girl draped upon it, breasts and body bared for all the world to view. There was a total of twelve superb colour pictures, one for each month, and each was a woodland scene. I recognized eight of them – all eight had been photographed in those woods.

I saw from the credits that the photographer was a local man called Anthony Gourlay from York; it was then that I realized who the mysterious visitor had been. The sketchy descriptions I'd received did match his general appearance. I felt sure the mystery man had been Gourlay, reconnoitring the landscape in the morning light before deciding upon his precise locations for his calendar.

I did not tell anyone about this. After all, I did not want the lake to become a tourist attraction.

* * *

That brief but very pleasant experience highlighted the fact that our waterways, whether in the form of the seaside or inland rivers, lakes or ponds, can hold a promise of untold bliss. This is recognized by many. If there is a convenient stretch of water, the British will spend time beside it, even if only for a day. Yorkshire's dramatic coastline, its huge rivers and countless streams or becks, all bear witness to this longing for waterside leisure, especially during the summer when the people evacuate their cities and towns for a day beside the sea, a picnic near a moorland stream or a holiday beside a river or lake. It was an appreciation of our inbred escapist needs that persuaded a local farmer to make good use of some derelict buildings.

He was Arthur Fewster of Riverside Farm, Lower Keld. This remote Ryedale hamlet is a couple of miles west of Crampton and overlooks the gentle River Rye. It has no shop, post office or pub and is known for its underground springs, the Yorkshire word 'keld' meaning a spring. Much of the district's domestic water supply is pumped from Lower Keld's never-ending flow of deliciously crisp and pure water. I had very few reasons to call at any of the half-dozen houses which comprised Lower Keld, but did visit the farm each quarter to check Arthur's stock registers.

After one visit, where I had indulged in the 'lowance, i.e. the usual mid-morning snack of teacakes, fruit cake, cheese and biscuits, washed down by a huge mug of hot tea, Arthur said, 'Here, Mr Rhea, Ah'll show you summat.'

He led me across his spacious yard to what had been an old disused and tumbledown building, full of farmyard junk. Now it was sparkling with new paint and freshly pointed brickwork. There were five new doors, all glistening with fresh paint, and the windows shone in the morning sunshine. He opened one of the doors and led me inside; the transformation was astonishing.

There I saw a neat kitchen with a newly fitted sink and

cooker, and it was furnished with new pine chairs and a table.
Two easy chairs stood in the far corners while a narrow
wooden staircase rose from the floor. He led me into a small
upstairs room and there I saw a double bed, a wardrobe,
dressing-table and two easy chairs, all in fashionable pine. A
small bathroom and toilet completed the accommodation.

'Holiday cottages,' he said proudly. 'Ah've converted this
awd tile shed into five cottages, two doubles like this 'un, and
three singles. T'other double's at yon end, singles are in
t'middle. Fishermen, tha knows. They come for a weekend or
longer, so Ah thowt Ah'd convert this awd spot into rooms for
'em. What do you think, Mr Rhea?'

'A great idea, Arthur,' I enthused. 'You've done a good
job.'

'One day, farmers'll have to do summat other than farm, Mr
Rhea,' he said. 'What with folks getting more leisure time and
longer holidays, well, it makes sense to me to cater for 'em.
Ah've done it all proper, planning consent and all that. So if
you know anybody who's looking for a quiet spot beside the
river, well, just you give 'em my name and address.'

'I will,' I promised him.

Arthur began to advertise his holiday accommodation, with
special emphasis upon the opportunities for angling in this
lovely river, and I did pass details to one or two people who
inquired. I was later to learn they had been very happy in
Arthur's old tile shed. He sold them fresh farm produce such
as milk, eggs, potatoes and vegetables and they thought they
were living the life of a rustic yokel. For some townies, the tile
shed represented bliss of a kind not associated with city streets
and concrete gardens. Arthur had hit upon a winner.

But from a police point of view, the assemblage of total
strangers in an alien environment, where they must live and
sleep in close proximity to one another, can often lead to
problems. Police officers in holiday resorts are well aware of
this and although I welcomed Arthur's initiative, I did wonder
when there would be trouble at t'tile shed. I forecast someone
going off without paying, or someone getting drunk and

smashing Arthur's furniture or someone fighting with his neighbour over parking places, girl friends or something equally silly.

But I think Arthur must have chosen his guests very carefully because I received no complaints, either from the few villagers who lived nearby, or from Arthur or his guests. As time went by, the old riverside tile shed did appear to be a genuine haven of rural delight.

The fact that, when full, the tile shed accommodated only seven people might have had some bearing upon this happy state of affairs. Had it accommodated seventy, then there may have been occasions for aggravation. But even so, for some forty weeks of the year, Lower Keld's population was swollen quite considerably. The entire hamlet had less than twenty residents, and so Arthur's enterprise regularly increased its population by about a third. It was a large percentage increase, if a modest numerical one. The shop and pub in nearby Crampton approved and so the situation was never a problem.

That state of bliss continued until I received a telephone call from Miss Neville, a retired spinster of uncertain years whose cottage was very close to Arthur's tile shed.

'Mr Rhea,' she breathed into the telephone late one night, 'do come to Lower Keld, please. I'm sorry to ring so late, but I fear there is trouble at Arthur's tile shed and he is out, you see, with his wife. There is an awful noise and lots of arguing with people shouting. It's terrible, it really is most out of character. I do fear there is trouble.'

'I'll be there in ten minutes,' I assured her.

I'd just completed a late route and was in my office writing up my pocketbook when her call came, otherwise I might have been in bed. I noticed it was approaching 11.30.

'I'm just popping down to Lower Keld,' I called to Mary who was already in bed. 'I won't be long, it sounds like a domestic row in Arthur's holiday cottages.'

Domestic rows are an aggravating feature of a police officer's life. Where possible, we endeavour to avoid them because if we enter the fray (usually at the request of a

neighbour), the warring husband/wife/boy-friend/girl-friend/
lovers join forces and attack the peace-keeping constable. Our
attitude has always been that minor domestic wars are best left
to play themselves out in the family home, although we are
sometimes concerned about an outbreak of something more
serious, such as physical attacks or injuries.

So to what was I heading at Lower Keld? I wondered what
horrors lay before me. Domestics are never pleasant, they
seldom provide the slightest degree of job satisfaction....

In my little police van, I chugged along the lane towards the
tile shed, enjoying the peace of the late-night journey. When I
arrived at Riverside Farm, it was in darkness except for the
tile-shed block, and there I noticed lights in two of the units. I
knew that at this time of year, the early spring, things were
quiet; in fact, I was to learn that only two of the units were
currently occupied. I parked and walked through the gate and
into the courtyard, but there was no noise.

Two cars were parked there and I did see a light shining
from Miss Neville's cottage beyond the parking area; her
curtains fluttered as the gate clicked upon my entry, but she
had not ventured into the battleground to greet me. But when
I entered the paved courtyard, once a muddy portion of
Arthur's farmyard, I saw in the light cast from the units, two
silent figures lying on the stone flags. Had vile murder been
done?

I hurried to them, fearing the worst. To my surprise, I
found two women, both unconscious, and they were
surrounded by empty bottles ... gin bottles, Martinis, wine
bottles.

At first glance, I reckoned they'd be in their thirties. They
were casually dressed: one wore jeans and the other had a
short skirt; both wore thick sweaters. I checked their pulses
and listened to their breathing as I sought any signs of injury.
My brief examination convinced me that neither was hurt; the
problem was that they were very, very drunk.

I looked around for any indication of other trouble, but
found none, the only clue being that two chalet doors were

standing wide open, flooding their light into this courtyard. Hurriedly, I entered the first and searched it, noting that the single bed was unoccupied ... more empty bottles littered the kitchen.

Next door, I knew, was the double chalet, the one I had inspected with Arthur some time ago. Its door was also open and the lights were on. I now entered that one, stepping gingerly through the open door.

I walked past a pair of thigh-length waders and some fishing equipment stacked in a corner, then went up the stairs. I opened the bedroom door and was surprised to see a man on one side of the bed, fast asleep. He was totally oblivious to the situation outside and an empty malt whisky bottle stood on the floor at the side of his bed.

From the available evidence, I could imagine what had happened. The three of them had had a wild party with lots to drink, and I guessed they'd been laughing and shouting outside. Poor Miss Neville had misunderstood the situation; she'd interpreted the noise as the sound of trouble whereas it had been the sound of fun. There was no damage anywhere, no injuries and no cause for alarm. Even so, it must have been quite a party ... these three, friends by the look of it, had enjoyed an almighty binge, but the two women had been unable to regain their respective chalets. The husband had managed to stagger upstairs with his bottle and had crashed into bed. That was my assessment of the situation.

I could return each woman to her chalet, but which woman should be sleeping with the man? I went upstairs to rouse him, but failed. All my shouting and shaking had absolutely no effect – the whisky had sent him into the deepest of sleeps. But I could manage. I went outside and studied the drunken, snoozing pair. For some reason I thought of Cinderella and decided that shoes might provide the answer, so I went into the single chalet and found a pair of high-heeled shoes.

I fitted them to each of the women's feet – they slid easily on to the girl in the jeans, but were far too small for her companion. The problem was solved! The next thing was to get them to safety. I went into the double chalet and again tried to rouse the sleeping man, but with no success, and so I went to the girl wearing the mini-skirt, hauled her to her feet and slung her face down across my shoulder in the fireman's lift. It was a technique taught us at training school and it meant I could carry her quite easily.

She groaned a little and wheezed a lot while making other weird noises as I settled her on my shoulder with her head and arms hanging down my back. I clamped my arm around the back of her dangling legs, and in this way bore her into the chalet. I would drop her in bed beside her husband; it was the only safe and warm place. Without much trouble, I mounted the stairs, entered the bedroom and with my free hand, rolled back the sheets. The man was as naked as a new born babe. Then, as carefully as possible, I deposited the unconscious woman beside her unconscious husband; he groaned and turned to face her, still asleep, as she began to snore. Although she was fully dressed, I covered them and left them, dropping the Yale latch as I made my exit.

I repeated the exercise with the other woman, placing her fully dressed into her single bed, and then dropped her latch as I went out. I left each of their lights burning just in case they had to wander to the loo during the night.

And that was it. I was quite proud of the ease with which I had dealt with that little problem and turned to leave, only to find Miss Neville standing near the gate, clutching a coat about her.

'It was a party, Miss Neville, a somewhat drunken party by all accounts. They'll all in bed now, fast asleep.'

'I hope you didn't mind me calling …'

'Not at all,' I assured her. 'That's what I'm here for.'

'I'll tell Mr Fewster when he returns, I think he and his wife are attending someone's silver-wedding party.'

'Yes, you tell him,' I smiled, looking at my watch. It was nearly quarter past twelve. 'But so far as I'm concerned, the matter is closed and I'm going home. Goodnight.'

It would be about ten o'clock next morning when a man

arrived at my police house. I welcomed him into my little office and settled him down. In his early forties with thinning sandy hair, he was smartly dressed in what were clearly a countryman's clothes – heavy greenish tweeds with brogue shoes bearing studded soles. He was smiling at me.

'You are the village constable, I understand?' he said in a gentle Scots accent. 'You patrol Lower Keld?'

'Yes, I'm PC Rhea,' I confirmed.

'I came to thank you,' he beamed. 'For last night.'

'Oh!' now I realized who he was and the purpose of his call.

'I saw Miss Neville this morning,' he enlightened me. 'She said she had called you, and that you had dealt with the problem.'

'It was nothing,' I assumed a modest pose. 'Just part of the service.'

'It was bloody good service if you ask me,' he chortled, his accent growing stronger. 'I go there to have a spot of quiet fishing, to get away from the pressures of work, you know, and what happens – some kind constable plonks a woman in bed beside me. I don't know her, and she doesn't know me ... but what a time we had....'

'I thought she was your wife ... '

'No, I have nae wife. I'm divorced. I spend my time fishing, it's relaxing. And last night, well, I drowned my sorrows with a good stiff whisky or two ... but then I thought I was having a wonderful dream ... stripping a woman, making love, it was some dream ... then I woke up and found a woman at my side, naked, asleep ... then she woke, saw me, screamed, grabbed her clothes and ran off ... God knows where she went. But she was most friendly and co-operative during my dream, I can assure you ... so I came to say thanks. Now, I'm going home feeling very happy and fulfilled – and I've had the best break of my life, thanks to you.'

When he'd gone, I pondered over the two women. Who was the one who'd entertained the fisherman? Some time later, I was talking to Arthur Fewster and referred to the incident.

He chuckled.

'By gum,' he grinned. 'You cheered that bloke up no end, Mr Rhea. Never had a time like it, he reckons. He asked if I could fix him up with another holiday like it.'

'But those two women ... I mean, I thought ... '

'Don't let it worry you, lad, no harm done. The one in my chalet comes from Brighton, t'other's her pal. The pal has a cousin in Lower Keld, Mrs Bayes down by t'bridge. She stayed there while her pal rented that spot from me. They'd had a bit of a farewell party last night ... now yon fisherman never locks his door. I reckon they'd strayed into his spot instead of hers when they were past caring ... that's why his door was open ... anyroad, it's all over. A good time was had by all.'

But I still do not know who that fisherman was, nor do I know the identity of his surprise partner that night.

But every Christmas for five or six years afterwards, a bottle of beautiful malt whisky would arrive at my house, anonymously. I raised my glass to him and to her, for she had made one man very happy and another very curious. Perhaps she is reading these words now?

I may never know.

* * *

That story of a strange party was echoed in another case which occurred in the hillside hamlet of Shelvingby, high on the southern escarpment of the North York Moors.

This tiny community of stone-built houses nestles deep in the moors beneath the sheltering slopes of a huge rounded hill. Once, not long ago, the village was the stronghold of local Methodism, John Wesley having preached here during one of his Yorkshire tours, and this might explain why the tiny village church reclines in the valley at a discreet distance from the village. Now, Methodism has virtually vanished from the district and the church is enjoying a revival, if only from visiting tourists. It stands beside the Shelf Beck, the village and beck being named after the strange step-like formation of the limestone landscape. In this case, the stream tumbles and roars down a series of stone shelves, but as it flows past the tiny church, it becomes calm and serene.

The churchyard borders the stream, and in late winter it is brilliant with masses of snowdrops; in the spring, it is the turn of the daffodils, for thousands of them bloom in this remote and quiet spot. Owing to its situation close to the beck, a public footpath passes through the churchyard, and consequently it is busy with hikers and ramblers for many weeks in the year. This does mean, however, that many passers-by pop into the church to contemplate its long history, and then they slip a coin or two into the offertory box. In this way, the little church enjoys a useful supplementary income.

It was a regular but local walker who drew my attention to a small problem in that churchyard. He was Timothy Pepper, a retired clerk.

A meek man, he had come to live in Shelvingby in his retirement. He was so meek and mild that when he heard strange noises emanating from the centre of the churchyard, he did not rush to investigate. Instead, he hurried home with his dog, an equally timid Yorkshire terrier called Garth, and wondered what to do about the noises. His wife, not eager to push Timothy to the limits of his valiant nature, advised him to forget it – it might have been nothing more than children playing or dogs skylarking. So Timothy obeyed her. For the next few weeks he walked his dog through the churchyard only during daylight hours, but as the autumn drew nearer, so the days grew darker.

Gradually, Timothy began to walk again in the darkness, but by now he'd forgotten about the noises and had resumed his night-time walks with Garth. Then around ten o'clock one night, he heard the noises again; he rushed home without seeking an explanation and this time his face was pale and his hair stood on end. Even Garth appeared to be worried about something because he refused to leave his master's side.

'It's awful,' Timothy stuttered to his wife. 'Terrible noises, shrieks ... weird laughter ... in the darkness ... '

'You're not telling me it's haunted?' Mrs Pepper was horrified at the possibility.

'No, I think it was humans,' he said. 'I wondered if there was some awful ritual being practised by incomers ... devil worship even, desecration of our churchyard or graves ... '

'It might be children playing,' she put to him.

'It didn't sound like children,' he said. 'Besides, it was late and we've no teenagers in this village, have we? One or two of infant school age, but it wouldn't be them, and there were no cars or motor bikes parked nearby ... '

Without an on-the-spot investigation by Timothy, it seemed that the cause of the noises would never be ascertained, and those who knew Timothy were quite aware of his shortcomings. When faced with an incident where positive action was required, Timothy would always seek someone else to take over. And so I was told of the problem during a routine visit to Shelvingby.

I popped into the shop, as was my practice, and was told all about Timothy's experience. I promised Mrs Belt, the shopkeeper, that I would keep an eye on the churchyard and I knew that news of my assurance would quickly reach the entire village. Shortly afterwards, when I came across Timothy taking Garth for his daily constitutional, I stopped my van and climbed out for a chat.

'I've heard about these noises in your churchyard, Mr Pepper,' I began. 'I thought I'd keep an eye on things. I've not heard them, so what can you tell me?'

He told me his story, but, after some prompting, did say that the noises were happy ones, like a party, with laughter and loud voices. But there were no lights. Most parties would have been illuminated by torches or lanterns, but he'd not seen such things.

He did say, however, that he was sure he'd heard a woman's voice, and added that he'd been to the centre of the graveyard in daylight but had seen no discarded bottles and no damage. The intruders did not seem to be vandals. On both occasions, the noises had occurred after 10 p.m.

'It's certainly mysterious,' I agreed. 'But thanks – I'll keep an eye open.'

Thereafter, each time I patrolled the village during the hours of darkness, I would leave the van at a discreet distance and take a walk along the public footpath which led to the churchyard. But on each occasion, I heard and saw nothing suspicious. After about four months, I had almost forgotten about the churchyard noises when I chanced to drive into Shelvingby late one night. I had no particular reason for being there but the village was on the route of one of my patrols. I parked in the village centre and walked around when, to my surprise, I saw Timothy making extreme haste towards me. He was dragging Garth by his lead and was clearly rushing about some urgent business – in fact, he was galloping home after undergoing another terrifying experience.

'Ah, Mr Rhea, thank God!' he panted. 'What a blessing I came across you ... those noises, they're there, now. I've just come from there....'

'Show me,' I requested. 'Then we can get the thing sorted out.'

'Oh, well, I ... er ... '

He was terrified, and so I didn't force him to accompany me; if the noises were still there, I would soon trace them. I took a powerful torch from my van and made my way to the graveyard; Timothy watched me for a few seconds, and then went home. On reflection, I'd be better without him – he might develop into a nervous wreck, faint on the spot or produce some other kind of problem. I walked towards the church with my soft-soled boots making no sound, and as I entered the churchyard I could hear some peculiar sounds. They were indeed coming from the midst of the gravestones, somewhere near the centre. I halted and listened.

It *did* sound like a party, albeit a small one, with a woman's voice laughing and talking. At this distance, the words were indistinct and I could not hear what she was saying, but as I stood and listened in the gloom of that October night, I could not see any lights nor could I discern the presence of any other people.

In some circumstances, particularly in such a location, the noises might frighten the faint-hearted, but police officers must not be afraid of the unknown, and so I moved quietly towards the sounds. On the soft grass between the tombstones my feet made no noise, and because my eyes had grown accustomed to the darkness I did not require my torch. Gradually, I moved closer to the noises, being guided by them. By now, they had been reduced to a softer chatter, as if the woman was talking to a friend.

I wondered if it was someone with a radio perhaps; a tramp maybe, sleeping rough, or some youngster seeking an opportunity to indulge in Radio Luxembourg after being forbidden to do so at home. But it was none of those.

As I approached, I could see a woman sitting against a tombstone, and she was alone. She was babbling away in her low voice and suddenly she shrieked with laughter, as if someone had told her a joke, and then she resumed her one-sided conversation. She had grey hair; I could see its light shade against the all-embracing darkness, and even now, as I stood only feet away, she was not aware of my presence.

I could see a bottle in her hand, a gin bottle I guessed, and all around the grave I could see beer bottles, empty ones. I had to make her aware of my presence and so I shone my torch. She blinked into the light, smiling up at me.

'Who's that?' her voice showed no fear, nor was she drunk.

'The policeman, PC Rhea from Aidensfield,' I said, switching off the light. 'I heard noises … '

'Sorry, officer,' she said. 'I was just having a drink … it's my husband's birthday, you see. We were just having a nice quiet drink together, and telling stories like we used to do … that's all.'

'I thought you were alone,' I could see no sign of her husband. 'So where's he?'

'Down here,' and she patted the earth beneath her. 'He's down here, and I've given him his eight pints … it's his birthday, you see, we always go out for a drink or two or three on his birthday, and on mine.... '

'So who are you?' I asked.

'Helen,' she said. 'Helen Brough. Alex's wife.'

I shone my torch on the gravestone and highlighted the inscription. I saw that the grave beneath her was that of Alexander Brough who had died three years earlier, aged sixty-four.

I did not know what to do with her. She was hardly drunk and disorderly; she was well dressed and she lived in the village, but she had this bizarre desire to drink at her husband's grave on celebratory occasions. And she made sure he got his share by pouring the contents of eight pint bottles on to his grave, but always removed the empties. I felt sure he would be happy with the arrangement – and he wouldn't have to stand anyone a round either!

My mind raced over the legislation I had been taught – I knew of the Ecclesiastical Courts Jurisdiction Act of 1860 which made brawling in a churchyard an offence. This was hardly 'brawling', i.e. any riotous, violent or indecent behaviour. She was not disturbing any divine service or troubling any minister or religion during divine service, although I did recall a provision which forbade the use of churchyards for secular purposes. Was she using it for a secular purpose by sharing a drink with her dead husband?

That, however, was not a police problem; it was the responsibility of churchwardens.

If she had been drunk, I might have considered the offence of being drunk and disorderly in a public place but she was not really disorderly, nor was she drunk and incapable, and it was questionable whether a graveyard at night was a public place.

I could think of no offences under the Noise Abatement Act, the Civic Amenities Act, the Litter Act, the Public Health Act, the Burial Act or the Burial Laws Amendment Act of 1880. The most likely offence was one under the Cemeteries Clauses Act of 1947 which made it illegal to play sports or games, or to discharge firearms (except at military funerals) or to commit any nuisance in a cemetery.

Was she committing a nuisance? What was a 'nuisance'?

I thought the wisest approach was to wait until someone made a formal complaint about her specific behaviour and then we would decide what to do about it. In the mean time, I told her to raise her glass to her husband and as she did, I said, 'Cheers, Alex,' then left.

As I have never received any formal complaint from the churchwarden or anyone else, Helen Brough might still be drinking with her husband on those private celebratory occasions. And I think the beer must have acted as a fertilizer because there was always a splendid crop of snowdrops on his grave.

2 Stolen Sweets are Always Sweeter

What would be theft in other poets is only victory in him.
John Dryden (1631–1700)

Theft is surely the most common of all crimes. It is committed by so many people in so many circumstances that it is impossible to record or even estimate an accurate total. The number of crimes known to the police bears little resemblance to the actual number committed, and this is particularly so where theft is concerned. Lots of us suffer thefts without reporting our loss to the police, either because we know the person responsible or we do not think any useful purpose would be served in making an official report.

There can be little doubt, however, that if every theft was reported to the authorities, then it would result in a more accurate and perhaps terrifying assessment of the nation's criminality. In that way, it might persuade the Home Office to permit police forces to recruit more constables in an attempt to combat the seemingly unstoppable growth of lawlessness. In spite of official denials, there is an acute shortage of uniformed, patrolling police officers.

As the village constable at Aidensfield, however, I was aware that my patch comprised a high proportion of law-abiding folk, but there were some felons among them.

Some operated stealthily while others were more open about their crimes; some got caught either by me or by their victims, but several did evade the majesty of the law. Some did not regard their thieving activities as either unlawful or even sinful, somehow convincing themselves that their actions were justified or not the action of a criminal. Many thieves do persuade themselves that they have a right to purloin their ill-gotten gains. Some shoplifters certainly think along those lines, but shoplifting is just one form of theft, and it is a serious crime with a maximum penalty of ten years' imprisonment.

I think it is fair to say that, in some cases, the act of stealing is an addiction – sometimes I wonder if there should be Thieves Anonymous just as there is Gamblers Anonymous and Alcoholics Anonymous. But the scheme would surely fail because thieves would steal from one another at their meetings....

Most police officers can give examples of compulsive thieves, people with the magpie mania. In Maddleskirk, for example, there was a milk roundsman who could not resist stealing things left in the yards and gardens of the houses to which he delivered his pintas. He had a penchant for children's trikes, but as the villagers all knew of his weakness, they never reported his crimes. They simply went to his house and reclaimed their missing goods. He stole anything and everything he could carry home, his range of trophies varying from zinc horse troughs to garden tools via trikes.

If it was left out in the open, Gold Top Gareth would pinch it. He never sold or disposed of his ill-gotten goods, and so it seems it was a genuine addiction.

But can theft ever be justified? For example, is it wrong for a man to steal a loaf of bread when he is starving? Is it wrong for him to steal a loaf for another man who is starving? This type of question is guaranteed to produce argument and discussion, with Robin Hood being quoted as an example of the merits in stealing from the rich to provide for the poor.

Such a Robin Hood type of character did operate on my beat, and I nicknamed him the Pilfering Poet. His crimes were never really serious, but they were annoying and, of course, they did not improve my crime statistics. Furthermore, they made my crime detection returns look positively sick!

The Poet's first reported crime was the theft of some hens. I was called to the premises of a poultry farmer at Elsinby and he led me to one of his henhouses. It stood in a large field some distance from the farmhouse and was one of dozens of similar wooden structures upon the premises. Jonathon Murray of Whin Bank Farm showed me the scene of the crime. He had locked up his hens the previous night at dusk, but when he'd come to let his birds out that morning, there was only one left in this particular henhouse. The door was closed and it was evident that the raid had occurred during the night. He'd lost twenty-three Rhode Island Red crossed with Light Sussex hens.

Hens of this breed were famed as good layers, but of that henhouse-full, only a solitary bird remained, clucking with pleasure at his arrival.

But the thief or thieves had left a curious note. It was hanging on the door and read,

> *We've taken your hens to feed the poor*
> *But we've left you one to breed some more.*

It was written in blue ballpoint pen on lined writing paper and hung from a hook inside the door. I took it down and asked,

'Any idea whose writing this is, Jon?'

'Nay, Mr Rhea.' He had lived on these premises all his life as man and boy, and shook his grey head. 'No idea.'

'And your other henhouses?'

'All present and correct, Mr Rhea. They've not raided any o' them.'

'Have you had any other hens stolen recently?'

Again he shook his head, 'Nay, lad. Never a one.'

I searched the ground around the henhouse for indications of any unusual boot prints or other clues, but found nothing. We returned to the farmhouse where Betty Murray produced three plates of scones and cakes, with a mug of coffee apiece, and I waded through this mammoth 'lowance break as I took written details of the crime. I kept the poetic note and promised I'd do my best to find the culprits.

Although the note was couched in royal 'we' terms, I suspected the thief was a lone operator. I had no idea why I felt this but later thefts reinforced that original gut-feeling. Jonathon did not honestly feel he'd get his birds back, but had had the sense to let me know about the crime in case similar ones were occurring nearby. But there weren't any others. I'd had no poultry thefts reported for some time, certainly none with this particularly poetic *modus operandi*. I made the usual inquiries at butchers' shops, hotels and other likely outlet points, but produced a blank. Nobody had seen Jonathon's poultry, dead or alive, dressed or undressed.

The next poetic theft was from the garden of a retired agricultural mechanic called Clive Gill. His garden was always a showpiece for he grew and exhibited a range of splendid flowers, specializing in chrysanthemums and dahlias. In his retirement, he produced gorgeous blooms which were in demand at weddings, funerals and every kind of special occasion.

Everyone liked Clive: he was a most friendly and jolly man. He rang me at nine one morning.

'Mr Rhea,' he said in his slow voice, 'you wouldn't believe this, but somebody's pinched my best spade. It's a stainless steel one, worth a few quid of anybody's money ... '

'Are you sure?' was my first question. 'You've not lent it to anyone, have you? Or put it in a different place?'

'No, nowt like that. In fact, the thieves have left a daft note behind ... '

'I'll come straight away,' I promised him. Already, I had the feeling that this would reveal another of those poetic MOs. I was right.

Clive lived in a delightful stone-built roadside cottage between Aidensfield and Elsinby and so I walked the mile or so, enjoying the sparkle of the mild spring morning. I spotted a wren busy with his nest building; a woodpecker hammering at an elm and a weasel darting across the road ahead of me. I arrived at Clive's cottage just before 9.30 and his wife greeted me. Pretty with her rimless spectacles and round, rosy face, she was a modest, tiny lady in her early sixties whose skills with flower arranging were invariably in demand at the local churches and chapels. She was also a keen member of the WI and was always prominent at WI events.

'Clive's in his greenhouse, Mr Rhea,' and she pointed in the general direction. 'I'll have some 'lowance ready when you've done.'

I found him re-potting some young green plants, and I marvelled at his natural skills as he upturned the plant pots and tapped out the small growths before transferring them to larger ones. He never spilt a bit of soil – I'd have had soil all over the floor if I'd been attempting that.

'There's the note, Mr Rhea,' he nodded towards a shelf at the other side of his greenhouse. I found a note on lined writing paper, written in blue ballpoint pen. This one said,

> *We've taken your spade, your garden is weedy*
> *we'll make sure it's used to till for the needy.*

'They've a bloody cheek,' he said. 'My garden's never weedy!'

I asked the usual questions about where he'd left the spade, what it looked like and whether he recognized the handwriting of the note, and then adjourned to the house for a hefty bout of eating Mrs Gill's sumptuous 'lowance. In addition to everything else, she produced a delicious slab of apple pie and this kept me busy as I compiled my crime report.

'If they'd wanted an old spade for the needy, I could have given 'em one,' Clive said. 'I've dozens in my shed, but that was my best 'un, a newish 'un, an' all.'

I told him about the missing hens and their note, and promised I'd do my best to recover his lost spade, albeit with little confidence in my own ability to retrieve it. Even if I did find it, it would be difficult proving its true ownership.

Looking at the poem, I realized once more that the note was couched in the plural and I began to wonder about the identity of the poor and needy who were recipients of this odd selection of stolen property. Were the goods genuinely being handed over for some charitable purpose, or was this just a poetic ploy by the thief or thieves?

Within the next few months, more stolen goods vanished at the hand of the mysterious poet. A fruiterer lost some of the stock from his wagon and this note was left:

> *Apples, pears and plums galore,*
> *We've given them away, you can get some more.*

A lady who had been spring cleaning her cottage had left a kitchen chair outside the back door. She intended taking it to a local upholsterer for repairs to its cane seat. One night, the chair vanished and a note said:

> *The chair you left outside your door*
> *Will come in handy for someone poor.*

A greengrocer discovered that part of his delivery of fresh vegetables, left outside his shop doorway in the early hours by the wholesaler, had vanished. The note said:

> *We've taken some peas and artichokes*
> *To be used in soup for our old folks.*

When a florist found several vases of display flowers missing at Ashfordly, a note was left which said:

> *Your lovely flowers will cheer the room*
> *Of one who has to live alone.*

In many cases, the stolen goods were items of food or associated with food. Without exception, the victims said that if the thieves had only asked, they would have willingly donated the items, or something similar, if it would ease the plight of someone less-well-off than themselves. None could understand why the thieves bothered to steal goods which would have been freely donated.

Within a space of about nine months, dozens of these minor thefts occurred, the hallmark of each one being the poetic MO.

My Pilfering Poet was certainly causing me a headache, but not once did I get any clue as to his identity; no one had seen or heard anything which might lead to him, her or them.

No vehicles had been heard or seen at odd hours, although it did seem that the crimes were the work of someone who was around at night, or in the very early hours of the morning. I did wonder if it was a driver regularly passing through the district, someone who was not local. My colleagues and I made inquiries at all the charitable and welfare organizations in the locality in the hope that we might identify the destination of the stolen goods, but we produced no information. The handwriting was never identified, while the writing paper could have come from any cheap pad.

Then, as suddenly as he had started, the Pilfering Poet ceased his activities. For weeks, no more notes were left and I wondered if it was someone who had moved from the district, or if the travelling pilferer had had his route altered. But I had to submit progress reports to show that I was continuing to investigate the crimes. Then, just before one month's end, I got the following note from Sergeant Bairstow:

> *The Inspector hopes you'll make the time*
> *To trace the suspect of your poetic crime.*

I decided to enter the spirit of the occasion and submitted the following progress report:

> *I've made inquiries all around*
> *But not a single clue I've found.*
> *The crimes all happened in the night*
> *With victims safely out of sight.*
> *Done with guile and some great stealth*
> *To benefit those who lack the wealth*
> *To make their own ends meet with ease.*
> *From garden spades to tins of peas –*
> *The range of thefts is quite bizarre*

But no one's seen or heard a car
Or van or bike or other steed
To carry spoils to those in need.
Our villain's silent, clever and shrewd
I think it must be Robin Hood.

I did not receive any response to my own modest poetic effort, but neither did I trace that thief or thieves.

* * *

All criminals use an MO. The Pilfering Poet's MO was his habit of leaving behind a suitable verse. The initials MO mean *modus operandi*, which translated into English is 'method of operation'. In many cases, it is possible to identify a criminal through his or her MO; some burglars, for example, always break in through a rear window, some use an upstairs window, some climb fall pipes and break in through a bedroom window. Some smash their way in while others drill holes in the woodwork of windows; some use master keys.

Others always have a meal in the attacked house, some write graffiti on walls, while highly nervous types will pee or do worse on the floor or carpet. Many a burgled householder has found a heap of stinking excrement on their finest rug – and it wasn't left by the dog.

Just as each of us has our own way of doing things, whether it is cleaning the house, performing our routine tasks like dressing ourselves or locking up at night, so villains all adopt a pattern in their crimes, often without realizing it. This enables the police to identify a criminal, even if, at times, it is not possible to prove his or her guilt.

One example was a local burglar with a very curious MO. He rejoiced in the unlikely name of Octavius Horatio Calpin and came from a very good but very large family in Ashfordly. As his name suggests, Octavius was the eighth child; the seventh was Septimus Brutus while the sixth was Sixtus Cletus, but I never did learn the name of their earlier brothers and sisters. However, his younger sister, the tenth in the family, was called Decima Prudence.

For some reason, Octavius turned out to be a wrong 'un. Even at school, when aged only six and three-quarters, he was caught stealing sweets and dinner money from his classmates, and when he persisted with his dishonesty in later years, his actions puzzled everyone. The family, local farmers, oozed love and affection for all their children, they were well fed and decently clothed and were among the happiest of people.

Octavius was the only one who went off the proverbial rails. What had persuaded him to turn to crime may never be known, but he did develop into a criminal of considerable skill. There was clearly some character defect, for outwardly he was a charming and likeable young man. As a criminal, he was fairly successful – by that I mean he was not often caught or prosecuted although we knew he was responsible for a high number of local housebreakings.

We became aware of his crimes through his MO. Octavius was a housebreaker and burglar, those two crimes being quite distinct from each other until the legal changes of 1968. Burglary was the name then given to the crime of breaking into someone's dwelling house *only at night*, i.e. between 9 p.m. and 6 a.m. If the house was broken into at any other time, the crime was classified as housebreaking and carried a lesser penalty. Other similar crimes were variously known as shopbreaking, garage breaking, office breaking, warehouse breaking and so forth. Since 1968, however, all such offences of breaking into property have been reclassified as burglary, whether or not the attacked premises were houses or other buildings.

In the main, Octavius tried to restrict his crimes to housebreaking, tending to enter good quality homes during the daylight hours while the occupants were away or at work. Very occasionally, he committed a burglary, but those crimes were rare – he knew the prevailing high penalties for burglary and rarely took that risk.

But his MO was rather peculiar. He insisted on tidying up

the houses which he entered. He did not merely tidy up his own mess, but tidied the entire premises, putting things straight. He would wipe the dust off shiny surfaces, place magazines and newspapers in a neat pile, pair off shoes, straighten pictures, replace jam jars and condiment sets in kitchen cupboards and perform a whole range of similar tidying-up routines.

This was in direct contrast to many other housebreakers who would smash up a house, spray paint on the walls and generally vandalize the premises to leave a terrible, heart-rending mess. On occasions, some of Octavius's victims reported things stolen when in fact they had been tidied away by their burglar – one lady reported the theft of a jar of marmalade, a packet of corn flakes and two china mugs because they'd vanished from her kitchen table. Later, she found them in a kitchen cupboard – Octavius had tidied them away.

He achieved most of this without leaving any fingerprints, but from time to time he did make mistakes, and in the months before my arrival at Aidensfeld, he had been arrested and sentenced to two years' imprisonment for housebreaking and theft. Thus he had a criminal record and, as a consequence, his fingerprints were on file.

For a time, Octavius went straight but eventually his old desires returned and we learned of this when a country house near York was raided and a large quantity of silver stolen.

The crime had all the hallmarks of a professional housebreaker, but the local police found something odd – the kitchen had been tidied up and papers on the desk of the occupier had been neatly re-arranged. From this, we knew the culprit was Octavius, but when his home was searched, nothing incriminating was found. He had speedily disposed of the proceeds. Other than the MO, we had no way of proving his guilt, and he denied responsibility. We knew we were now having to deal with a rather clever and professional criminal. His time in prison had taught him the doubtful skills of raiding a better class of house, as well as providing some useful tips for avoiding conviction. Having served his apprentice-ship, Octavius was now a professional.

Soon, other houses of quality were raided; antiques, silverware, glassware and pottery, all of a high quality, were stolen. In each case, the place was tidied up; in each case, Octavius was questioned, and in each case, we were unable to prove his guilt. He left no fingerprints, and no incriminating evidence was ever found upon him or in his possession. Octavius's time in prison had been very well spent – it had been his University of Crooked Skills.

The local CID, crime prevention officers, crime squads and detectives from neighbouring forces held a meeting to pool their ideas to 'target' Octavius Horatio Calpin. One outcome was that all rural beat officers, like myself, were issued with information about the scale of Octavius's crimes.

We had instructions to alert all the occupiers of large country houses and stately homes on our beats. I had several on my patch, some occupied and owned by national figures and some containing very valuable sculptures, paintings and antiques. I decided to visit each in turn and advise their owners to be more security conscious. I issued leaflets and drew attention to the vulnerable points of their homes, calling in specialist crime prevention officers where appropriate.

One of the householders was Sir James Schofield, who lived at Briggsby Manor on the north-west corner of my patch. With interests in brewing, horse-racing and property development, he and Lady Schofield owned a beautiful home set among trees on the outskirts of Briggsby. It overlooked Briggsby Beck, a delightful moorland stream which rippled across a rocky bed as it flowed into the Rye. I made an appointment to visit Sir James and upon my arrival was shown into his richly furnished study. A maid brought coffee and biscuits on a silver tray, inviting me to help myself as I awaited the master of the house. He arrived in a good mood, his cheerful grey eyes smiling at me as he poured himself a coffee. He sat behind his large desk, his small figure almost concealed by its bulk, but his personality was large and happy.

'So,' he boomed in a voice far louder than anyone would have expected. 'What brings the constabulary to Briggsby Manor?'

I explained my purpose, alarming him with stories of burglaries and housebreakings in houses similar to his own, and voicing our belief that one man was responsible. I told him a little about Octavius. I advised him on security, on the need for window locks and for care by his staff whenever they retired for the night or vacated the house. He listened and thanked me, then said, 'But I have a good alarm, Mr Rhea, for my cash and my wife's jewellery. Here, I'll show you. But first, let me de-activate it.'

He took me into the hall where he pressed the switch to cut off the alarm, then I followed him into the massive drawing room with its polished wooden floors. I admired the huge open fireplace, the oak panelling and the sumptuous furnishings as he led me to an oil painting on the south wall. He lifted it up and beneath was a wall safe.

'Total security,' he said proudly. 'Not even a thermal lance would get into that – and if anyone does try, the alarm will go off. It's a silent alarm; it's linked to your headquarters so that if a burglar does come here, your officers will be alerted without the criminal being aware of it. And so, God willing, you'll catch him.'

I realized that a lot of luck was needed – a patrolling officer would have to be in the vicinity if he was to catch a villain quickly, but it was not impossible. Sometimes luck could be on our side. I explained to Sir James that he had many other valuables that could not be accommodated in that safe. These included his many pictures, his antiques, his everyday items like TV set, binoculars, radio and so forth; they were all valuable and so he promised he'd review his overall security arrangements. Having shown me the wall safe behind the coaching scene, which was some three feet long by two feet deep, he replaced the picture.

'Sir James,' I asked, 'how is that alarm activated? The one that protects the wall safe?'

'By the slightest movement of this picture,' he said. 'That's why the alarm must be switched off when the maid dusts it.'

'So if someone tried to straighten the picture when the alarm was set, it would react and issue a warning?'

He was quick to see my plan.

He smiled. 'So if I leave this picture slightly skew-whiff, you think your tidy-minded housebreaker might attempt to straighten it? And set off the alarm? And so get himself arrested?'

'Yes,' I said. 'If he comes here … I've no information that he will attempt to break into your property, Sir James, but you are vulnerable and well, it would be nice to catch him red-handed.'

'I'll leave that picture out-of-true,' he laughed. 'I'll tell my staff not to touch it. It'll be a good story at the club if we do nail him, eh?'

And so the trap was set.

There were two further raids on country houses within the next five months, and then one evening when I was on patrol in my official mini-van at Stovingsby, I received a call over my radio. The alarm at Briggsby Manor had been activated – intruders were on the premises. I knew Sir James and Lady Schofield were away at Cheltenham races for the Gold Cup and so the house would be unoccupied because the staff lived out in their own homes. The intruder had known this. The call instructed all mobiles to attend Briggsby Manor but not to arrive like a cavalry charge with flashing blue lights and a lot of noise. If there was an intruder, we must catch and detain him through stealth and cunning. I reckoned I was nearest but I was alone, and it is difficult for one police constable to surround a mansion as large as Briggsby Manor and to supervise all its exits.

I was more than relieved, therefore, to hear the call-sign of a CID car which was just leaving Ashfordly Police Station with two detectives on board. They had heard the call and were on their way. I suggested a rendezvous point out of sight of the manor, and said that as I was familiar with the grounds and the layout of the house, we could probably arrest our raider red-handed. Without going into a lot of detail, we did just that. In the darkness, we found the break-in point and chummy's parked van; we waited and jumped on him while he was in possession of a suitcase full of silverware. And, as expected, it was our friend Octavius Horatio Calpin.

He had been unable to resist straightening the crooked picture and had consequently trapped himself. We never told him how we had trapped him – we knew we could set the same trap again, at some future date when he got out of prison because, as sure as God made little thieves, Octavius would go a-burgling and a-housebreaking in the future. And, because his long-suffering mum, with all her children, had insisted that each of them tidied his own room, so Octavius would tidy up some future house in which he found himself, lawfully or not. I wondered what sort of job they would give him in prison – whatever it was, he'd certainly leave the place tidier than when he arrived.

For the crime at Briggsby Manor, he was sentenced to five years' imprisonment which meant he had a long time to get the prison as tidy as he wished.

* * *

Surely the strangest thief was a scruffy individual in his mid-forties who lived alone in a prefab in Crampton. He had no regular work and described himself as a general dealer; we called him a scrappie for he dealt in all kinds of scrap junk and waste metal which he collected in an old van.

Over a wide area he was known as Tin Lid Talbot. His real name was James Edward Talbot, but very few knew that, for he had earned his nickname through hoarding a bewildering range of old tin lids. They fitted everything from oil drums and dustbins to tea-pots, kettles and jam jars.

As police officers, we knew he was not against the occasional bout of petty thieving; if he called at a house or farm and there was no one about, he would steal things from the premises.

Usually, it was stuff that the owner was glad to get rid of but from time to time he would overstretch their generosity to make off with cash or something of real value. And then we would call on him. As a consequence, he was one of the regulars at the local magistrates' court, somehow avoiding any custodial sentence, but invariably being put on probation or being fined small sums, which never deterred him. I think the Bench felt sorry for him; he wasn't really a criminal, not in the nasty sense of the word, for his thieving was mainly restricted to things he found lying about and which were considered almost useless. Furthermore, he would never, for example, break into a house or outbuilding nor would he dream of using violence against anyone or anything.

He would, however, sneak into a house if the door was standing open and take whatever he found inside – and in the country districts, people did leave their doors open with money placed ready for collection by people like the insurance man, the milkman and catalogue collectors. Sometimes, the available cash was a temptation for Tin Lid and he would take it.

As a result, he had a huge list of petty convictions and a friendly relationship with the magistrates, the clerk of the court and the prosecuting officer. I think they all felt vaguely sorry for Tin Lid Talbot.

He was a pathetic fellow really, with his unkempt, lank and dark greasy hair, his mouth full of bad teeth, his dirty finger nails, clothes which were always too large for his small figure, plus his eternal wellington boots which he wore even in summer. But his long list of convictions was due largely to his strange response when questioned by the police – he would always deny his guilt while simultaneously but unwittingly admitting it. If that seems odd, I can give the first example I encountered.

A company director called Owen Robertson rang me to complain that his garden roller had been stolen. It was a large roller in good condition and it had been taken from his front lawn. A vehicle was obviously required to carry it off. When I interviewed him, he said the house had been visited by Talbot's General Dealers that very afternoon – he knew this, because Tin Lid had left a printed note to that effect.

The note said that if the housebuilders had any surplus metal, Mr Talbot would be glad to call and take it away. I drove straight to Tin Lid's old shack; his van was there and I saw a plank still in position, leading from the rear to the ground. It was just the thing for the removal of a garden roller. I found him in his shed and, knowing how to deal with him, said, 'Now, Tin Lid. What have you done with Mr Robertson's garden roller?'

'Not me, Mr Rhea,' he shook his dirty head.

'You called this afternoon and stole it,' I said.

'Look, do you think I've taken it to roll my mother's lawn or something?'

His equally scruffy mother, in her dotage, lived in similar conditions next door and so I went through the gate. And there was the roller on her lawn. He hadn't even had the time to use it.

'Come along, Tin Lid, back into your van with it, and take it straight back to where it belongs. Now! This very minute.'

'Yes, all right, Mr Rhea, but I just wanted to borrow it … '

'Then you should have asked,' I said. I helped him to roll it up the plank and we secured it in the back of his old van, then I followed him to Mr Robertson's house. Robertson declined to prosecute. He felt sorry for the pathetic little figure standing before him and was just happy to have his roller back. Tin Lid was lucky on that occasion.

Over the years, I assembled a catalogue of his curious denials. Once, he stole some cash from an unlocked house – it was £5 left out for the insurance man by a lady in Aidensfield. She'd left her door standing open when Tin Lid happened to be visiting the village, and he'd been tempted. When I interviewed him, he said, 'Not me, Mr Rhea. Do you think I'd steal her fiver and spend it in the pub or something?'

When I saw George Ward, the landlord of the Hopbind Inn at Elsinby, he recalled Tin Lid entering to buy drinks and using a £5 note for the purpose.

Tin Lid was fined £3 and ordered to pay restitution for that episode.

On another occasion, a fine brass coach lamp disappeared from a builder's yard in Maddleskirk. The builder, John Grant, had bought it to embellish his own front door and had left it unattended for twenty minutes while he took a phone call. In that time, Tin Lid had entered the yard, seen the lamp and taken it. As it was known he was collecting scrap in the village at that time, I found myself driving to his yard once again.

'It's about a lovely brass coach lamp, Tin Lid,' I announced. 'Taken from Grant's yard in Maddleskirk this morning. What have you done with it?'

'Not me, Mr Rhea,' he said. 'You don't think I'd take a thing like that and sell it to an antique dealer, do you?'

I recovered it from an antique shop in Ashfordly, and on this occasion Tin Lid was fined £5.

I do know that other officers had occasion to interview him and they all knew of his strange form of denial, but, from my own view point, I found this quirk of character to be most fascinating. He never did learn any other way of denying his guilt and over the years he told me a succession of stories like:

'You don't think I'd steal a thing like that and hide it up my chimney, do you, Mr Rhea?'

'You don't think I'd nick a pile of tiles like that and bury them in the garden, do you, Mr Rhea?'

'You don't think I'd steal milk money from a doorstep and put the cash on a horse or something, do you, Mr Rhea?'

'You don't think I'd steal a spare wheel and put it on my own van, do you, Mr Rhea?'

'You don't think I'd steal a coil of rope from that cow shed and use it as a tow rope or something, do you, Mr Rhea?'

'You don't think I'd stoop to stealing a Christmas tree, then give it to the children's home, do you, Mr Rhea?'

If his denials had not been so pathetic, they would have been funny, and I know that all of my colleagues could tell similar stories about dear old Tin Lid. But the inevitable happened. He was arrested by a new detective because he was suspected of stealing seventeen dozen clay plant pots in assorted sizes. It was alleged he had taken them from a garden centre he'd visited on his scrap round, but they were not to be found anywhere. Most certainly, they were not on his premises.

I became aware of this when visiting Eltering Police Station because I saw his name in the charge book. He was then reclining in the cells, having been unsuccessfully interrogated by the new detective, a man called Littleton. Sergeant Bairstow hailed me.

'Nick,' he said. 'We've got Tin Lid down the cells, he's been lifted for nicking some plant pots but denies it. Littleton's sure he's our man, but he's admitting nothing.'

'Was he caught with the stuff?' I asked.

'No, and it's not on his premises.'

'Then why involve me?' I asked with interest.

'You know him, have a word with him for us. He talks to you. Get him to admit the job, that's all. Take a voluntary from him, then we can wrap this case up. When he coughs, we'll release him on bail.'

I read up the case papers and learned that Tin Lid had been seen near the garden centre in question; furthermore, he had been there around the material time and he'd been in possession of his van. It did seem possible that he was the culprit and it was the sort of thing he'd do, although I suspected he'd be content with one plant pot rather than two hundred. Full of curiosity, I went into his cell, taking with me a cup of hot sweet tea.

'Now then, Tin Lid,' I said, sitting on the hard bed at his side. 'What's all this about you stealing plant pots?'

'Not me, Mr Rhea. I never touched 'em. I was near that spot, I'll admit that, but I never took the pots.'

'I believe you, Tid Lid,' I said.

I went out and told Sergeant Bairstow that in my opinion, Tin Lid was not guilty – I knew that because he had not delivered his usual strange denial. That omission convinced me. I don't think that either Littleton and Bairstow immediately accepted my view for each went into the cell to re-interview Tin Lid, but he never admitted that theft.

I do know that Sergeant Bairstow spoke to Tin Lid in words to the effect that, 'If PC Rhea believes you, Tin Lid, it's good enough for me.'

He was released without charge. Next day, he was passing my police house when he halted and knocked at my door.

'Hello, Tin Lid, this is a surprise!'

It was, because he never volunteered to visit the police.

'You told them you believed me yesterday, Mr Rhea,' he said. 'You know an honest man when you see one. I'm not a copper's nark, Mr Rhea, but the chap that pinched those pots is Sacky Conway from Eltering. That's my way of saying thanks.'

'Thanks, Tin Lid.' I invited him in for a cup of coffee, but he said he had to dash off. I rang Sergeant Bairstow who was on duty at Eltering and gave him the tip.

'Thanks, Nick. Somebody tipped you off, eh?'

'An old friend, serge,' I said. 'A chap who just can't tell a lie!'

3   Artful Deceivers

Of wiles more unexpert, I boast not
John Milton (1608–74)

When it comes to the practice of dishonesty and deceit, the human being shows extraordinary skill. It is a fact of life that some very shrewd and clever people turn to dishonesty as a livelihood or hobby, and one wonders what satisfaction they achieve by denying others their lawful and rightful ownership of goods or services. Criminals are usually very selfish people.

Police officers are very aware that where money is involved and where any new thief-proof procedure is developed, some cunning rogue will devise a method of beating the system in order to steal. Their cunning is legendary. Nothing is foolproof; no procedure or security system is totally secure against the wiles of a cunning and persistent criminal, and society will always have to tolerate dishonest people.

I've come across seemingly meek old ladies who were skilled shoplifters; I've come across people who never paid their grocery bills or other debts – and in these cases, the police are powerless to act because these are civil debts.

But sometimes I wonder if the criminal law and its interpretation of the word 'dishonesty' should now apply to those who deliberately obtain goods or services with no intention of paying. One's actions are often proof of one's intent and where a person regularly and systematically defrauds tradespeople of their just monies, then surely a crime is committed?

It is a sad fact too that so many dishonest people appear to be trustworthy and as such are the last that anyone would suspect of roguish deeds. Examples of this occurred in two interesting cases on my patch at Aidensfield. Neither reached the courts for in both cases it was impossible to prove any breach of the criminal law, but the morals of each case were certainly of the lowest kind. For that reason, they are worthy of record.

The first involved a spinster lady called Penelope Stirling who was highly respected in Ploatby where she lived. A church organist, she arranged the ladies' flower rota and it was known she had worked in London before retiring to Yorkshire. She'd be in her early sixties when I moved to the area. Her home was a neat little detached house known as Miller's Cottage, and she ran a small, pale-blue Austin mini saloon. She was a fussy little person, always popping in and out of houses in Ploatby, Elsinby, Maddleskirk, Aidensfield and elsewhere, giving a helping hand to those less fortunate than herself.

When Meals on Wheels became so popular, it was Miss Stirling who volunteered to operate it in our district.

In short, Miss Stirling was a treasure, a wonderful volunteer helper in all kinds of ways, even if she was very prim and rather humourless. I became aware of her through her voluntary work for I'd noticed her going busily about her many social activities. In winter, she was very recognizable in her fur coat, fur hat with ear warmers and the curious fur muff which kept her hands warm. She wore heavy tortoiseshell spectacles, and when she was fully clad in her furs, all that I could see of her features was her sharp nose and rosy cheeks. She darted about the villages like a busy jenny wren. In summer, she wore a light-coloured belted raincoat and a plastic headcover.

She called at my house one day seeking donations for the Red Cross, and introduced herself. Afterwards, I often noticed her little car parked outside houses around my patch. Everyone spoke very highly of her – she shopped for the elderly and infirm, she ran errands for the sick, she dusted and tidied the homes of those unable to fend for themselves and took elderly ladies for trips into the countryside or to the seaside. The old folk all loved her and she demanded nothing in return. Her actions were entirely voluntary and done out of good will.

In spite of her help to others, I came to realize that Penny, as everyone called her, was a very lonely woman.

Although she visited the homes of so many people, I knew of none who had been invited into her house and none who had actually stepped inside. Even regular callers such as the milkman, the butcher and the insurance man had never been inside. She dealt with each on the doorstep. Her home life seemed sacrosanct and almost secretive.

Another intriguing factor was that I never saw her with any of her own family – she seemed to have no aged mother or father, no brothers or sisters, no visiting cousins. Even more curious for a woman in her position, was that there seemed none of that range of nephews and nieces who might call. Lots of maiden ladies had nephews and nieces who visited them. But Penny Stirling hadn't anyone; she was totally alone, and in time I realized she had neither a cat nor a dog. There was no living thing in her quiet home, apart from herself. I wondered if she was happy there.

I never did discover precisely what her occupation had been, other than she made it known she had worked in London; those to whom she had imparted this information assumed she had been employed in a big office somewhere, a civil servant perhaps, a top secretary or something similar.

Among her interests beyond social work was attending sales of furniture or house contents at local farms and cottages. These occurred on a fairly regular basis and I was usually informed by the auctioneers about an impending sale in case there was a traffic problem. Some farm entrances, for example, were on dangerous bends in the road, and, in some cases, house contents were displayed prior to the sale by making use of village greens, roadside verges and any available space. Minor problems could arise.

These sales were very popular, with one species of sale-goer being the city antique dealer who came into our villages in the hope of securing some hitherto unrevealed treasure. There is no doubt some did buy wonderful things – I once saw a book dealer flush with pride at buying a job lot of old books in a cardboard box. His earlier inspection had shown it to contain a rare old Bible. Auctioneers and buyers are full of such stories.

As I attended these sales, I became aware of Penny Stirling's familiar figure. She attended most and almost always bought something. She seemed to know her antiques, often buying glassware, china and books; I also noticed that she was most willing to purchase incomplete sets of objects. While most of us would wish to purchase a complete set of glasses, cutlery or books, Miss Stirling bought incomplete ones. At Elsinby one day, I saw her bid successfully for an incomplete set of the works of Charles Dickens. Two volumes were absent, and so the price was far lower than it would have been for the full set.

It was her purchase of that set of books that alerted me to her devious and highly suspect behaviour, because within a month I saw that same set of books for sale in a York shop.

This time, the set was complete. The missing volumes were present and I knew it was the same set because of the name inscribed in the front of each volume. Old folks would write their names inside their books and each of these contained the signature 'R.J. Stewart'. So where had the two missing volumes come from?

It was the contents of the Stewarts' home that had been sold recently, and at which Penny had bought the incomplete set. I knew, from local knowledge, that Penny had been caring for the old and widowed Mrs Stewart before her death, undertaking such chores as driving her to the shops, washing her clothes and cooking her meals.

My suspicious police mind began to operate and, for a time, I did wonder whether I was grossly wrong in my assessment of Penny's character and motives. I hoped I was; after all, she did do an enormous amount of charitable and beneficial work, but

I had to find out whether there was more to her – and I had to do so with the utmost discretion.

I was uncertain how to begin my inquiries, for I did not want to give even a hint of my suspicions to another soul. But providence was on my side because, within the month, another of Penny's 'patients' died and the contents of her house were put up for auction. She was Mrs Elsie Baker and I made a point of attending that sale.

Mrs Baker lived in a terrace-house in Aidensfield and, before her death, she had left instructions that her house and its contents be sold and the proceeds given to cancer research. She had not been a wealthy lady, but since her husband's death had kept a nice house with some interesting glassware. She had no immediate family who might inherit her belongings.

Having ensured there would be no obstruction of the highway due to the crowd and the furniture, I watched the proceedings. There was little of interest until some very fine engraved wine glasses were held aloft – and the auctioneer announced that it was an incomplete set. There were only two glasses instead of the required three. The bidding proceeded slowly and, sure enough, Miss Stirling was making her bids. I joined in with one or two bids, if only to push up the price she would pay to cancer research, but the glasses were knocked down to Penelope Stirling. I noticed the fierce glow of pride on her sharp features.

When it was all over, I managed to find a quiet corner for a chat with the auctioneer, Paul Sandford. I asked about the wine glasses.

'They're beautiful,' he said. 'I saw you bidding, but if that set had been complete, they'd have been worth much more.'

'Does Miss Stirling often buy incomplete sets of things?' I asked.

He glanced at me as if reading my mind or knowing of my suspicions, then said, 'She does. I must admit that over the years I've noticed her doing that. Sets of books, glassware, china objects, cutlery, condiment sets, candle sticks … mainly household things you'd expect to find in complete sets. I can guarantee that if I offer an incomplete set of any worthwhile objects in this locality, she'll bid for it – and get it. Anyway, Mr Rhea, why are you interested in her deals?'

I told him about the Dickens volumes and of Penny's charity towards those whose goods were later put up for auction. I decided to voice my suspicions to him. 'I think she's borrowing things from those people while they're alive – and not returning them. She's doing so when she knows they'll soon go to meet their heavenly maker, and then she goes to the auction to buy the rest of the goods. She then makes up a complete set and trades it in for a massive profit. She's clever, Mr Sandford. She's too crafty to remove the entire sets because that would raise questions.'

'People aren't as devious as that, surely!' he protested.

'They can be,' I assured him.

'If it's true, what can we do about it?' he asked. 'There's nothing illegal in borrowing things, is there? And if the owner dies before the object is returned, so what?'

'Precisely!' I said.

'I'll keep an eye on her,' he promised. 'If she is doing that, she's denying lots of relations and other benefactors their dues. And as we handle most of the local auctions, I can check her easily enough. Pop in to my saleroom when you've time to spare and we'll have a look at the records of some recent sales.'

It was several months later when I called, his commitments and mine conspiring to prevent us meeting earlier. There had been no further local house content sales in that time, and when I settled before his old desk, it was clear he had already done his own research.

'I've checked back several years,' he said. 'We keep detailed records of our sales and, in the past four years, your Miss Stirling has regularly bought part sets of all manner of things. There is a definite pattern – she obviously knows her antiques and knows exactly what to buy. As we said earlier, it's chiefly domestic stuff – glasses, cutlery, volumes of books and so forth. She seems to know when the person is going to die because I remember one or two families' relations asking where certain items had gone – they'd visited their aunts, mothers, dads or whatever shortly before their deaths and some had noticed things were missing. The old folks couldn't remember what they'd done with them – in fact, I do wonder if that woman was taking them without the knowledge of her old folks. But she does seem to know the very personal circumstances of each old person and whether there will be a future sale of house contents – it's often folks who have no dependent relatives or those who want to donate something to charity.'

'It wouldn't surprise me if she was systematically stealing from the old folk,' I ventured. 'Being a so-called friend, she could take away bits and pieces without them knowing or being suspicious about her motives. She could do that by asking to borrow things – everybody does it.'

'Can you proceed against her for that?' he asked.

'It's almost impossible to prove her guilty intentions,' I said. 'All she need say is that either she borrowed the objects intending to return them, or that the old person had given her the items. Besides, some old folks don't remember their actions very clearly.'

'So it's not theft to borrow a book and not return it?'

'It's theft to borrow a book with the intention of not returning it,' I said. 'But to prosecute in such a case, we must prove that intention. That's virtually impossible. How could it be proved that a person took it with the intention of *permanently* depriving the owner of it? It's the proving of the taker's intention at the time of taking it that presents legal difficulties. Borrowing, in itself, isn't theft … '

'Could you prosecute her to frighten her off? Even if you failed to get a conviction, it might stop her antics.'

'We'd have difficulty, all our key witnesses are dead!' I smiled ruefully. 'Our prosecution department would never let it proceed. Besides, no court would convict her.'

'So what can we do?' he asked. 'I'd like to stop her, if only for the sake of the genuine benefactors.'

'I'll give the matter some thought,' I promised him. 'And I'll keep in touch.'

Over the ensuing months, I watched Miss Stirling continue to visit her old folks, and there's little doubt she was a kindly and hard-working volunteer. And then I learned that poor old Abraham Salter was dying. He was a retired schoolmaster, a bachelor with no known relatives, and he lived in a rented estate cottage at Crampton. He had cancer, I discovered, and was not expected to live beyond Christmas. And, I noticed, he was being visited regularly by Miss Stirling.

This situation had all the hallmarks of those earlier episodes, and so I decided to keep an eye on developments. I decided I must visit old Mr Salter and found a reason when there was yet another scare about bogus council workers; men were entering the homes of old folks under the pretence of checking their water supply, and they were then stealing money and other goods. I toured all the old folks on my patch, warning them about these villains. And one of the old men on my list was Mr Salter.

The nurse was with him when I arrived, and she made us a cup of tea, saying it was nice that he had a visitor. In spite of his severe illness, he was mentally alert and I had an enjoyable talk with him. Our conversation turned to books, for I saw that his room was lined with them, and it transpired that he was an authority on the Brontës, but, owing to his work, the fact he had never owned a car and now his state of health, he had never revisited the famous parsonage since seeing it as a child, nor had he joined the Brontë society. He reckoned membership would not be of benefit to him.

He pointed to a space on his shelf. 'Over there, Mr Rhea, is a scarce edition of six volumes, a complete collection of all seven novels of the Brontë sisters.'

'There are only five volumes here,' I said pointedly. 'Perhaps you are reading the sixth?'

'No, that nice Miss Stirling asked if she could borrow it – she loves the Brontës, you see. It's Charlotte's *Jane Eyre* that's missing. I let her take it – she'll return it soon, she assures me.

She does call a lot, you know. She looks after me, she's very nice.'

I saw the nurse glance at me and I knew what was going through her mind; without her saying anything, I knew she had encountered Miss Stirling's 'borrowings' before. Other patients must have mentioned it.

'Mr Salter wants to have the contents of his house sold, and the proceeds given to the Brontë society,' she told me.

'But those volumes, well, surely you'll donate those as they are?' I suggested. 'You'd not sell them.'

'Miss Stirling, who knows antiques, said the Brontë society already has a set of these, and she said she'd been in touch with them at Haworth and they'd said that cash from the sale of my collection would be of greater benefit,' he said. 'In the future, they need to extend the visitors' part of the premises at the parsonage, you see, and are keen to raise funds for building work.'

'Did she say that?' I said, my own eyes reflecting my scepticism. 'I'll check for you, shall I? If I ring them and mention your books, they'll tell me what's best – but don't tell Miss Stirling what I'm doing!'

'I think Mr Salter would appreciate that,' said the nurse. And the alert Mr Salter smiled.

The society did say that, of course, all bequests were most gratefully received and that funds for improvements to the facilities were always welcome, but that his complete set of the sisters' works was a 'must' for their library and museum. If Mr Salter would donate those books, the society would be forever grateful ... and he was invited to visit the parsonage to make the presentation.

I had great pleasure, therefore, in knocking at Miss Stirling's door one day to ask for the return of *Jane Eyre* as Mr Salter was being taken to Haworth, with his nurse, to present the entire set to the Brontë Society. If looks could have killed, I would have shrivelled and disappeared, but she did produce the volume and hand it over.

'I always intended giving it back to him,' she snapped.

'And all those other things you've borrowed from old folks,' I heard myself saying against my better judgement, and I then heard myself running through a list of the things I knew she'd borrowed. And then I added, 'And I'll be visiting the old folks to see what's missing, and the auction rooms....'

She spat at me, her tiny features a picture of hate and spite as she slammed the door in my face. Three months later, she sold her house and went to live in Scotland. But she did not arrange a sale of her own house contents. I suspect it would have been like Aladdin's Cave.

* * *

Among life's parasites is a high proportion of idle and useless siblings who sponge off their parents. One man who silently suffered the waywardness of his two sons was a shopowner called Leonard Carroll. His two sons were Raymond and Graham, Raymond being the elder by some two years. Mrs Carroll had died several years previously, before I was posted to Aidensfield, and so I never knew her.

Following her death, Mr Carroll's domestic chores were undertaken by a cleaning lady.

Leonard Carroll had opened a shop in Ashfordly just after the Second World War; it was originally a one-man business which sold household goods like pots and pans, cleaning materials and some garden equipment. Through his hard work and enterprise, the business had flourished until it had grown into the market town's only department store. Gradually, Mr Carroll had purchased the adjoining properties until his store, old fashioned though it was, sold almost everything that might be required to furnish a home or dress a family. Carpets, curtains, soft furnishing, dining suites, bedroom suites, ladies' and gents' clothes, shoes, school uniforms – all could be purchased from Carroll's.

My acquaintanceship with Mr Carroll began when I was posted to Aidensfield because we bought a lot of our furniture from his shop; he always allowed generous credit with time to pay when we were short of cash. He treated everyone like that, especially young people trying to establish their own homes, as we then were. Len Carroll was a kindly man who was liked by everyone.

Over the months, I was to learn that his sons had always taken advantage of his generosity. At school, they'd never been short of pocket money but had constantly been in trouble for disorderly behaviour in class. Raymond was something of a bully while Graham teased small boys; he did tricks like throwing their satchels away or pouring ink over their books. When these horrors left school, they drank heavily and drove fast cars.... Len found them posts within his own store, but they proved to be useless and also a liability. Two members of staff had refused to work alongside them. There was some talk of Raymond fiddling the accounts in his department. Some said Leonard had been too soft with the boys after the death of their mother; some said he'd spent too much time with the business and not enough with his sons, but whatever the reason behind their rotten behaviour, they continued to sponge off their kind-hearted father as they grew into objectionable adults.

Local knowledge, gleaned through keeping my ears and eyes open, informed me that Len had frequently paid their debts, Raymond once running up a huge bill with a local bookie and Graham owing a fortune to a garage for a succession of damaged cars and their petrol. By the time I arrived in the district, Raymond was in his late forties, unmarried but with an eye for the women, while Graham, in his early forties, had unsuccessfully tried to run his own shops. Each of his many schemes had failed because of his inefficiency and mismanagement.

Not many months after our arrival at Aidensfield, I discovered that Leonard was approaching retirement and had decided to end his active involvement with the store. He would continue to own it, however, but would appoint a manager.

When these new plans were put into operation, his two sons

rapidly found themselves no longer able to sponge from him. He made sure his own money was beyond their reach and was known to have said he intended to enjoy his few years in retirement without their parasitic demands. He openly said he had done enough for them – now they were on their own.

In the months that followed, I got to know him fairly well because he sold his large house in Ashfordly and came to live in a more modest home at Aidensfield. There he began to attend Mass at St Aiden's Catholic Church. Until that time, I did not know we shared the same faith and I was pleased when he joined the work of the parish with great enthusiasm.

He had reached sixty-five years of age by that time and we all knew he had made his will. We knew because he had stipulated that upon his death his entire estate, except for the shop, be sold and that the proceeds should go to the NSPCC. He felt that many deserving children would benefit. The shop, he said, was to be made into a trust, the trustees ensuring that it continued for the benefit of the town and its people. In the event of the shop failing to remain a viable business, then it must be sold and the proceeds donated to the NSPCC.

The two wayward sons were left entirely out of his will. He openly said they had had enough from him; they had had their opportunities, they had enjoyed his generosity and they had failed to make good use of his fatherly assistance. Now it was too late – they would not inherit his shop or his money.

It was no secret in the village that they were very hurt and angry; they were bitter and they argued with their father, saying they'd reform if he would change his will in their favour. But he had heard it all before and steadfastly refused. His mind was made up.

This information filtered to the villagers, as such information is wont to do in close communities, and we were all pleased. No one had liked the sons' treatment of their kind-hearted father and we all felt they had been justly rewarded for their past stupidity and the hurt they had inflicted on their father. But they did not give up. They began to visit him at his home, even staying for the weekend under the pretext of caring for him. He told me,

'They keep on at me to change my will in their favour, Nick, but I'll not give in, not now. I know they're my own flesh and blood, but I've given them lots of chances to make good, more chances than most lads would ever get.'

Their pressure clearly worried him and I felt pleased he was able to talk to me about his concern. Then he had a heart attack. Father Luke, the parish priest, had found him collapsed in his kitchen and had rushed him into intensive care. Len had rallied; his sons did visit him as did many villagers, including myself. In time, he was back at home, albeit under doctor's orders to take things easy.

He was a long way off seventy years of age, but the pressures of work had finally made him pay the price and he was never fully fit again. He did potter in his garden, he did visit the store once or twice a week, and he did work for the parish, making sure the grass and paths about the church were tidy, doing running repairs to the fabric and so on. But he was far less active than the Leonard Carroll we all knew. Whenever I saw him, he looked pale and under pressure. We discovered that the reason was Raymond, his eldest son.

'He never lets me alone,' Len confided in me one day. 'Always harping on about changing my will ... he says he'll reform, he'll run the store like I wanted him to ... but I can't trust him, Nick, not now ... he's made such a mess of his life, he's let me down so often. I'd far rather my money went to help some poor kids who'll appreciate it.'

'It's your decision,' I said. 'No one can advise you, Len, no one.'

'I just wish they wouldn't keep on at me, it's so bloody tiring, Nick. I'm dreading their visits now. Graham's at it as well – I think Raymond's persuaded him to nag at me.'

I did my best to console him, and was tempted to warn off the roguish sons, but knew that such family matters were really no concern of mine, however unpleasant the sons' treatment of their ailing father. Sadly, we all knew that Leonard was very ill indeed, we knew that he was dying.

He suffered further heart attacks and it wasn't long before he was confined to his bed, with a nurse calling regularly. One Sunday, after Mass, I called in to see him and was surprised to see both sons leaving, each looking happy. When I arrived at his bedside, his nurse made me a coffee and I settled down for a chat. I said I'd seen Raymond and Graham departing.

'I've altered my will,' he said with resignation. 'In their favour ... I had to, Nick, they just kept on at me ... mind, I haven't signed it yet. My solicitor's drawing it up in legal jargon, and he'll fetch it as soon as it's ready. Will you be a witness when I sign it? I've asked Father Luke to be the other witness....'

'Yes, of course, but are you sure you want to do that? To alter it in their favour?'

'Aye,' he said wearily. 'Aye, I am. I've just told the lads, I want a bit of peace now.'

The next thing I knew was that there was an urgent call for my presence at Len's bedside. I was on patrol at the time and Mary, my wife, managed to ring Divisional Headquarters who called me on the radio in the van and diverted me to Len's house. When I arrived, I saw the doctor's car, the nurse's car and those of his two sons. I hurried inside. A solicitor met me on the stairs. I recognized him as Mr Mitchell from Eltering whom I'd often encountered in court and he said,

'Mr Rhea, Mr Carroll is dying. Father Luke is with him now. He's given him the last rites. The doctor says there's no hope. I'm here with his will ... as you know, he changed it at the last minute, and the sons are here ...'

'They would be!' I said. 'Has he signed it yet?'

'No, we're waiting for you. He wanted you to be one of the two witnesses – Father Luke is the other. Father Luke specifically asked that you be here.'

'I'll do it,' I said somewhat reluctantly, for I had no wish to overtly delay things, even if it did mean the sons benefiting. That would have been against Len's last wishes and the priest knew that. I followed Mr Mitchell into the bedroom, but in those short moments, things had already happened. Len had died.

'He's dead,' Dr Archie McGee stood up as we entered. 'I'm sorry … he just went … '

'But he signed his will before he died,' said Raymond coldly, and no one could miss the look of triumph on his face.

Father Luke had the document in his hand and nodded. 'It was touch and go … Raymond had to hold his hand, he moved it … I'm sure Len was still alive when he signed … just … '

I could have felled Raymond there and then, forcing a dying man's hand like that … but I could not argue because I had not been in the room at the precise moment and neither had the solicitor. But Father Luke seemed content with this bizarre turn of events.

Dr McGee closed Len's eyes. 'The precise moment of death is never easy to determine,' was all he contributed.

Whatever the precise moment of Leonard Carroll's death, his sons now had the amended will which bore their father's important signature. But it was not yet witnessed, and no one, other than the solicitor, knew the precise contents of that will. I was later to suspect that Father Luke did know something of his parishioner's deepest wishes.

'I've signed it,' said Father Luke as we assembled downstairs. 'You need not shrink from being a witness, Nick. This is his will and you know his signature.'

The solicitor handed me the document and I saw the wavy handwriting of the deceased man; I had seen his writing often enough and did recognize it as Len's work, even if it was very shaky. I looked at the priest; he knew my views on the two sharks lurking in the background, awaiting the moment their lives would be changed. But Father Luke merely smiled at me and nodded. 'Go ahead, Nick, it was Len's wish.'

'If it's his wish, I'll sign,' and so I did.

Later, I was to be very pleased that I did witness that signature and that the will had been made. Len had altered his will in his sons' favour, but not in the way they had envisaged. He had still left his shop in trust and had left the bulk of his estate to the NSPCC as he had originally decided. But he had changed his will to set aside enough money for each of the sons to be buried in church. And that was all.

Upon their deaths, their funerals would be paid for out of his estate, and when it was all over, any residue would be paid to the NSPCC....

I felt they would remember their father and their own waywardness for a long, long time.

4 The Devil Looks After His Own

Suddenly, as rare things will, it vanished.
Robert Browning (1812–89)

The sight of two women locked in mortal combat is never a pretty sight, even if the women involved are ravishingly beautiful. They fight vigorously with a lot of screaming, oath-laden catcalls and other accompanying noises: there is much swishing of handbags and hair-pulling.

A female joust can result in skulls being dented by hand-held high-heeled shoes and facial flesh being bloodied by lethal finger-nails which are like rapiers. To say that women fight like spitting, claw-wielding wild cats is a fairly accurate description, as those who have witnessed violent feminine contests can testify. After such hostilities, the contestants look like savaged rag dolls that have, quite literally, been dragged repeatedly through a hedge of vicious thorns.

A woman fighting a man is quite different – she will throw cups and saucers at him, or fling the first thing that comes into her hands even if it does contain treacle, tomato soup or wet nappies. There is generally a good deal of shrieking and other sound effects, plus the inevitable gallons of tears. If she knows the man well enough, this bout will end in oceans of salty tears and lots of urgent, healing kisses.

But the wise man will not consider the contest to be finished at that stage – one careless word can re-activate the entire war machinery.

But if there is anything worse than two women fighting in

the privacy of their own homes, it is the sight of two women doing battle in a public place. Most police officers have had to cope with female wars, often contested over garden walls or in backyards, and waged with weapons like rolling pins, clothes props and broom handles. Over the years, these bouts have provided some good entertainment, with the added bonus of some juicy gossip to follow. This is especially so if the objective of the battle was a man beloved by both parties.

But if the war-zone is a public place, then a new dimension is added and, in legal terms, the matter can become a Breach of the Peace at the very least, or involve a serious wounding offence or an affray at the most.

Like most of my colleagues, I'd sorted out a few border skirmishes between neighbours or relations but I must admit I was surprised at the sight of one particular feminine combat. It burst into action one Friday afternoon when I was on duty in Ashfordly. At the time, the market-place was full of colourful stalls as the traders shouted and sold their wares. Crowds of people, locals and holidaymakers alike, were milling around the market-place, chatting and enjoying the hot June sunshine when the double doors of the King's Head hotel burst open with a resounding crash.

It was the prelude to some great entertainment. The doors of well-designed pubs always open outwards to facilitate any necessarily swift ejection processes, and those of the King's Head then proved ideal for this purpose. As the twin doors crashed against the outer walls, there tumbled from the depths within a spitting, claw-wielding leopard and a ferocious tooth-gnashing grizzly bear. Each was endeavouring to tear the other to pieces; their warring was like a cross between bear baiting and gladitorial sparring, with a few spitting wild cats thrown in for good measure.

As the townspeople and shoppers halted to observe this circus act, they realized it wasn't a couple of wild beasts in the throes of mortal combat. It was a couple of women in fur coats. One coat was yellow and spotted like a leopard and the other was thick and brown, for all the world like the hide of a grizzly bear. And this was a summer day in June! Their wearers were fighting in a manner reminiscent of a bout between a lioness and a tigress. Even the noises and clawing were similar.

That it was a duel to the death was not in doubt. Nothing else could have produced such a rabid outcome, and so the crowds of the market-place and the people of the town wandered across to watch. Some were already striving to find the best vantage point as several from the hotel emerged to watch. Among them were more women in expensive fur coats and large, outrageously silly hats.

Here was entertainment of a very superior kind. As the pair of women, fur coats flying, legs askew, skirts above their waists and shoes cast into the far corners of the market-place, buckled down to their conflict, so the crowd began to cheer them as they would have done in bear-baiting days.

Some shouted for the leopard lady, others for the grizzly, and that was the situation which prevailed as I hove to. It was the cheers of the enthusiastic crowd that attracted my attention as I was parking my mini-van to commence a foot patrol of the market square. At first, I had no idea what was happening, thinking that the crowd's interest was in the antics of a market trader. Some stallholders were greatly entertaining, like the one who juggled with full dinner services or performed magic deeds with sharp knives and turnips. As I strolled across to the crowd, I became aware of the shrieking and screaming that was rising from the depths of the cheering masses. Here indeed was something of great interest.

'What's going on?' I asked a man standing at the edge of the crowd.

'It sounds like a bloody scrap between a couple of hundred farmyard cats,' he laughed. 'But it's two snooty women tearing themselves to pieces.'

If his assessment was correct, I had to halt the affair – brawling in a public place was definitely not the sort of thing to entertain market-day crowds, and it did seem worse because it was between two women. One did not expect this from ladies.

I pushed through the crowd, my uniform creating a buzz of

conversation from the onlookers, and when I reached the ringside, I appreciated the attraction and extent of the tournament. With the expanse of thigh, suspender, stocking-top, all revealed by rising skirts, this had the sex-appeal of women wrestling naked in mud, because these two were literally tearing the clothes off one another's backs.

The exceptions were the fur coats which seemed impervious to damage. But blouses and skirts had been ripped off, stockings shredded, shoes kicked away, handbag contents scattered....

There were a few boos and unwelcome whistles when I stepped forward to bring the proceedings to a dignified halt; I waded in, wary of course that both protagonists might turn on me with their nails, high heels and handbags. On reflection, I think I arrived just as each was realizing they were tiring rapidly, that no outright winner was likely and that they were making themselves look ridiculous. And it would be a costly bout so far as replacement clothes were concerned.

I shouted to them, demanding that they halt their battle, but at first their shrieks drowned my voice and so I had to push into the scrimmage and seize each by the collar of her fur coat. There wasn't much else left to grab at that stage, but I held them apart at arm's length. Each was now six feet from the other with me in between.

For a few brief moments, their arms flailed, their feet kicked and their voices rose to a pitch of high excitement, but all to no avail. They were now fighting thin air. It was a technique we used to separate fighting dogs. I simply held them apart until they had calmed down.

They were a sorry sight, their smart hair-styles gone, their make-up ruined, tears and mascara running down their cheeks, their feet bare and even bleeding, their reputations gone, and their fine clothes in tatters. It had been a considerable affray, but now, as I held them apart wondering what to do with them, both began to weep. The gross embarrassment of those public moments began to eat into their silly brains.

I decided to take them into the hotel whence they had emerged, albeit keeping them firmly apart. By now, the crowd was silent, wondering firstly what had started the rumpus and, secondly, what I was going to do about it. Those were my thoughts too. I decided the onlookers would never know the answer to either question, hence my decision to take the aggressors indoors. As I propelled the female gladiators inside, I saw the hotel manager hovering in the background looking decidedly worried, but he did step forward to close the door against the inquisitive crowd, some of whom were on the verge of following the drama to its lawful conclusion.

Inside the hotel's foyer, I released my grip on the furry collars, but stood between the two women.

Each was in her mid-forties and each looking decidedly humble by this time.

'Well,' I said, wondering if I sounded like a schoolmaster lecturing his erring pupils. 'What was all that about?'

Neither of them spoke. Each stood with her head hung low, in half-attire, as if the awful shame of the past few minutes had suddenly dawned. The manager, a smooth-haired man called David Sanderson, stepped forward.

'It was about an umbrella,' he said quietly.

'An umbrella?' I asked in disbelief.

'It had been left here, last month in fact. These ladies are members of the Ashfordly Ladies' Luncheon Club, you see. They love to parade in their fur coats and expensive hats ... well, one of them left an umbrella behind after the last meeting.'

He paused as if to imply that the brolly was a Very Important Thing, then continued, 'Today, when I showed it to the ladies, this lady,' and he indicated the one in the leopard-skin coat, 'said it was hers. She thanked me and was walking out with it ... '

'It's not Rebecca's, it's mine.' the one in the grizzly-bear coat now came to life. 'I said it was mine all along ... I left it behind last time I came ... it is mine, I keep telling her that.'

'It's not, you silly bitch, it's mine,' spat her foe. 'I'd know it anywhere, it's mine … '

'Hold on,' I shouted, stepping between them again lest battle be resumed, 'We're not going to suffer another fight, so just keep quiet, both of you. I've never seen such unruly behaviour from anyone, let alone women who pretend to be quality examples of their sex. You fight like alley cats instead of acting like the sophisticated women you pretend to be.... So, Mr Sanderson, where is the brolly now?'

'Mrs Fenner took it out with her … '

'And she snatched it from me … '

'No I didn't, I just wanted to look at it … '

I shouted at them again in my schoolmaster's voice, and said, 'Well, if neither of you have got it, then it's still outside, so it seems. After all this commotion, you've dropped it, one or other of you. And your shoes are still out there, as well as things from your handbags and bits of clothing … ' They looked at themselves, now horrified.

'I'll send someone out to collect their belongings,' offered Sanderson, and I said it was a great idea. The women, chaperoned by Sanderson and I, then adjourned to a more private place, a small ante-room away from the stares of hotel staff and residents. The two warring women sat with their backs to each other as Mr Sanderson and I waited for the residue of their cannonade to be brought in.

'I hope this disgraceful display does not detract from the high reputation of the hotel,' Sanderson said. 'This is most certainly not the sort of behaviour one expects … '

'It's all her fault,' hissed Mrs Fenner.

'It's not mine, it's yours,' shrieked the other, whose name I later learned was Mrs Porter.

'Quiet, the pair of you,' said I.

Sanderson went on, 'I must really take a long hard look at the luncheon club's future with us. I thought they were ladies – they call themselves ladies, but they behave like alley cats.... '

We were denied any more of his ramblings when a waitress from the hotel's dining room staff entered bearing shoes, handbags and other assorted belongings which had been gathered from the battlefield outside.

'Has the crowd gone?' I asked her.

'Yes, Mr Rhea, they've all gone,' she smiled.

'Thanks for searching for all these things,' I smiled. 'Did you find the missing umbrella?'

'No,' she said. 'I searched everywhere, it's gone. I think someone's stolen it,' she added.

And so they had. I went out and made another very thorough search, even looking under parked cars, into the branches of trees and along the patch of garden in front of the hotel, but it had gone. Now they would never know who was the true owner, but because I did not know who owned it, I could not record it as a crime. After all, who was the loser?

Sanderson and I talked to the two warriors but neither would admit being at fault, nor would they agree about ownership of the missing brolly. From my own point of view, the theft of the umbrella had been fortuitous. I'm sure that if we had recovered it, the dispute would have continued. Now, they had nothing to fight about and I said that I would take no action against them. If either wished to claim the other had assaulted her, then the remedy was to take out a private summons. I explained this could be done by contacting a solicitor. I knew that the police would not wish to become involved, and I suggested that any claims for damage to clothing should be sorted out between them. This had a calming effect and, quite surprisingly, the two women suddenly turned and clung to one another, sobbing their sorrows into the thick fur of their respective coats before going to the ladies' room to repair some of the damage.

I did hear later that both had resigned from the luncheon club, but I never did find out who really owned the disputed umbrella. But why did they fight with such determination over something as trivial and replaceable as an umbrella? I did wonder if there was another aspect to the story, whether, for example, the husband of one was illicitly seeing the other. But I did not pursue the matter.

Due to their high-profile fight, however, the luncheon club had become a laughing stock, the townspeople chuckling for many months over that drama.

They made fun of the women and their ridiculous behaviour in trying to outshine each other with their expensive and outlandish hats, fur coats, gloves and shoes. Discerning ladies were suddenly quite embarrassed to be associated with it.

The umbrella story became part of the folklore of Ashfordly, and today the missing object is probably hanging upon someone's coat hook. Perhaps it was removed by the true owner? But where did it go? And what was so special about that umbrella? The mystery remains.

* * *

Umbrella owners will know that objects of that size can easily disappear without trace, even within one's own home, but an infinitely more puzzling event involved the disappearance of something considerably larger. And, like that umbrella, the mystery remains.

I was on patrol one winter's night, working a late turn, i.e. from 2 p.m. until 10 p.m., when the puzzle developed. That tour of duty promised to be pleasant because my beat was quiet and I had no pressing commitments. I could check on vulnerable premises, visit a few friendly farmers and cottagers, make inquiries about any outstanding crimes and generally perform useful public relations duties by visiting pubs, popping into shops and other places open to the public. I'd show my uniform where it mattered; I'd visit old folk who were alone or worried and generally reappraise the welfare of those at risk.

Such work is an important part of the rural bobby's duty; consequently, leisurely patrols of this kind provided an opportunity to maintain vital contact with a wide range of people.

The afternoon passed without incident and I did fulfil many of my plans. By the time I returned home for my meal break, from 5.45 p.m. until 6.30 p.m., darkness had fallen and freezing fog was threatened. When I left the house, however, the sky was clear with the stars twinkling in the blackness above, but the air contained that distinctive hint of an imminent hard frost. I was cosy in my official van with the heating system working at peak level but was determined not to be lulled into any false sense of security, because there was a threat of ice on the roads. The forecast warned of a severe frost later that night and said it would persist for several days. The council's gritting lorries had been out earlier in the evening to spread salt along the roads and I decided I would park my van and walk where possible.

I would undertake the main part of my evening patrol on foot, making calls in Aidensfield, Elsinby, Ploatby and Crampton before knocking off at 10 p.m. There was no point in risking a motor accident on the icy roads, although I did need the van to travel between the villages.

It would be shortly after 8.30 p.m. when I received a radio call from the Control Room.

It seemed that a man from Crampton, Mr Geoffrey Dixon, who worked for a petrol supplier, had been walking his dog between Crampton and Thackerston a few minutes earlier when he had discovered a serious traffic accident. It had happened at the foot of Oak Lea Bank just outside Crampton. A small car appeared to have collided with a horse; the car was on its side in the ditch while the horse was lying injured at the scene; the car driver was not with his car and appeared to have wandered off, probably suffering from concussion. His car, it seemed from the report, was badly damaged. Mr Dixon had rushed to the nearest house from where he had telephoned. I was directed to the scene, and Control reminded me to drive carefully because of the ice. It seemed that the accident had occurred on a very slippery road surface. A vet had been called too, but the horse had no rider with it.

I knew the hill in question. It was steep and the downward slope terminated in a sweeping corner to the left; drivers often experienced trouble negotiating it and in winter it was made worse because water oozed from the fields above and ran across the highway. In severe conditions, it froze to produce a very slippery and sloping surface. I had no doubt that this was the cause of the accident. It would take me ten minutes to arrive at the scene and I gave that ETA (estimated time of arrival) to Control; they did say that owing to the probability that the driver had wandered off in an apparent concussed state, an ambulance had been called.

What looked like concussion could sometimes conceal a more serious internal injury.

Off I went to deal with the accident, driving very carefully through our narrow lanes with the stars twinkling above. My route took me through Thackerston and thus to Oak Lea Bank from its lower end. I parked the van on a wide grass verge some distance from the foot of the hill, took a powerful torch from the van and walked to the notorious corner.

But there was nothing to be seen. I saw the anticipated patch of thick ice which spread across the road, but there was no sign of an injured horse or a damaged car. The beam from my torch played across the road ahead of me and then, in the ditch just below the corner, I found evidence of the car's recent presence. There was damage to the hedge and the fence behind it, with some broken headlamp glass and red light glass upon the frozen grass and the inevitable twisted pieces of chrome strip. Chrome strips always seemed to fall off accident-damaged cars. These bits had come from a Ford Anglia. I searched everywhere along that roadside and even ventured into the adjoining fields, thinking the impetus of the car might have propelled it across one of the hawthorn hedges. But there was no damage to any of the hedges and the car was nowhere to be seen. Neither was the horse. I spent some considerable time in the darkness, checking and re-checking in my search, but the scene was deserted.

I walked the entire length of that hill with my torch, examining the ditches, gates, hedge-bottoms and all places that either a horse or a car might be concealed. But I found nothing, nor did I find the concussed driver. As I hunted, the ambulance arrived and I explained the situation to the driver; then a vet from Harrowby, a Mr Marriott, turned up to attend the horse.

Together, using the headlights of our vehicles and with torches blazing, we undertook another search of every inch of that hill and its verges, but found neither horse, car, nor man. We did, however, discover a large spot of fresh blood in the road and guessed it had come from the horse. We also found further fragments of smashed glass in the centre of the road and I noticed some piles of mud, good indications of the precise location of a collision. In a collision which involves a motor vehicle, such piles of mud invariably fall from the undersides to identify the point of impact.

'So what do you suggest, constable?' asked the vet in his light Scots accent.

'First, I'll check with Control,' I said. 'They might have given me the wrong location.'

I called them on my radio and they confirmed the location. According to them, we were all standing precisely at the scene of the reported accident.

'So what next?' persisted the vet.

'I need to have a word with Mr Dixon, the man who reported it. He didn't ring me, he rang our Control Room,' I explained. 'They diverted me here. He lives in Crampton, I know his house. I can be there and back in two minutes – I'll ask him to come and show us where it happened.'

The vet looked at the ambulance driver and both agreed to wait for those extra minutes, just in case we had been directed to the wrong place. If we had, then their skills may be needed elsewhere. I hurried off to Geoff Dixon's cottage in my van and he answered the door.

'It's about the accident you reported, Geoff,' I began.

'It's at the bottom of Oak Lea Bank, Mr Rhea. I rang your headquarters.'

'Yes, but there's nothing there. I've got a vet and an ambulance down there, as well as myself, and we're all looking for casualties – but there's nothing. Can you come and show us exactly where it happened?'

'Sure, I'll get my coat.'

He directed me to the place I'd already visited and stood in the road, baffled. We all stood and looked at him.

'It was definitely here,' he pointed to the mess in the hedge. 'The car was there, on its side, and it was pretty badly damaged ... but there was nobody with it. And the horse was lying down there, on that wide bit of verge. There was blood on its flank – it looked like a bad stomach wound and it was panting heavily, but alive.... I ran to call the police.'

'I got the call at 8.30 p.m.,' I said, looking at my watch. It was now ten minutes past nine. We'd spent the interim searching.

'It would take me a good five minutes to run and make the call, but the accident might have happened some time before I arrived. Maybe the man in the car rang from somewhere, or a pal was with him or something....'

'So it might have occurred an hour ago?' I said, thinking that that left sufficient time for someone to come and clear away the damaged car and remove the horse. With Dixon helping us, we made another complete search of the neighbouring fields and road verges, but found nothing. I thanked the vet and the ambulance for coming all this way on icy roads for nothing, but said I had no idea where the casualties had gone.

I took Geoff Dixon home and he invited me in for a cup of coffee; I went over his experience once again, getting a detailed description of the car and the horse, just to satisfy myself that the incident *had* occurred, but of that, there was no doubt.

Even today, I do not know what happened to that car driver or his Ford Anglia car, nor do I know what happened to the injured horse. I am convinced that Dixon had not imagined the accident – the evidence at the scene confirmed his experience. But of the casualties? They vanished on that frosty night in January.

* * *

Another curious instance of disappearing property occurred

when someone allegedly stole sheep from Frank Huggett. Frank ran a huge flock on the open moors above Gelderslack, his black-faced ewes living almost wild upon those bleak and heathery heights. They had no fences to keep them in and they spread themselves across a spacious area of heather and bracken, fending for themselves for most of the year. Then, every three months or so, Frank would ride the range upon his horse, accompanied by his team of three dogs, and he would bring his flock down to the lower reaches for clipping or for counting or dipping when required.

But these sheep did not stray from their pastures because they were heeafed, pronounced hee-affed. This curious dialect word comes from *heaf* meaning home, and in this case it means that the sheep know their own territory and will remain there without the need for fences. Whole flocks are heeafed and the local name for these sheep is therefore heeafed yows (heafed ewes).

Frank claimed he could recognize every one of his ewes, even though all were black-faced with horns, and had the distinctive black legs. To anyone else, they were like peas in the proverbial pod, except that there were hundreds of them. But Frank knew their individual faces as a head teacher knows the faces of all the school's pupils; he could remember which ewe had had twins or triplets, which had been ill or missing in the counting sessions and which needed the greatest care.

That Frank loved his sheep was never in doubt. Some said he was sheep-fond or sheep-daft, meaning he thought of nothing else, just as some Yorkshire lasses are known as lad-fond. Certainly, every minute of Frank's life, whether working or at leisure, was dominated by his flocks, and it was equally well known that he was regarded as an expert on moorland sheep and was a leading member of the Black-faced Sheep Breeders' Association.

He judged at shows and was often called by his friends to give advice, and yet his formal education had been virtually nil. He'd left the village school at fourteen to follow his father into moorland sheep-farming and had been willing both to work hard and to learn from his highly experienced father. With his father and mother long dead, Frank and his wife did keep some other animals – goats could be seen about his farm buildings and his wife bred geese, ducks and poultry. Frank even reckoned to be able to identify every hen on the premises.

* * *

So far as his sheep were concerned, people would often put Frank to the test, asking him to identify a particular ewe and to provide its history. And he would oblige. He'd say,

'Yon awd lass had triplets two year back, and she's been wi' me nigh on fower year. Ah gat her at Eltering Mart. Ah calls her Elsie Seven and she's allus given a good fleece, thick and full. She's been a good lamber an' all, and Ah reckon there's a year or two in her yet. She's a grand awd lass is yon.'

The name of Elsie Seven intrigued me. He did give names to most of his ewes, but because he had such a huge flock he ran out of names. Thus, several sheep bore the same female Christian name, with a numeral for their surname. He would often point out a sheep in the distance, saying she was Kate Three, the daughter of Mary Nine and that she'd had three lambs in three years, the other two being Nancy Two and Brenda Eight. It was a joy to hear him counting his sheep, shouting at Joan Eleven to 'git oot o' t'rooad' or Lily One to 'sharpen thisell and git between yon fences'.

Frank's individual system of identification was, of course, in addition to the standard one which is used for moorland sheep. Because several farmers run their flocks on the open moors, the animals must be identified as belonging to a particular person. Quite often, the sheep of one farmer mingle with those of another and confusion would occur without a simple and highly visible identification method. That method involves the use of coloured dye; thus moorland sheep will have splashes of red, green or blue dye upon their wool. One farmer might mark all members of his flock with a red left foreshoulder; another might use a green rump or another a blue right hand quarter. I have heard townspeople cry with alarm at seeing a sheep with a bright red patch on its belly wool – they thought it had been injured, but it was just the owner's mark.

Tups are also marked with dye under their bellies before they embark upon fatherhood. As they serve each ewe, so they leave behind a brightly coloured patch on the ewe's rump – red is a favourite colour – and so the farmer knows which of his ewes have or have not been charmed into future motherhood by the busy tup. Ear clipping is another means of identification, with members of each flock having distinctive marks upon their ears.

But in Frank Huggett's distinctive method of naming his sheep, who could prove him wrong? If he made such claims about knowledge of his animals, how could anyone prove otherwise? Not that anyone would – they all trusted him and I had no reason to doubt his expertise. If he said he knew every single one of his sheep by their first names, then neither I nor anyone else doubted him. He was a fine man, a solid, likeable moorland farmer who stood no nonsense from anyone. Now approaching fifty-five, he was a thick-set character with a surprisingly pink complexion beneath his head of wavy greying hair. Bright blue eyes gave him a baby-faced look, and he was always particular about his appearance, never going unshaven and always having neat haircuts.

You'd rarely find him indoors; whenever I called, morning, noon or night, Frank would be somewhere on the moors with his dogs and shepherd's crook, checking his flock for one thing or another. On one occasion, he went out in blizzard conditions, to take a supply of hay to some of his flock who had been marooned on the windswept heights. He learned they had found shelter in an old barn on the moors high above his farmhouse.

Nonetheless, he went out in appalling conditions to see to them and to take them food. He reckoned the safety of his sheep was more important than sitting cosily beside his blazing kitchen fire. It's not surprising that his friends called

him Awd Moorender. Moorender is a slightly derogatory term
for a rough character who lives on the moors and who is not
sophisticated like townspeople. Indeed, lots of townies refer to
country folk of this region (like me!) as moorenders, the
implication being that moorenders are simpletons.

The word is also used for rough sheep or even horses that
live on these heights. If a man had a tired, shaggy old horse,
people would describe it as a moorender. In spite of this, I'd
say that Frank was a moorender, but he was by no means a
simpleton. His wife never complained of his devotion to the
sheep, for she had produced three lovely children, now in
their twenties, and occupied herself with village organizations
like the WI and the PCC of the small parish church.

I do not know if the sheep responded to the dedication that
Frank lavished upon them – they are rather stupid animals,
unlike dogs who will respond to a master's love and trust. But
Frank seemed to think that they knew him and loved him, and
that they welcomed his constant care and affection. Perhaps
they did. That thought made him very happy and contented.

It was therefore a most hurtful experience when he
discovered that two of his flock had been stolen.

For Frank, it was tantamount to someone kidnapping his
child, and the matter clearly upset him. He was upset rather
than angry. I learned of this crime through a telephone call.

'Somebody's ta'en a pair of my sheep, Mr Rhea,' he told me
shortly after eight one morning. 'Can thoo come and see me?'

I said I'd be there within twenty minutes. As I drove across
the moor, I wondered if they had really been stolen. Sheep did
go astray; some got stuck in ditches and others wandered into
distant corners of their heeaf. Some were run down by
motorists and some simply died in isolation. Few farmers
could supervise every single inch of the huge open area of
countryside in which their flocks lived and so we had to treat
every case of reported theft with just a hint of caution.
Nonetheless, sheep rustling did occur. Thieves armed with
.22 rifles would shoot the animals which grazed near the
roadside. The carcasses were immediately skinned on the spot

and placed in the rear of a van, the discarded skins being thrown far into the heather. Thus, if we caught a thief in possession of a carcass, it was impossible to prove where it had come from, and virtually impossible to locate the discarded skin and fleece. Such slaughtered carcasses were sold to butchers in the surrounding towns. Was this the fate of Frank's animals?

When I interviewed Frank in his cosy kitchen, enjoying the inevitable 'lowance and huge mug of tea, I had to cast doubt upon his theft theory.

I did so by asking whether the sheep could be stuck in a ditch, whether they might have wandered into a neighbour's heeaf, whether they had simply died or whether they were victims of a road accident. But he was adamant.

'Last night, t'pair on 'em was up near Holm Intak, doon bi t'stream. Ah knows 'em, Mr Rhea, them two's been pals since they were lambs. Maud Seven and Doris Twelve, they go ivverywhere together them two, cousins they are. You'll nivver see yan withoot t'other, so if yan had been trapped or run over, t'other would be standing by, bleating for me to come and do summat. They've both gone, Mr Rhea, and in my book, that means somebody's pinched 'em.'

I had no option but to accept his word. I could not visit the scene of the crime because they might have been stolen from anywhere within thousands of acres, but after convincing myself that Frank was correct, I decided to 'crime' the report of the missing sheep. That meant it was officially recorded as a crime and I was sure Frank would then be able to claim from his insurance if his animals were not recovered alive.

'Frank,' I said, 'you realize we stand very little chance of recovering your sheep? If the thieves have clipped off your dye marks, we'll never prove they are yours even if we catch the thief.... To be brutally honest, I think they'll probably be lamb chops by now, on sale in some butcher's shop in Middlesbrough or Sunderland. But I'll circulate the theft to all our officers and we will make wide inquiries.'

'Ah know there's nowt much you fellers can do, but

t'insurance says we must report thefts to you blokes. But Ah's off to Eltering Mart this morning, Mr Rhea, and if them sheep o' mine are there, Ah'll recognize 'em even if t'markings have been shaven off. If their faces are there, Ah'll know 'em!'

'If you do see them, call us,' I cautioned him. 'Don't take the law into your own hands!'

On my return journey to Aidensfield, I popped into the police office at Ashfordly to record the crime and decided to spend a few moments in that office, typing up my initial crime report. It took me about an hour, and as I was finishing it off, the telephone rang. It was Frank Huggett.

'Ah rang your house, but your missus said you'd likely be there,' he began. 'Ah've found them sheep, Mr Rhea, like Ah said. Maud Seven and Doris Twelve. At Eltering Mart. In a pen. T'licence bobby 'as isolated 'em; t'pen belongs to awd Ernie Stubbs. Thoo knaws as well as me that we've suspected 'im for years. 'E's pinched more sheep that Ah've had hot dinners, and nut once 'as 'e been caught. Well, we've got him red-handed, Mr Rhea, you'll be pleased to know.'

'Where are you ringing from?' I asked.

'T'mart office,' he said.

'I'll come straight away,' I told him. 'Tell the Mart PC I'm on my way and ask him to keep Ernie Stubbs and the sheep there.'

'Right ho, Mr Rhea.'

At every cattle mart, there used to be a constable on duty and his task was to issue pig licences as well as to keep a general eye on the proceedings. That system operated in my time as a village constable and it was fortunate that a constable was there on this occasion. When I arrived twenty-five minutes later, I went to the office and found PC John Rogers of Eltering Police. He had isolated the suspect animals and had also detained Ernie Stubbs; he was now in Eltering Police Station cells, under arrest for suspected theft. 'I had to lift him on suspicion,' said PC Rogers to me. 'Mind, he says he didn't steal those sheep, says he's never been near Frank Huggett's spot.'

'He would say that, wouldn't he?' I smiled.

'But, Nick, you can't prove those are Mr Huggett's sheep, can you? One sheep looks just like any other … '

'Ah know my sheep,' said Frank stolidly. 'Them's mine, Mr Rogers, there's neea doubt aboot it.'

'Let's have a look at them,' I suggested.

The tiny pen contained two timid looking sheep, both black-faced ewes with horns and black legs, but neither bearing any ear clipping marks or dyed wool. To my inexpert eye, they looked like identical twins; I could see no difference in them.

'He's clipped my colour off,' said Frank, touching each animal on its shoulder to indicate the site of the missing dye. 'Thoo knows, Mr Rhea, Ah's a red right shoulder man. Thoo can see where t'fleece 'as been trimmed.'

He was right. The wool around that shoulder had been recently cut short, but whether a court would accept that as evidence of the removal of identifying marks and thus an indication of theft, remained to be seen.

'But these sheep don't respond to you,' said PC Rogers to Frank.

'They do!' he cried. 'They know me, but sheep are not daft, Mr Rogers, they don't show emotion like dogs, they don't make a fuss.... Them two's my ewes, mak neea mistake.'

'Frank is an expert on moorland sheep,' I informed Rogers. 'I'm sure that if he gave evidence in court, as an expert witness, it would be treated with great respect.'

Thus we were faced with something of a dilemma, for I doubted whether our own prosecution department would accept Frank's opinion that these were indeed his animals. After all, anyone could claim ownership of anything if absolute proof became an unnecessary prerequisite. But I did believe Frank and felt that the decision should rest with a court. As Frank had said, we had long suspected Stubbs of sheep stealing; indeed, we were positive he was a regular thief but we had never been able to prove a single case against him. We'd never caught him in possession of the stolen animals.

To cut a long story short, Stubbs was charged with theft of

Frank's two ewes and, in court, steadfastly denied any responsibility for that crime.

He refused to reveal from where he had obtained the two ewes in question and denied clipping off the red identification mark. The magistrates listened to Frank's simple explanation of his reputed ability to identify every animal in his flock of over eight hundred, and the court accepted his status as an expert on moorland sheep. I felt sure the court would decide that there was reasonable doubt about Stubb's guilt and that they would acquit him of theft, but as one of the magistrates was himself a moorland farmer, I reckon the bench knew of Ernie Stubb's reputation and of Frank's legendary skill. So he was found guilty and fined £50.

About a month later, I called at Frank's lonely farm for my quarterly visit to sign his stock register and I was invited to join him and his wife for 'lowance. I mentioned that we'd had no subsequent reports of sheep stealing since Stubbs's conviction and thanked Frank for his efforts in convicting him.

'Somebody 'ad to sort him out, Mr Rhea.' A knowing smile flickered across his pink face. ' 'E's been at it for years without getting caught.'

'But now he's been convicted of sheep stealing, the local markets will be less keen to take stuff from him?'

'Aye,' beamed Frank. ' 'E'll not pinch sheep unless 'e can sell 'em, and 'e can't sell 'em if nobody'll take 'em off 'is 'ands. Ah reckon we fettled him good and proper, Mr Rhea.'

'It still baffles me how you can tell one sheep from another, Frank,' I laughed.

'He can't,' commented his wife. 'He makes it all up, it's his party trick!'

'But two o' my ewes were missing ewes and Ah've get two back. If Ah say they're mine, then mine they are!' grinned Frank. 'And we've stopped Stubbs. Moorenders aren't so daft after all, are they, Mr Rhea?'

'Fortunately, no!' I heard myself saying. 'And I can record a crime as being detected.' It was all that I, as another moorender, could think of adding.

5 Fellowship and Social Assembly

Their judgement is a mere lottery
John Dryden (1631–1700)

The legal name for tombola or a raffle is a *lottery* and in my time as village constable at Aidensfield there were only four types of lottery, other than premium bonds, which were legal in this country. Every other lottery was unlawful.

The definition of a lottery is 'a distribution of prizes by lot or chance', the important element being that there should be no skill involved. A lottery is won by sheer chance or good fortune, hence the need for legal control.

To conform to the then prevailing law, there were sets of rules to govern each of the four legal types of lottery. One which rarely featured in police work was the lottery of an art union. Members of an art union drew lots, the winners being allowed to retain certain works of art for a specified period.

The other three types of lottery were more widespread i.e.: ·

(1) *Small lotteries* which were incidental to popular entertainments like jumble sales, dinners, dances and sporting events. Tickets for those were sold and drawn on the premises during the event and it was a rule (often broken) that no cash prizes could be given. The prizes were generally things like boxes of chocolates, groceries, toiletries and similar gifts.

(2) *Private lotteries* which were restricted to members of a

society, say a football supporters' club. In this case, all the proceeds, less expenses, had to be donated to the charity and certain rules had to be followed.

(3)   *Registered lotteries*. These had to be registered with the local authority and organized for charitable purposes, but the prizes could be larger, like holidays overseas or TV sets, provided the value of each prize (at that time) did not exceed £100. Tickets for these lotteries could be sold before or during the event, and sold off the premises. Each ticket had to contain the name of the charity, the promoter of the raffle and the cost of each ticket (which should not exceed one shilling – 5p).

From time to time, organizations wanted to stage a massive raffle with a huge prize like a motor car, but the trick was to remove the competition from the status of a lottery. This could be done by incorporating some act of skill, like estimating the number of peas in a jam jar, estimating how many yards a car could be driven on one gallon of petrol, estimating the weight of a cake or a baby, or calculating the time the pointers of a clock would stop if it wasn't wound up. All kinds of skilful deeds were introduced to remove such contests from the lottery laws. Lots of organizations ran these so-called prize competitions instead of raffles, but the good old village raffle continued to flourish in spite of any newfangled ideas.

At most village raffles, numbered cloakroom tickets in various colours were sold to people at social functions, but the rules of these small lotteries were generally ignored or not even considered. Little old ladies cheerfully broke the law by organizing raffles for cash prizes or selling the tickets around the village before the event took place. It would not surprise me if committees continue to break the law concerning small lotteries, but who complains? And who knows what those laws are? Who, apart from the village constable, was then familiar with the Betting, Gaming and Lotteries Act of 1963?

A village constable had to close his eyes to some breaches of that statute, such as those occasions where, for example, a teddy bear was raffled by tickets sold in the village shop. As this was not 'incidental to an entertainment' like a dinner, dance, social event or sporting fixture, it was an unlawful lottery. It might be argued by some that shopping was 'entertainment', but it is doubtful whether the courts would agree with that interpretation. But as the proceeds were going to charity, who would complain?

If, on the other hand, some wily character was making money for himself by this means, then, of course, we would step in and prosecute. It's a matter of applying the law with common sense, because to rigidly enforce every rule and regulation, as some politicians demand, would result in a police state.

In such cases, suitable advice was often given to the unwitting law-breakers. I did hear of some strange raffles – one man who worked in a large factory always raffled his wage packets and made more from that than he did from his wages. As the dastardly deed was not on my patch, I was not concerned with that enterprising illegality. Another man, again not on my beat, decided to raffle his house when it was on the market for a long time, but I don't think it was a successful venture. He failed to sell enough tickets to cover the value of his property.

To give most of the village raffle organizers due credit, they did come to me for advice when they were about to embark upon a new project. In many cases, I was able to help, sometimes suggesting that an act of skill be incorporated to provide greater appeal, especially when it was for a worthwhile cause. And, as Aidensfield's chief raffle consultant, I was invariably asked to buy tickets, but my record of wins was abysmal. Some people always win and some never do; I was in the latter category, while a friend who worked in a turkey factory always won several turkeys at Christmas, and a local publican always won bottles of whisky.

It was during my involvement with raffles in Aidensfield and the surrounding villages that I noticed a curious phenomenon. The strangeness did not make itself immediately apparent, but materialized only after I'd attended about a dozen social events in various village halls.

I noticed that every raffle prize list contained a tin of sardines. I guessed the donor was a local grocer. The local licensees always gave bottles of whisky or gin, the butchers gave hams or pheasants, the garages gave cans of oil or vouchers for free petrol, the hairdressers gave vouchers for free hair-styling and local restaurants offered free meals for two in cosy candlelit places. As the village constable, there was little I could offer by way of a professional prize – I could hardly offer fine-free vouchers for speeding or the chance to drink after hours without being caught – and so I tried to buy something different for each raffle, like an ornament, perfume, book, picture and so forth. With about a dozen villages and hamlets on my patch, it was an expensive indulgence because there was usually a raffle somewhere every month, either for the WI, a football or cricket club, gardening club, playgroup and one or other of the churches, but never the chapels.

Mary and I tried to socialize at these events as often as we could, our appearances being heavily dependent upon baby-sitters and my odd working-hours, but it did become clear that the villagers keenly supported one another's raffles. They attended each other's WI meetings, whist drives, dances and so on. It was very heart-warming to see them supporting one another.

It was during these events that I came to notice that whenever a tin of sardines was won in the raffle, there was an almighty cheer from the audience. It was surely because no one really wanted to win it!

While not wishing to show my curiosity or ignorance about it, and never wanting to appear silly by asking why everyone cheered the tin of sardines, it was then that I realized that almost every local raffle had a tin of sardines as a prize. There were one or two exceptions, usually when two events occurred simultaneously in different villages. I began to wonder about the identity of the supplier – which benefactor had all those tins to spare, I wondered? Where were they coming from? Was there something odd going on? Something that I ought to be familiar with? That sardine-cheering was a puzzle.

Then the inevitable happened. Mary and I attended a dance in aid of church funds and, sure enough, raffle tickets were on sale. I bought some and resigned myself to the fact that I would never win. I never did – I regarded that investment as a donation to church funds.

It is not difficult, therefore, to imagine my surprise when I found I had a winning ticket, the last one of that evening – and that my prize was a tin of sardines. As I strode forward to claim it, there was an almighty cheer. From past experience, I had expected the cheer, but as I bore the small tin triumphantly back to my seat, Mary asked,

'Why did they cheer like that?'

I told her about the custom I'd witnessed at other events but added, 'But I don't really know why they do it – it's just that every time a tin of sardines is won, everybody cheers.'

'There must be a reason,' she said.

'It's like dropping a plate or a cup in a works canteen – everybody cheers when that happens!' I told her.

Without really inspecting the tin, I slipped it into my jacket pocket and joined the dancing. It was a pleasant evening and we enjoyed it, but as the dance was drawing to a close, the organizer, Charles Thackray, approached me.

'I was glad you and Mrs Rhea could join us socially,' he said. 'I hope we'll see you again.'

'We've enjoyed it.' I meant every word. 'If my duties allow, and we can find a baby-sitter, we'll come again.'

'And you've no more worries about what to give as the next raffle prize,' he laughed.

'The sardines?' I realized what he was talking about and knew it was the perfect time to ask about the cheering custom. 'Tell me, Mr Thackray, why does everyone cheer when tins of sardines are won?'

'You don't know?' he sounded surprised.

'Well, to be honest, no I don't.'

'I'll warn you,' he chuckled. 'Don't try to open that tin and don't eat the contents!'

I took it out of my pocket and looked at it.

Then I realized that the design of the label was ancient – it was like those tins of sardines I'd seen when I was a child – and apart from that, the label and indeed the tin looked worn and shabby. It was an extremely old tin of extremely old sardines.

'That tin's more than thirty years old,' he laughed. 'It's been going around these villages since before the war. It's always given as a raffle prize, Mr Rhea – whoever wins it gives it back as a prize. It's not for opening, you see, it's for winning in raffles.'

'You mean this is the same tin I've seen at all those raffles?'

'Aye, that's why they all cheer. So when you're asked to give a prize next time, you give it back.'

'Thanks for warning me!' I said. 'We might have opened it.... '

'You'd have had to buy a new tin,' he said. 'We always have a tin of sardines at all our raffles. It's a good prize, you know, it saves you having to find a prize for the next raffle!'

As I looked at it, I wondered how many more of those raffle prizes were never opened, being recycled in village raffles. It was less than a week later when Mrs Allen stopped me in Elsinby and asked,

'It's our WI raffle next month, Mr Rhea. I wondered if you might give a prize – I hear you've got the tin of sardines?'

'I'll fetch it along,' I promised her.

And until I left the area, that tin of sardines was still being won in local raffles.

* * *

Among the 'entertainments' at which raffles were held was the village whist drive, a most serious affair. Every week, on whist night, the village hall was prepared with green-baize card tables in readiness for this major social event. A supper was arranged and people from the surrounding area would arrive to compete with one another. There was immense honour in winning first prize. The prize itself, something like a brace of pheasants or a box of groceries, was secondary to the pride and honour in actually beating all-comers in this most honourable of contests. There was sometimes a First Man prize and a First Woman prize, and occasionally, if the organizer had a sense of humour, a wooden spoon for the lowest scorer. As opening time arrived, men, women and children, all gripped with the fever of winning, arrived early to ensure a good seat at their lucky starting table.

Almost every village had its own whist drives, their popularity being legendary. The moors were rich with stories of this card game, with certain players never losing, others always winning when hearts were shinners (trumps), some being lucky at full moon or some only when there was an 'r' in the month.

Stories would circulate far and wide about Awd Isaac who never had an ace in his hand but won nonetheless, of Awd Mrs Blenkin who thought spades were omens of death and always lost when she got the ace, and of Awd Jack Harrison whose winning streak lasted over five years until somebody trumped his king of diamonds with the two of clubs. He was ill for months afterwards, blaming himself for not correctly reading the other's hand.

Whist drives were often varied to give added spice to the proceedings. For example, there would be military whist drives in which the players formed teams which represented nations. Each team was allocated a little flag and thus nation was pitted against nation in a very serious kind of war. Another kind of whist drive was the partner drive. Two people played as a team throughout the evening and in this case one had to be very careful about the choice of one's partner. One had to select someone with whom one had a strong rapport and someone strong enough not to become antagonistic if your abysmal playing helped to lose the game.

With close partners, there was always a temptation to cheat but the MC was always alert for this. He'd keep his sharp eyes open for the man who'd wink the left eye if he had the ace of shinners or the right if he hadn't a shinner in his hand. But a genuinely good whist partner had no need to cheat; a good partner was akin to a companion who was so close that the couple could almost thought-read. By the way one partner played his cards, the other could calculate which cards were held by the friend and which were held by the opposition. In this way, a tremendous amount of skill entered the game, and consequently whist, like many card games, was not classified as a lottery. It is a game of skill and chance combined, the chance being the hand of cards one is dealt, and the skill being the way in which the hand is played. The same applies to dominoes and cribbage, two very popular games, especially in pubs.

The villages around Aidensfield, therefore, were rich in highly skilled whist players. These moorfolk, men and women alike, had played whist since childhood and knew each other's game as if it was printing in large letters on their foreheads. So skilled were they, that they knew which cards the other would play in any given circumstance; they knew how to read the facial features, hand gestures, signs of worry like foot-tapping or nail-biting. And by memorizing the cards which had been played and the sequence in which they had fallen, they knew which cards remained to be played in any of the hands of the others at the table.

Players of this calibre, therefore, were steeped in the game and they could not tolerate unseasoned players joining 'their' whist drives. This was because those unseasoned players had not competed locally over an extended period, and so the established player did not know how to 'read' their game.

The result was that the strangers often won, simply because their unorthodox or amateurish style of card play completely perplexed and disorientated their more studious opponents. Many an old player has regaled a newcomer because of an awkward style of play, and so many new players refused to attend local whist drives. The aggravation, with its open criticism and rude comments, was just not worth it.

The result was, of course, that whist drives of that kind gradually ceased to exist; as those old players went off to that ever-winning whist drive in the sky, no young people took their places.

But schoolchildren are impervious to the niceties of adult behaviour or culture and, quite often, brash youngsters would attend these drives just for the sheer fun of annoying the hardened adult players. A rampant schoolboy with a hand full of shinners was indeed a menace, as was the quiet kid who knew how to read the game and confound his seniors by playing contrary to their own system.

It was memories of this kind that flooded back to me when I was visited by an old school friend called Dave. He had been working as an accountant for a British company in Africa for a few years and had returned to England for a three-month break, staying with his parents. We invited him to visit us for a few days. On the second day of his visit, I walked him through Aidensfield, showing him the historic church and other interesting parts.

We met some of the local people too, and had a lunch-time drink in the Brewers' Arms. It was there, on the pub notice board, that he spotted the poster which announced that a partner whist drive was to be held that evening in Aidensfield village hall.

'I think we ought to go.' His eyes twinkled as he read the details. 'Remember when we were kids, going to those partner drives and winning everything!'

It all came back to me. Dave and I would be about fourteen at the time, both living in a tiny moorland village where the only entertainment was the snooker table and the weekly whist drive. One night, we ventured into the hall as a whist drive was about to start and there happened to be two seats vacant at one of the tables. The MC spotted us and invited us to join the drive. It was a partner drive, he warned us, so we would have to play together as a team throughout the evening, but at least we did make up a full table. Thus we were regarded as useful.

Ever ready for a bit of juvenile excitement, we joined in and we actually enjoyed it. We could play whist – we played every day on the half-hour train journey to school and so this more formal approach held no fears for us. We did not, of course, bargain for the extremely serious approach which was adopted by these regular attenders; whereas our schoolboy game was a bit of fun, this was a very solemn affair.

But on that first occasion, we did our best; we didn't win anything, but we were invited back if and when there was a couple of spare seats. As it happened, there was often a couple of vacant seats and so Dave and I became regular players. And we began to win. We knew each other's play; very quickly, we learned to 'read' the method of play of the others and were soon attaining high scores, winning regularly and moving from table to table to tackle fresh opponents. We did not win at every drive, but we did do extremely well. We were good whist partners.

And so, all those years later when Dave visited me at Aidensfield on the very night of a partner drive, it seemed that this was an omen. We would attend for old time's sake, just for a bit of fun as we had done all those years ago. To be sure we wouldn't make complete fools of ourselves, we had some practice games at home with Mary and a dummy hand, and it was surprising how, after a dozen or so rounds, we regained most of our old skills. I found myself knowing how Dave would play:... I grew quite excited about tonight's game.

As we left the house that night, Mary warned me not to show off, for one of my long-time interests has been card manipulation and sleight-of-hand. I knew a lot of false deals, card-sharping and vanishing tricks but had no intention of using that knowledge or my conjuring skills at the village whist drive. But I did know enough about card-sharping never to play cards for money with total strangers.

At the door, Randolph Burley, the local auctioneer, hailed me and took our money.

'I didn't know you were a whist man, Mr Rhea,' he said.

'I'm not.' I decided to play down my past experience. 'But this is Dave, an old school friend. We used to play a bit on the train, on our way to school, so we thought we'd revive a few memories tonight.'

'It's a big night,' he said solemnly. 'There's a lot at stake – it's Steel Cup night.'

Joe Steel was the village shopkeeper and had donated the Steel Cup; it was to be won by the most successful partnership over the past year, and tonight two teams were competing for it. Each team had won on five occasions over the year; in twelve partnership drives, each had won five times. There'd been a stray winning team last November, thus ensuring a cliff-hanging finale. Tonight, the twelfth and last drive in the series, was the deciding match. Now two teams were drawing, but if neither of them won tonight the cup would be held over and they'd all have to start again next year. But some felt there would be a clear winner.

'It'll be Mr and Mrs Dunstone,' said Randolph. 'I reckon they've the edge on John and Mary Potter. It's a full house. Folks have come from far enough, so we've put out extra tables.'

And so we paid our entrance fees, obtained our score cards and entered the throng.

The gleaming silver Steel Cup stood on a table on the stage, and there was an array of other lesser prizes for tonight's game. A lot of the players raised their eyebrows at the sight of me among the tables and I'm sure they wondered what on earth I and the unknown man were doing there. In fact, Dave did look rather like a policeman and I'm sure they thought we were undercover constables on the look-out for cheats, this being such an auspicious occasion.

Dave and I did lose a few hands, but it was astonishing how the cards fell; we got some very good hands and we found that our past skills had not deserted us. If we weren't careful, this might be an embarrassingly successful evening.

It was.

We won.

In fact, we won handsomely, with me coming away with a bottle of malt whisky and Dave winning a box of groceries. But we had scuppered the Steel Cup. For the Dunstones and the Potters, the outcome remained a draw and they would have to start all over again next year.

In the days that followed, I found that I received a very cool reception from certain villagers; the warmth I'd experienced in the past had quickly evaporated and I wondered what I had done wrong. I hadn't arrested anyone for a trivial matter, I hadn't upset anyone that I could recall and neither had Mary.... I puzzled over this for a day or two and mentioned it to Mary.

She said I was imagining things, but I knew I was not; the current state of chilliness was real enough. There was definitely a new air of disdain towards the village constable in Aidensfield and district.

It was Randolph who enlightened me.

'They weren't at all happy about you and your pal winning that night,' he said. 'That's upset the regulars, Mr Rhea. No stranger ever comes in and wins like that, not even in a partner drive. And you're a stranger at whist-drives, not being a regular attender. You weren't supposed to win, Mr Rhea, with all due respect. Worse still, you and your pal stopped the Dunstones or mebbe the Potters winning that cup.... They said Mrs Dunstone was in tears afterwards – it would have been the culmination of a year's work for her and Alfred.'

I didn't know how to react or what to say. We'd played fairly and won fairly.

'We just went for a bit of fun, Randolph,' I told him. 'We didn't go to win or to deny anyone a cup or anything. We didn't even know about the contest till we got there.'

'Those players didn't see it like that,' he spoke solemnly. 'They reckoned you'd come in deliberately. Some said you were skilled whist men, you and that other chap, the way you played. They reckoned you were not beginners … '

'We played as school kids,' I told him, and explained why we had decided to attend. Then I asked, 'So, how can I make amends?'

'There's no need,' he said. 'Forget it, they'll get over it. They start again next month, another year of couples aiming for the Steel Cup. It has to be won outright, you see. It's not given for draws.'

I went home and told Mary, but she said it was all my fault

for inviting Dave. 'You might have known you and he would cause trouble. Think of all those folks you beat as kids.... '

I thought about it and when I saw the following month's posters advertising the next partner drive, I called Dave. He was still staying with his parents in England and when I invited him over to Aidensfield to take part in another partner drive, he was delighted.

'My mother was pleased with those groceries,' he said.

'This time, it's not to win,' I cautioned him. 'I must let them beat me, they're not talking to me.... ' And I told the sorry tale.

'You're joking?'

'I'm not – just you come and see the reception we get if we go into the Steel Cup this time.... '

He came, as I knew he would. A frosty reception greeted us, but when we played hopelessly and lost game after game, the frostiness began to evaporate and the players, especially the Dunstones and Potters, began to smile. They nodded to one another with knowing grins ... these two men were not real players ... last time, it had just been luck ...

I could almost read their minds. I must say that Dave and I played magnificently. It was probably the finest partnership whist that we'd ever played, for we lost game after game most handsomely. We believed we'd played with extraordinary skill – I know the others thought we played like idiots and that our earlier win had been nothing more than a flash-in-the-pan. When I went to collect the wooden spoon on behalf of Dave and I, for achieving the lowest score of the night, I heard an old-stager say in a loud whisper.

'That'll teach 'em not to play whist against them who can play proper, them what really knows their cards!'

I smiled but decided I wouldn't show him my bottom deal or my range of false shuffles. Next day, the warmth had returned.

Indeed, a few whist fanatics invited me along to future drives, saying they'd teach me how to play properly if I was really interested, but I declined. 'It's far too complicated for me,' I said.

The wooden spoon was a most useful asset in our kitchen.

* * *

I'm sure one of our poets has said that love is a form of lottery, and when one learns how couples meet it seems it can be argued either that their meeting comes about through sheer lot or chance or that there is some other unknown power which brings them together. When I was a lad deep in the North York Moors, a high percentage of romances began through chance meetings at village dances which were always held in draughty halls.

The girls, like the wallflowers that many became, sat along one side of the hall while the youths stood at the other side, no shy youth daring to walk across that expanse of deserted floor to select a dancing companion. As the band, sometimes comprising only a fiddle and a piano, played waltzes, foxtrots, military two-steps and dashing white sergeants, so the lads tried to pluck up the necessary courage to ask a girl to dance. To do so meant a lonely walk across no man's land before the assembled audience, and that walk demanded courage of a very high order, especially if there was a likelihood that the girl would refuse the honour of dancing with such a noble fellow.

As a consequence, there were many occasions when the band played their entire repertoire for a particular dance and no one actually took to the floor. But the proverbial ice was usually broken when some youths, having obtained artificial courage at the pub, arrived to whirl the girls around to screams of delight. At this, the shy lads would respond and rush to the rescue of maidens whom they believed to be in distress.

One youth who was more shy than most was Geoffrey Stafford with whom I went to school. We were friends, but not close friends; perhaps a better word would be acquaintances for we never went around together as pals. But, like me, Geoffrey joined the police service and so, from time to time, I would come across him during my duties.

Geoff was memorable for several reasons. The first was his

inordinate shyness with girls, a second was his height for he was six feet seven inches tall, and a third was the size of his hands and feet. Quite literally, his hands were like shovels protruding from the sleeves of his clothing, sleeves which always seemed too short. At school, his jackets were always too short, with an enormous length of bare arm filling the space between the end of his sleeve and his wrist. Things hadn't changed as an adult – his police uniform sleeves were always too short, and when he stood to attention, it seemed as if his hands were so heavy that they were stretching his arms and drawing them out of their sleeves.

There were times when I wondered if the weight of his hands would drag his arms from their sockets.

But if his hands were huge, then so were his feet. To say they were colossal is an understatement. They were gigantic and fulfilled all those hoary old jokes about policemen having big feet. He took size fourteen in shoes, for example, and when his specially made uniform boots stood beside those of his colleagues, they looked like a pair of dug-out canoes each with a submarine conning tower at one end; they were large enough to have inspired the nursery rhyme about the old lady who lived in a shoe.

To witness Geoff patrolling down the street was indeed a sight to be treasured as those massive hands and feet worked in unison to propel his tall figure through the crowds.

To see him standing in the middle of the road directing traffic was equally memorable, for his huge mobile hands were like mechanical carpet-beaters, while his splendid feet anchored him safely when it was windy.

But for all his massive appendages, he was a charming fellow. He really did try to please people, and those who knew him did like and respect him, but his painful shyness with girls always militated against a successful romance. In an otherwise very happy life, that was the missing element, and he remained a reluctant bachelor. After all, for a neat-footed girl to do a quickstep with Geoff must have been like grains of corn trying to avoid being battered by flails.

I think it was his lack of success with girls and painful shyness that prompted him to join the Salvation Army. That uniform was just as ill-fitting as his police outfit, but I understand he was pretty effective with a pair of cymbals. His new-found faith, however, tended to restrict him even further in his search for romance because he ceased to join his colleagues in their pubs and clubs and stopped drinking alcohol.

It was one November when I met him during my duties. He had been seconded to the Crime Prevention Department and was going around shops and business premises advising them on internal security when he chanced to pass through Aidensfield. I was walking down the street in uniform and he hailed me. He, on the other hand, now wore civilian clothes, but they were as ill-fitting as his uniforms.

As he clambered out of his car, I was aware of that continuing gap which exposed a chunk of bare arm between his hands and his sleeves. He never did seem able to obtain jackets with sleeves long enough to cope with his endless arms.

We reminisced, as one always does on such occasions, and I reminded him of those village dances. He said he'd always enjoyed them, whereupon I said that Mary and I were going to the hunt ball next week: it was to be held in Aidensfield Village Hall and I was off duty that night. Several of us were forming a party – and I heard myself asking Geoff if he'd like to join us. Much to my surprise, he said he would. He did remind me that he was a teetotaller now, but I said it was nothing to apologise for; besides, the bar would offer soft drinks.

I said we'd meet him inside the hall at 9 p.m. that Friday night, then I went home to tell Mary the glad tidings. Her only comment was that she hoped he didn't ask her for a dance – she had memories of his efforts as a young man, for he'd ruined more than one girl's shoes by trampling all over them in his gallant attempts to musically co-ordinate the movements of his colossal feet.

Later, while reflecting upon that particular hunt ball, it was

Geoff's presence that caused me to ponder upon the lottery of life. Also attending the ball was Catherine Schofield, the daughter of Sir James and Lady Schofield of Briggsby Manor. She was up from London where she worked in an art gallery and had decided to accompany her parents. They were keen supporters of the hunt, but for Catherine it was a brave decision because she was not really known as a local girl – she'd been away at school and had also worked away, in addition to which her upper class lifestyle had segregated her from the attention of village Romeos. It was not surprising, therefore, that she was still single at the age of twenty-nine.

If one asks why she had not found a husband in London or among her own class, then it might have been owing to her appearance. Although her father was tiny, Catherine was well over six feet in height, and she was far from pretty. As featureless as a flagpole and just about as thin, she had no discernible breasts or hips and wore peculiar spectacles and a hairstyle that made her look twenty years older than she really was.

Her light brown hair was worn in a tight bun and she had a penchant for sensible shoes and all-embracing shapeless dresses. The villagers called her Keyhole Kate after a character in the popular comics of the time. The poor girl did look like something from the past, but, like Geoff, she was charming and she was blessed with a delightful sense of humour.

On the night of the hunt ball she needed every ounce of that humour because I was suddenly aware of Geoff advancing towards her, arms and feet carving a wide swathe through the crowds.

To this day, I have no idea what caused him to pluck up the courage to make that move, but I was amazed to see him asking her to dance. It was an Eva three-step. To say they presented an astonishing sight is perhaps an understatement, but the truth is that the lofty couple did circumnavigate the dance floor head and shoulders above the rest of us, and Geoff did so without Catherine or anyone else tripping over his feet.

By some miracle, he kept them under control. And an even more astonishing miracle was that, at the end of it, Catherine was actually smiling with pleasure.

After another two dances with her, he brought her across to our group and introduced her. He bought her a drink and escorted her to supper. Mary and I were delighted....

And so a most unlikely romance was born. As I watched them that night, I did wonder whether this particular lottery did have some unknown force controlling it, or was it sheer chance that brought Geoff and Catherine together?

During the evening, I could see Geoff relaxing, I could see his shyness evaporating before our eyes and I could see the happiness in Catherine's eyes too. Here was a man, taller than she, who could make her laugh and be happy. If he stood on her toes, she laughed about it and he laughed about it too. Afterwards, we invited him back to our house for coffee before he drove home, but he declined, saying he had been asked to visit Briggsby Manor for a good-night drink. I wished him well.

'Will he be able to come to terms with Catherine's family?' Mary asked me as we drank our nightcaps.

'I don't see why not,' I responded. 'Class barriers aren't so restrictive these days. And he is an intelligent lad, you know.'

'I wasn't thinking so much of that,' she said. 'I meant his non-drinking stance. They own a brewery – I think Catherine's a big shareholder in it. Will he find himself facing a conflict of conscience?'

'True love will overcome that!' I laughed.

And so it did. Geoffrey left the police force to marry Catherine and he gave up being a teetotaller; he drank champagne at his reception and they went to live in London. He was found a position within the family brewery business and is now managing director. He is no longer a member of the Salvation Army and his suits are not only made to measure – they are actually made to fit him!

The last time I saw him, there was no long gap between his cuffs and those gigantic hands. In life's lottery, Geoffrey had drawn a winning ticket.

6 *Every Dog Has His Day*

Brothers and sisters, I bid you beware,
Of giving your heart to a dog to tear.
Rudyard Kipling (1865–1936)

Although the strong and friendly relationship between an Englishman and his dog is almost legendary, there are those who mistreat Man's Best Friend. Town and country police officers, the RSPCA, veterinary surgeons and many others can relate horror stories of our inhumane treatment, not only of dogs, but of cats, pets of all kinds, farm animals and even wild creatures. Even in these enlightened times, sadists go badger hunting and killing domestic cats for fun; they torment tiny creatures with whom they come into contact and tease the docile. Villains have been known to set fire to the manes of horses in fields, to poke out the eyes of trusting donkeys, inflate frogs with straws and shoot crossbow bolts into swimming swans and ducks. And there is worse.

But so far as dogs are concerned, the dogs' homes of this country are full of tragedies. Unwanted Christmas presents and birthday gifts are abandoned and left to die; dogs are left without food and water or denied veterinary treatment. Happily, many of them find their way into the caring hands of the RSPCA and other good homes, but some are not so fortunate.

The on-going catalogue of cruelty is far too extensive to include in a book of this type, but it is fair to add that police officers do care for the ill-treated animals they encounter. For example, constables on patrol frequently come across stray dogs, and they are obliged to care for them, if only temporarily, until they can be provided with a new home or humanely put to death. Country police officers in particular come across wandering dogs which have been thrown out of cars in remote places simply because their owners no longer want them. Why go to the trouble of driving into the countryside to abandon one's pet? Why not take it to a dogs' home or some other animal sanctuary? The sick logic behind such callousness is baffling.

After living in a domestic situation, the miserable, confused animals, some little more than pups, are unable to fend for themselves in the wild. Some are shot in the belief they are sheep worriers, but many simply starve to death or get killed in accidents. Some are trapped in snares set for rabbits; others die painfully through eating poisoned carrion. A few of these castaways are fortunate because they are found and cared for, either by country folk and farmers or by those who take them into formal care.

If a person genuinely cannot cope with a dog, then it is refreshing when they do make the effort to find it a good home, but it ought to be said that police stations are not repositories for unwanted dogs, nor indeed any kind of animal.

On a temporary basis, the staff of a police station will care for a lost or stray dog, but eventually the unwilling visitor will be removed to the nearest dogs' home or, failing that, destroyed. A police station, therefore, is not the place to which one takes an unwanted dog for convenience.

I was faced with such a problem while performing a series of half-day duties in Ashfordly. I was in the market town during the absence of one of the local constables, and at 9 a.m. one morning in early June was in the office typing a report about a traffic accident when the door opened and a scruffy child appeared at the counter. She was a girl of about ten with beautiful dark brown eyes and lank, unwashed hair which might have been a stunning shade of auburn had it been clean and cared for. She wore a faded old dress with a floral pattern upon it and her thin legs and arms were bare. She had a pair of old sandals on her sockless feet and a silver-coloured bangle on her right wrist.

'Yes?' I peered over the counter at her.

'Oi've found this dog,' she said with more than a hint of an Irish accent. She was hauling on a length of rope at the end of which was a large and beautiful dog; it followed her into the office. I recognized the breed – it was a borzoi, otherwise known as a Russian wolfhound, and was something like a large, silky haired greyhound, standing almost three feet high.

The borzoi was once a favourite of the Russian royal family and was introduced to this country just over a hundred years ago when it became a fashionable dog to possess. Although it was bred in Russia specifically for wolf-hunting, it was welcomed in this country for its beautiful, elegant appearance. Ownership of a borzoi soon became a status symbol.

The dog's predominant colour is white, and the one standing before me had patchy fawn-coloured markings about its body. Its tail was silky and it had a long snout with the most gentle of eyes peering up at me. It looked nervous as it stood in the police station and was somewhat grubby in appearance. I reached over to pat it, but it shrank away from me. A sign of ill-treatment perhaps?

'Where did you find it?' I asked the child.

'On the road, near our camp.' She did not smile.

'Which camp's that?' I asked.

'Oi don't know what it's called,' she said.

'By camp do you mean those caravans just up the road from here?'

'Yes, we're travellers. Moi ma said Oi had to bring the dog in here.'

'Ah!' Now I remembered something. I recalled an entourage of filthy lorries, vans and caravans which had turned up one day about a fortnight ago. These were not true gipsies, but didicois, tinkers, scrap merchants, travellers or whatever. The council had been trying to move them on and we kept an eye on them because of their petty thieving and unsocial behaviour. Some of the smelly menfolk were prone to causing trouble in the pubs.

It was while I looked at that girl, that I realized I had seen the dog before. It was a striking animal, not one to be easily overlooked, and in my various patrols past that collection of awful vehicles, I had seen the dog tied to a tree. It had been there the whole time, for several days in fact, so this was no stray dog! This child was trying to get rid of it, I was sure!

I decided to put her to the test.

'What's his name?' I asked.

'Carl,' she said instinctively.

The dog did respond to the name, but not in the way that a loved dog would do: there was no wagging of its tail or signs of happiness, just a slight reaction, a twitching of its ears and a slight movement of its head.

'So your mum doesn't want Carl any more and told you to bring him here, eh?' I said.

'She said to say Oi'd found him ... '

'Then I'm sorry, young lady, but we do not take dogs in just because people don't want them. You need the dogs' home. Now, what's your name?'

'Leela,' she said.

'Leela what?'

'Smith.' She had a captivating smile. It was amazing how many travellers were called Smith. Try serving a summons on one Jake Smith and dozens will step forward, smiling a challenge; they are impossibly cunning.

'OK, Leela, you take Carl back to your mother and say I would not take him. If she wants to part with him, she must take him to a dogs' home – tell her there's one in York. They'll look after him, we can't do that. Do you understand?'

'But mum said you look after lost dogs.... '

'We do. We look after lost dogs, Leela. Lost ones, not unwanted ones. So take him back to your mother, OK? He's a lovely dog, Leela. You can't want to give him away, surely?'

She shrugged her thin shoulders. 'He's all roight but he wants a lot of food and exercoise ... '

I did not ask how the family had obtained Carl, but I did persuade the child to leave the station and to take the lovely dog with her. I just hoped Carl would not be abandoned and that these travelling people would take him to a home where he would be cared for.

Two hours later, a squat, heavily built and very untidy woman stomped into the police station, and I saw that she was towing Carl behind her. She had the striking black eyebrows and hair of the Irish and dark brown eyes; once she would have been pretty. Now she was gross, unwashed and perspiring.

'Oi want yous to take this animal.' She plonked her end of the rope on the counter. 'It's a stray dog, mister. It's been following us for days.'

'It's not a stray, Mrs Smith,' I used what I guessed was her name. 'It's your dog and we are not a dogs' home. You'll have to take it to York or give it to a good home. We take in strays, he's not a stray.'

'He would be if Oi bloody well turned him loose ... '

'I think you care too much for him to do that,' I suggested. 'At least you tried bringing him here instead of just abandoning him. It shows you feel for him.'

'Look, constable, he needs a good home, a better home than we can give him ... '

'Where did you get him?' I asked.

'Oi told you, he's a stray, he just turned up,' and she waved her hands in an expression of helplessness. 'Oi don't know where he come from but we can't keep him. We're travelling all the time and there's nowhere for him.... '

I must admit I had mixed feelings about this. I would have liked to have taken the dog off her hands because her motive was sound. I was sure we could publicize Carl's plight so that someone would come forward to offer him a home. But I also knew that Sergeant Blaketon and the others had been keeping an eye on those grotty vehicles and had seen the dog. They would know he was not a stray and I would get myself into trouble if I accepted him. Besides, police stations were never intended to be alternative dogs' homes. I had to be firm; to accept him might start an avalanche of unwanted dogs. These travellers might want to dispose of other animals!

'I'm sorry, Mrs Smith,' I said. 'But I just cannot accept him, it's not allowed. If you take him to the RSPCA or some other sanctuary, I know they'll be delighted to receive him, he's such a lovely animal.... '

She glared at me for a long time, her subdued fury being contained in that massive body, and I expected a torrent of powerful Irish oaths to flow, but they did not.

'You'll be sorry for this!' and she snatched the rope and stalked out of the building and past the railings with the magnificent dog trotting at her heels. I watched her go along the street with just a feeling of regret. If I'd wanted a dog of my own, I wouldn't have refused that one ... he was a real beauty and he looked so docile, albeit in need of a good home.

When she'd gone, I locked up the office to undertake a foot patrol around the town before knocking off at 1 p.m. It was now approaching 11.45 and I had a few calls to make; there would be no problem filling that hour or so.

But when I returned to the station just before one o'clock I saw Carl sitting on the footpath. One end of his rope was tied to the police station railings. He looked at me as I approached and I detected just a flicker of a wag from his tail. I stopped at his side and patted his silky head.

'So who brought you this time, Carl?' I asked, looking up and down the street. There was no sign of the Irish woman or any other travellers, so I loosened his rope and led him into the police office.

We kept some tins of dog food and biscuits to feed our canine guests and I gave him something to eat while I completed my written work. He ate with some sophistication, not wolfing down the food as I might have expected, and wagged his tail when I offered him a bowl of water.

Before I left the office, I placed him in the kennel behind

the building and left a note to inform the incoming constable that we had a guest. I put an entry in the Stray Dog Register, saying the dog had been left tied to the police station railings and that I was trying to locate the owner.

On my way home for lunch, I drove past the site of the travellers' camp, but they had gone. All that was left was a pile of ghastly rubbish and some scorched earth where they had lit their fires. It was no good chasing them for I had no idea of the direction they'd taken and they probably had a long start anyway.

From home, I rang Ashfordly Police Station to tell PC Alwyn Foxton that I'd looked for the dog's owners without success.

'What a gorgeous dog!' he enthused over the telephone. 'Isn't he a gem?'

'He is,' I said. 'But what can we do with him, Alwyn? I'd hate to have him put down … '

'Leave it to me,' he said. 'I think I know someone who'll give him a good home. Remember that chap last week, the one whose Afghan hound was killed by that bus? He said he'd never find a dog as good as the one he'd lost, and he couldn't afford to go out and buy one. Well, I might persuade him to have a look at this one.'

'Carl's his name,' I said.

'No, it was something like Newport … '

'The dog I mean!' I laughed.

'How do you know that if it's a stray?' he asked pointedly.

So I told him the detailed story and he praised the travelling woman for her efforts to secure a place for Carl, but said he'd treat the dog as a stray. If Newport did not want Carl, then we'd make a fuss about him in the local papers. That would surely produce someone who'd love and cherish him.

That evening, Alwyn rang me.

'Carl's gone to a good home,' he said. 'Mr Newport said he looks like a pedigree animal … he's delighted.'

And so the story did have a happy ending. Some two weeks later, I saw Mr Newport walking Carl beside a local stream.

The dog's lovely silky coat had been beautifully groomed and Carl appeared to be in superb condition; dog and master looked the picture of happiness and contentment.

And when I said, 'Hello, Carl,' the dog wagged his tail.

* * *

Ownership of a large dog is one way of ensuring a moderate level of physical fitness.

Because large dogs must have regular exercise and lots of activity, then their owners can also benefit; they receive beneficial exercise and activity. It was this simple logic that came to mind one evening when I found myself off duty and having a drink with Chris Ellis.

Until that time, I knew him chiefly by sight. In his early thirties, he was a quiet, well-dressed man who worked for a local department store. He lived in Aidensfield and drove his second-hand mini into Ashfordly every day to work. His home was a tiny stone cottage tucked under the lee of the hill, where he had two small children and a charming, but mousey wife. She rarely mixed with the other young women but did send her two children, a boy aged three and a girl four and a half, to playgroup. As some of my children also attended the same group, I was acquainted with the family.

I liked Chris. He was a pleasant-mannered man who took life seriously, perhaps a little too seriously, but he did his best for his family. Although his wage was low, he kept a clean, tidy home and ensured that his family were well fed and content. And I knew his wife had a part-time job which helped to clothe the family.

On the evening in question, he and I were among half a dozen men who had volunteered to do a little maintenance to the Catholic church we all attended: the roof gutters needed cleaning, the path needed weeding, some woodwork needed a coat of paint and several other jobs demanded attention.

Father Luke had recruited a band of volunteers, and as we worked, I found myself alongside Chris Ellis. Afterwards, we all adjourned to the Brewers' Arms for a pint or two. I found myself telling Chris about my love of the North York Moors and highlighting some of the sights and scenes to be explored. He surprised me by saying he had never ventured onto the moors – I told him there were isolated streams where the children would love to play, castles and old abbeys to visit, some picturesque walks to undertake, beauty spots to admire, villages to potter around and craftsmen's premises to examine. I told him about some particular places where we took our children – places where they could roam without hindrance and paddle in the cool waters of crystal clear moorland streams. There were wild bilberries and brambles to pick in the autumn and basking adders to observe in the summer....

But although Chris had lived all his life on the southern edge of those moors, he had never ventured into their depths.

'I'd love to go, Nick,' he confessed to me over our drinks, 'but I haven't the time now. As a kid, we never had a car so Dad couldn't take us, but now that I manage to run an old car, I never have time to take a ride out there … '

'But you must have!' I cried. 'What about weekends?'

'I work Saturdays,' he said. 'All day, in the shop. Wednesday is my half day, but Marie goes out on Wednesday afternoons to her little job while I look after the children. She takes the car, you see. She works for a plumber, does his book-keeping. It's not much, four hours a week, but it helps with clothes for the kids.'

'And Sundays?' I persisted.

'We go to my mother-in-law's for lunch and stay the afternoon.'

'Every Sunday?' I asked.

'Yes,' he said quietly. 'Every Sunday after Mass.'

My heart felt for him. 'You mean she asks you … '

'Yes,' he nodded, sipping at his pint. 'We can't get out of it. She gets upset if we suggest not going. She can't see why we don't want to go … to be honest, I'm pretty fed up. I mean, once every fortnight wouldn't be too bad, but every week … ' and he shook his head almost in despair.

'You've tried to break the routine?' I asked.

'You bet I have. I have no parents now, so I can't use them as my excuse. But she's a widow, Marie's her only child and she insists on doing Sunday lunch for us all – she loves seeing the bairns. Sometimes, I think we're doing a Christian duty towards her, and sometimes I think it's a real pain ... '

'She sounds very selfish to me,' I muttered. I could appreciate the woman's loneliness, but she ought to have some respect for her daughter's own needs and recreation. Marie's mother was rapidly making herself into a burden.

'I mean,' Chris went on. 'It's not as if she hasn't friends, she has lots. She goes to the WI, she's busy with flowers for the church and that sort of thing, so she's not totally alone like some old folks. She could invite some of her friends in – some other lonely person would love the chance for company at lunch.'

I commiserated with him and we bought more drinks. He poured out his agony to me and I felt it was probably the first time he had been able to do this: his wife would be biased towards her mother. As we grumbled into our pint pots, I heard myself saying,

'What you need, Chris, is a dog.'

'A dog?' he was puzzled.

'Yes, a big dog. One that needs lots of exercise. One that would benefit from long walks on the moors. One you could train to your own standards, or even show in local dog shows.... '

'Why would I want a dog like that?' he puzzled.

'To get you out of your mother-in-law's house on a Sunday,' I smiled. 'You'd need to train it, exercise it ... '

'I can't afford to buy a dog like that,' he sighed.

'You'd get a good one from the dogs' home in York,' I told him.

And so he did. That February, he turned up with a beautiful golden retriever called Cassius and promptly set about training him and exercising him.

Very soon, Chris and Cassius were familiar figures about the village and along the neighbouring footpaths, often strolling beside the village stream or through the fields. One day, I asked how his new mother-in-law avoidance scheme was working.

'So far so good,' he beamed. 'I'm taking things slowly. I've not put it to the test yet, but I've told mother-in-law that big dogs need exercise and training. I said there are dog training classes at weekends and that I might have to miss lunch one of these Sundays.'

'And?'

'Well, she agreed, funnily enough. It seems her husband kept labradors and had to exercise them, so she knows about dogs … '

In the weeks that followed, I kept in touch with Chris and his plot. Then, one Sunday, he'd told his mother-in-law that he could not come to lunch. Marie and the children would come as usual, but he had to attend a one-day dog-training course with Cassius. It was to be held in Malton.

Having been primed to that notion, mother-in-law accepted his story without question. It was the break he needed. Within a month, Chris was saying that Marie was needed at some of the classes. The instructor suggested she attend to familiarize Cassius with any regular commands she might have to make – the dog needed to know all his human companions for it must not become a one-person dog.

And so mother-in-law found herself looking after the children while Chris and Marie took Cassius to his classes. Then, quite deliberately, they omitted to tell her that there was no class on one Sunday. They let her believe there was. And so Chris and Marie went off for the day, alone.

That single outing, following the challenge of training Cassius at Malton, had finally persuaded Marie that they ought to have more time to themselves, more time away from her mother's constant and not-so-subtle demands.

With Cassius quoted as the reason for missing that Sunday lunch, it was Marie who suggested to Chris that they take the children out and show them the moors, to show them sights she had only just discovered. They could play with Cassius in the streams and among the heather, and with summer coming along there would surely be some wonderful outings....

Chris was delighted, especially as the idea had come from Marie, but it backfired. Marie's mother insisted on coming too. Once she heard that Chris, Marie and the children were going out for a picnic, she invited herself along. It was a crush in the car, with mother-in-law, two children and Cassius on the rear seat, but there was no option.

Thereafter, mother-in-law inflicted herself upon Chris and Marie – she even went to the dog-training classes when they resumed.

'At least we get out of doors,' Chris smiled ruefully one day when he told me all this. 'It's better than sitting indoors all day, and we do see something of the countryside. But she won't leave us alone ... not even for a day!'

'You'll have to take Cassius for very long walks, then,' I laughed.

And so he did.

He told mother-in-law that they were going for a twelve-mile hike across the moors with Cassius, and invited her to join them. She declined, saying there was no way she could cope with such a trek at her age, and offered to look after the children. And so off went Marie, Chris and Cassius once again, but it seems the children were not too happy about that arrangement. Having tasted a world beyond granny's front room, they made their noisy, argumentative presence felt until she did not enjoy them at all. They wanted to be with their mum, dad and Cassius and they let their grandma know in no uncertain way – the good children of those earlier days had changed into noisy, demanding kids.

Then, one week, mother-in-law suggested that Chris and Marie take the children out with them; she'd stay at home, by herself, alone, with nothing to do and no one to see. If nobody wanted her, she would cook lunch for herself. She'd sit and watch television, all by herself. She'd do some knitting. She might do the washing, seeing she was alone....

'I know she's piling on the agony, but we've got to make the break,' Chris had told Marie yet again. And so they did. Marie now appreciated that they must not allow her mother to dominate their lives, and so they left her alone that Sunday while they took the children and Cassius onto the moors.

The last time I saw Chris, his weekends had fallen into a new pattern – he had given up dog-training classes, but he and his family did avoid the trap of being committed for lunch every Sunday with mother-in-law. It was not easy – they had to be alert to all her ploys – but they did visit her, they did take lunch with her once a month or so, and they did have picnics with her and the children. But all were enjoyable occasions, not imposed upon them by Royal Command.

'It's all thanks to Cassius,' he smiled one day.

But I did wonder what would happen when Cassius was too old to go for long walks. Would mother-in-law look after him while the others went out?

No one knew, but I was pleased to see that this young couple had learned to be as cunning as mother-in-law.

* * *

Britain is rich in stories of dogs whose faithfulness to their master or mistress has become part of our folklore. One of the best known is surely Greyfriars Bobby, a terrier owned by a Borders shepherd called Jock Gray. When Mr Gray died in 1858, Bobby went to his grave in Greyfriar's churchyard in Edinburgh and watched over it.

He remained at that graveside until he died in 1872, an astonishing period of fourteen years. He was fed by the local people and adopted by the city as a mascot. Upon his death, he was buried beside his master. A fountain near the church bears a statue of Greyfriars Bobby and that tiny dog's unfailing loyalty to his master has been a talking point ever since; his statue is now one of the tourist attractions of Scotland's capital city.

But many villages and towns offer similar stories of dogs,

albeit lacking the sheer endurance of Bobby. One such dog was a Border collie owned by a retired Aidensfield farm worker. The dog was a black and white sheepdog, locally known as a cur. These dogs are very popular with the sheep farmers of the Yorkshire dales and moors for they are hard working, very devoted and highly intelligent. The dog's name was Roy. His master was called Douglas Grisedale. Doug had laboured on local farms all his life and had retired, with his wife, to an old folks' bungalow in Aidensfield. He was a frail-looking man, hardly the robust character one tends to associate with heavy farm work. Very slender, with gaunt cheeks and dark eyes, he had retained his black hair even though he was going on for seventy. Doris, his wife, was a round and cheerful lady with pink cheeks and plump legs; she liked being busy and involved herself with all manner of organizations. She helped to run the village hall, she cleaned the church, joined the WI, became a parish councillor and so on.

Doug, on the other hand, was a quiet man who preferred to be alone, a legacy of his years of solitary work in the fields. He occupied his time with his bees and his garden and seemed quite content with his very peaceful retirement.

His constant companion was his dog, Roy. Although Roy was a sheepdog, he had never been used for shepherding, although from time to time he did reveal his natural instinct by rounding up hens and ducks in the village, then lying to watch over them as he contained them in the corner of a paddock. Doug would call him away and the dog would release his captives.

Man and dog went everywhere together. If Doug walked down to the post office for his pension or across to the pub for a pint and some tobacco, then Roy would accompany him. Doug seldom spoke to Roy, although he would sometimes say 'sit' or 'stay' and the dog would obey without hesitation. At other times, we would hear Doug say, 'Come on, awd lad', or 'Shift thysen, awd lad'. Awd lad was a term of endearment, meaning 'old boy'.

Roy was not a young dog; he had accompanied Doug during the latter years of his work on the farm and I guessed he would be around nine or ten years old when I first encountered him and his master. In observing them, it seemed as if there was some mental telepathy between the two because if Doug turned left or right, the dog did likewise at exactly the same time. Sometimes, it was uncanny to watch them.

On one occasion I saw them walking towards the post office when the dog suddenly stopped outside a cottage and sat down on the footpath. There had been no command from Doug; indeed, he continued along his way to leave Roy sitting alone. Then I saw a lady calling from the upstairs window of that cottage. She was trying to catch Doug's attention. Within seconds, her loud voice had halted him, but Roy was already waiting ...

The lady, a friend of Doug and Doris Grisedale, had seen him passing and wanted him to bring her some stamps. Had she called to Doug from inside the house so that, at first, he had not heard her voice? Could that call have been heard by the dog? Did the dog respond to a call of 'Doug' as it would have responded to its own name? Or maybe Doug had heard the call and was spending a few moments debating whether or not he should obey it? Had Roy made up his mind for him? We shall never know. It was a minor incident, but rich with interest; a curious example of the rapport between Doug and his dog.

In following his master everywhere, Roy's patience was endless. Whenever Doug went to the toilet, for example, Roy would lie outside the door and wait, even if it took Doug half an hour. I was to learn that the dog even slept outside Doug's bedroom door and that when he sat in at night to watch television, Roy would lie at his feet; but if Doug moved, Roy was on his feet in an instant, ready to follow wherever his master went.

Whenever Doug went to the post office or into Ashfordly for some garden seeds or equipment, Roy would go with him and wait outside the premises.

Their companionship spanned the years and then, one fateful morning, I spotted Roy lying outside the surgery. He was stretched out with his chin on the threshold of the door which stood open and I knew Doug must be inside. Indeed he was; it was a rare event for him even to speak to a doctor let alone visit one, and I wondered what was the problem. But I didn't ask. After all, in the twilight of their years, many men did have problems and ailments which could benefit from a doctor's wisdom.

But the next thing we knew was that Doug was being whisked off to a hospital in York for tests. It was decided to detain him there. No one spoke openly of their worries about Doug because one never likes to air one's hidden fears, but it was Doris who hailed me soon afterwards. She caught me as I was filling the tank of the police van at the garage.

'Mr Rhea,' she said, 'Roy's run away. I've tried to keep him in but he got out the day before yesterday. I've looked everywhere Doug used to sit or go, but I can't find him.'

'He'll be pining for Doug, is he?'

'Aye.' There were tears in her eyes. 'Aye, he is,' she said quietly. 'They're inseparable, those two.'

'I'll put a note in our books. We'll ask our lads to keep their eyes open,' I promised her. 'Has he got a collar on?'

'Aye, with our name and address on it,' she nodded. 'Doug said we'd better do that if Roy was coming to live in a village.'

'Good. It'll help if he has wandered off.'

It was next day when I got a call from York Police.

'PC Stevenson, York City,' said the voice. 'We've got a stray dog here, a sheepdog, with the name Grisedale, Aidensfield on the collar. They're not in the telephone directory so can you call and ask them to pick him up? He's a lovely dog, but a bit thin and dirty. We wouldn't want to see him stuck away in the dogs' home.'

'Where was he found?' I asked.

'Hanging about at the County Hospital. He's been trying to get inside. They found him in one of the corridors and brought him down to us.'

'His master's in there,' I said softly, with more than a hint of tears in my eyes. 'Keep him safe, will you? I think he's walked all the way to York to be with Doug … '

'You're joking! It's all of twenty miles!'

'I'll be in touch,' I assured him after telling him about Roy's devotion.

Doris did not drive, and I could hardly justify use of the official van to drive into York to collect the dog, so when I went to inform Doris that Roy had been found, I said,

'Doris, you'll be wanting to visit Doug, won't you? So if I drive you in this evening when I'm off duty, I can leave you at the hospital while I pop down to Clifford Street to collect Roy. Then I can fetch you both back home.'

'That would be nice, Mr Rhea,' she smiled. 'I get the bus in as a rule.'

While I was with her, I remembered to pick up a lead for Roy.

Our local bus went to York on Tuesday, Thursday and Saturday mornings and returned in the afternoons, so poor Doris would not see much of Doug, although I knew that several of the villagers would take turns to drive her in. My offer was therefore accepted with pleasure. It was during that drive into York that I learned the truth about Doug's condition – he had cancer of his intestine. It had only just been discovered but it was so far advanced that he would not survive. It must have been eating away at his innards for months, perhaps years. But he had never complained. If only he'd gone to a doctor earlier … he must have known things weren't right … I learned he had only a short time to live, six months at the most. Doris was very brave about it.

I dropped her off at the hospital and went to the Clifford Street headquarters of York City Police to collect Roy. He recognized me, but he was thin and dirty, not the handsome dog I knew so well. But he jumped into my car without any trouble and sat on the front seat as I drove back to the hospital.

Even as I approached, his mood began to change; he

whimpered and wagged his tail, looking at me as if trying to ask me something, and I knew what he wanted. He wanted to visit Doug. That's why he had walked all the way to York, without food or shelter....

'I'll see what I can do, awd lad.' I used Doug's own phrase as I patted Roy on the head.

I went into the office on Ward 4 and was fortunate to find the duty doctor, Dr Holt. I explained about Roy's adventure and I could see the doctor was moved. He went so far as to say that the presence of the dog might cheer up Doug who was miserable in his enforced inactivity. I did explain that Roy was, at this moment, somewhat dirty after his escapade, and did remind him that Roy had already been here of his own accord, hoping to visit Doug. Holt remembered the dog ...

'We had no idea.' He shook his head. 'We thought he was just another stray nicking scraps from our wastebins ... but even if we'd caught him and seen the name on the collar, I doubt if anyone would have linked the two.... '

I felt sure that Roy's visit would not be a surprise to Doug because Doris would have told him, but as I led him into the ward and released his lead he galloped directly to the room in which Doug lay. He knew exactly where to go. The emotion of their reunion was overwhelming, not only for Doris and me but for all the occupants of that small ward, men who had learned of Doug's attachment to his dog. They and their visitors wept as the crying Doug fondled his dog's ears and the happy Roy made a fuss of his master. The meeting had a powerful effect upon all of us. Then everyone cheered up. The other patients wanted to meet Roy, they wanted Doug to tell them about him; some were city people who knew nothing of the relationship between a farm worker and his dog. They wondered how on earth he could have found his way from Aidensfield to York – that was something no-one could determine. And as I watched, wiping my own eyes, I knew we could not separate the two, not now. Not after what Doris had told me. As the couple and their dog made friends with everyone, I slipped out to find Dr Holt.

'I saw what happened,' he said quietly. 'It's astonishing.'

'You know my next request?' I put to him.

He nodded. 'It's not been done before – hygiene, you understand. Dogs are not really allowed in the hospital, let alone in the wards, and he is more than a bit scruffy.'

'Doug would soon put that right,' I said. 'Roy is house trained and he would not come into the ward unless he was allowed. This really is an amazing relationship. Roy would lie outside all day, just waiting. He'd need the occasional walk, that's all, and some food … Doug would see to that.'

'Doug's not fit to see to that, Mr Rhea,' said the doctor. 'He is a very sick man, more than his wife realizes, more than he realizes.'

'But not more than Roy realizes?' I said.

'Point taken. OK, the dog can stay,' Dr Holt said. 'I will clear it with the authorities … '

'Doug will tell Roy what to do, how to behave and so on,' I assured him.

And so, contrary to hospital regulations, Roy was allowed to remain. The nurses fell in love with him and he had no shortage of walks. One of them bathed him to clean him up and they took turns to feed him. Another found some old discarded blankets and made him a bed outside the ward door. But Roy never ceased his observations of Doug. As predicted, he spent his time lying just outside the door of the ward, his nose to the floor as he watched the passing events inside.

At visiting time, he was allowed in – he went in whether or not anyone escorted him, following the other visitors even if Doris was not there. In those final days of Doug's life, man and dog were happy; there was no doubt that the dog's presence did help to ease that time for Doug. But after less than two weeks, the ailing Doug passed away in his sleep. Dr Holt knew because Roy began to whine and ask for admission to the ward, but there was nothing anyone could do.

At the funeral, Roy walked beneath the coffin as the bearers carried it towards the altar, and during the service the vicar allowed Roy to lie on the altar steps, his eyes always on the coffin. After the service, he again walked beneath the coffin on the way out to the churchyard, tail between his legs.

He whined miserably as the coffin was lowered into the dark earth and uttered a weird, heart-rending howl as the vicar threw a handful of loose earth onto the coffin. Then, like Greyfriars Bobby, Roy lay down beside the grave and refused to move. In spite of pleas from Doris and her friends, he would not go home to eat or drink nor would he touch any food brought to him. He simply faded away.

Roy died three weeks after Doug and the vicar allowed him to be buried in the same grave. Later, when the family erected Doug's tombstone, there was an addition to his epitaph.

Beneath the inscription to Doug's memory, there were the simple words: '*Roy, his friend – 1953–1966.*'

7 Men of Letters

It is a place with only one post a day.
Revd Sydney Smith (1771–1845)

Aidensfield and the villages which surround it are most
fortunate with their postmen and postwomen. The service
they provide has always been infinitely more than the mere
delivery of letters and parcels, and this is because the postie, as
he or she is affectionately known, visits every home in the
area. The postie does not visit every home *every* day of course,
but because of the nature of their job, these uniformed
messengers are in a unique position to meet everyone and to
become aware of any social problems that might arise. This is
especially so among the lonely, the elderly and the infirm.

One of the finest ways for a lonely pensioner to gain the
attention of the postman is to offer him a cup of tea or coffee
during his rounds. Here in North Yorkshire, our mail comes
early – mine arrives between 7.15 a.m. and 7.45 a.m. as a rule
and we do receive it on time. Some Londoners think our
papers arrive a day late and our letters spend a week in transit!
This is not the case – in my morning mail, I receive lots of
letters date-stamped the previous day in London and
elsewhere, even those bearing second-class stamps. For us, the
service is superb, especially as it is carried out on such a
personal basis.

The postman knows us and we know him. I know that if we
are away, he'll leave the mail next door or even keep it until we
return; if we're still in bed when he arrives, he'll tuck it under

the front step or even call back if the morning weather is likely to harm any mail he leaves for us. He will take the trouble to decipher difficult handwriting or incorrect addresses, and he'll share our joy when postcards arrive from friends in exotic places, or commiserate with us when we get final reminders from the income tax authorities or the electricity people. He'll say 'I see your Aunt Agatha's leg is getting better' or 'What's that lad of yours doing in Sri Lanka?' This kind of relationship is not regarded as prying, for, in a village community, knowledge of another's life-style and habits can sometimes be a life-saver. Any good policeman knows that – as does the nurse, the doctor, the vicar and, of course, the postman.

Even in the depths of winter when snow, ice or fog can render other services impotent, the post manages to get through and so it maintains the enviable reputation of the Royal Mail. Few of us bother to say 'thanks' for this remarkable achievement – but we do blame the postman if the letters we are expecting bring bad news! This harks back to primitive times when emperors executed messengers who delivered bad news! We still blame the man who carries the letter rather than the person or organization that wrote it.

Here in North Yorkshire, with vast uninhabited areas to cover along with daily visits to isolated farms and cottages, our postmen must begin their day very early. Some occasional deliveries involve a trek of up to two miles through countryside that is rough enough to make a fine training ground for tanks, or remote enough to be utilized as a practice range for firing cannons. Consequently the delivery of some letters can be a tiring and long-drawn-out affair. By ten o'clock in the morning, therefore, most rural postmen (and in that term I include postwomen) are ready to sit down with a cup of hot tea and a biscuit. And it is a wise person who offers that kind of sustenance and sanctuary. The benefits can be tremendous.

This is where the lonely or house-bound person can score lots of Brownie points with the postman. A cup of tea or coffee and a hot, buttered scone can be like a feast to a tired and footsore postal delivery operative, especially on a wintry day. And, in return, the postman will offer to undertake small chores. I know one lady pensioner in a moorland village who feeds passing postmen with meals large enough to be described as banquets; in return they do her shopping and run her messages. As she cannot easily get to the shops or call on tradespeople, the postman of the day will take her order and obtain the necessaries, delivering them when next he calls for his coffee and buns. It is an admirable arrangement.

I know of postmen and postwomen who light fires for pensioners, who feed dogs and cats for people at work, who collect laundry, shopping, dry-cleaning and pensions, who change library books, collect eggs and deliver sacks of potatoes or turnips. One collects fish-and-chips on Fridays and another checks the snares laid by a farmer who is rather lame – that postie's reward is the occasional rabbit or hare. This is a most useful kind of barter system, and it helps to keep a community happy and in touch with one another. In these modern times, the postman can quite easily store a sack of potatoes or a case of wine in his van for delivery to a local house; in the good old days, it would not have been so easy, for there was a limit to what could be carried on a postman's bike or in the sack on his back.

But there was one postman who had another kind of regular commitment, one which I did not know about for some time. He was Postie Win. His name was Winston Charlesworth, a man whose unfortunate initials had earned him the childhood nickname of Closethead. Even at that time, the mid-1960s, not every village home had a water closet or WC as they were known; some continued to use the earth-closets, sometimes known as thunder-boxes, johns or necessaries, abbreviated to nessies.

Winston had the sense to make fun of his own name and initials, and this confounded those who tried to mock him. As he matured, he wooed and married a local girl, but for some reason they had never produced any children.

This was sad because Winston had come from a large and

caring family and loved children – he was Father Christmas at village parties and was a friendly character who bred rabbits and guinea pigs in his tiny back garden.

Winston earned his living as the postman for Elsinby, covering several tiny villages, including Waindale, Ploatby and Thackerston. He knew everyone and they knew him; he was the kind of good-hearted fellow who would undertake any of the chores I have already mentioned but who expected nothing in return. His tastes were simple and he was always whistling and singing as he went about his multifarious jobs. And to do his work, he rode a red post-office bicycle with a large front tray which sometimes seemed too full of parcels to be safe on the roads. Yet he coped, even if he did sometimes wobble.

Like all his rural colleagues, his round began very early each morning, about 6.30, and when I was undertaking any of my early patrols, we would often meet. We would stop for a chat and would swop yarns – we'd mention people we knew who might have developed the need for a quiet helping hand, or if there had been any crimes in the locality; I would ask if he'd seen any suspicious characters in the area. In his work, he saw far more than I, and so I could warn him of outbreaks of housebreaking, damage or vandalism, and he told the householders to beware of strangers and to lock up their goods. He kept a constant eye open for malefactors and we had a good mutual understanding.

I found it odd, therefore, one Friday morning, when I couldn't find him. There had been a hit-and-run accident near Elsinby; I knew he would be in the village, so where had he gone? I needed to find him urgently to ask him about the incident.

The reason for my anxiety began about 7.15 a.m. one late January morning. A 22-year-old girl called Jenny Green was riding her bicycle from Ploatby to Elsinby along the narrow lane which linked the two communities. It was a frosty morning and there were patches of ice on the roads; furthermore, it was dark, but Jenny knew the dangers and was riding carefully. She was on her way to Elsinby to catch the 7.30 a.m. bus to York where she worked in a shop. It was a trip she undertook every working day, even on Saturdays. She returned early on Wednesdays, however, that being her half-day. Each day, she left her bike in a shed behind the Hopbind Inn and rode home after work, her return bus arriving just after six o'clock. It was a long day, but she claimed she enjoyed the work and the chance to be involved in a city environment.

On that Friday morning, she had been riding along the correct side of the road, with her bike properly illuminated, when a car had approached her from behind. Jenny, upon hearing the car and seeing the spread of its lights about her as it came nearer, had eased to the left so that she was almost riding on the verge. But the front wing or some other part of the car had collided with her right handlebar; the impact had unbalanced Jenny and thrown her off her bike and into the hedge. The offending car had not stopped, but in her distress, Jenny had not noticed any material details; she couldn't even say whether it was a large or small, red or blue, Austin, Ford, Vauxhall or Rolls-Royce, nor had she noticed its registration number.

Fortunately, Jenny wasn't badly hurt although she did suffer a few cuts and bruises and a lot of scratches from the thorns of the hedge. Her clothes were also torn, she had ripped her nice winter top coat, and the front wheel of her bike was buckled. She was more angry than injured and hurried to a nearby cottage for help. I was told about the accident some twenty-five minutes after it had happened, long enough for the offending car to reach York and get lost in the traffic, but I hurried to Jenny's parents' home in Ploatby. I found her battered bicycle outside with Jenny in the kitchen, sipping a cup of hot sweet tea as her mother fussed like a broody hen. I established that she did not need medical attention; Mum would see to the scratches.

I tried to take firm details but Jenny could not provide me with any hint as to the identity of the car; the only thing she could say was that it had never passed her on any previous morning. Normally, no one passed her during that short ride. Only when she reached Elsinby did she see other people and cars.

That morning, of course, she hadn't got as far as Elsinby and so no one there could help.

She was adamant that the car's nearside mudguard or even its wing-mirror had touched her handlebar and unbalanced her, and from that I doubted whether the car would be damaged. Maybe the driver had no idea he'd touched her? That was possible – if his wing mirror had caused the problem, the smallest touch could have unbalanced Jenny. I finished up with no description of the offending car, other than it was well illuminated and it was not driving at excessive speed. That tended to rule out a stolen vehicle being used by a joy-rider.

Nonetheless, I rang our Sub-Divisional office to circulate the car as being involved in a hit-and-run accident, thinking that if the car was going about some illicit mission it might attract attention elsewhere. I realized that it must have driven through Elsinby moments after upskittling Jenny, so perhaps someone there had noticed it? Someone like Postie Win?

By the time I had taken Jenny's statement, measured the scene and circulated details, it was almost nine o'clock, and when I began inquiries in Elsinby, most of the people who'd been around at 7.30ish had gone to work. But Postie would be around.

I began to look for him, hoping to catch him emerging from a cottage, but I never saw him. Nor did I see his familiar red bike. I began to grow concerned – I hoped the offending car had not knocked him off his bike too!

Was he lying hurt in a ditch somewhere? Had he been knocked into the stream which ran through the village? Was he lying in a hedge, or unconscious in someone's back garden? I toured Elsinby in my van, looking for Postie and his bike, but failed to find him. I must admit I was growing worried, for he was *always* delivering in the village around this time. Just after 9.15, I decided to call at his home. Perhaps he was ill? I had to know.

Mrs Charlesworth answered my knock. 'Is your Win about?' I asked.

'He'll be at the school,' she smiled, checking her watch.

'Of course!' I had forgotten about the school. It lay half a mile out of Elsinby along a narrow lane, and because there were no cottages there, I'd forgotten he might call there with any letters and had omitted to search that area. I told Mrs Charlesworth the reason for my call and she said she'd ring the Greens to ask after Jenny; maybe she'd need some ointment picking up from the chemist's? Win would see to that if she asked him....

As I drove towards the school, I was relieved to see the familiar red bike leaning against the wall with its front tray full of parcels and letters. As I climbed from my van to walk towards the school I could hear the children singing their morning hymns: it was assembly time. And then, as I reached the gate, I could see Postie Win.

He was standing at the head of the class, conducting the children and singing louder than them, thoroughly enjoying a spirited rendering of 'Dear Lord and Father of Mankind'. And he had a superb voice. I wondered whether to go in ... but he spotted me and beckoned me inside. I decided I could justify this intrusion because I could ask if any of the children had seen the car – it was hardly likely, but some youngsters did get up early to feed their ferrets or rabbits, walk their dogs and milk their goats.

The headmistress smiled a welcome.

'Hello, Mr Rhea. Come in. We're just finishing assembly.'

'I see you've got a good singer there!' I laughed.

'Winston always comes to sing with us,' she said. 'Every morning. He leads the children in their hymns.'

At this, Winston joined us. 'I love a good sing-song,' he said. 'Well, I must be off.'

I halted him and told the story of the hit-and-run, but he couldn't help – he hadn't seen the car. With the teacher's help,

I asked the children too, but they all shook their heads. I thanked them for helping me and the headmistress asked me to call back sometime, by prior arrangement, to tell them about my work. I said it would be a pleasure. I walked out with Winston and he said he'd keep his eyes and ears open for the car; maybe it was a newcomer to the area, maybe this was his first day at work and he was rushing ... it was all maybes.

'Thanks,' I said. 'And well done, singing like that with the children.'

'I love a good sing-song,' he laughed. 'Singing with those kids gives me a marvellous start to the day. I call in every morning. You can't beat a bit of hymn-singing with the bairns to remind you what life's all about. Well, I must be off.'

'Where to now?' I asked.

'Old Mr Coates,' he said. 'I light his fire for him every morning. Then it's Miss Bowes. Her washing machine's playing up – I think it needs a new belt so I said I'd fix it ... '

'It's a busy life, being a postman,' I laughed.

'Being a postman's the easy bit!' he chuckled as he rode off. And then he called, 'I'd better pop in to see if Jenny Green wants anything, eh? Maybe her bike needs fixing!'

I was to learn that he had straightened the buckled front wheel by the simple expedient of laying the wheel flat on the ground and jumping on its rim. It had sprung back into shape. Jenny took the following day, a Saturday, off work and resumed on the Monday, riding her bike as usual to catch the bus.

I had learned a little more about the philosophy and routine of a local postman, but we never did find that offending car.

* * *

Mortimer Micklethwaite was another rustic postman, but his achievements did not meet the high standards of those undertaken by Postie Win.

In fact, Mortimer's achievements were practically nil because he was no good at anything. Born to ageing parents, and having suffered the trauma of being born in an era when medical care was not of a high standard, poor Mortimer was one of life's losers. Some said that if he'd been a tup lamb or a bull calf, he'd have received better care from the vet than he did from the aged midwife who'd delivered him.

Some said his mother had been frightened by a mad donkey just before Mortimer's birth, some said she'd seen a ghost as Mortimer was entering the world, and others claimed she'd seen the devil himself, but whatever had gone wrong at birth had resulted in Mortimer being rather simple. His mental capacity was likened to that of a frog, so by no stretch of the imagination could Mortimer be described as a bright lad. Locally, it was said he was as fond as a scuttle, as empty as a blown egg, as daft as brush or as soft as putty. In Yorkshire, the word *fond*, in this instance, means stupid. Poor Mortimer was rarely flattered or praised.

He and his parents lived in Crampton where his father had a joiner's shop tucked away behind a huddle of red-roofed limestone cottages just off Dale Street. Arthur Micklethwaite was a craftsman, there is no doubt about that, and one of my joys was to visit his workshop, there to watch him at work amid the powerful scents of seasoned timber and wood shavings. His workshop was always warm, even in the depths of winter, and he never seemed to hurry yet always delivered commissions on time.

He did a lot of work for Crampton Estate and his immaculately finished products ranged from superb dining furniture to five-bar farmyard gates via coffins and church benches. He'd even made cart-wheels as a lad and was still a proficient wheelwright, sometimes creating them for people who wanted them to adorn their gardens and patios. A visit to Crampton today will reveal many of Arthur's cart-wheels still adorning village walls and gardens.

But when I first knew Arthur, he was well into his eighties, albeit still working, while Mortimer was getting on for forty. To Arthur's credit, he had tried to teach Mortimer his craft, but I knew from village gossip that Mortimer could not absorb any of his father's tuition. He was just too thick, but he did continue to help his father, often being allocated simple tasks like sweeping the floor, chopping up end-bits for firewood or even priming bare timber prior to being painted. But he could never be trusted to make anything, not even something basic like a toothbrush holder or bookends.

Within a couple of years of my arrival at Aidensfield, Arthur had died, leaving his business to Mortimer. After all, he was Arthur's only son, and with a bit of coaxing from his mother, Annie, the lad might just be able to scrape a living. But Annie was also in her eighties and a little frail and although she did know a lot about the running of the business, she was unable to provide Mortimer with the necessary full-time guidance. But Mortimer did try.

One brave householder, a newcomer to the village, commissioned Mortimer, now hailing himself as Crampton's Cabinet Maker, Undertaker and Wheelwright, to replace some rotten window frames. A local person would never have taken that risk but Mr Slater, a retired businessman from Liverpool, did not know of Mortimer's weaknesses and believed in making use of rural craftsmen. The task was simple – three cottage-style windows along the front of Mr Slater's country home had rotten frames which must be replaced. Mr Slater would be away for two weeks during which time the work could be done. Mortimer, so proud at being asked to do such an important job, said he'd fix them.

I was in the village when Mortimer's handiwork was being fitted into the gaping hole from where he had removed the first window. I halted out of curiosity, my interest being aroused by the sight of the diminutive Mortimer actually doing some work. One of his father's old friends was helping.

Mortimer, a mere five feet tall with a long face and thin, sandy hair, was clad in his father's old apron with an array of tools in the front pocket like a kangeroo's pouch. The two men were attempting to fit the window frame into the gaping hole. But from my vantage point at the other side of the road, it was clearly impossible. Mortimer's newly made window, devoid of glass, was far too small for the hole they had created by removing the existing one, and it was the wrong size for either of the remaining two window spaces.

'Thoo's got all t'measurements wrong!' grunted the helper.

'Turn it round sideways then,' said Mortimer.

'Thoo daft ha'porth, that's neea good! Tonning it sidewards only makes it worse! Onnyroad, some of these spaces thoo's made for t'glass is inside out! By, thoo's made a right pig's ear of this job, Mortimer!'

To cut a long story short, Mrs Micklethwaite hired another local carpenter to make and fit the new windows; she would pay him out of the fees to be paid by Mr Slater.

And so the job was done in time for Mr Slater's return.

When Slater saw the handiwork, he was delighted.

'You know,' he said in the pub later, 'it's nice to see the work of a genuine craftsman. You don't get such skills in Liverpool. So, I shall be asking Mr Micklethwaite to undertake more work for me.'

Everyone was so astonished that they said nothing. In fact, due to his mother's influence, Mortimer did just that. Everytime he was asked to do a carpenter's task, his mother commissioned a neighbouring craftsman, and so Mortimer became a middleman and, with his mother's help, did manage to earn a meagre living. In the meantime, while his 'workers' performed their craft, Mortimer chopped up bits of wood for sale as firewood and kindling, sometimes inadvertently demolishing valuable antiques or pieces left by his father for incorporating in fine furniture.

He also spent a lot of time sweeping his shop floor, and so effective was he that his shop became known as the tidiest and cleanest in Yorkshire. One reason was that it was never used.

His enterprise as the village undertaker came to an abrupt end when a local man, Jonathan Holgate, became terminally ill. Mrs Micklethwaite prepared Mortimer for the task of building the coffin by explaining what would happen when Mr Holgate did eventually pass away, but the silly Mortimer upset the family by going to the house to measure Mr Holgate while he was still alive. Some said the shock killed Mr Holgate.

And then Mortimer's own mother died. As a final act of love, Mortimer built her a coffin which would have accommodated a giant, but the vicar allowed the funeral to go ahead even if the resultant grave looked large enough to be a communal one. But Mortimer was proud of that job. Upon his mother's death, however, the problem was – what would Mortimer do now that his mother had gone? She had done her best to sustain him by helping him with the business, but she had had limited success.

Acting alone, Mortimer was incapable of running the workshop, useless at performing the necessary craftsmanship and incompetent at organizing his business and personal life. Then an answer came, as if from heaven. The village needed a postman.

The postmistress, Dorothy Porteus, put a notice in her shop window to say that her husband, Lawrence, was retiring as the delivery postman and that a new one was required.

It was a part-time post because Crampton was a small village; the job demanded some four hours work each day except Sunday, and it was a permanent position. The small wage ruled out most family men and it would not be easy filling the position; then someone suggested Mortimer. He had the time, he needed the money, he never left the village and he knew everyone. It seemed an ideal answer. He went to see Mrs Porteus and she filled in his application form, knowing the right words to use. She said she'd have a word with the head postmaster in York and would recommend Mortimer for the job. She'd remain as postmistress to issue stamps, postal orders, pensions and so forth as she continued to run her general store and newsagency, and Mortimer would deliver the mail.

And so, with the minimum of fuss, Mortimer got the job.

There was only one real problem.

Mortimer could not read.

His mother and father must have known, but Mortimer had managed his own affairs without anyone realizing that particular deficiency. When Mrs Porteus had filled in his application form, Mortimer had signed it, something he had learned to do, and thus no one in the post office had discovered his secret. It was revealed on his first morning's duty. The Ashfordly post-office van delivered a pile of letters and packets to Crampton village shop-cum-post office, as Mortimer arrived to begin the day's delivery.

His first task was to sort the letters into some kind of logical sequence for his walk around the village, and that's when Mrs Porteus realized what she'd done. But she did not want to appear a fool by admitting her error and so she told Mortimer where to deliver his first few letters, advising him to ask a householder if he reached a confusing stage.

For several blissful years, therefore, Crampton was served by a postman who could not read. Mrs Porteus would set him off with his first handful of letters, telling him which houses to visit, and then he would ask for advice at one of the houses for his next directions. The villagers soon realized the problem, but they decided never to reveal it – after all, they would look a bit silly if they told the world about Mortimer.

Through this mutual aid from the villagers, the post was always delivered; that incredibly efficient network of advisers kept Mortimer's secret and it provided him with a welcome and necessary income and occupation.

I must admit that I knew nothing of this until I went into Crampton to deliver a summons. It had been sent to me from Manchester City Police with a request that I deliver it personally to a Mr Charles Finney who lived at Snowdrop Cottage in Crampton. It was for a careless driving charge in the Manchester area, but I did not know Finney, nor did I know where to find Snowdrop Cottage. Most of the houses did not have names or did not display their names, the logic being that the villagers all knew one another.

As I drove into Crampton that morning, who should I see but Mortimer in his postman's uniform and carrying a big sack of letters. I halted my van and approached him with the address of the summons uppermost.

'Where's this house, Mortimer?' I showed him the address. 'There's no street name given.'

He peered at the typewritten address and shook his head.

'No idea, Mr Rhea. Sorry.'

'But you do know the man, surely?'

'What man, Mr Rhea?'

'This man, the man named here. Mr Finney.'

'Oh, that man! Yes, he lives in Moor Street, third house along. Used to be called Jasmine Cottage till the jasmine died … now it's Snowdrop Cottage because the garden's full of snowdrops in February … '

I looked at him.

'You can't read!' I realized. 'You've no idea what it says here, have you?'

He blushed and hung his head; he'd been brought up never to lie to a policeman and I could see he was acutely embarrassed.

'Does the post office know?' I put to him.

He shook his head.

'And so, for the last few years you've been delivering the mail without being able to read the addresses?'

'Aye,' he said. 'They help me if I'm stuck. I know a lot now, by the shape and colour of the envelopes … regular stuff, you know.'

'Well, if you've managed all this time without the post office knowing, I'm not going to tell them, Mortimer.'

'Thanks, Mr Rhea. It's a good job for me, is this one.'

I smiled and nodded. 'The best,' I said, going into Moor Street to deliver my summons.

8   Currents of Domestic Joy

'Withindoors house – the shocks!'
Gerard Manley Hopkins (1844–89)

'The decorators are coming in a couple of weeks, Rhea,'
Sergeant Blaketon rang at half past eight one morning to
inform me. 'I'll send you the official notification – it's internal,
all rooms upstairs and down, and the office. You'll be given
some wallpaper sample books to make a selection from, within
the official price range that is. The decorator will see you
about your choice of paper and paint, but don't go mad, we
don't want the police house looking like a sleazy night club, do
we? But the office will be in the official colour, cream walls
and woodwork. We want none of your psychedelic pinks in
there.'

At this news, my heart sank. Several times during my
service, Mary and I had suffered the intrusions of the official
decorators, both internally and externally. They came as an
army, van loads of white-overalled men who plonked huge
smelly cans of paint all over the place, followed by rolls of
wallpaper and paste buckets, and who ignored the domestic
routine which had to continue midst the mayhem. They came
at eight in the morning and covered everything with protective
sheets, then left at 4.30 in the afternoon after consuming
gallons of coffee or tea. This invasion lasted for about ten
days, i.e. two whole weeks discounting weekends.

The internal decoration of our police houses was scheduled
once in every seven years, with the external woodwork being

repainted every four years. The outside work was never a real problem unless the days were very cold – the painters seemed able to work only when all doors and windows were standing open. It was the internal decorating which was more disruptive; it was worse than moving house. Some officers managed to avoid internals – by being transferred around the county and exchanging police houses on a regular, short-term basis, some had never experienced the trauma of being internally decorated. At times I wondered if they engineered their transfers simply to avoid the decorators.

But others, like me, seemed to arrive at a house weeks before the decorators were due; even though we seldom occupied our police houses for more than three years, we always contrived to be resident when they were due to be decorated internally. Once I had to tolerate the wallpaper choice of the previous tenant because he suddenly moved out after making his selection and had gone to pastures new before the decorators came to honour his and his wife's wishes. Fortunately, their choice was tolerable. Conversely, we had one of our houses decorated shortly before we moved out: our bedrooms were done in nursery rhymes and fairy-story pictures, not very welcoming for the teenage lads who followed us.

On this occasion at Aidensfield, however, things were likely to be more difficult than usual.

One problem was that we had four tiny children, and the second was that I was working shifts, including nights, which meant on occasions I'd be trying to sleep during the daytime while the painters were working. The logistics of getting the painting done in tandem with our frantic domestic routine promised more than a few headaches. I could anticipate finger-marked doors, upturned paintpots and lost tempers from all parties. Much of the aggravation would fall on poor Mary for, unless I was on nights, I would be out of the house on duty, and thus out of the way, for some eight hours of most painting days.

For me, it was a strange experience having decorators to do

the work, for I'd always been brought up to do my own painting and decorating, household maintenance, repairs of domestic machinery, fitting of tap washers, installation of wall lights and so forth. For me as a child, DIY was not a new fad – it had always been my father's mode of living and so it was with me. It was odd, therefore, watching others do what I would have normally done myself, but, in an official house, one had to abide by the rules. Even if a tap wanted something as basic as a new washer, the job had to be done by a professional engaged by the county council. What I could have done for the cost of the washer would cost the ratepayers a large amount. Nonetheless, we were allowed to decorate our own interiors within that seven years, and indeed I did so when convenient. In spite of that, seven-year internals had to be done on schedule.

The constabulary sought tenders from private contractors for this work and, because it was linked so closely to the county council, the police were compelled to accept the lowest offer. Thus quality did not enter into the bargain – the job was done on the cheap. Cheap paint, cheap paper and cheap labour was employed. When a contractor was awarded the work, it meant he usually had many other police houses to decorate as part of his contract. As a consequence, he would rush around them all to strip off the old wallpaper and check the old paintwork, then he'd tear about with undercoats, followed by gloss paint, probably decorating five or six houses at the same time.

It did take about ten days to complete one house, but those ten days were not always consecutive, sometimes being spread over a month or more. This also meant that if he said he'd come to our house on Monday, it might be Friday by the time he arrived owing to some unexpected delay, but we had, in the meantime, cleared the rooms in readiness. The disruption could be considerable and there is little wonder we never looked forward to our nice new decor.

But that was the system and we had to abide by it. Some of us grumbled; some of us said if the authorities gave us the money it cost to complete that seven-year internal, we could do the work ourselves. This was looked upon with some scepticism for one senior officer asked, 'But if we give you the money, what guarantee have we that you'll do the job?'

Such was the trust among one's fellow officers. Another suggestion was that we did the work and obtained receipts for the expenditure on materials, with inspection of our handiwork being welcomed. This was also frowned upon, one excuse being that some officers might not be very capable DIY decorators. So none of our suggestions was considered. The system would not be altered – the houses would be decorated internally every seven years by the contractor who submitted the lowest tender, and that was that.

Within a couple of days of Sergeant Blaketon's call, therefore, we received large books of sample wallpapers with a note that we had to return them the same day because they had to be circulated among several of my colleagues. We had to make a note of the reference numbers for each room and the decorator would call shortly; we had to give him those numbers and inform him for which room each paper was intended. He would inspect the rooms to determine the precise number of rolls required. The kitchen would not be wallpapered – its walls would be glossed and so would those of the bathroom/toilet upstairs and the downstairs toilet. We could wallpaper each of the three bedrooms, the lounge, the dining room and the entrance hall/staircase/landing. The cost must not exceed the stated total amount, but if we had cheap paper upstairs we could have more expensive designs in the reception rooms downstairs.

And so we laboured over those books, having to rush our selection from the somewhat limited range, but Mary and I did find some papers which met our joint approval. And there were papers for the children's bedrooms which they helped to select – nursery rhyme scenes, Disney characters and so forth. Now we awaited the visit of the decorator who had won the contract and we knew what to expect – he would try to persuade us to accept different, cheaper papers. He would highlight those of similar colour and design, and if we succumbed to his charms, he would make more profit.... We'd experienced this technique many times before and so we knew the tricks of their trade.

Shortly afterwards, I received a telephone call from a Mr Rodney Osbourne of Osbourne's Decorators, saying he'd like to call and discuss our requirements. We arranged a time when I'd be at home and, on the day in question, Mary had the kettle boiling and some home-made buns ready. We would show Mr Osbourne some hospitality at this early stage. We reckoned that would shorten pressurized discussions with him – if we were nice to him, he would respond with efficient service.

At the appointed time of eleven o'clock, a scruffy white van arrived in our drive from which a short, round man emerged. Thin strands of dark hair formed a bizarre network on his balding head; he wore rounded spectacles with heavy rims and a brown dustcoat with pens in the breast pocket. He had a clip-board in one hand and a book of wallpaper samples in the other.

I opened the front door and invited him to enter. He shook my hand and said, 'Osbourne.'

'PC Rhea,' I introduced myself. 'Nick. And this is Mary, my wife, and the children.... '

All four emerged from the lounge where they were playing and stood staring at him. He patted them on their heads and said, 'They'll be going to stay with their granny, are they? When my fellers come?'

'No,' I said. 'They'll be here.'

'I don't do this for a profit, you know,' he began. 'There's no profit in doing police houses. I just take the job on to keep my men in work and you know, when times are slack. Kids can cause delays, get in the way, you know, and I don't want delays, I can't afford delays, not on a cut-price job like this ... '

'Their grandparents are all at work,' I said. 'We can't expect them to take time off to look after our kids. Besides, they're well behaved ... '

'They all say that. I could tell you some tales about

policemen's kids ... '

'Cup of coffee, Mr Osbourne?' asked Mary quietly.

'Wouldn't say no,' he said, following her into the kitchen as I shooed the children back into the lounge. I told them to stay there until we had finished talking to the gentleman and asked Elizabeth to keep an eye on the others. Even at her tender age, she could control her brother and sisters. But their excitement was too great – they had all been told about their new bedrooms, about the new paint and wallpaper, and were anxious to see the miracle-worker who would achieve all this. Four tiny heads appeared around the kitchen door, but they remained quiet, watching him as a cat might watch a playing mouse. Mary's coffee and buns achieved their intended purpose and he said he'd tolerate the bairns if they were kept in one room while his men operated.... The more controlled the children were, the sooner his men would finish.

Then followed the anticipated 'advice' about our selection of wallpapers.

'Now for that back bedroom you'll need seven rolls of that one you've picked.' He scribbled on his pad. 'But in this book here, there's one the same colour as yours, but the pattern's smaller, which means we can use less rolls, you know, one less mebbe on a room that size ... that's a saving, you know ... it all adds up and we don't make a profit on these jobs ... '

'Then we could have more expensive paper in the lounge,' said Mary, smiling at him with all her feminine charm.

'Now I wasn't quite thinking like that,' he countered. 'I mean, there's little enough in this for us as it is, and so far as the lounge is concerned, I think this one here ... ' and he flicked to another in his book, 'is better than your choice – smaller pattern, lighter background, prettier an' all, hard wearing, you know, where the kids'll touch it ... '

'We were told not to exceed the sum allocated,' I said. 'And our choice does that, Mr Osbourne, even allowing for big repeat patterns and extra rolls ... '

'Aye, well, I was just trying to be helpful, you know, not restricting you to that first book, you understand.'

'Thanks, but we are happy with that book,' I said. 'We've made up our minds.'

'Oh, well, so long as you're happy,' and he closed the pattern book with a snap of its pages. 'Well, if you let me see the rooms, I'll work out the number of rolls … '

Having been decorated many times, the Force records contained the numbers required because all local police houses had rooms of a standard size and that had already been taken into account in allocating the contract to Mr Osbourne. But we did not object. He went round the rooms, jotting things down on his pad and making a fuss of measuring windows and doors.

'Magnolia,' he said, tapping a window ledge in the main bedroom. 'Gloss.'

'Magnolia, in here?' Mary looked at me.

'It won't go very well with our bedroom paper,' I said. 'Magnolia's a creamy off-white, isn't it? We were thinking of something that would be a better match.'

'Magnolia goes with anything, you know,' he said. 'That's why we use nowt else, gloss and matt, emulsion and paint.'

'We'd like a pinkish tint on this woodwork,' Mary tried. 'Something that's more in keeping with the new bedroom paper.'

'Put a pink bulb in your bedside lamp, Mrs Rhea – it'll give out a lovely glow, and your magnolia'll look grand. It'll pick up surrounding colours, you know – get a red sky in the morning and that magnolia'll look lovely. Blue skies make it look good, even grey skies give it charm, so they say.'

'But I don't want magnolia,' she said.

'It's in the contract.' He tapped his pad with his pencil. 'Magnolia on all interior wood surfaces. It says so in writing. It's been agreed.'

I had no way of countering that statement and winked at Mary. I said we'd accept it. Magnolia it would be – all over!

'When will you be coming?' I asked. 'I need to know so that I can clear the rooms and make them ready.'

He pulled a tattered diary from his rear pocket and flicked through it.

'Three weeks on Monday,' he said. 'Eight o'clock sharp.'

Mary did a quick calculation.

'That's the week my mum's coming to stay,' she said. 'Can you make it a week later?'

He checked his diary again. 'Right, yes. No problem, I can do a job in Eltering that week. Right. Four weeks on Monday it is.'

And off he went.

'You shouldn't have agreed to magnolia all over!' Mary grumbled afterwards. 'I'm sure we can choose colours, within the price range.'

'I know, but I'll have words with the workmen when they arrive. They'll ignore their boss – he doesn't paint any more, he just organizes things. We'll get our pink paintwork, you'll see.' I felt sure I could persuade them towards our wishes.

Mary's mum came on the Sunday evening a week before the painters were due and said she'd help to prepare the house for them. There were carpets to take up, furniture to remove, paintwork to wash down and so forth, and the painters wanted us to live in one room while they prepared and decorated all the others.

But at eight o'clock that Monday morning, the painters arrived. I was in bed, having worked half-nights until 2 a.m. A very anxious Mary knocked me up.

'They're here!' she cried. 'The painters. And mother's here, and you're in bed and they said they weren't coming till next week … '

'Tell them to come back next week,' I groaned.

'The foreman says no, he's been told to come here now, today. They're already moving paint pots and all their stuff into your office … '

I struggled out of bed and went down to greet the invaders. By then, they'd half-filled my office floor with tins of paint and rolls of wallpaper. I succeeded in identifying the foreman.

'We weren't expecting you. Your boss said you'd come next Monday,' I tried valiantly. 'You're a week early!'

'Well, he was wrong, mister. Our schedule says today, and

he said nowt about a change. If we miss today we'll be out of work a week and we can't afford no wages, not like you blokes with secure jobs, and if we wait till next week, you might have to wait months because we'll have to re-schedule our rota, and then Harry's going on holiday and it'll cause a right cock-up in our office and things are bad enough there as it is, what with Sandra getting pregnant and being sick every morning, and there's nobody to order the paper and paint, and the police and fire brigade all wanting houses done, and them nurses' homes.'

I began to wish I hadn't asked.

'Right, you can stay.' I decided that the sooner we got this job finished, the better. 'We'll cope. But can you do a favour for me?'

'Depends,' he said.

'We'd like delicate pink, blush pink I think they call it, on the bedroom woodwork instead of magnolia.'

'We've only got magnolia. It's magnolia in here, your office that is, and the kitchen and bathroom, glossed walls, matt emulsion wood and ceilings ... the contract says magnolia on all woodwork. I've got my orders.'

'If I get my own pink paint, could you put it on?'

'We're not allowed to use other folks' materials, but seeing as we've caused a bit of hassle, I'll see if we've any pink in our warehouse, or red. We might mix red with magnolia ... '

And so they stayed. It was chaotic. To enable them to whizz around the house with brushes flailing, and to give them a clear run in as many rooms as possible, we had to live and eat in one room. The snag was it was a different room each day. As Mary, her mother and the children huddled in one room during the day while I was out in the countryside, the painters slapped on gallons of magnolia undercoat and gloss; it would dry overnight and then they'd use the gloss. But at night, I had to move all our furniture into the room they'd just done, watchful of wet paint, because the next day, they wanted to be in the room we were using.

Like nomads, we moved about the house to allow

undercoating and moved all over again to allow the glossing and then the papering. We lodged in the office, we sat on the stairs, the children cried, our meals were either like picnics or burnt offerings, and the office, newly painted in glorious magnolia, became an overflow second home/granny annexe. The children touched wet magnolia; they got magnolia in their hair and on their clothes; they left their fingerprints on magnolia door pillars, magnolia door frames and the magnolia staircase. But, surprisingly, the house did look better – except for the downstairs toilet. Our predecessor had painted the interior walls with a very dark blue gloss paint, but these men decided that it would have to be magnolia gloss. They slapped on a coat – and the blue showed through, making it a dirty kind of sea-green. It looked like the interior of a grimy fish-tank.

'You'll be putting another coat on that loo?' I said.

'No, only one coat of gloss,' said the foreman. 'That's the rule.'

'But it looks awful!' I grumbled.

'Some folks are never satisfied!' he said. 'Free decorating and still they're not pleased. By gum, I don't know what the world's coming to! Craftsman-decorated loos ... they'll be asking for hand-carved toilet seats next ... '

I gave up. I'd paint it myself when they'd gone because it was too ghastly for any of our visitors. It could put them off the purpose for which they resorted to this little room. The last room to be done was the main bedroom, partly because I was on night duty on that final Thursday and Friday.

I'd be out of the house from 10 p.m. until 6 a.m. While they were completing the decoration of my usual bedroom, I would sleep during the day in the tiny back room with its Snow White and Seven Dwarfs paper. In spite of our reservations, the two weeks had flown and the house was looking much better, even if it did smell of new paint and in spite of having to cope with mother-in-law and four children. In fact, she was an enormous help in keeping them occupied, taking them for walks and helping to organize the ritual shifting of furniture every night while poor Mary coped with all the other domestic chores.

And so, on that final Friday morning, I returned from my tour of duty at 6 a.m., had a light snack and climbed thankfully into bed.

The decorators would be here at eight and I would rise around 2 p.m. or so. As I climbed into my warm bed in the back room, Mary and the children were in our marital bed, with mother-in-law in the middle room, and I did not disturb them. Mary, the children and her mum would get up early to ensure everything was ready for the men to finish their work today and, by tonight, the house would be ours again. It would be smart and clean, fresh and new, albeit smelling of paint.

But I must have been shattered because I overslept. During the day, I'd been vaguely aware of movements on the stairs, of painters working and children trying to be quiet. Those disruptions and my night without sleep had conspired to keep me in bed until five o'clock. I woke in the knowledge that I was on nights again at 10 p.m. that night, but would cope easily after my restful sleep. But now the house was quiet. I peeped out of the bedroom window and saw that the decorators' van had gone, as had their ladders and other equipment. I smiled as I walked to the bathroom, but decided to inspect our lovely new bedroom.

It was covered with magnolia paint.

It looked awful against the colour scheme we had selected and I groaned. With officialdom, the little man can never win. I'd do it myself within a week or two ... when I had time. As I sat down to my evening meal with the scent of new paint all about me, I said to Mary,

'Darling, promise me one thing.'

'What's that?'

'When we get a house of our own, promise you'll never grow magnolia in the garden, that we'll never buy a house called Magnolia House and we'll never use magnolia paint in any of our colour schemes.'

'Oh, I don't know,' she smiled. 'I quite like it, now it's on.'

* * *

Being the wife of a policeman is never easy. There are the pressures of a unique kind of work, with the added menace of danger, and there are the unsocial hours that must be tolerated. If a policeman's tour of duty is scheduled to end at a given time and then, minutes before he is due to finish work some urgent task crops up, then he must attend to it. Unlike so many jobs, we cannot walk away from work when the hooter sounds. And, fortunately, police officers do maintain a sense of responsibility towards the public and will continue to work when needed.

This means that many officers work very long hours, especially those who serve in the CID: they can't cease their inquiries just because it's five o'clock and time to go home. Happily, many police wives understand this necessary commitment, and Mary was one of them. She knew that I had a responsibility to the public whom I served even if, at times, this did mean sacrificing a normal social life. It was very difficult to make definite plans for anything.

Even when I was off duty, in the evenings or at weekends, or perhaps having friends in for a meal, the public was not to know this, and if people came to the house I had to deal with them. If a man knocked on the door while I was enjoying time off and said he'd just been involved in a traffic accident in the village, then I couldn't ignore him.

It was a similar story even when I was not at home. If I was out on patrol, the police house remained a police house. Its continuing role was announced by its blue POLICE sign in front of the adjoining office and noticeboard. So when people wanted help, they would come to the house even if the sole occupant was a young, untrained woman with four tiny children. And, like me, Mary could not ignore anyone with a genuine, urgent problem. In such cases, she was always a tower of strength, always operating as my devoted unpaid assistant. From time to time, while I was away on duty, she'd coped with callers in trouble – like a woman who complained of rape, a man who had found a house on fire and a dead man inside, a lorry driver who had run off the road, victims of petty crime and all manner of other routine chores. In all cases, she'd coped with calmness and efficiency.

But the wife of a country policeman receives no pay or reward for her supportive work, save that her efforts are appreciated, coupled with the knowledge that the public hold her in high regard.

It follows that there were times when it was difficult for both Mary and I ever to be free from such responsibility. The only way to avoid continuous duty was to get away from the house altogether during my leisure hours. Mary and I therefore did our best to take time away from home during my days off, even when those days off occurred mid-week. I was always aware of the difficulties this caused, particularly when the children started school, and Mary's tolerance meant that I endeavoured to compensate her whenever I could. In spite of the demands on us, I liked her to go out alone, to get involved with village events, to drive into town or to have a life of her own.

I was delighted, therefore, when she was asked by the ladies of Aidensfield WI to attend one of their monthly meetings and talk about her life as the wife of a village policeman. I knew she would do a good job, even if she felt some reservation about speaking in public, and I persuaded her to accept the challenge. When the secretary suggested a date, I checked with my advance duty roster and found I was scheduled to perform duty from 10 a.m. until 6 p.m. on that day. Mary's talk was to begin at 7.30 p.m. in the village hall and so I could return home in time to baby-sit. The meeting was still two months away and so I could ensure I'd be off duty; if my duties were re-scheduled, I could ask a colleague to swap shifts if necessary. But my duties were not tampered with and Mary's big day arrived.

'You'll be sure to finish on time?' Mary requested as I prepared to leave home that morning.

'I've nothing pressing today,' I assured her. 'I'll be home at six.'

'But sometimes we've had to cancel things, dances, dinners and so on, when you've had to stay on to deal with a sudden death or an accident or something ... '

'There'll be other men on duty this evening,' I said. 'If something happens last minute, I'm sure I can get somebody to take over from me.'

The fear of some unexpected occurrence was always present on such occasions and I could understand Mary's concern: we'd had to cancel so many outings because of last-minute changes to my duty or through last minute official dramas ...

But that day, I set off with confidence, manoeuvring my little van onto the road. My first job was to visit the Section Office in Ashfordly to collect any waiting correspondence, and then I would drive to Crampton and Gelderslack to deal with several applications for renewals of firearm certificates. It was going to be a gentle routine day of non-urgent duties.

And so it was – until quarter to five.

My official radio crackled into action as I was ordered to attend a traffic accident on the road between Ashfordly and Brantsford. Initial reports suggested that a van had emerged from a side road directly into the path of a fast-moving car.

I groaned.

'Ten four,' I acknowledged. 'Will attend. Any report of casualties?'

'Negative,' said Control. 'It is a minor accident. A breakdown vehicle has been called and is en route. What is your ETA?'

'16.55,' I said, calculating that it was a ten-minute run from my present location at Crampton.

When I arrived at the scene, I found a small grey van in the ditch and a Ford Cortina on its side nearby. The two drivers were waiting, their anger long spent, and neither was injured. It seemed the van driver was at fault, thinking he'd had the time to emerge from a side road ahead of the oncoming car, when in fact he had not. The car driver had taken swift evasive action, but in spite of his efforts, had collided with the front nearside of the van, spinning it around and hurtling it off the highway. Neither man was hurt but each of their vehicles was badly damaged.

I obtained details including a statement from each, and decided that consideration would have to be given to prosecution of the van driver for careless driving. I told him in the formal jargon of the Notice of Intended Prosecution and was pleased when the breakdown truck arrived. It lifted the car onto the rear platform and hoisted the van onto its front wheels, then departed with both. The drivers went too. They would make their own arrangements to get home.

The immediate necessities of the incident were over; my typing of the report, my production of a scale plan of the scene and my preparation of the case papers could wait until tomorrow. It was now five minutes to six – I'd be a few minutes late booking off duty, but at least the job had been completed in good time. Mary would get her night out. I radioed Control to up-date them on the outcome of the accident and reported that the matter had been dealt with. I concluded by saying I was en route to Aidensfield to book off duty.

I'd only covered three miles when the radio burbled into action once again. This time it was urgent.

'Control to All Mobiles in Ashfordly/Brantsford/Eltering district. Urgent. All mobiles and foot patrols to rendezvous at Ashfordly Police Office immediately,' was the instruction. 'Await further orders there. Acknowledge. Over.'

I groaned aloud. I couldn't believe it! My heart sank as I wondered what on earth had happened, but I did recognize that the voice of the Control Room operator carried a note of real urgency. I responded by giving my call-sign and saying I was en route and would arrive within ten minutes. Mary's night out was in jeopardy once again but I could not intrude on the airwaves to ask what it was all about. I'd be blocking valuable transmissions. I would have to wait to find out more when I arrived at Ashfordly. I turned the van around and hurtled through the lanes.

When I arrived at the police station, other cars were assembling and Sergeant Blaketon was jotting down the names of those who had arrived.

'What's happened?' I asked Alwyn Foxton, the duty constable at Ashfordly.

'Two men raided the pub at Stovingsby,' he said. 'After hours. Not long ago in fact. They got in through the back door, tied up the licensee and his wife and got away with cash and jewellery. They crashed their car into a tractor while escaping – their car's a write-off and they've taken to the moors on foot. We're the search party. We're assembling here. The dog section's been called out. Once we're all here, we'll get our orders.'

My dismay must have been evident. I thought of poor Mary.

'Where were these characters last seen?' I asked.

'Heading across the moor towards Gelderslack. On foot,' he said. 'We've got other cars coming in from the north and traffic division's establishing road blocks, but finding those two won't be easy. The dogs might catch them,' he added.

'Have I time to ring Mary?' I asked, wondering if there was a free telephone.

'Sure, there's a few more of us to come before we get briefed. Use the one in my house,' he offered, for his house was next to Ashfordly Police Station. Mary was not at all pleased.

'But you said you'd definitely be home.' I could hear the disappointment in her voice. 'And I promised those ladies that I'd go … I can't let them down. How long will you be?'

'I don't know.' I couldn't offer any indication of a home-coming time, but added, 'I might be away all night, it depends.'

'What can I do then?' There was a note of desperation in her voice.

'Try Mrs Quarry,' I suggested. 'Surely she'll baby-sit at short notice, if she knows the reason … '

'But we put on her far too much, she's so good.'

'I'm sorry, darling.' Through Alwyn's window I could see Sergeant Blaketon calling everyone indoors. 'I must go, we're assembling for our briefing now. And good luck with the talk.'

She didn't reply as she put down the telephone and I knew she must be both angry and upset, but what could I do? I just hoped that Mrs Quarry was able to baby-sit. I had no way of keeping in touch with Mary as I received my briefing for the search. From the information received, the two men had broken cover to run into the hills above Lairsbeck, heading for the forests and open moors of Lairsdale. A farmer had seen them running and had called Eltering Police, and so one dog unit, two cars and eight officers had been directed there instead of attending our briefing. They would maintain contact. The hunt was on, and with the aid of radios and police dogs, we felt sure we would trace and capture the villains.

My brief was to patrol the higher points of Lairsdale, touring the isolated farms and cottages in that remote, widespread community to warn the widely scattered residents of the fleeing robbers and to record any possible sightings. It was seven o'clock when I left the office armed with a list of names taken from the electoral register and a map showing the position of remote farms and cottages in the higher reaches of Lairsdale. I wondered how Mary was getting on, but our official radios could not be used for contacting home. Although we had a radio on our official vehicles, the rural constables did not have official radios in their offices. Sometimes, if we were engaged in anything exciting, our wives would listen on our own portable radios – coded messages might sometimes be transmitted!

Mary would sometimes listen to my voice at work by tuning in to the police wavelength. Lots of people used this technique, including journalists, and so they could listen to a very one-sided commentary as we went about our more exciting duties. There was nothing illegal in listening – it became illegal if anyone, other than the police, acted on the information thus acquired. But Mary would not be listening tonight – hopefully, she'd be entertaining the WI members. I raced into the hills, anxious to get this job finished as soon as possible – I was hungry too, having been dragged away from any chance of having my evening meal on time! The sooner we got this job over, the sooner I would eat.

As I motored high into the dale with my radio burbling constantly, I saw a lonely roadside telephone kiosk. I'd ring Mary from here. But when I got through, Mrs Quarry answered.

'She's gone,' I was told. 'Not five minutes ago. Your supper's in the oven for when you get back…. How long will you be, Mr Rhea?'

'I don't know,' I had to say. 'But thanks for stepping in at short notice.'

'She said she should be back by ten,' Mrs Quarry told me.

'I might be in before then.' I was hopeful of an early finish. 'Or I might be later. I'm heading for Lairsbeck – we're hunting two robbers,' I added for dramatic effect.

'It was on the news,' she told me. 'But watch out and be careful.'

'I will,' I assured her.

'Don't forget to search Low Holly Heads while you're up there,' she added.

'Why, what's at Low Holly Heads?'

'Nowt,' she answered. 'It's a ruin now. My grandfather used to farm there years ago, for the estate. It's not far from the track that goes over those heights, though. A good hiding spot, I'd say, especially if those chaps are heading that way like the radio said they were.'

'Thanks, I'll check it out.' I was pleased to be provided with this piece of local information. All I had was a list of occupied farms, not ruins.

I'd bear it in mind, and a glance at my map showed it was close to my intended tour of the occupied premises. My initial visits produced no information; none of the farmers or cottagers had seen the runaways but at least they now knew of our interest and promised they'd contact us if the men did appear. By the time I'd visited all those outlying places, it was almost 8.30; darkness would fall around nine and if the men had not been traced, they might go to ground for the night. From reports over my official radio, I knew there had been no more sightings in other areas and our dogs had lost the trail near a stream. I decided it was now time to look at Low Holly Heads. I could take the van to within some three-quarters of a mile of the ruined farm, the final stretch of the old road being impassable to cars now. And so, as darkness began to fall, I walked down the track.

It led through a steep field, across a stream in the gulley below, and then climbed up the far side through a pine wood. The old farm lay on the slopes above that wood. I could see it in the distance, a stark stone-built house with most of its roof missing and its walls tumbling down. But parts were tiled and it did offer some shelter. As I hurried down the steep track, I heard voices and then a shout – they'd seen me! Two men were running away from the farm, climbing higher along the steep hillside. I'd be quarter of a mile away from them ... should I chase them, or call for help?

If I chased them on foot, I'd lose them, of that there was little doubt in this rough, expansive terrain, and so I ran back to the van, waited a moment to gain my breath and then reported to Control. I explained the difficulties due to the rough nature of the landscape, the lack of tracks, the steep hillsides leading to open moorland, the acres of heather and bracken, the gulleys and streams. Dogs would be needed, lighting would have to be available, a field radio system would be an asset – this was before the advent of personal radios for police officers.

I was told to wait at my van and to rendezvous there with the members of search party as they arrived. Two units of dog handlers had been despatched and the dogs would be put on the trail, consequently no one must interfere with the scent which led from Low Holly Heads. I confirmed that I had not trampled upon the men's tracks and this pleased Blaketon: so many villains have escaped due to police officers confusing the dogs by trampling all over the fresh scent trails.

I looked at my watch. It was nine o'clock. The sun had set and darkness was beginning to envelope the dramatic landscape as I wondered how Mary was faring with her talk. She should have finished by now. My radio was in constant action by this time, asking me for updates, for directions to the scene and for a recommendation as to the use of specialist vehicles, like a four-wheel drive truck which could be borrowed from the mountain rescue service.

Was there any track for such a vehicle to use? My own knowledge of the area combined with judicious use of the Ordnance Survey map suggesting the fleeing men would quickly reach the bridleway which formed a northern boundary to Lairsdale Moor; the track formed a semi-circle around the bulk of the rising moor and led to both east and west. It was used by Forestry Commission vehicles, ramblers and horse riders. I suggested that units be despatched to each end of that bridleway....

Within half an hour, Sergeant Blaketon arrived, rapidly followed by a mass of other police vehicles and officers, some of whom had been called out an hour early to begin their night duty. They'd started at nine o'clock instead of ten – I wondered how many of those had missed their suppers! The inspector had been dragged away from his and had opted to operate from the western end of the bridleway, taking with him several more officers. And so a huge search was mounted. Blaketon despatched two units of dog handlers to Low Holly Heads Farm where they succeeded in picking up the trail. Off they went, noses following the scent like bloodhounds, while I remained with my van and its radio, acting as co-ordinator for this end of the search because of my knowledge of the terrain.

It was a dog handler who caught the men. Having fled at the distant sight of me trekking towards their hiding place in Low Holly Heads, they had crossed the open moor to find shelter in an old sheepshed.

The absence of officers in hot pursuit had convinced the men they had evaded us and so they had settled down, whereas in fact we had been consolidating our search. The triumphant dog handler and his happy Alsatian escorted the captives back to their vehicle and so to Eltering Police Station. And they were still in possession of the stolen property; their guilt would never be in question.

It was 10.30 when I returned to Ashfordly Police Station to record my part in the search, and quarter past eleven by the time I arrived home. Mary was back, I was pleased to say. I kissed her and said I'd be with her in just a few moments, when I had taken off my uniform and booked off duty. I knew she had rustled up a fresh meal for me – I knew that the moment I walked in from the scent of cooking which wafted from the kitchen. I then realized how famished I was. Now (hopefully) finished for the day, I put on my slippers and settled down to ask Mary about her evening. I found that, in spite of the late hour, she had set the table in the dining room; there was a candle in the middle and a bottle of wine already opened....

'Hey!' I was very pleasantly surprised. 'What's all this for?'

'They gave me a bottle of wine for talking to them, and, well, I thought I'd been unreasonable with you earlier, you know, getting cross with you when you're only doing your job ... so I did this, for both of us.'

I kissed her and cuddled her warmly, thanking her for this generous thought, and then we settled down to the meal. I asked how she had coped at the WI meeting. She smiled.

'Great!' she beamed. 'I took our portable radio.... I told them about the demands on us both, on you especially, not knowing what was going to happen next, and then we listened to that manhunt on the radio. I used it as an example of the things you get involved in, switching it on and off every so often to illustrate points. We could only hear one side of the broadcasts, but we did hear your name mentioned several times, especially just after you'd seen those men and were co-ordinating the chase ... the ladies loved it.... '

'What a brilliant idea!' I congratulated her and we discussed our respective evenings as we enjoyed that romantic and very welcome meal. But as we were just finishing the coffee, the telephone rang. Mary looked at me and I looked at her. I groaned and said, 'Oh, not again!'

Mary said, 'I'll answer it. I'll say you're still out … '

She went into the office to take the call and returned moments later.

'It was just Mrs Quarry,' she laughed. 'She wanted to know if you'd got back safely and if you'd searched Low Holly Heads Farm like she told you to.'

'What did you say?'

'I told her you had. I said you'd pop in to thank her and tell her all about it sometime. I said you'd caught the two men who had been there … '

'It's been a very successful night.' I felt content now.

'It's not over yet,' she said, taking my hand and leading me upstairs. I hoped the telephone wouldn't ring now.

9 Brotherly Feuds

Peter and Paul were brothers. Peter was the elder at forty-nine years of age, while Paul was two years younger. Both lived in Crampton and were neighbours, each boasting a fine detached house in the upper part of the village, not far from the church. Their homes had extensive views over the dale to the north and east, with open fields to the south; the ancient church with its fine tower blocked their view to the west. Both had nice wives and two children, a son and daughter each. Peter's wife was called Emma and Paul's was called Sandra.

Their surname was Almsgill, their father being Percy Almsgill, then in his mid-seventies. Percy also lived in Crampton, albeit in a pleasant bungalow whose lawns reached down to the banks of a stream which flowed into the gently moving river. He and Mrs Almsgill had handed over the family firm to their sons some ten years ago, hopefully to enjoy a peaceful retirement. They were keen gardeners and, having made a success of their building business, now had the wealth and the time to make their garden a showpiece.

P. Almsgill and Sons had been a prosperous and thriving local building firm, but some eight years ago the two brothers, each called P. Almsgill, had fallen out. Peter and Paul had had an almighty row.

No one knew the reason for the dispute, although the villagers had their own ideas, some based on rumour and some on speculation. It is doubtful whether anyone knew the truth. The rumours and speculation included tales that Peter had been found in bed with Paul's wife; that Paul had been found in bed with Peter's wife; that Paul had been fiddling money from the business; that Peter had been fiddling money from the business; that Peter worked hard while Paul spent his time socializing; that Paul had made a disastrous deal which had cost the firm lots of money and that Peter had invested the firm's profits in stocks and shares that had failed. But all these and sundry other notions were unproven – there might have been a little piece of truth in every tale, or they might all have been totally false. No one really knew.

Whatever the cause of their split, the two brothers each decided that they would continue with their building business and so there were two builders in Crampton, each still known as P. Almsgill and Sons. Each claimed theirs was the original P. Almsgill and Sons and neither would change the name of their business. They even continued to share the same yard. Old Mr Percy had acquired some derelict farm buildings years ago and had converted them into a very useful builders' yard. Here were his piles of stones and tiles, roof timbers and doors, kitchen sinks, bathroom suites and toilets, some under cover and some in the open air. He also acted as a builders' merchant, selling items to customers who called.

But in their feud, the brothers had agreed to use separate parts of the yard, although they did share a common entrance. Each had an office in what had once been pigsties, and each had his own stocks of commodities and equipment.

How the postman and those who came seeking work found the right P. Almsgill remains a mystery, although everyone suspected that it was the two wives who sorted out the mess. Somehow, the right bills reached the right office and the right orders arrived upon the right desk.

There was little doubt that Emma and Sandra were responsible for keeping sanity in the yard and helping to sort out problems that would otherwise be intractable. Two charming and lovely women, they had not fallen out and there is every reason to believe they regarded their husbands' behaviour as childish. The wives remained good friends and each acted as secretary to her husband's firm, dealing with representatives, taking orders, arranging deliveries to their premises and sites currently in work and generally retaining sanity among the work force, the villagers and the customers.

The older and original P. Almsgill, i.e. Percy, kept out of this altogether – his view was that he had retired and if those b— stupid sons of his were daft enough to throw away their prospects by dividing the business, then it was their loss, not his. And he and his wife remained on good terms with both sons and their wives.

In time, the village had grown to accept this nonsense. Somehow, most of the villagers knew whether to deal with Peter or Paul on any given matter – they went to Peter if they wanted a house built and to Paul if they wanted a cowshed. They asked Peter to fix the tiles of their roofs and Paul to lay a new drive. Peter would build a conventional cemented wall around a garden while Paul would construct a drystone wall around a field or paddock. Somehow, the local people created their own demarcation lines and so the two builders found themselves specializing in certain types of work – Peter did domestic work while Paul seemed to deal with agricultural matters.

Outwardly, therefore, the two businesses appeared to thrive in a peaceful manner; certainly, the two sets of workers co-operated with each other, sometimes helping one another when the occasion demanded. I'd seen Peter's workers helping Paul's to finish a new stable block before the onset of one winter, but was later to learn that this had arisen due to the common-sense attitude of the respective wives. The brothers had known little of that deal.

As the village constable, this kind of dispute was no real concern of mine. I was aware of the problem, even if I did not know or understand the root cause, but such family matters were of no professional interest to me unless, of course, they resulted in trouble of the kind that might bring the matter into the realms of a breach of the peace.

From the outbreak of the feud, there had been no such bother, the brothers managing to contain their problems within their own bounds, but for some unaccountable reason, the underlying cause of the feud suddenly resurrected itself. No one outside the family knew why this had happened or what had prompted the sudden eruption of feeling, but the first I knew was when someone dumped a lorry load of sand in the middle of a road in Crampton. It was right outside Peter Almsgill's house.

I was told by a gamekeeper who lived nearby.

'Mr Rhea,' he halted me as I drove towards the village. 'Some daft bat's dumped a load of sand near the church. It's blocking Church Lane. I thought I'd better tell you.'

'Right, I'll see to it,' I promised.

As the mound of sand was outside Peter's home, I went to the door to ask if anyone knew about it. The house was deserted so I went to the builders' yard and found Mrs Emma.

'Sand?' She was puzzled. 'We're not expecting any sand, Mr Rhea.'

'Well, it's blocking the road outside your house,' I told her. 'And it's blocking your drive.'

She groaned.

'I bet it's Paul,' she sighed.

'Paul?' I asked.

'They're at it again, Peter and Paul,' she told me with some resignation. 'I don't know what's set them off, but they've started to play stupid tricks on each other again.'

'I'll have words with Sandra,' I offered.

Sandra was in her office at the other side of the yard and nodded. 'It'll be our Paul, wanting to annoy Peter,' she said. 'I'll get our men to shift it, Mr Rhea, straight away, with a JCB.'

'Thanks,' I said. 'And tell Paul that if he does it again, I'll book him for obstructing the highway!'

'I wish somebody would bang their heads together, Mr Rhea. Can you do that?'

'They'd have me up for assault!' I laughed.

That episode marked the beginning of a series of ridiculous nuisances which were perpetrated by some unknown persons, but we all knew it was the work of one brother against the other. Unwanted logs were dumped in their drives; shoals of unwanted mail arrived; delivery men turned up with unwanted and unordered goods like tons of liquid cement, coffins, greenhouses and paving stones. Somebody sent Paul five dogs from the dogs' home; someone else sent Peter a load of useless furniture from an auctioneer's store; Paul was sent to measure a site for a pigsty and it turned out to be at a ladies' fashion shop in Ashfordly, while Peter was asked to begin negotiations for a new house: when he went to inspect the site, it was a village pond. And so the catalogue of fun continued, with Peter playing the bagpipes outside Paul's house at six in the morning and Paul buying a pet peacock which cried all night and day in its paddock next to Peter's bedroom.

Eventually, some of the villagers did complain because these silly pranks caused them annoyance – the peacocks got out and invaded all corners of the village, stealing hen food and calling incessantly to the distraction of people living nearby; Peter's bagpipe music, which he claimed was legitimate practice for his musical tastes, was disruptive and upset the vicar, while some of the bizarre range of dumped goods did cause blockages and obstruction to footpaths and lanes. A lorry load of surplus tiger dung from the local zoo was not welcomed, nor was a dumped cartful of raw slaughter-house waste considered suitable manure for Peter's garden. I warned the brothers from time to time, always avoiding a prosecution where possible by asking them to clear away their mess – which they always did.

Then, one day, I found Paul shovelling a heap of horse manure from his drive, throwing it into a lorry which stood nearby.

'Another prank?' I asked.

'That bloody daft brother of mine,' was all he said.

'What set all this off?' I asked.

'He sent me a bill for his bloody newspapers!' Paul said. 'I wouldn't have minded, but it was more than mine. He was trying to get me to pay his paper bills!'

'How much more?' I put to him.

'Ten bob,' he said.

'In a month?' (That was the equivalent of 50 pence today.) I added, 'It was probably a mistake.'

'Never. There's never been a mistake before!'

'Who sent it to you?' I decided to get to the bottom of this now that he was talking; it was the first time I'd heard him talk of the feud.

'It was delivered,' he said. 'By hand. It always comes by hand, but I reckon he swopped them.... Why should I get his bills, eh?'

'You know Laurie Porteus has retired, don't you?' I put to him.

'So what?'

'Well, poor old Mortimer's delivering the post now, and he can't read. Now, just suppose he slipped the wrong bill through your letter box, and Peter got yours ... it could have happened. Have you asked anybody? Peter? Emma? Mrs Porteus? Mortimer?'

He hadn't asked. I don't know whether that error had been caused by Mortimer's mistaken delivery, but Paul did shrink a little at my suggestion and then went indoors.

I didn't see him for a long time afterwards, but the series of pranks ended. Even so, the feud continued and still now, there are two building firms in Crampton, each called P. Almsgill and Sons. Old Mr Percy has passed on, but Peter's son, Percy, has since joined his father's business, and so has Paul's son, also called Percy. The confusion continues.

*   *   *

But the brothers Almsgill were not the only ones to create a mystery for me. If local gossip and innuendo was to be believed, it was the brothers of the local Freemasons' lodge whose treatment of one of their brethren, if it was true, gave cause for concern.

Due to the mystique surrounding the rituals and rules of

Antient Fraternity of Free and Accepted Masons under the United Grand Lodge of England, there is bound to be a lot of unjust and unsubstantiated rumour about them and their brotherhood. Not being a Freemason, I am not in a position to confirm or deny any of that speculation, nor am I in a position to criticize or praise the brotherhood. I do not know the scope of their work, but I understand that they do perform many acts of charity, particularly towards their own brethren and their widows or families. That work is done through their Board of Benevolence. Their desirable good and humane qualities are encompassed within the Antient Charges and Regulations which are read to the Master Elect prior to his installation.

Similar charges of behaviour apply to members of lodges while at their meetings or elsewhere – for example, any Freemason must agree to be a good man who strictly obeys the moral law. He must be a peaceable subject and cheerfully conform to the laws of the country in which he resides. He must promote the general good of society and cultivate the social values, guarding against intemperance and excess. He must work honestly and live creditably.

He must view the errors of mankind with compassion and strive by the purity of his own conduct to demonstrate the superior excellence of the faith he professes. And, like all Freemasons, he may enjoy himself with innocent mirth and avoid all excesses, always saluting his brothers in the courteous manner in which all masons are instructed. And, in the presence of strangers, he is told that 'You shall be cautious in your words and carriage, that the most penetrating stranger shall not be able to discover or find out what is not proper to be intimated.' Hence the secrecy of the handshakes and other salutes, and the mystique which surrounds the brotherhood.

In the course of my work, I did come across Freemasons, because several officers, both senior and junior, were members and so were many of the local businessmen who lived and worked within my compass. The introductory handshake, with the thumb pressed into the back of the recipient's hand, is their way of finding out whether a stranger is a member – a lot of police officers who are not members recognize that handshake and return it, just to see what happens next.

Some outsiders regard the Freemasons as a harmless and curious club for men, while others see it as something sinister because of its rituals, its secrecy and the wearing of specified jewels, aprons, chains, collars, garter-blue or red silk gauntlets and other regalia.

Knowing of the high standard of behaviour required, and of their acknowledged benevolence towards their brothers, I was surprised to hear of the ill-treatment of one of them.

Maybe stories of this suppposed treatment were inaccurate, or maybe the treatment was justified. I do not know, but I can only relate the story as it appeared to me, an outsider.

The gentleman concerned was called Clarence Denby and he owned a thriving music shop in Eltering. For a small North Yorkshire market town, it was a superb shop, selling everything from pop music to the classics by way of sheet music, records, books about music and musicians, instruments and portraits of artistes and composers. Clarence's shop was popular with young and old alike for he was knowledgeable about all aspects of his art and could talk pop with teenagers just as he revealed a remarkably deep knowledge of the classics, including opera and ballet.

Clarence did not live above the shop, however. He owned a very pretty cottage beside the stream in Elsinby and he shared it with his mother. Mr Denby, senior, had died many years ago, leaving what was then a young widow with a small boy. Mother and son had lived together ever since, even though Clarence was, at the time of this story, getting on for fifty years of age. His mother was still alive and approaching her eighties, and still caring for her son. She washed his clothes, cleaned the house and prepared his meals.

Clarence had never married, but in its wisdom, nature had not made him very attractive to the opposite sex, or even to his own sex. In short, Clarence Denby was not a very pleasant man. Despite his musical knowledge and his expertise at running his business, and despite the business rapport he enjoyed with his customers, he was without any close friends.

For one thing, his appearance and general demeanour militated against him. He was a short, very fat man, barely five feet tall, who perspired persistently and heavily. On a hot day, this made the atmosphere in his tiny shop somewhat pungent and the townspeople often asked one another whether Clarence ever bathed. No one asked him directly – if they did make remarks about the midden-like atmosphere which wafted among the quavers and crotchets, they'd ask if he had a dead rat under the counter or whether someone's dog had either died or had an unfortunate accident among his LPs. Clarence's only response was to allow the shop door to stand open in high summer. His ill-fitting clothes were always shabby and greasy too – his enormous rounded belly required him to wear braces upon his trousers, and he wore a belt as well, but it appeared to be a useless girdle about his huge stomach. The belt had no known purpose, while his jacket was never fastened. Customers were greeted by a massive expanse of grubby white shirt which was eternally bursting at the buttons, a soup-stained tie with a loose knot, and acres of dark, greasy material which comprised his jacket and trousers.

Clarence's face, often described as pudgy, matched his overall appearance. It was round and fat with a multiplicity of chins, giving his eyes a distinctly piggy appearance. He wore tiny steel-rimmed spectacles which perched on the end of his bulbous nose, while his dark, greasy hair was sparse upon his balding dome, but thick about the ears and back of the neck. To add insult to injury, he had a very high-pitched voice and a peculiar wart to the left of his main chin.

In spite of all these unavoidable handicaps, Clarence's shop was popular, if only for the quality of his musical wares and his own superb knowledge. That he was an expert in musical history was never in doubt, but it seemed he did not play any instrument – at least, no one had seen or heard him in action.

In the shop, he had a middle-aged woman assistant called Peggy who tended the counter while he looked after his books during busy times, and, in local terms, it seemed that Clarence was a success. His shop was always well stocked and always busy with customers, and this aura of success was confirmed when he became a member of the Freemasons.

I would sometimes see him pottering along to meetings in Eltering, carrying his little bag of regalia, and would pass the time of day with him. He never paused for long, for he always seemed to be anxious to go about whatever business it was in which he was currently engaged. Sometimes I wondered whether he was afraid of policemen, perhaps because his mother had threatened to call one whenever he was a naughty boy.

Then, nasty rumours began to circulate about Clarence. I was never sure how the stories began, but because he lived on my beat, they did concern me. It was said that Clarence was interfering with small boys. It was claimed that part of his reason for stocking the latest pop music was to encourage young boys to visit his shop and to go upstairs to a private room to listen with Clarence.

As police officers, we were all interested to know whether or not there was any substance to these reports, but in spite of maintaining very discreet observations in and around the shop in Eltering, we could never produce any real evidence of this behaviour. I kept an eye open at Elsinby, looking out for Clarence bringing young boys home or taking them for rides in his car, but I never saw anything that would cause me to be suspicious. He was also a keen supporter of the Anglican church in Elsinby, acting as church warden and being a member of the Parochial Church Council, and so I kept an eye on his behaviour with choirboys. But, again, I saw nothing that would give rise to concern.

Not once did we receive any complaint from the parents of small boys about his behaviour, and yet, in spite of our absence of evidence and the lack of any complaint, the rumours persisted. All of us, including the CID, tried to pin down the stories; we tried to ascertain whether or not there was any substance to the tales, but found absolutely nothing.

So far as we were concerned, Clarence was not harming the children, but the public continued with their innuendoes and veiled allegations against him. I do know that we were criticized for not prosecuting him, but for what? Unlike the public, we had undertaken observations and a very comprehensive investigation into his behaviour without finding any cause for concern. We could not proceed against a man on the strength of unsupported rumours.

I do not know whether Clarence knew of these scurrilous tales, but his business did not seem to suffer. People still patronized his premises and bought his musical offerings. And then, one night, someone broke into the shop.

The broken glass of the door was discovered by one of our night patrols and the constable rang me, asking if I would rouse Clarence and ask him to come to the shop. This was the procedure we adopted for informing keyholders of breaks into their premises; we preferred the personal touch rather than a cold phone call in the dead of night. It was 6.30 that morning when I called at his house; he was at home and answered my knock. I gave him the bad news and he said he would go immediately. His presence was needed so that the constable who'd discovered the break-in could tour the shop and determine if anything had been stolen.

Having been aroused early, I made a tour of my beat before going home for breakfast but I did not see Clarence until that evening when he came home from the shop.

'Hello, Clarence.' I was in Elsinby when he turned his Morris into the drive of his house. 'What was the outcome of this morning's alarm? Anything stolen?'

He shook his fat head. 'Nothing, Mr Rhea. The door's glass panel was smashed through. I think your people are recording it as malicious damage, not shopbreaking.'

'You've not been upsetting anyone, have you?' I put to him. 'Someone having a go at your shop out of revenge?'

He shrugged his shoulders. 'No, not that I know of.' He was open with me as he added in his high-pitched voice, 'I thought it might have been kids, hard-up teenagers pinching current hits, but none's been taken. It could be damage – it might even be an accident, Mr Rhea. You know the sort of thing. Some couple courting in my shop doorway and one of them puts an elbow through the glass.'

'You could be right. Well, we'll keep our ears and eyes open, Clarence, and if you hear anything from your customers that might explain who did it and why, give us a call. We'd like to get the matter cleared up.'

'Yes, of course, Mr Rhea,' and he vanished indoors to a hot meal lovingly prepared by his aged mother.

A couple of days later, I was talking to the constable who had discovered the smashed glass and discussed it with him.

'It wasn't an accident,' he told me. 'That glass was smashed near the lock, and when I got there, the lock had opened and the door was standing ajar. It's a Yale, chummy had reached inside the broken door to release it.'

'But Clarence says nothing was stolen?' I put to him.

'I saw no signs of larceny,' he admitted. 'The till hadn't been touched and, so far as I could see, none of the stocks of records had been touched. I wouldn't know about instruments – some of those guitars, for example, are worth a lot. But Clarence reckons nothing was touched.'

'And you? What's your gut feeling?'

'I think something was taken from that shop,' he said. 'I'm sure Clarence lost something he doesn't want to talk about – you do know about those rumours?'

'Someone wanting to blackmail him, you mean?' I asked. 'Had he got something there, I wonder, that would associate him with little boys?'

'It's a thought,' my colleague acknowledged. 'But what can we do? If he says nothing has been taken, how can we trace it?'

And so the mystery of the damage to Denby's Music Shop remained unsolved. Meanwhile, I had noticed a new development – Clarence was no longer attending his Masonic lodge in Eltering. For a time, this seemed of little or no significance because, so far as I knew, a Mason could resign his membership at any time.

I knew also that a Mason could be excluded from his lodge if there was sufficient cause, provided that a notice in writing was served upon him. That notice had to contain particulars of the complaint made against him. So had someone made a complaint against Clarence?

Other than to make a mental note of Clarence's changed circumstances, I did not pursue the matter; after all, it was not of any professional concern to me.

It would be some four months later when I called at his Eltering shop to buy some records. I wanted a selection of Chopin's music, in particular an album containing his Nocturne in E Flat, Opus 9, No. 2. I like all piano music, but this is one of my favourite pieces. Clarence was not in the shop that day and so Peggy, his voluble assistant, served me. I made my choice and said,

'Has he heard any more about his break-in?'

'Not a sausage, Mr Rhea. But then he wouldn't, would he?'

'Why not?' I was puzzled by her remark.

'It was the Freemasons,' she said. 'Everybody knows that. They want him out – he refuses to resign.'

'Why do they want him to resign?' I asked.

'Those rumours about him, little boys and that. You must have heard.'

'Yes, but there was nothing in them, was there?'

She shrugged her shoulders. 'The folks hereabouts all thought there was.'

'And you?' I pressed.

'I just work here,' she said. 'I've nothing against old Clarence, not personally, and I've seen nothing that would make me worry. But, well, you know what gossip is.'

'But the Masons wouldn't base their decisions on gossip, would they?'

'Maybe some of the Masons have little lads, Mr Rhea. Maybe they couldn't bear to think of him being one of them when the town was rich with rumours, bad though it might be.'

I thought fast. If the Masons had no proof of Clarence's

sexual misbehaviour, then they could not exclude him from
the lodge. They could not base such a decision on mere
speculation, and if he refused to resign, then they were
compelled to retain him, however embarrassing.

'So how does this break in link him and the Masons?' I
asked, now that she was so chatty.

'His regalia, Mr Rhea. He's not told anybody this, I know,
but he kept it upstairs, in a cupboard. When he went to the
lodge, he called here first to collect his little bag, then off he
went to the meeting. Whoever broke in took that bag, that's
all. No money, no records. Just his regalia.'

Now I could see what she was telling me. The rules of the
Freemasons say that no brother shall be admitted to a meeting
without the clothing appropriate to his rank. Without his
clothing, he could not be admitted, and unless he was
admitted, he could do nothing about the loss.

If what Peggy said was true, then poor old Clarence had
been denied admission to his Masonic meetings in a way that
barred him completely. But why? Because of rumour?
Because his conduct now lacked the necessary purity, or
because he had offended against the Freemason's concept of
moral law? Or had his loss been the action of a rogue
Freemason, someone acting without the knowledge of his
brothers? Or was it someone unconnected with the
Freemasons? Someone who knew how to inflict the maximum
embarrassment upon Clarence? I do not know – I could not
believe that the Brotherhood would stoop to this kind of
behaviour.

Clearly, I could not question Clarence on this delicate
matter – he was adamant that nothing had been stolen. Even
so, I did tend to believe Peggy's version of events.

Clarence continued to live in my beat and to run his
constantly successful music shop, but not once did I have
cause to suspect him of improper behaviour with children.
Then he died. It was a very sudden death: when driving to
work one day, he had a heart attack in his car, crashed through
some railings and ended that final journey on the banks of a

stream near Brantsford. His death revived all those memories of the veiled allegations against him, and even then, we had no proof that he had ever committed such low crimes. Clarence was buried in Elsinby churchyard and it was a big funeral, with his mother in attendance, for she was still alive.

I attended out of respect for him and watched his coffin being lowered into the earth.

That night, I was on duty from 10 p.m. until 6 a.m., and my patrol area included Eltering. At half past four in the morning, I was checking lock-up premises, one of which was Clarence's Music Shop. Peggy was running it until his will was executed – we all thought she would inherit it, which in fact she did.

As I reached into the dark recess of the doorway to turn the doorknob in my check on its security, I was aware of a parcel on the floor. I picked it up; it was wrapped in brown paper with no name on it, so I opened it, thinking it was an item of lost property.

But it contained a number of Masonic items and on one of the leather apron pouches inside the box was the name 'C'. Denby'.

Someone had returned Clarence's regalia.

10 The Feast of Christmas

Lay thy sheaf adown and come,
Share my harvest and my home.
Thomas Hood (1799–1845)

Christmas is a time for forgiving and for giving and in the country districts especially it is a period of true happiness and genuine friendliness. People visit one another, they help one another, they invite one another into their homes to share a drink or a meal and they give presents to people who have befriended them or helped them during the year. People such as the dustman, the milkman, the postman, the paper delivery lady and others are duly rewarded with suitable gifts, and we all go around with happy smiles on our faces.

Country policemen get Christmas gifts too. Some unwise souls regard these as attempted bribes, something to persuade the constable to turn a blind eye to minor breaches of the law, but in the mind of the rural dweller, there is no such evil intent. The present is given as a means of saying a sincere 'thank you', and if the constable persists in not accepting it, then the donor may be hurt or offended. Some givers will say it is not for the policeman, but for his wife and family, but whatever the circumstances of such a gift, it is never intended as a way of diverting the constable from doing his duty. City constables might have different views on such actions.

The truth is that country people know their constables as individuals and would never respect one who shirked his duty for whatever reason. Without their respect, he could not undertake his work. If the constable has to summons a countryman who has just given him a brace of pheasants, then that must be done without fear or favour. The pheasant-giver would not expect any favourable treatment, nor would he get it.

I became acutely aware of such matters about a week before Christmas when I called on a farmer called Dick Ferguson who lived at Thackerston. His well-tended farm was called Broom Hill and the house stood high above the village; the hillside below was covered with acres of broom, as it had been for centuries. It was a riot of brilliant golden yellow in the early summer.

Dick, a stockily built man in his early sixties, had long specialized in pig farming. He exhibited his best stock at local agricultural shows and was a frequent prize-winner, but he was a down-to-earth and highly practical man. I don't think Dick had an enemy in the world either. This might have been owing to his great honesty or even his generosity – at shows, he could be found in the bar, buying drinks for friends and competitors alike, while at home he was generous to the village hall, the WI, the church and all the local organizations. He always ensured they had enough prizes for their raffles or enough fresh food for their entertaining.

He'd even go down to the hall to help set up tables or sweep the floor if necessary. Nothing was too much trouble for Dick.

Just before that Christmas, I had to visit him to obtain a witness's statement. He'd been driving home from Harrogate when he'd witnessed a minor traffic accident in Knaresborough. Two cars had collided and a man had been injured. Typical of Dick, he'd stopped at the scene to help and had given his name to the injured man before the ambulance had carried him off. I had to interview Dick to establish exactly what he'd seen. It was a chill day in early December and I called at mid-morning.

'Come in, Mr Rhea. Sit thyself down and have a drink – it's very near Christmas,' were his opening words.

'A soft drink, thanks,' I said. 'I'm driving!'

'Sensible chap, thoo's as wise as a jinny owlet.' And his wife, Dorothy, produced two mugs of coffee, two buttered scones and a slice of gingerbread each with a slice of cheese to accompany it. Thus fortified, I settled down to the interview, first eliciting the story as Dick saw it. He was a good witness, giving me a clear account of precisely what had occurred, and I wrote down his words, getting him to sign his statement which would be sent to Knaresborough Police for whatever action they deemed necessary.

'Will I have to go to court?' he asked.

'It depends,' I said. 'If that man in the Ford Cortina is prosecuted for careless driving – and it does seem he was at fault – then you might have to give evidence. That's if he pleads not guilty. If he admits careless driving, I don't think they'll call you, but what you've just told me will help the Prosecution Department to decide whether or not to summons him.'

'So if I do have to go to court, I'll just tell 'em what I've told you, as straight as a bulrush?'

'Just that. Give them facts, not opinions,' I advised him, and then I explained a little of the procedure in a magistrates' court, detailing what would occur if a careless driving case was heard. He'd never been in court before and I felt he'd benefit from a little foreknowledge. I answered a few of his questions about the intricacies of giving evidence and warned him of the sort of cross-examination he might have to endure. He seemed to understand it all and thanked me for my guidance.

I remained a few more minutes chatting to Dick and Dorothy in their comfortable lounge about local matters, and he offered me a Christmas whisky, a lovely malt. Most reluctantly, I had to refuse – to drink whisky in uniform and then drive a police vehicle would be very stupid, but I did appreciate his gesture. I accepted a bitter lemon, however, a token of the proffered Christmas spirit, and wished them both seasonal greetings.

As I got up to leave, he said, 'Come wi' me, Mr Rhea.'

He led me into a huge beamed kitchen, and hanging from

the ceiling on strong metal hooks were dozens of cured hams. At that time, some people, like Dick, still did their own pig-killing and ham-curing, using methods handed down from generation to generation. A strong home-cured Yorkshire ham was one of life's great treats and the farmers in this region would slice off pieces as they required them and cook them for breakfast. I'd been brought up to similar practices, surviving the Second World War with the fruits of the countryside – pheasants, grouse, salmon, home-cured ham, home-grown potatoes, soft fruit and apples, home-produced milk, cream and cheese, brambles and wild mushrooms – it all formed part of the luxury of rustic living. Broom Hill, thanks to Dick and Dorothy, was perpetuating that highly desirable style of life.

'Somebody's been busy,' was all I could think of saying as I gazed on this forest of suspended hams.

'Heat from working kitchens is good for 'em,' he said. 'They allus used to hang hams in t'kitchen rafters. You have to know t'right method, right time to salt them, and then t'right amount of salt, saltpetre, vinegar and a spot o' sugar – then hang 'em up like this, where there's a bit of smoke from t'kitchen fire, not so as they get too dry mind or too hot.... If they get too dry and hot, t'skin gets as tough as bog oak ... '

He stood on a chair and lifted one of them down, passing it to me. I took it in my outstretched arms and almost dropped it – it was so heavy, like a huge, weighty stone.

But I held on to it. I could smell the strength of that ham; I could imagine it sizzling with roast potatoes ... it was mouth-watering.

'This is what a ham should be like,' I complimented him. 'I'll bet it tastes smashing ... '

'It's yours,' he said. 'Take it. For Christmas, for t'missus and your bairns.'

'No,' I protested weakly. 'I can't, not all this!'

'Well a few slices isn't any good to anybody,' he said. 'It's yours, take it.'

'How much?' I asked.

'How much he asks ... nowt, dammit man. It's Christmas,

you've been good to me, explaining about that court business, so it's me saying thanks to you, Mr Rhea. Nowt no less, nowt no more.'

I persisted with my weak refusals, but succumbed. A ham this size would last us months. I bore it home in triumph and Mary was overwhelmed – like me, she was born and bred in the Yorkshire countryside and knew the wholesome value of a home-cured ham. There was a hook in the pantry and I hung it there to await the time we cut the first slice.

About a week later, there was a knock on the door and when I opened it, Dick was standing there, carrying another equally huge ham on his shoulder. For the briefest of moments, I thought he'd forgotten about giving me the first one, and that this was another ...

'Come in,' I said.

He stomped in and I helped him to lift the enormous ham from his powerful shoulder, still wondering why he had come.

'You've still got that ham I gave you, have you?' he asked in his blunt Yorkshire way.

'Yes, untouched, Dick. We're saving it for a special occasion.

'Aye, well, good. Well, I hope you don't mind me coming like this, but I'd like it back – and this 'un's yours, not that first 'un.'

I was puzzled for a moment, and said, 'But they look the same to me.'

'Aye, well, they're not. That first 'un's for t'Brewers Arms, so I'll leave this new leg and if you give me t'old 'un back, then we'll say no more about it.'

I took the new one and went to the pantry where I lifted down the original, then as I handed it to him, I asked,

'Dick, just what is the difference, if you don't mind me asking? I can't see anything different.... '

'Salt, Mr Rhea. That 'un for t'pub, 'as got a lot more salt on it. Salt's good for beer sales, you see, Mr Rhea. When t'regulars eat sandwiches made from that ham, they'll guzzle gallons o' beer afterwards. It's an arrangement I have with

George – I allus gives 'is hams an extra dollop or two of strong salt. They're as salty as Lot's wife.'

'So it's a good job we didn't eat it!' I laughed.

'Aye, you'd have been as dry as our vicar's sermons!' he chortled.

Having accepted the swop, I asked, 'How about you then, Dick? You'll be a bit dry after lugging that ham up here?'

'Just a bit,' he said.

'I've got a nice malt whisky,' I said. 'How about having a Christmas drink with me?'

'If I get as tipsy as a fiddler's bitch, I can allus walk home,' he said, following me into the lounge.

* * *

Dick's generosity was in direct contrast to the attitude of old Mr Morley. Well into his seventies, he lived alone in a neat but somewhat isolated brick-built bungalow beside the road leading from Thackerston to Ploatby, and few of the villagers, if any, knew his Christian name. Everybody called him Mr Morley – when his wife was alive, she had always referred to him as Mr Morley, and never as 'my husband' or 'our Fred', or whatever his name was.

Because of the loneliness of his bungalow, I would pop in when I was passing, especially if the weather was wintry, because his route to the shops was easily cut-off by snow. I would ask if he needed anything from the shops and, from time to time, he would ask me to bring something back, such as a tin of baked beans or packet of corn flakes. I know the other callers did likewise. His only mode of travel was an old black bike which he'd had for years, but he rarely left his home – he had no need to. When he did emerge, he always wore a black beret. The sight of the little man in the black beret, aboard an old black bike, was a familiar one in those lanes, especially in the summer months. I think he sold some of his flowers in the local shops.

His neighbours, distant though they were, were kind to

him, doing his errands, shopping for his clothes, giving him food and sometimes taking him hot meals. A nearby farmer's wife always cooked his Sunday lunch, for example, and took it to him on a tray, a journey of about a mile and a half.

Mr Morley did have relatives, but they lived in the Midlands and, in any case, were not very close to him. He had no sons or daughters, those relations being distant cousins so far as I could establish. He had never been to visit them, and, so far as anyone knew, they had never come to see him. His only link with most of them was the occasional Christmas card, but one of them, the daughter of one of his distant cousins, did send him a Christmas cake every year.

For all the kindness displayed by his neighbours, old Mr Morley never returned their generosity, not even asking them to sit down for a cup of tea or to share a Christmas drink. I don't think he was mean or distrusting; I think he simply did not think about inviting any one to share a few quiet moments with him.

On the few occasions I had been inside his house, I had found it clean, tidy and well decorated. Some elderly men, living alone, tend to ignore the appearance of their paintwork and wallpaper, but to give Mr Morley his due credit, he did keep a nice home. His garden was also neat and tidy, for he spent a lot of time among his flowers and vegetables, but never gave any to his callers.

Conversely, they did not expect anything for their generosity, but sometimes I felt that the farmer's wife who brought his Sunday lunch would have enjoyed the occasional gift of a bunch of his lovely flowers, and some of the ladies who did his shopping would have welcomed a bag of carrots or sprouts.

But those thoughts were not important; the important thing was to make sure he was cared for, and in that we all took our turn, albeit without any requests either from Mr Morley or anyone else. He was alone and so the villagers looked after him.

Then, one day, just before Christmas, I received a

privileged insight into his character. It was a bitterly cold day as I halted my van outside his garden gate. I was passing and thought I'd pop in to ask whether he needed anything, but as I walked up the path to his back door, I saw that it was standing open. I rapped and called out, 'Anyone around? Are you there, Mr Morley? Hello?'

He was not in the kitchen and so I checked his garden and outbuildings before going into the bungalow, but there was no sign of him. I returned to the kitchen door and repeated my knocking and shouting, and then I thought I heard a soft cry.

I was slightly alarmed. I called his name and went into the house, announcing my own name as I progressed to minimize any alarm he might experience. I found him in his living room, slumped in an armchair, and he seemed to be dazed.

'Mr Morley?' I called to him, and he responded, his grey eyes blinking at me. 'What's happened?'

'Oh, hello, Mr Rhea. Glad you've come ... it was a dizzy spell ... just came over me ... '

'I'll get the doctor to look at you,' I said.

'He's been. I've some tablets.' He pointed to the kitchen. 'Above the sink, in a brown bottle, heart ... it's my age, you know.'

'And you've not taken one this morning like you should have done, is that it?'

'Aye,' he said.

I went into the kitchen for the required tablet and a glass of water, but couldn't find the brown bottle. I looked in various other cupboards – and found a miser's hoard! One cupboard, clean and neatly arranged, was full of Christmas cakes, all looking very much alike. I counted a dozen – twelve Christmas cakes all sitting there. And in another, there were bottles of spirits – whisky, gin, brandy – all unopened. I counted six bottles of whisky alone, and then in another cupboard, there were boxes of chocolates, dozens of them, all neatly stacked in piles.

Then I found the tablets, read the instructions and tipped one into the palm of my hand. I ran a glass of water and took the treatment to him. He swallowed the tablet with a grunt and thanked me.

'I'll get the doctor to pop in,' I said. 'Now, your fire's not lit, and it's cold outside, so I'll light it while I'm here.'

'Mrs Pennock'll do it when she brings my dinner,' he said. 'It's Wednesday, you see.'

'I'll do it, Mr Morley. It'll save her a job.'

And so I buckled down to the task of cleaning out his grate and lighting the fire, finding that he did have a stock of chopped kindling in an outside shed, and a large stock of coal. So he was not a miser in the sense that he did not want to spend money, so I wondered about his massive stocks of cakes, chocolates and booze.

As I worked on lighting the fire, I chattered to him, asking what he would be doing this Christmas and whether he'd be seeing any of his relatives. He said he'd be at home like he always was, but that Mrs Bowes had invited him to share Christmas dinner with her and her husband. He'd accepted.

'I see you're all right for Christmas cakes,' I said, my curiosity getting the better of me. Why did he keep so many?

'It's our Alice's lass,' he said. 'She sends one every year.'

'But you don't eat them?' I smiled.

'No, I'm allergic to dried fruit – it brings me out in spots, so I can't eat fruit cake, Mr Rhea.'

'You ought to tell her!' I suggested, sweeping up the dust from his hearth. 'You've enough cakes to feed the whole of this dale!'

'They keep well,' he said.

'They're for eating, not for keeping,' I chided him. 'You could send some into York, for the poor folks there. There's loads of charitable organizations would welcome them, Mr Morley, and you'd know they'd gone to a useful place. Are you allergic to whisky as well?'

'Aye, I can't drink spirits, you see, so when folks give me bottles, I never drink 'em. I don't mind a bottle of beer now and then, but not spirits.'

'And chocolates?'

'Allergic to chocolate an' all, so I keep them … '

By that time I had finished the fireplace and ensured that a good roaring fire was warming the room, the pill had achieved its purpose and he had recovered from his dizzy spell. I told him where the bottle was and warned him to make sure he took his pills on time in accordance with the doctor's instructions. He promised he would, but, being an old man, I felt concerned that he might forget from time to time. But I was reassured by the number of people who called in – like me, one of them would probably find him if he needed help.

After getting the fire going, I asked if he'd like a cup of tea or coffee, and he smiled. 'Aye, I would,' he said. I had to ask him – he'd never think of asking me! I made two mugs of coffee and sat with him for about an hour; we talked about Christmas time, about it being a time for giving, about the events that had been arranged in the surrounding villages like the old folks' parties, the church events, the children's parties, whist drives and so on.

'You know, Mr Morley,' I said, 'those parties and events would welcome anything you don't need for raffle prizes – like those bottles of gin or whisky and some of those boxes of chocolates, and Christmas cakes for sharing with the old folks.'

'Aye, but them's all presents to me.' He shook his grey head. 'You can't go about giving presents away, can you?'

'What happened to the earlier cakes, then?' I asked.

'My missus used to give 'em away. Them in my kitchen's come since our Elsie passed on, Mr Rhea – she'd have handed 'em out to somebody … '

'But you could do the same! If Mrs Morley did it, then so can you. You could always give people like Mrs Pennock a box of chocolates, as a thanks for bringing your dinners in.'

'Aye, well, I'll think about it.'

I left him, now confident that he would survive, but I did tell both the doctor and the district nurse about Mr Morley and they said they'd make regular calls.

But the next time I called was after that Christmas. There

had been a heavy fall of snow overnight and I popped in to ask if he was all right. He was – his fire was blazing, someone had brought in some logs and I could see the remains of a hefty meal on the table.

'I was just passing, Mr Morley, and thought I'd check to see if you're all right.'

'Very well, thanks, Mr Rhea. I had a nice Christmas.'

'Did you get any nice presents,' I asked.

'Aye, three bottles of whisky, two bottles of gin, a lovely cake from our Alice's lass and some chocolates from the neighbours.'

'And what have you done with them?' I asked him.

'They're in the cupboards,' he said. 'With the others.'

And so they were. He had not given any of his earlier gifts away, and so his stock had now increased. And it increased every year. I did try to persuade him that he should give generously to local charitable organizations but, for some reason, he would never part with any of his presents, however unwanted they were. And not once did he give anything to any of his helpers – I realized that my solitary cup of coffee with him was indeed an unusual event.

But then I realized I'd had to ask him for it.

So suppose people asked him for a donation to their function? Would he then give generously?

Some weeks later, the Reverend Simon Hamilton, vicar of St Andrew's parish church in Elsinby, mentioned that he was arranging a spring fête to raise money for repairs to the tower. He would be staging a tombola and there would be teas, as well as the usual attractions.

'Do you ever pop in to visit old Mr Morley?' I asked him.

'Regularly,' he said. 'At least once a week.'

I mentioned my own visits and we shared experiences, and then I said, 'Look, vicar, if you need bottles of spirits, Christmas cakes or boxes of chocolates, he's got dozens stacked away. He never uses any of them – they're all unwanted gifts. If you were to ask if he had something for your fête, he might decide to part with one of his treasures! But you'd have to ask, he'll never volunteer a gift!'

'I'll try it!' he beamed.

A week before the fête, I saw the vicar in Elsinby and we discussed parking arrangements and other professional matters, then I asked.

'Old Mr Morley, did you ask him for something for your fête?'

'I did,' he smiled.

'And?' I asked.

'Nothing,' he laughed. 'He said he hadn't anything to give away.'

* * *

Another fascinating character was Miss Gertrude Midgley who lived in the end cottage of a row of cute terraced houses in Maddleskirk. The row comprises six tiny stone-built homes, each with only one bedroom, a bathroom/toilet, a kitchen and a lounge. There were no garages, although each house had a tiny yard and a patch of hillside garden behind. The front doors opened onto the village street and each of the cottages was occupied by a solitary elderly lady. Six old ladies therefore occupied the entire block known as Field Houses, with Gertrude in No. 6.

She had worked in service during her youth, being employed in several country houses in Ryedale, first as a servant girl and later as a housekeeper. Her latter years had been spent as the dinner lady in the primary school in Maddleskirk, from where she had retired some twenty years earlier. Many of the villagers remembered her time at the school – she was a strict, no-nonsense lady who could keep the children in order during their dinner break. Now about eighty years old, she was spritely for her age and managed to do all her own shopping by using the local buses or pottering down to the village shops.

She was a plump person, perhaps typical of ladies who cared for the appetites of country gentlemen and their friends, and, latterly, schoolchildren. She wore her grey hair in a neat bun, tied with a coloured ribbon. Her face was round and she had ruddy cheeks, but she lacked the perpetual smile of so many cooking ladies.

In some respects, she was a grey figure – she always wore long grey dresses which came to below her knees, and seemed to perpetually wear sandals over her thick grey lisle stockings. She wore greyish cardigans, too, and seldom seemed to enjoy bright colours upon her, except for that ribbon in her hair – it would be red one day, blue another, then yellow, green or even purple or white.

So far as anyone knew, there had never been a romance in her life and she did not appear to have any family who might visit her or whom she might call on. I know she did visit people in the village, and they called on her, either to check that she was all right or to have a cup of tea or a natter with her. But it never occurred to me that I should call. After all, she was hale and hearty, she had a stream of callers and was not the sort of person who would come to the notice of the police or the social services for any reason.

It was with some surprise, therefore, that I saw her waving to me from her front door some two weeks before Christmas. I was walking along the village street on one of my foot patrols when she hailed me.

'Mr Rhea,' she beckoned. 'Can you spare a minute?'

'Of course,' and so I followed her into her cottage. A fire was blazing in the black-leaded grate and an old-fashioned kettle, large and black, was singing on the hob. A rocking chair stood at one side of the fireplace, and a comfortable old easy chair was at the other.

A clip mat lay before the fire, while the mantelpiece was full of brassware – lots of candlesticks large and small, vases, animal figures and so on. It looked very cosy.

'Sit down.' She pointed to the easy chair. 'You'll have a cup of tea?'

As it was more of a command than an invitation, I obeyed and indicated that I'd love one. She disappeared into the kitchen and returned with a plate of scones which she placed on the hearth, followed by two mugs, a bowl of sugar and jug of milk. She poured the hot water into the tea pot and sat down in the rocking chair, allowing it to move as she settled down.

'You never came last year,' she said. 'So I thought I'd better remind you this time.'

I was puzzled by her comment. 'Last year?' I shook my head. 'I'm not sure what you mean, Miss Midgley.'

'The policeman always calls to cut my cake,' she said.

'Your Christmas cake, you mean?' I guessed that was the subject of her remarks.

'Aye, what else?'

'I'm sorry,' I tried to express my feelings by the movements of my hands, 'but I had no idea. I mean, if I had known, I'd have called especially.'

'Well, make sure you call this year then – Christmas Day or Boxing Day, not before. And before New Year. Make sure you get it cut before New Year.'

As I pondered over my newly imposed duties, she poured the tea and handed me one of the mugs and the sugar.

'No sugar, thanks,' I smiled, but accepted one of the scones. 'So who did cut your cake last year?' I ventured.

'Nobody, so it's still in my pantry. You'll cut it before you leave, I should think.'

'Yes, of course.' The scone was delicious, home-made with lots of rich butter oozing into it. 'I'll be delighted.'

She produced the delicious-looking cake which stood on a large wooden board; it would be about eight inches square by two inches deep, but lacked any icing. A knife lay beside it. She placed the board on the table in her lounge and I went across, wondering if there was any ceremonial method of performing this task, or speech to be made, but there did not seem to be any formalities. I simply slid the knife into the cake in the centre and sliced it through.

'Cut yourself a slice,' she said. 'And me.'

I chopped two slices and we returned to the fireside where I tasted the cake. It was delicious, moist and very highly flavoured with brandy or malt whisky so far as I could tell. That had preserved it well.

'Happy Christmas for last year,' I said.

'And you,' she returned.

As I chomped the year-old piece of cake, I wondered what all this was about, and decided to ask. I guessed she would never enlighten me unless I did ask.

'Why does the policeman have to cut your Christmas cake?' I ventured.

'It's my custom.' She actually smiled this time. 'My grandad was a policeman. He rose to be sergeant,' she added with pride. 'I had no brothers or sisters, and Dad died early – he was a railwayman. But I allus say, if I'd been a lad, I'd have joined the force. Girls didn't do that in my day, Mr Rhea, you see. Anyroad, Grandad allus cut our cake for Christmas, and when he passed on, I got other policemen to do the job. Last year was the first time I'd missed ... '

'I'm sorry, I had no idea, otherwise I would have called in.'

'I'm not grumbling,' she said. 'There's no point in grumbling about things, but I've got it done now, and I know you'll call this year come Christmas.'

'I will, I promise,' I assured her.

I remained a few more minutes and learned that she would spend her Christmas alone. She had no relations, and had no wish to inflict herself upon any other family who did have friends or relations to visit them. I made a determined vow to visit her on Christmas Day – at least she'd have a visitor on that very special day.

'You could always come to us,' I heard myself saying. 'We always have a crowd in – my wife and I are both from big families.'

'No, Mr Rhea, I know what family life is like at Christmas and I will not intrude, but thanks for the thought.'

'You could pop down to one of the hotels, perhaps? Or contact one of the charities who arrange dinner for lots of people like yourself ... '

'I'll have no charity, Mr Rhea!' she was firm. 'I'm fit and

healthy, and I can cook myself a nice Christmas dinner without relying on other folks. No, you forget me, leave me alone and I'll manage. It's my lot in life to be alone, without a husband or kids, and I'll not grumble about it. So just you mind on and come to cut my cake, that's all I ask.'

I tried to persuade her to allow me to make an approach on her behalf, to ask around to see if there were any gatherings to which she might be invited for Christmas Day, but she steadfastly refused. In some ways, I had to admire her sturdy determination, but I did feel she must be a very lonely old lady.

I left with a slab of her Christmas cake in my pocket for Mary and the children, and continued my patrol of Maddleskirk before heading for home in Aidensfield. In the days that followed, I did learn that she always spent Christmas alone and that others in the village had invited her to join them – her neighbours in Field Houses, for example, had extended lots of invitations. She did visit them at other times, but because each had their family in at Christmas, or went to their family, Miss Midgley refused to be a 'nuisance' as she put it.

It would be about a week after my visit that I found myself embroiled in the preparations for the Eltering Sub-Divisional Police Children's Christmas Party. It was to be held in the Whistler Hall at Eltering and all children of police officers in Eltering Sub-Division were invited. It would be held on the Wednesday between Christmas and New Year from 3 p.m. until 7 p.m. The mums would share the chore of making cakes and jellies, dads would decorate the hall and organize games, and the parents had arranged some music and entertainment, my part being that of the magician. I hoped my famous Chinese Rings would survive the assault of many hands as the kids tried to separate them after I had magically joined them. Sergeant Bairstow was to be Father Christmas and all the children would receive a present.

Mrs Bairstow was in charge of the feeding arrangements, co-ordinating the work of all the other ladies, and it was always a very happy, if very tiring, occasion. Then, two days before the party, Mrs Bairstow's mother was taken ill – Mrs Bairstow had to rush off to care for her. Sergeant Bairstow was not needed at her side and so remained to fulfil both his police and Yuletide duties.

'We could do with another pair of hands,' he said to me. 'My missus did a good job at that party, you need somebody to organize things.... '

It was then that I thought of Miss Midgley.

'I think I know somebody,' I told him, and explained about Gertrude and her association with policemen.

'Isn't she a bit old?' That was his only reservation.

I shook my head. 'She'll be tired afterwards, we will all be,' I said. 'But I'll bet she'll be happy.'

'OK, Nick, ask her. We can fetch and carry her.'

When I went on Christmas Day to cut her Christmas cake for the current year, therefore, I took her a small present from Mary, me and the children, and then put the proposal to her.

'Nay, Mr Rhea, I'm too old for that sort of thing – I've lost my touch now.'

But I could sense the wistfulness in her voice and began to convince her that she could do the job. I reminded her of her days organizing school dinners, her work in the country houses, her knowledge of food, her ability to get along with others ... In time, she weakened.

'Well, if you honestly think I could do it,' she said.

'I do, otherwise I wouldn't be here, asking!' I said.

She hesitated and then nodded. 'I'll do it,' she smiled.

'Right, I'll pick you up at one o'clock,' I said, and then explained the overall arrangements. When I called for her, she had changed into another frock, a pretty pink and blue one, and I saw she'd had her hair done too. This was clearly a very important outing. Her reserve was broken when one of the mums recognized her as her own dinner lady at school, and from that point, Gertrude entered the spirit of our party.

She organized the plates for the children, making sure none got two plates and that they all got a jelly and a beaker of orange squash. Her no-nonsense manner endeared her to the other women for she was a natural organizer, being able to spot the need for extra food long before it arose, keeping the children in order and ensuring that they all cleared away their own plates – just like they did at school. Afterwards, when Father Christmas distributed the presents, there was one for Gertrude, from all the children. I could see she was truly moved.

As I drove her home, I asked, 'Well, did you enjoy that?'

'Mr Rhea, it was lovely, the best Christmas I've had for, well, I daren't say. I really did enjoy myself – and I know my grandad would have been pleased to see me there. And a present as well. It was really lovely, a marvellous day.'

'We were all pleased to see you there,' I said, for it was true. She had been marvellous. 'So how about next year?'

'If they'll have me,' she said.

'They will,' I assured her. I let her out of the car and helped her up the steps into her cottage.

'Happy Christmas, Miss Midgley,' I said, holding open her cottage door.

'And you – and don't forget to come next year!' she reminded me, disappearing inside. 'I'll have another cake waiting.'

More Enthralling Fiction from Headline:

HEARTBEAT

CONSTABLE ACROSS THE MOORS
AND OTHER TALES OF A YORKSHIRE
VILLAGE BOBBY
NOW AN ITV SERIES
NICHOLAS RHEA

Of the millions who have enjoyed ITV's popular series
HEARTBEAT, none will forget characters such as Claude
Jeremiah Greengrass, Sergeant Blaketon and PC
'Vesuvius' Ventress. And they will be familiar with the
village of Aidensfield, at the heart of Constable Nick
Rowan's North Yorkshire beat. Set in 1960s Aidensfield,
this omnibus collection of stories, which together with
Nicholas Rhea's other tales of a village policeman
originally inspired the HEARTBEAT tv series, tells of all
these characters and many more: of Claude Jeremiah's dog
Alfred and his unfortunate incident with the budgerigar,
of young PC Nick's first merry New Year's Eve in
Aidensfield, and of the funeral of the ancient tramp,
Irresponsible John. Humorous, touching and imbued with
a deep affection for the Yorkshire countryside and its
people, this heartwarming collection is a treat no
HEARTBEAT fan will want to miss.

'Witty, warm-hearted and full of lovable rogues'
Northern Echo

Heartbeat is a Yorkshire Television series derived from the
Constable Books by Nicholas Rhea

YORKSHIRE
TELEVISION

Don't miss *Heartbeat: Constable Among the Heather*, the first
volume of *Constable* stories, also available from Headline

FICTION/TV TIE-IN   0 7472 4125 2

More Thrilling Crime Fiction from Headline:

MARTHA GRIMES

THE HORSE YOU CAME IN ON

Richard Jury is supposed to be on holiday when the telephone call comes. And in any case, what has sudden death on American soil to do with an English police superintendent? But when the victim turns out to be British by birth, and to have a distant connection with Jury's old acquaintance, Lady Cray, he reluctantly acknowledges that his marker is being called in. Enlisting the aid of reluctant peer Melrose Plant, and accompanied by the irrepressibly lugubrious Sergeant Wiggins, Jury crosses the Atlantic to see what he can find out.

Baltimore turns out to have many attractions – not least that it is the home of avant garde novelist Ellen Taylor, last encountered at The Old Silent inn. Ellen is painfully engaged upon finishing her new book, but takes time out to introduce the trio to the delights of the city – football, Edgar Allen Poe, Bromo-Seltzer and a bar called The Horse You Came In On.

A case of plagiarism, a blind and deaf street-dweller, an engaging child who bears a strong resemblance to Scarlett O'Hara – these are just some of the elements in a complex puzzle whose solution looks set to defy the combined talents of the visiting team and put an end to a very promising writing career...

Also by Martha Grimes in Headline
THE DIRTY DUCK   JERUSALEM INN   THE DEER LEAP
THE FIVE BELLS AND BLADEBONE   HELP THE POOR STRUGGLER
THE OLD FOX DECEIV'D   THE ANODYNE NECKLACE
THE OLD SILENT   THE MAN WITH A LOAD OF MISCHIEF
THE OLD CONTEMPTIBLES   I AM THE ONLY RUNNING FOOTMAN

FICTION/CRIME   0 7472 4221 6

P.C. DOHERTY

AN ANCIENT EVIL

THE KNIGHT'S TALE OF MYSTERY AND
MURDER AS HE GOES ON PILGRIMAGE
FROM LONDON TO CANTERBURY

As the travellers gather in the Tabard Inn at the start of a pilgrimage to
pray before the blessed bones of St Thomas à Becket in Canterbury,
they agree eagerly to mine host Harry's suggestion of amusing
themselves on each day of their journey with one tale and each
evening with another – but the latter to be of mystery, terror and
murder. The Knight begins that evening: his tale opens with the
destruction of a sinister cult at its stronghold in the wilds of
Oxfordshire by Sir Hugo Mortimer during the reign of
William the Conqueror and then moves to Oxford some two
hundred years later where strange crimes and terrible
murders are being committed. The authorities seem
powerless but Lady Constance, Abbess of the Convent of St
Anne's, believes the murders are connected with the legends of
the cult and she petitions the King for help.

As the murders continue unabated, special commissioner Sir
Godfrey Evesden and royal clerk Alexander MacBain uncover clues
that lead to a macabre world sect, which worships the dark lord. But
they can find no solution to a series of increasingly baffling questions
and matters are not helped by the growing rift between Sir Godfrey
and McBain for the hand and favour of the fair Lady Emily.

P.C. Doherty's previous novels (medieval mysteries featuring Hugh Corbett) are also
available from Headline: SATAN IN ST MARY'S, CROWN IN DARKNESS,
SPY IN CHANCERY, THE ANGEL OF DEATH, THE PRINCE OF DARKNESS,
MURDER WEARS A COWL, THE ASSASSIN IN THE GREENWOOD;
'Medieval London comes vividly to life...Doherty's depictions of medieval characters
and manners of thought, from the highest to the lowest in the land, ringing true'
Publishers Weekly

FICTION/CRIME   0 7472 4356 5

More Compelling Fiction from John Francome

JOHN
FRANCOME

OUTSIDER

'Francome writes an odds-on racing cert'
Daily Express

'Spirited stuff' *OK* magazine

'Pacy racing and racy pacing – John Francome has found his stride as a solo novelist' *Horse and Hound*

Already a leading jockey in his home country, Jake Felton comes to England to further his career and avoid confrontation with New York's racing mafia. But his plans to combine the life of an English squire with that of a top-flight jockey look like coming to a sticky end when he falls victim to a series of accidents that begin to seem all too deliberate.

Aided and abetted by typical English rose Camilla Fielding, Jake discovers that he's been targeted by a ruthless and professional killer. And now he urgently needs to find out why...

With an intricate and thrilling plot and all the drama and excitement of Derby Day, *Outsider* shows John Francome at the top of his form in this new novel of danger and skulduggery on the race track.

Don't miss John Francome's previous bestsellers, ROUGH RIDE, STONE COLD and STUD POKER, and, with James MacGregor, RIDING HIGH, EAVESDROPPER, BLOOD STOCK and DECLARED DEAD, also available from Headline

'A thoroughly convincing and entertaining tale' *Daily Mail*

'The racing feel is authentic and it's a pacy, entertaining read' *The Times*

FICTION/CRIME   0 7472 4375 1

More Thrilling Fiction from Headline:

TELL ME NO SECRETS

THE TERRIFYING PSYCHOLOGICAL THRILLER

JOY FIELDING

BESTSELLING AUTHOR OF *SEE JANE RUN*

'People who annoy me have a way of... disappearing'

Jess Koster thinks she has conquered the crippling panic attacks that have plagued her since the unexplained disappearance of her mother, eight years ago. But they are back with a vengeance. And not without reason. Being a chief prosecutor in the State's Attorney's office exposes Jess to some decidedly lowlife types. Like Rick Ferguson, about to be tried for rape – until his victim goes missing. Another inexplicable disappearance.

If only Jess didn't feel so alone. Her father is about to re-marry; her sister is busy being the perfect wife and mother; her ex-husband has a new girlfriend. And besides, he's Rick Ferguson's defence lawyer...

Battling with a legal system that all too often judges women by appalling double standards; living under the constant threat of physical danger; fighting to overcome the emotional legacy of her mother's disappearance, Jess is in danger of going under. And it looks as though someone is determined that she should disappear, too...

'Joy Fielding tightens suspense like a noose round your neck and keeps one shattering surprise for the very last page. Whew!' *Annabel*

'The story she has to tell this time is a corker that runs rings round Mary Higgins Clark. Don't even think of starting this anywhere near bedtime' *Kirkus Reviews*

Don't miss Joy Fielding's *See Jane Run* ('Compulsive reading' *Company*), also from Headline Feature

FICTION/GENERAL   0 7472 4163 5

More Thrilling Crime Fiction from Headline:

TAKEOUT DOUBLE
A CASSIE SWANN MYSTERY
SUSAN MOODY

Two years of teaching biology had been enough. Two years of dissecting frogs and reeking of formaldehyde had finally persuaded Cassie Swann to set up as a bridge professional instead. So far, she has managed to make a reasonable living, operating from her Cotswold cottage.

And then, during a Winter Bridge Weekend at a country-house hotel, she finds three of her punters dead around the green-baize table. And at least one of them is indisputably the victim of murder.

Nothing to do with Cassie – or is it?

When she realises that her livelihood is now threatened by the unwanted notoriety, she is forced to undertake some investigations of her own.

Set amid the eccentricities of English village life, *Takeout Double* is the first in a marvellous series featuring an amateur sleuth in the obsessive world of bridge players.

FICTION/CRIME   0 7472 3946 0

More Crime Fiction from Headline:

KATE CHARLES

Appointed to Die

A clerical mystery

**Death at the Deanery – sudden and unnatural death.
Someone should have seen it coming.**

Even before Stuart Latimer arrives as the new Dean of Malbury
Cathedral shock waves reverberate around the tightly knit
Cathedral Close, heralding sweeping changes in a community
that is not open to change. And the reality is worse than the
expectation. The Dean's naked ambition and ruthless behaviour
alienate everyone in the Chapter: the Canons, gentle John
Kingsley, vague Rupert Greenwood, pompous Philip Thetford,
and Subdean Arthur Bridges-ffrench, a traditionalist who
resists change most strongly of all.

Financial jiggery-pokery, clandestine meetings, malicious
gossip, and several people who see more than they ought to: a
potent mix. But who could foresee that the mistrust and even
hatred within the Cathedral Close would spill over into
violence and death? Canon Kingsley's daughter Lucy draws in
her lover David Middleton-Brown, against his better
judgement, and together they probe the surprising secrets of a
self-contained world where nothing is what it seems.

Also by Kate Charles and available from Headline
A DRINK OF DEADLY WINE 'Bloodstained version of Barbara Pym...could
make one late for evensong' *The Guardian*
THE SNARES OF DEATH 'The writing is elegant...the kind of emotion that
stirred murder throughout the works of Agatha Christie' *Sunday Telegraph*

FICTION/CRIME   0 7472 4199 6

More Compelling Fiction from Headline:

SPECULATOR
ANDREW MACALLAN

THE NEW EPIC OF ADVENTURE FROM THE AUTHOR OF
SUCCESSION AND *DIAMOND HARD*

SPECULATOR
The speed and the spirit

From boyhood, Richard Rowlands speculates on his theories about making engines of all types work more quickly and efficiently than their designers ever thought possible. But after two world wars, when both sides use and abuse his inventions; when he sees his brilliant ideas pirated, he discovers – perhaps too late – that the human spirit matters more than speed at any price.

SPECULATOR
When one young woman takes wing

As a girl, Carola Marsh is fascinated by the skill of a stunt flier in a travelling fair and becomes determined to learn to fly. She meets the hugely wealthy and childless Lady Warren, who speculates that Carola could do what she has only dreamed of, and bankrolls the girl's ambitions. But when Carola takes off on a solo round-the-world flight, she discovers that for a woman with wings, the sky can be a terribly lonely place.

SPECULATOR
A desperate obsession with money – and with love

And all the while, manipulating their lives like a malign puppetmaster, is the shadowy figure of Sir James Mannering, for whom money is god. He speculates in human lives, providing arms for any country, any cause – at a price. But this ruthless merchant of death has a secret and desperate obsession with a woman he dare not even approach – one for whom his millions have no meaning...

Spanning continents and chronicling the dramatic world events of the first half of the twentieth century, *Speculator* is a compelling celebration of the pioneering men and women whose vision and courage laid the foundations of our modern technological world.

Don't miss *Succession, Generation, Diamond Hard* and *Fanfare* by Andrew MacAllan and available from Headline.

FICTION/GENERAL   0 7472 4181 3

A selection of bestsellers
from Headline

APPOINTED TO DIE	Kate Charles	£4.99 ☐
SIX FOOT UNDER	Katherine John	£4.99 ☐
TAKEOUT DOUBLE	Susan Moody	£4.99 ☐
POISON FOR THE PRINCE	Elizabeth Eyre	£4.99 ☐
THE HORSE YOU CAME IN ON	Martha Grimes	£5.99 ☐
DEADLY ADMIRER	Christine Green	£4.99 ☐
A SUDDEN FEARFUL DEATH	Anne Perry	£5.99 ☐
THE ASSASSIN IN THE GREENWOOD	P C Doherty	£4.99 ☐
KATWALK	Karen Kijewski	£4.50 ☐
THE ENVY OF THE STRANGER	Caroline Graham	£4.99 ☐
WHERE OLD BONES LIE	Ann Granger	£4.99 ☐
BONE IDLE	Staynes & Storey	£4.99 ☐
MISSING PERSON	Frances Ferguson	£4.99 ☐

All Headline books are available at your local bookshop or newsagent, or can be ordered direct from the publisher. Just tick the titles you want and fill in the form below. Prices and availability subject to change without notice.

Headline Book Publishing, Cash Sales Department, Bookpoint, 39 Milton Park, Abingdon, OXON, OX14 4TD, UK. If you have a credit card you may order by telephone – 0235 400400.

Please enclose a cheque or postal order made payable to Bookpoint Ltd to the value of the cover price and allow the following for postage and packing:
UK & BFPO: £1.00 for the first book, 50p for the second book and 30p for each additional book ordered up to a maximum charge of £3.00.
OVERSEAS & EIRE: £2.00 for the first book, £1.00 for the second book and 50p for each additional book.

Name ....

Address ....

....

....

If you would prefer to pay by credit card, please complete:
Please debit my Visa/Access/Diner's Card/American Express (delete as applicable) card no:

Signature .... Expiry Date ....